CW00952022

CONSPIRACIES AND CONSPIRACY THEORY IN EARLY MODERN EUROPE

Conspiracies and Conspiracy Theory in Early Modern Europe

From the Waldensians to the French Revolution

Edited by

BARRY COWARD
Birkbeck College, UK

JULIAN SWANN
Birkbeck College, UK

ASHGATE

Published by
Ashgate Publishing Limited
Gower House
Croft Road
Aldershot
Hampshire GU11 3HR
England

Ashgate Publishing Company
Suite 420
101 Cherry Street
Burlington, VT 05401-4405
USA

Ashgate website: http://www.ashgate.com

British Library Cataloguing in Publication Data
Conspiracies and conspiracy theory in early modern Europe :
    from the Waldensians to the French Revolution
    1. Conspiracies – Europe – History – 16th century – Congresses 2. Conspiracies –
    Europe – History – 17th century – Congresses 3. Conspiracies – Europe – History –
    18th century – Congresses 4. Persecution – Europe – History – 17th century –
    Congresses 5. Europe – Politics and government – 1517-1648 – Congresses 6. Europe –
    Politics and government 1648-1789 – Congresses 7. France – Politics and
    government – 1789-1799 – Congresses
    I. Coward, Barry, 1941- II. Swann, Julian
    940.2

Library of Congress Cataloging-in-Publication Data
Conspiracies and conspiracy theory in Early Modern Europe : from the Waldensians to the French Revolution / edited by Barry Coward and Julian Swann.
        p. cm.
    Based on a conference held at Birkbeck College in July 2001.
    Includes bibliographical references and index.
    ISBN 0-7546-3564-3 (alk. paper)
    1. Europe – History – 1492- 2. Conspiracies – Europe – History. 3.
Conspiracy – Europe – History. I. Coward, Barry. II. Swann, Julian.

    D210.C68 2004
    364.1'094'0903—dc22

                                                                    2004000030

ISBN 0 7546 3564 3

Printed and bound in Great Britain by MPG Books Ltd, Bodmin, Cornwall

Contents

List of Contributors

Nigel Aston teaches at the University of Leicester. His research interests and activities centre on the history of religion (including Judaism) in Western Europe during the late early modern era of *c.*1660–1790 (especially in France and Britain), with a particular focus on the place of the clergy in politics and intellectual life. He is the author, amongst other things, of *Christianity in Revolutionary Europe, c1750–1830* (2002).

Wolfgang Behringer is Professor of History at the Saarland University, Saarbrucken. [umlaut over the u] Amongst his major publications are *Witchcraft Persecutions in Bavaria. Popular Magic, Religious Zealotry and Reason of State in Early Modern Europe* (translated by J. C. Grayson and David Lederer. Past & Present Publications, Cambridge University Press, 1997), and *The Shaman of Oberstdorf. Chonrad Stoeckhlin and the Phantoms of the Night* (translated by H. C. Erik Midelfort. Virginia University Press, Charlottesville 1998).

Dr Peter Campbell is Senior Lecturer in History at the University of Sussex. He is the author of *Louis XIV* (Longman, 1993) and *Power and Politics in Old Regime France*, 1720-1745 (Routledge, 1996).

Stuart Carroll, Senior Lecturer in Early Modern History at the University of York, is currently finishing a book entitled 'Rage of the Gods: Blood and Violence in France, 1450–1700'.

Barry Coward is Professor of History at Birkbeck College, University of London. His most recent books are *The Cromwellian Protectorate* (2002 and the third edition of his *The Stuart Age: England 1603–1714* (2003). He has also edited *The Blackwell Companion to Stuart Britain* (2003).

Colin Haydon is Reader in Early Modern History at King Alfred's College, Winchester. He edited, with John Walsh and Stephen Taylor, *The Church of England, c.1689–c.1833: From Toleration to Tractarianism* (Cambridge University Press, 1993) and, with William Doyle, Robespierre (Cambridge University Press, 1999), and is the author of *Anti-Catholicism in Eighteenth-Century England, c.1714–80* (Manchester University Press, 1994).

Mark Knights teaches early modern history at the University of East Anglia. He has published a book on the succession crisis of 1679–81 and his next book,' Representation and Misrepresentation in Later Stuart Britain: Partisanship and Political Culture', is forthcoming from OUP in 2004. He is also part of an editorial team producing an edition of the 'Entring Book of Roger Morrice, 1677–1691', which is to be published in 2005. Both these works have further discussions of the conspiratorial mentality of the later Stuart world.

Peter Lake is professor of history at Princeton University. His most recent book (written with Michael Questier) is *The Antichrist's Lewd Hat*. He is currently working on a book about Catholic accounts of the Elizabethan regime as a tyranny and a conspiracy.

Marisa Linton is a senior lecturer at Kingston University. She has published a book on the political culture of eighteenth-century France, *The Politics of Virtue in Enlightenment France* (Palgrave, 2001). She has also published several articles on French revolutionary politics on sic subjects as Robespierre's political ideas and on revolutionary projects for the future.

Kate Lowe is Professor of Renaissance History at Goldsmiths College, University of London. Her research interests are in Italian and, to a lesser extent, Portuguese Renaissance history. She has a particular interest in cultural, religious and social history, and their interactions, including an interest in political history. Amongst her publications are *Church and Politics in Renaissance Italy: the Life and Career of Cradinal Francesco Soderini*, 1453–1524 (Cambridge University Press, 1993) and *Marriage in Italy*, 1300–1650 (Cambridge University Press, 1998).

Dr Jason Peacey is Senior Research Fellow at the History of Parliament Trust, London. His publications include *Politicians and Pamphleteers: Propaganda During the English Civil Wars and Interregnum* (Ashgate, 2004), and he is editor of *The Regicides and the Execution of Charles I* (Palgrave, 2001), and co-editor (with Chris R. Kyle) of *Parliament at Work: Parliamentary Committees, Political Power and Public Access in Early Modern England* (Boydell, 2002).

Munro Price is Reader in Modern European History at Bradford University, and specializes in late eighteenth-century and Revolutionary France. His most recent book is *The Fall of the French Monarchy: Louis XVI, Marie Antoinette and* *the baron de Breteuil* (Macmillan, 2002), and he is currently working on a study of French politics between 1814 and 1848.

Penny Roberts is Senior Lecturer in History at the University of Warwick. She has published extensively on the religious and social history of sixteenth-century France. Amongst her principal publications are: *A City in Conflict: Troyes during the French Wars of Religion* (Manchester U.P., 1996), and *The Adventure of Religious Pluralism in Early Modern France*, ed. (Peter Lang, 2000).

Malina Stefanovska is professor of French and Francophone studies at U.C.L.A. She is the author of *Saint-Simon, un historien dans les marges* (Paris, 1998) and has published extensively on the literature and cultural history of seventeenth and early eighteenth century France.

Julian Swann is Lecturer in early modern European history at Birkbeck College, University of London. He is the author of *Provincial power and absolute monarchy. The Estates General of Burgundy, 1661–1790* (Cambridge University Press, 2003), and is currently writing a history of 'Disgrace: internal exile and political punishment in early modern France'.

List of Figures

Acknowledgements

We are very grateful to Greg Neale, editor of the *BBC History Magazine*, for helping to sponsor the conference held at Birkbeck College University of London in July 2001 where the essays in this book were first presented. We should also like to thank our students on the Birkbeck College MA in the History of Early Modern England and France, whose enthusiasm for this period provided the initial spark for the idea of this collaborative venture.

Barry Coward and Julian Swann

Chapter 1

Introduction

Barry Coward and Julian Swann

While organising the conference, held at Birkbeck College in July 2001, that was the inspiration for this volume, the editors were asked to participate in a number of radio broadcasts discussing the theme of conspiracy. Hopes of debating the finer points of early modern conspiracy theory were quickly dashed, as successive interviewers sought our views on whether or not the Americans had really sent a man to the moon, or asked for clarification of various aspects of the Kennedy assassination. The fascination with such topics and the underlying suspicion of official versions of the historical record or received scientific wisdom are a perennial feature of our supposedly rational modern world. Indeed the proliferation of scientific knowledge and the seemingly endless expansion of access to information provided by resources such as the internet appear to be widening the scope and appeal of conspiracy theory. Thankfully grappling with the causes of these contemporary phenomena is beyond the scope of this study which is instead devoted to conspiracies, real and imagined, and conspiracy theory in early modern Europe. There is, however, one very clear link between the modern and early modern worlds, namely that conspiracies did and do exist and that, if anything, belief in their existence seems as pervasive in popular culture today as at any time in the past. If there is a clear demarcation line between the two, it is the separation between elite and popular attitudes towards conspiracy theory, which on its own is no longer seen as an intellectually respectable means of explaining the seemingly inexplicable.

The causes of changing attitudes towards conspiracy theory are many and complex, but it is clear that early modern Europeans lacked the sophisticated tools of modern historical, economic or sociological analysis. In a devoutly religious age, divine providence offered a potentially all-encompassing explanatory model, but total submission to the Lord's mysterious ways proved difficult, especially when events seemed to be pointing in an unwanted direction. As a result, when they confronted such perplexing questions as why bad luck, ill-health or other misfortunes befell those whose morals and behaviour seemed not to merit it, or why sudden or unexpected political or religious upheavals occurred, many turned to conspiracy theory for a plausible and convincing explanation. There was a general tendency to blame human agency for these events, an intervention that was understood in terms of the individual, or groups of individuals, and not as the result of impersonal socio-economic forces. In this respect, conspiracy theory performed a similar function to accusations of magical practices, and it is not a coincidence that so many alleged plots combined accusations of sorcery as well as treason. For the elites, unwelcome change was explicable by reference to, amongst other things, the plotting of courtiers, ministers, favourites, heretics or freemasons, while the lower orders believed that famine was not simply the result of bad weather, or poor distribution methods, but of the nefarious actions of speculators. Events were explicable in terms of individuals, whose moral or religious virtues, or vices, were assumed to offer an insight into both their motives and the results of their actions.

The emphasis on the individual made particular sense to the inhabitants of an intellectual world shaped by the classical and Christian traditions. Whether considering the actions of Brutus, Catilina or Judas, the educated elites could find concrete proof of conspiracies that had led to the overthrow of governments or the betrayal of the just. Examples of conspiracies were, of course, widely available from more recent times and for writers like Machiavelli conspiracy was an integral part of politics, the principal means by which rulers were deposed. As an astute observer of the Italian city-states, where conspiracies were endemic, he was close to the truth and it is probably fair to say that for most of the early modern period political change could only be effected by force.

These lessons were not lost on English Catholics as they contemplated the triumph of their Protestant adversaries towards the end of the reign of Elizabeth I. As Peter Lake demonstrates, they believed that they were the victims of a plot, orchestrated by the 'two English Machiavel Catilines', Cecil and Leicester. Elite political discourse was punctuated throughout with these classical references. English MPs in the early seventeenth century, for example, often drew on Tacitus and Roman history to interpret the politics of their own day,[1] while members of the Parlement of Paris fondly thought of themselves as a modern senate whose benches were adorned by the worthy heirs of Cicero.

This classical culture was reinforced by the visual and performing arts. Malina Stefanovska's discussion of seventeenth-century French drama and, in particular, her analysis of Corneille's *Cinna*, Tristan L'Hermite's *Seneca's Death* and Cyrano de Bergerac's *The Death of Agrippina* reveals how classical themes were adapted to carry a clear message about the contemporary political scene. Other playwrights also exploited the possibilities offered by conspiracy, and Shakespeare's *Macbeth*, *Othello* and *Richard III* all remind us of how early modern culture helped to reinforce the conspiratorial mindset. Indeed, during the eighteenth century, the importance of the classics to elite education, the lessons drawn from their reading of the classical period by authors such as Montesquieu and Rousseau and the effects of the neo-classical revival may have acted as a counterweight to an Enlightened critique of conspiracy theory. As the French revolutionary generation sought to conceptualise politics, it turned continually towards classical models. Attempts to create a virtuous republic after 1792 were predicated upon the existence of virtuous citizens and to achieve that end it was necessary to purge the body politic of the morally corrupt whose actions were alleged to be the mainspring of counter-revolution.

In addition to these literary and classical references, early modern commentators had plenty of examples from their own times to draw upon. Such infamous events as the Tumult of Amboise or the Gunpowder Plot simply confirmed what most contemporaries had long suspected, namely that conspiracy was an ever-present threat. In a sense, their analysis was correct. As Peter Campbell's contribution to this volume demonstrates so effectively, conspiracy was integral to early modern political life and any attempt to understand why conspiracy theory prospered has to accept that on one level it was a perfectly rational way of understanding a court centred political culture in which a relatively small number of people actively participated.

Power at court derived from access to the monarch, or to those who exercised authority on his or her behalf, and the great aristocratic clans that dominated the courts of London, Madrid or Versailles formed into factions and cabals to compete for royal favour. Based upon, amongst other things, personal, familial and regional interests, these factions sought control of the wealth and patronage power of the crown and their membership frequently resembled a kaleidoscope of constantly changing interests. It was not a coincidence that monarchs such as Philip II or Louis XIV, who were alert to the need to conciliate the interests of court factions through even-handed distribution of patronage, were amongst those who were least troubled by plots against their authority. Less politically astute rulers, or those who entrusted government to favourites, risked provoking revolts and conspiracies, and ministers such as the cardinal de Richelieu, the duke of Buckingham or the count-duke of Olivares were the targets of almost constant plotting. Their monopoly of royal favour forced disgruntled grandees to adopt extreme measures, involving attempted assassination and armed revolt. However, conspiracy became almost endemic at a time of succession crisis or religious division.

One of the key themes to emerge from this volume is the impact of the reformation in reinforcing the conspiratorial mindset. Both majority and minority groups interpreted the actions of their religious rivals in terms of plots and within individual churches the same pattern was repeated with Jansenists denouncing Jesuits and Anglican conformists attacking Puritans and dissenters with equal fervour. Religion could also provide an ideological dimension to factional quarrels, and the French civil wars of the sixteenth century were, in part, the result of the sectarian conflict that divided the grandees no less decisively than the rest of society. The Saint Bartholomew's Day Massacre provided a terrible warning of what could happen when courtly conspiratorial politics combined with popular fears to produce bloodshed and violence.

As Stuart Carroll remarks 'conspiracy was integral to factional politics', and both he and Kate Lowe draw our attention to the fact that it was also connected to wider patterns of noble and masculine behaviour. In the period before 1650, in particular, codes of honour and vengeance produced not only a passion for duelling, but also for revenge killings which almost inevitably involved conspiracy. Such activities were by definition violent and dangerous, and Lowe makes the intriguing suggestion that in Italy it was a masculine crime appealing to young men, in part, because of the frisson provided by an activity that quite literally involved dicing with death. It certainly seems probable that similar sentiments were shared by noble plotters elsewhere, although it should not be forgotten that aristocratic women were amongst the most active conspirators. In France, the duchesses of Chevreuse, Montbazon and Longueville were inveterate plotters and as they were all but immune from serious punishment they were amongst the most persistent thorns in the sides of Richelieu and Mazarin.[2]

In his introduction to an important collection of essays discussing early modern conspiracies, Yves-Marie Bercé has argued that the rise of the centralised monarchical state led to the decline of a culture of conspiracy.[3] After 1650, the expansion of the military power of the major European states made armed revolt increasingly hazardous, but such a theory is clearly derived from a traditionalist reading of French history based upon the premise that the seventeenth century witnessed 'the birth of absolutism'.[4] It is true that the number and violence of aristocratic conspiracies declined after the Fronde, but Louis XIV's skilful management of French elites also contributed substantially to that process. Elsewhere the picture was very different. In 1688–1689, England witnessed one of the most successful conspiracies of the early modern period with the overthrow of the legitimate king, James II. His fall after the 'Glorious Revolution' offered a splendid example of how the authors of a successful conspiracy could rewrite history in their own image. Monmouth's failed rebellion of 1685 and the Jacobite risings of 1715 and especially that of 1745–1746 revealed that even the existence of the most powerful centralised state in Europe did not deter determined plotters. Peter I (the Great) of Russia was forced to curtail his grand tour of Europe in 1698 in order to crush an attempted palace coup, while Gustavus III of Sweden added another dimension to the picture in 1772. His successful coup against the authority of an increasingly despotic and unpopular Riksdag, demonstrated that a monarch could be the instrument and not just the victim of a plot.

Many more examples could be added to this list, but the violent struggles that periodically shook the great palaces of Europe help to explain why court politics was interpreted in conspiratorial terms. In theory, absolute monarchy left no space for public expressions of opposition or dissent and so the recourse to cloak and dagger methods was understandable. Indeed, even when not engaged in any illicit political activity, the life of a courtier was associated with secrecy and deceit. In the many manuals for would-be courtiers, or the memoirs of those who pursued that calling, the word dissimulation comes regularly to the fore. To succeed courtiers were expected to hide their true feelings behind a mask of civility and politeness, exuding an air of detachment and magnanimity, while secretly employing every available means to advance their own interests. Sentiments such as these help to explain why the term courtier was frequently treated as if it were a term of abuse. It also sheds light on why those who sought to analyse the behaviour of governments in the period so often resorted to a conspiratorial explanation.

Despite the relatively stable British parliamentary system established after 1689, English commentators or American colonists remained obsessed with the idea of plots. So pervasive was the idea of shadowy figures around the throne, who were aiming to subvert the constitutional or religious settlement, that historians have seriously considered the existence of a 'paranoid style' in Anglo-American politics.[5] On one level, this might be interpreted as a continuation of the attitudes associated with court politics, especially given the persistence of a discourse emphasising the nefarious role of courtiers allegedly gathered around the throne of George III that so frightened the American colonists. Yet, as Mark Knights reveals in an essay examining attitudes to conspiracy in the later Stuart period, there was more to the picture. As the English party system began to take shape, in the context of a more open, representative political system, conspiracy theory flourished. Whigs and Tories competed for support, each assuming that the other was employing the ancient art of dissimulation, seeking to advance their political ambitions by deceiving a gullible public.

As we have seen, historians of the absolute monarchy in France, on the other hand, have tended to downplay the importance of the conspiratorial mindset which had allegedly declined with the rise of a centralised state.[6] It is true that armed revolt was rare after 1661, but the political discourse of the old regime continued to contain a conspiratorial strand,[7] as even the most cursory glance at the voluminous remonstrances written by the parlements during the eighteenth century quickly reveals. In August 1756, the Parlement of Paris warned Louis XV of 'a plan ... to destroy the magistracy in France',[8] a theme to which the *parlementaires* returned in 1765 when they claimed to have 'glimpsed the object of a plot that has already attained such a degree of activity and maturity, that at the same time a blow struck against the magistracy reverberates from one side of the kingdom to the other'.[9] Finally, in March 1766, they were even more specific, declaring that 'the enemies of the magistracy have seized this occasion to destroy (the Parlement of Rennes) and to render suspect... to Your Majesty all the parlements of your kingdom, who have all attracted the hatred of the enemies of all that is good by proscribing this proud and intriguing society'.[10] The Society in question was, of course, the Jesuits, but the remonstrances were full of more general references to shadowy 'evil minded people' preventing the king's loyal subjects from approaching to the feet of the throne. Nor did the crown view things any differently. Louis XV and his ministers were obsessed with the idea that the parlements were concerting their resistance to his policies, a not unreasonable assumption given their claims to form a single national body through the doctrine of a *union des classes*.[11] Suspicion of a conspiracy involving leading members of the Parlement of Brittany and the Estates of that province in 1764–1765, led to the arrest of several leading magistrates, provoking a protracted political crisis that would culminate in the royal revolution of 1771.

These exchanges between the French king and his parlements were, in part, following an ancient convention, with the *parlementaires* invoking the threat posed by evil councillors or the supporters of the Jesuits to justify more wideranging criticisms of an unpopular royal policy. Yet it was more than just a rhetorical strategy, and plans to break the power of the parlements were a constant theme of discussion in government circles both before and after 1771. A similar pattern can be detected throughout Europe, and the problem for contemporaries as well as for historians is the need to distinguish the genuine conspiracy from the imagined, or even invented plot. Real fears and miscomprehension could make that process almost impossible, and as Jason Peacey's essay makes clear both Puritans and Laudians could accuse each other in good faith of being engaged in a plot to subvert the Church. With the abiding memory of Guy Fawkes and his accomplices to haunt them, the English were particularly susceptible to any revised version of the Popish plot and Titus Oates was by no means the only one to seek to take advantage of the fact. As Colin Haydon's chapter demonstrates, these fears continued to have a resonance throughout the eighteenth century, and the outlandish claims about the Catholic threat supposedly lurking behind such innocuous legislation as the Quebec or Relief acts continued to find a receptive audience.

In any given situation, certain individuals are wont to interpret events in a conspiratorial light, but those who required more substantial proof were always in a potentially difficult position. By its very nature plotting was liable to be of a clandestine, secretive nature and any firm evidence was difficult to obtain. Judicial authorities responded accordingly, employing torture extensively in order to extract confessions and further information from those who were accused of conspiracy. This was partly a result of the seriousness of the crime of treason, but all too often cases were manipulated as part of the factional politics of the time to incriminate opponents and their friends and families. Modern historians, like contemporaries, can therefore find themselves short of the proverbial smoking gun when it comes to deciding whether rumours of a conspiracy were well-founded. The problem is compounded by the fact that genuine fears of conspiracy were deliberately manipulated to further other ends. Rulers frequently used the accusation of conspiracy as a catch all device to pursue their wider aims as the Jesuits discovered to their cost in 1758, when the blame for an attempt on the life of king José I of Portugal was laid at their door. Although not directly implicated in what was essentially an aristocratic plot, they were subsequently expelled from the kingdom and crucially driven from their missions in South America where their defence of native interests conflicted with the monarch's colonial policies.

In the ruthless and competitive world of high politics, accusations of conspiracy were often fatal. Charles I's unfortunate favourite, Strafford, was sent to the block after having been accused of treason not against his king, whose confidence he enjoyed, but for 'endeavouring to subvert the ancient and fundamental laws and government … of England and Ireland, and to introduce an arbitrary and tyrannical government against law'.[12] Pym and his other principal antagonists were almost certainly aware of the dubious legality of the attainder bill that secured Strafford's fate, but it served their purpose of overthrowing a powerful enemy, and in a period when the king and his opponents were all engaged in a variety of military plots it was sufficiently plausible to secure a guilty verdict. Strafford deserves perhaps to be considered an early victim of the crime of *lèse-nation*, and such periods of intense political activity were (and remain) particularly prone to fears of conspiracy. Significantly, the parliamentarians' fear of conspiracies at the heart of the Caroline court that lay behind Strafford's attainder were mirrored by Charles I's belief (illustrated in a royal declaration of May 1640) that 'some few seditiously affected men' had seduced the people 'to bring ruin and confusion to the state, and render contemptible this glorious monarchy'.[13] This conspiratorial explanation of the crisis faced by the Stuart monarchy in the early 1640s was shared by the king's adviser, Edward Hyde. 'The number of those who really intended these prodigious alterations was very inconsiderable', he later wrote in his *History of the Rebellion*.[14]

The French Revolution offers another classic example, with fears of, amongst other things, aristocratic, counter-revolutionary and foreign plots succeeding each other with alarming regularity, but as Marisa Linton and Munro Price show in their respective chapters there was always enough evidence of genuinely conspiratorial behaviour to keep an already feverish political temperature at dangerous levels. Incidents such as Louis XVI's flight to Varennes or the discovery of the contacts between revolutionary leaders and foreign powers accentuated existing fears and uncertainties.[15] Perhaps more ominously they gave credence to the claims of those like Marat or Robespierre who saw conspiracy lurking around just about every corner. Indeed, both men sought to establish reputations for being able to identify conspirators, denouncing their opponents with all the deadly venom of secular witch hunters. The fratricidal behaviour of revolutionary politicians showed just how dangerous accusations of conspiracy could become and not for nothing is the Law of Suspects of September 1793 seen as one of the foundation stones of the Terror.

Real fear and suspicion were also integral part of the French religious wars of the sixteenth century, and Catholic French towns had good reason to worry about the machinations of the Huguenot population. The outbreak of civil war in 1562 had coincided with concerted attempts by the Calvinists to seize major cities such as Rouen, Toulouse and Troyes. Many of these attempted coups were only overturned after much bloodshed and it is hardly surprising that mistrust of Huguenots was endemic. As Penny Robert's chapter shows, attention was focused not only upon the local threat, but also the perceived danger of Huguenot collusion with foreign Protestants such as the English or the Dutch. Towns such as Dijon, Lyon, Mâcon, Marseilles and Toulon were constantly referring to the continued threat of conspiracy in order to wring concessions from the crown. Demands from towns such as Le Mans to be treated as a military border because of its proximity to Normandy, a province occupied by the English in the Hundred Years War, does, however, suggest that they occasionally protested a little too much, and that the threat of a foreign plot was being employed as a rhetorical strategy designed to protect local privileges, as much as to ward off any serious threat from the Calvinists.

Whatever the truth of the matter, the treatment of the Huguenots illustrates the wider practice of scapegoating and of attributing conspiratorial motives to minority groups in order to discredit them. In his study of the persecution of the Waldensians, Wolfgang Behringer offers us a chilling example of how they were accused of the 'monstrous ultimate conspiracy' of witchcraft. The false accusations against the Waldensians and their alleged involvement in a conspiracy mirrors that suffered by other religious minorities, notably the Jews, and brings to mind modern fabrications such as the infamous Protocols of the Elders of Zion. We might expect that the growth in religious scepticism would have been accompanied by a decline in such blanket condemnations, but the evidence is far from overwhelming. Instead, if anything, there was a broadening of the number of prospective targets for such accusations, and the eighteenth century witnessed the proliferation of, amongst others, Masonic, Philosophic and Jacobin plots. Moreover, the educated continued to use conspiracy theory to analyse unexpected political developments. As Nigel Aston's chapter illustrates, in the 1780s many conservative British thinkers believed that they had identified a link between the political radicalism of their own day and the Puritans of the 1640s. One might also draw parallels with the Tory campaign of 'Church and state in danger' waged around the figure of Doctor Sacheverell in 1710. In other words, there was a continuity in the conspiratorial interpretation with radicals cast as modern Puritans seeking the overthrow of church and king. Writers such as Edmund Burke or the abbé Barruel, who sought to analyse the origins of the French Revolution, shared this mindset, although it was a new Philosophic plot that came to the fore.

That a social and political upheaval on the scale of 1789 could still be conceptualised in terms of conspiracy theory underlines its continuing hold over the European mind. That hold was never broken entirely, but it was increasingly challenged by the rise of a scepticism whose origins were not dissimilar to that which chipped away at the notion of Christian providence. The development of both the physical and social sciences offered alternative methods of analysing human actions and their consequences, as did a conception of history that was increasingly connected to the movement of impersonal forces. As the European intellectual debate became focused upon movements such as the development of the modern bureaucratic state, capitalism, industrialisation and the conflict of social classes, conspiracy theory as an explanatory model had little to offer. As part of this process, elite attitudes towards causality were transformed and the intimate link between cause and effect was broken with a growing acceptance that individuals acting with the best intentions could produce unpleasant and unwanted results. Yet the extent to which such scepticism has ever permeated out beyond the world of academe should not be exaggerated, and both democratic and authoritarian regimes have, on occasions, employed conspiracy theory to deadly effect. Today, for a population that has become increasingly disenchanted with the words of politicians and other pillars of authority, and is confronted with an ever more voluminous and baffling array of conflicting opinions, conspiracies, real and imagined, continue to offer a means of explaining the seemingly inexplicable and they are likely to continue to do so.

Notes

1   M. Smuts, 'Court-centred politics and the use of Roman historians c.1590–1630' and D. Norbrook, 'Lucan, Thomas May and the creation of a republican literary culture' in P. Lake and K. Sharpe, eds., *Culture and Politics in Early Stuart England* (1994).

2   R. Briggs, 'Noble conspiracy and revolt in France, 1610–60', *Seventeenth-Century French Studies* (1990), pp. 158–74, esp. pp. 170.

3   Yves-Marie Bercé and Elena Fasano Guarini, *Complots et Conjurations dans l'Europe Moderne* (Rome, 1996), pp. 3–4.

4   Bercé entitled his recent textbook *La Naissance Dramatique de l'Absolutisme, 1598–1661* (Paris, 1992), which was published in English as *The Birth of Absolutism. A History of France, 1598–1661* (London, 1996).

5   The essential introduction is G.S. Wood, 'Conspiracy and the Paranoid Style: Causality and Deceit in the Eighteenth Century', *William and Mary Quarterly*, 3d ser., 39 (1982), pp. 401–41.

6   Bercé and Guarini eds., *Complots et Conjurations*, pp. 3–4. In his recent investigation into the origins of the conspiratorial obsession of the French revolutionaries, T. Tackett, 'Conspiracy obsession in a time of revolution': French elites and the origins of the Terror, 1789–1792', *American Historical Review*, 105 (2000), pp. 691–713, esp. pp. 698–9, has also written of 'the relative absence of conspiracy fears in French political culture' before 1789.

7   Peter Campbell reinforces this argument is his chapter below.

8   J. Flammermont, *Remontrances du Parlement de Paris au XVIIIe Siècle* (3 vols., Paris, 1888–1898), II, p. 140.

9   Ibid., p. 503.

10 Ibid., p. 843.

11 For a recent discussion of the *union des classes*, see J. Swann, 'Robe, sword and aristocratic reaction revisited: The French nobility and political crisis, 1748–1789' in R.G. Asch, *Der Europäische Adel im Ancien Régime. Von der Krise der Ständischen Monarchien bis zur Revolution, 1600–1789* (Cologne, 2001), pp. 151–78.

12 Quoted in A. Wooorych, *Britain in Revolution, 1625–1660* (Oxford, 2002), pp. 176–7.

13 Quoted in R. Cust, 'Charles I and popularity' in T. Cogswell, R. Cust and P. Lake, eds., *Politics, Religion and Popularity in Early Stuart Britain* (2002), p. 252.

14 Edward Hyde, earl of Clarendon, *The History of the Rebellion and Civil Wars in England* (ed. W.D. Macray, 6 vols., 1888), vol. 2, p. 182.

15 Here they give support to the position of Tackett, 'Conspiracy obsession in a time of revolution'.

Chapter 2

Detecting the Ultimate Conspiracy, or how Waldensians became Witches[1]

Wolfgang Behringer

A conspiracy of evil as a causal explanation for an increase of bad luck or accidents seems to be an attractive idea, not just in European history, but also on an anthropological level. In his most recent study of the rise of witchcraft anxieties and persecutions in the Republic of South Africa, the anthropologist Isak Niehaus has pointed out that since the 1980s a new pattern of witch hunting has emerged. He relates this to massive changes in the economic and political system, which shattered traditional authorities, economic hardship that threatened the people's subsistence, a religious movement - the Zionist Christian Church - which reconfigured the perception of evil, and pressure groups, in particular the Comrades of the ANC youth movement, who exploited the widespread uncertainties and anxieties of the common people to enhance their influence.[2] This may sound like an emulation of an old Malinowski-type functionalist approach, associating social stress with anti-witchcraft movements,[3] but from our perspective it is interesting that Niehaus analyses the growth of witchcraft fears in a specific region, fuelled by a number of factors into full-scale contemporary witch-hunts, and that he accepts that the native belief systems are an autonomous factor, and tries to identify the actors and their motives.

When the psychologists Carl F. Graumann and Serge Moscovici held their conference on 'Changing Perceptions of Conspiracy' some years ago, witchcraft played a prominent role.[4] Nicole Jacques-Chaquin contributed the chapter on the 'Demoniac Conspiracy',[5] but in addition Dieter Groh touched on the subject in his introductory chapter about 'The temptation of conspiracy theory, or: why do bad things happen to good people?'[6] The witches' conspiracy was well suited to answer this core question, and Groh even came to the conclusion that despite earlier fantasies about Jewish conspiracies, the witch pattern provided 'for the first time in European history a conspiracy theory as the kernel of a consistent interpretation pattern'.[7] However, witch beliefs need not lead automatically to persecution.

In South Africa before the 1960s, cases of witchcraft were handled carefully by chiefs and witch-doctors, and rarely led to violent retaliation. Similarly, in medieval Europe witchcraft was downplayed by the authorities. Systematic persecutions began only in the fifteenth century, sometimes encouraged by the authorities, secular as well as religious. It seems easy to conceive of evil as binarily opposed to a society of the good under the umbrella of a Christian church, based upon authorities like St. Augustine and his concept of 'Civitas Dei'. It is more difficult, however, to explain why this conspiracy was only detected in the later Middle Ages. Groh starts his story, rather traditionally, with Thomas Aquinas and the church's opposition to heresy, the Cathars in particular.[8] Norman Cohn, however, has demonstrated convincingly that Catharism was never mixed up with witchcraft,[9] and the accusation of a diabolical conspiracy of witches did not emerge until the fifteenth century, when it was first levelled against the Waldensians. Yet this movement seems less suited than Catharism to be confused with witchcraft. Whereas the Cathars could easily be classified as devil worshippers, because they had indeed claimed that the Devil was the God of this material world, the Waldensians denied the Devil's power. Furthermore, they denied the wonders of the saints, the power of relics, the sacraments, pilgrimages and offerings. Waldensianism – promoting the ideals of brotherliness, biblicism, pacifism, anti-papalism, and anti-feudalism – in no way resembles witchcraft.[10] As precursors of the Reformation, and as a persecuted minority, the Waldensians have gained the sympathy of many researchers. This may be one of the reasons why historians of Waldensianism have not made any useful contribution to our debate.[11]

In order to understand *why Waldensians became witches*, and why the existence of this ultimate conspiracy was constructed, it seems necessary to scrutinise the historiography of Waldensianism as well as of witchcraft, and furthermore to analyse in detail the circumstances of the first appearance of the new sect of Waldensian witches. As already mentioned, witchcraft has not played a prominent role in the historiography of Waldensianism, because Waldensianism and witchcraft seemed to be incompatible.[12] Historians of witchcraft could not avoid the subject so easily, but their explanation was simple. The leading scholar of the 'rationalist school' of research, Joseph Hansen (1862–1943),[13] claimed that Waldensians were forced into making confessions by the intellectual and physical power of the Inquisition.[14] According to this theory,[15] these outsiders were simply labelled as sodomites by the populace, as adorers of the Devil by Catholic theologians, and by both as witches, without themselves giving any reasons for doing so.[16] Hansen's explanation is still widely accepted, for example, with some modifications, by Cohn, Carlo Ginzburg, and William Monter.[17]

Recently I tried to demonstrate that this story is more complex, and before moving on I shall briefly summarise my argument: namely, that there are some possible bridges between witchcraft and Waldensianism. For instance, as radical pacifists and opponents of all bloodshed, they despised any form of capital punishment, and would not even accept the execution of sorcerers.[18] As we know from African societies, as well as from European demonologies like the *Malleus Maleficarum*, the protectors of suspected witches can easily be associated with witchcraft themselves.[19] The author of the *Malleus*, the Alsatian Dominican Heinrich Kramer (1430–1505) did indeed raise the question in one of his later publications on the Waldensian heresy.[20] With their nocturnal gatherings and secret meetings, necessitated by the danger of persecution, Waldensians could therefore arouse suspicions aside from their religious practices.

Furthermore, the Waldensian clergy were famous for their ability to cure diseases, as healers and diviners. However, I would suggest that the most important factor making it possible to equate them with witches was the Waldensian clergy's ability to get in to contact with the Otherworld. Almost unnoticed by scholars of Waldensianism, and unconnected to Waldensian theology, we find in trial records from the Baltic region to Southern France that the common folk believed firmly that the Waldensian leaders were visiting otherworldly places, which they identified as paradise, and gaining superior spiritual power from their direct encounters with angels, or even God himself.

The lower orders formed the majority of this religious mass movement, and due to persecution, resulting in the so-called 'marginalisation of Waldensianism', it was particularly strong among peasants and herdsmen, with a relatively high percentage of mountain farmers and shepherds.[21] Is it then likely, that the average *credentes* were early Rationalists, or Puritans, or that they were less superstitious than their Catholic neighbours? Even in Swiss towns like Bern or Fribourg suspicions of sorcery played an important role in trials against Waldensians.[22] And how about the peasants in the high Alpine valleys of the Piedmont, the Dauphiné, the Valais, or the Pays de Vaud? These are exactly the places where preachers of the high and late Middle Ages, reformers of the sixteenth century, rationalists of the seventeenth or eighteenth centuries, as well as folklorists of the nineteenth and twentieth centuries would expect the most exotic forms of folk-beliefs. And there is certainly historical evidence to support this stereotypical assumption.[23] Although Paravy painstakingly tries to keep witchcraft and Waldensianism separate, and has treated the two subjects in subsequent chapters, obviously avoiding any interrelations, trials for magic and sorcery were held in the Waldensian valleys of the Dauphiné.[24] From the Cathar village of Montaillou in the Pyrenees we hear about love magic, harmful magic, the belief in spirits, and the charming story of a soul leaving the body in the form of a snake, walking over a silvery bridge and visiting a castle in a mountain. And magic and divination were not only practised by the *credentes*, farmers and herdsmen, but also by the noblewoman Beatrice de Planissoles and her spiritual leader in heresy, Guillaume Bélibaste (?–1321).[25]

Is it not worth considering anew the role of the spiritual leaders of the Waldensians, the 'brothers', who like the Cathar *perfecti* managed to establish a peculiar spiritual élite outside the Latin church? What was their position within a peasant society? These brethren or *barbes* had been trained by other brethren, and despite all attempts to reconstruct their education and the customs of their secret society we do not know much about it.[26] What we certainly know is that they had to be accepted voluntarily by their followers, their communities. This implies charismatic abilities, which had to meet the spiritual demands of their followers. But what could the brethren offer that the Catholic priests could not? My suggestion is that at least some of them must have found a peculiar way to demonstrate their spiritual superiority. What I am referring to are the astonishingly large number of accounts of contacts of Waldensian brethren with the 'Other World'. Evangelically trained Waldensian theologians may have rejected the idea of ecstasies, like many of their Catholic counterparts, but spiritual contacts to the other world, to the paradise, to prophets, to angels, or God himself, at least in some areas were thought to be a specifically Waldensian affair by contemporaries. The Swiss historian of Waldensianism, Kathrin Utz-Tremp,[27] not only provides a profound criticism of Le Roy Ladurie's interpretation of the heretics' spiritual world, but also explores in her important essay 'Waldensians and revenants' the example of Arnauld Gélis who claimed to have contacted the deceased around 1312, with *revenants*, and could finally see the dead not only in his dreams, but while he was awake. As his inquisitor Jacques Fournier, later pope Benedict XII (1285–1342, r. 1334–1342), reported, Gélis served as a courier for the deceased, and he also received orders from the living before he went to the realm of the dead. This Waldensian brother worked as a communicator between the living and the dead, and he was well-known for his abilities in the region, serving as a medium to clients who wanted to get into contact with the other world. His spiritual qualities thus exceeded by far those of Catholic priests and met the demands of the common people in a very peculiar way.[28]

The belief in *revenants* was widespread and in no way peculiar to Waldensiansm.[29] As we can see, however, it was also believed among the heretics, and even more, it was believed that it was possible to visit the deceased, and to ask them about both the past and future developments. Gélis was not the only Waldensian with this ability, he was not even the only one within his family. Rather he was continuing the custom of his cousin, and thus we can conclude that this ability was considered to be hereditary within his lineage. As he explained during his trial in March 1320, his cousin had been able to walk with the dead, and sometimes she had gone with them for three or four days. Gélis acquired the same ability. After a while he began to walk - that means: to fly - with the 'good women and the souls of the deceased' [cum bonis dominabus seu animabus defunctorum], who visited the cleanest houses, to eat there and to drink good wine in the cellars.[30] Here, of course, we are very close to fairy tales in a literal sense, or housemaid's fantasies, as Keith Thomas interpreted it.[31] Clearly we are talking about 'extravagant' fantasies, but to many contemporaries they did not appear to be foolish. On the contrary they were treated with utmost seriousness and care, as they were for instance in the trial against two women in Milan in 1384, who had claimed to have ecstatic experiences with the 'good lady and her folk', and were therefore able to cure and to look into the future.[32]

Bernard Gui, the famous author of an inquisitors' manual did not include these kinds of stories in his chapter on the Waldensians, but he did refer to them a few pages later in his chapter about 'Sorcerers, Diviners, and Those Who Invoke Demons'. He was emphasising here 'the vanity of superstitious men, who turn their attention to spirits of evil and the teachings of demons', but in the eyes of an inquisitor this was probably much the same as what the brothers did. Furthermore the inquisitors were required to ask the suspected persons about 'the situation of souls of the dead; also, forecasts of future events; also, the fairy women, whom they call the "good folk", and who, they say, roam about at night; also, making incantations or conjuring with incantations using fruits, herbs, girdles, and other materials [...]. Also, [ask about] curing diseases [...]'.[33] Most historians of Waldensianism would claim that this has nothing to do with Waldensianism. But the stories of Arnauld Gélis, which could be related to Bernard Gui's catalogues of Waldensians as well as on witches, are not exceptional. In Austrian trials against the Waldensians stories of this sort emerged during an extensive persecution launched by the bishop of Passau, Bernhard von Prambach (1285–1313). With the support of the archbishop of Salzburg, Eberhard II von Regensburg (1170–1246, r. 1200–1246) and the Austrian archduke Friedrich der Schöne (1289–1330, r. 1298–1330), the bishop appointed for his diocese several inquisitors, who eventually included almost forty Austrian towns in their persecution. One trial in the town of Krems in the years between 1312 and 1315 is especially well documented.[34] And here the inquisitor's protocol summarises as one of the typical Waldensian errors, that two of the brothers had to go to paradise every year, to receive the power of binding and resolving, which they could afterwards transmit to their followers.[35] Bernard Gui's suggestions of the brethren's powers, which was thought to derive directly from God, comes to mind. This was not merely an inquisitor's fantasy, since Audisio and other scholars of Waldensianism have provided similar examples from trial records.[36] The priestly power of binding and resolving (Matthew 18,18) was central for the brethren's abilities, at least in the eyes of their followers. Many witnesses from all over Europe, and also from fourteenth and fifteenth-century Piedmont and Dauphiné, claimed that their masters owned this particular power.[37]

As Richard Kieckhefer has mentioned, in Northern Germany in the late fourteenth century ecstatic experiences were commonly thought to be a Waldensian affair.[38] Parts of Zwicker's records in Pommern and Brandenburg have survived, and they reveal that the Waldensian brethren were thought to make periodic trips to paradise. One Aley, the wife of Thyde Takken of Bowmgarten confessed in March 1394, 'that she had heard from a certain woman, that two of their apostolic and heresiarch brethren went to hell, and heard the pitiable cries and saw the devils attacking the souls in hell and saying, "that one was an adulterer, that one a usurer, that one a tavern-haunter", and so on of all the other sorts of vice-laden souls; and afterwards they came to paradise and heard the voice of the Lord God giving them wisdom and learning, with which they were to instruct the people committed to their care on earth'.[39] Confessions of otherworld-experiences of the Waldensian brethren were also found during the inquisition campaigns of Peter Zwicker in Bohemia and Austria in the last years of the fourteenth and the early years of the fifteenth centuries.[40] The Waldensian masters' journey to the otherworld, paradise, to receive supernatural powers, authority and wisdom from an angel, or God himself, was even a question of public debate. Some *credentes* assumed that they had to go there every seven years, others claimed to know that it had to happen more frequently, for instance every year.[41]

Such stories sound familiar to historians of witchcraft. Some of the most aggressive witch-hunts in European history were launched after confessions by witch-doctors with otherworld experiences, who have been regarded as witches themselves by the authorities. One example around 1500 is Hans Tscholi from Kriens, between Luzern and Bern in Switzerland, who had claimed to walk with the souls of the deceased. From their revelations he derived his authority as a witch-doctor. And as in the case of Gélis, Tscholi was not the only member of his family with these kinds of ecstatic experiences.[42] Another example is Zuanne delle Piatte, a wandering witch-doctor in the Italian Alps, well-known in many villages of the Dolomites, who claimed to visit regularly the *Venusberg*, where the fairy queen was living, and whose confessions led to a witch-hunt around Cavalese in the Val di Fiemme/Fleimstal.[43] Another example is Diell Breull (?–1632), who visited Frau Holle in her mountain castle and was therefore able to foresee the future. His tales caused a large witch-hunt with almost 200 victims within the small Calvinist county of Isenburg-Büdingen as late as 1630.[44] Chonrad Stoeckhlin (1549–1587), a herdsman from Oberstdorf in the German Alps, to whom I have devoted the microhistory *Chonrad Stoeckhlin and the Phantoms of the Night* fits this same pattern.[45] All of them were visiting 'the other world', and their peculiar position as messengers 'between the living and the dead' was obviously the precondition for their ability of healing and divining.[46]

None of these healers with otherworld experiences considered himself a witch, but due to their exotic stories each of them was tortured until they became adapted to demonological theory. Stoeckhlin's confessions in 1586 caused the largest witch-hunt within the prince-bishopric of Augsburg, and this impressed the surrounding territories so that finally the whole region was affected.[47] Investigating the stories of Chonrad Stoeckhlin about his 'Nachtschar', the 'Phantoms of the Night', which regularly flew to certain places in order to observe hell and paradise, and his ability to cure and to recognise witchcraft, which he claimed was obtained from his spiritual leader, an angel, I found more and more associated stories in neighbouring parts of Austria, and especially in Switzerland, where the vernacular terms *Nachtschar* and *Nachtvolk* (night-folk) were distributed from the German Alps in the Northeast to the Swiss Cantons of *Valais* and *Vaud* in the Southwest.[48] In part this was caused by the fact that Stoeckhlin's best friends were migrants from the Little Walser Valley to his home town Oberstdorf in the German Alps. The Walsers are an Alemannic group, who had migrated southwards to the Upper Rhone valley in the early Middle Ages, and had been settled in the Valais (Wallis) for centuries. Due to overpopulation some of them turned northwards in the late Middle Ages, to settle in the Swiss Upper Rhine valley, in the canton of Grisons (Graubünden) or as mountain farmers in its side valleys and some high alpine valleys in western Austria (Montafon, Walser Valleys), near the German border.[49]

They brought with them strange stories about the Phantoms of the Night (Nachtschar, Nachtvolk). The stories of herdsmen observing meetings of the 'good folk', who produced heavenly music, danced in blessed houses, cooked complete cows or oxen, which they restored to life from their skins and bones the next morning, of individuals who were invited to join the *bons hommes* or the 'good ladies' to walk and fly with them during the night and to obtain superior spiritual qualities, were widespread not only in fairy-tales, but also in late medieval and sixteenth-century Swiss sources.[50] It is striking to see how far popular beliefs contained ideas about otherworld journeys, independently of any allusions to witchcraft or Waldensianism. The Lucerne chancellor Renward Cysat (1545–1614), a devout Counter-Reformation Catholic of Milanese ancestry, reports in his chronicles dozens of stories of well-known contemporaries, who were members of the 'good society'. The decisive point seems to me that these examples are not treated like fairy-tales or fables, but as testimonies from reliable individuals, even at the end of the sixteenth century.[51] And it is in no way astonishing that the same subjects had been treated in the witch trials against Waldensians, or witches, or Waldensian witches.[52]

Starting my research into the case of Chonrad Stoeckhlin in the German Alps, my investigations have led me directly to the very region where the concept of the witches' Sabbat had emerged, the Swiss Cantons of Wallis/Valais and of Waadtland/*Vaud* - and this name may well have reinforced the use of the term *Vauderie* - and the former duchy of Savoy. At present it seems impossible to assess exactly how far confessions of ecstatic experiences during the persecutions of the Waldensians have contributed to the paradigm shift, the fusion of witchcraft and Waldensianism. If so, it must have occurred on the Italian or French side of the linguistic border, German theologians never used the term 'Waldensians' for witches. In the Francophone parts of Switzerland, however, the term *Vaudoises* was used in courts from about 1430, and it persisted around Fribourg until the present.[53] Since Hansen it has been obvious, that the crusade against the syncretistic traditions of a peasant world in Savoy, Piedmont, and the Dauphiné must have decisively contributed to this fusion, even more, since the inquisition was accompanied by propagandistic campaigns of charismatic preachers like the sanctified Vinzenz Ferrier. But on the other hand it has never been plausibly explained, why Waldensians should have been transformed into witches, while Jews, Cathars, Fraticelli, or other heretics were not. For historians of Waldensianism it remained an enigma, why the witches could be called *Vaudois*.[54]

But when examined from a comparative perspective this is less surprising. The Waldensian brethren, despite lacking any medical training, also worked as doctors and were asked to cure diseases. Reports from fifteenth-century

Dauphiné, for example, describe them prescribing their clients with recipes and herbs, but also using prayers. These might have been understood, or misunderstood, as magical spells. Also in healing their clients the 'barbes' probably thought to fulfil an evangelical mission (Matthew: 10,8),[55] but in the eyes of the common people this ability may have been connected with the brethren's reputation for holiness. One of their characteristics was their ascetic life, which exceeded by far the customs of their Catholic counterparts.[56] And this may have resulted in peculiar forms of veneration, and of expectations; the 'barbes' were reported to be *sancti viri*, 'holy men'. Their 'great appearance of holiness' was already mentioned by the *Passau Anonymous*,[57] and the term 'holy men' by Bernard Gui, but its usage is confirmed by the Waldensian believers themselves, in trial records from Pomerania, Bohemia, Austria, the Alsace, as well as in the Piedmont or the Dauphiné.[58]

The phenomenon of 'living saints' was not uncommon to contemporaries, it was well known in the Roman church,[59] where protagonists like St. Francis advertised the power of Catholicism. On the other hand the phenomenon is not solely a Christian affair, but is well-known in social anthropology.[60] And it reminds us of 'religious specialists' like Hans Tscholi, Zuanne delle Piatte or Chonrad Stoeckhlin, who served their communities as healers, diviners and messengers to the other world. These spiritual qualities are characteristic features of shamanism.[61] And although this may have been contrary to the intention of the gospel, at least some of the brothers were treated as, and seem to have worked as, shamans. Even Audisio points to the fact, that some narratives about the 'barbes' have been amplified with additional popular beliefs concerning the liminal experiences of fear, pain or death, thus resembling typical initiation rites of shamans.[62]

The 'brothers' were treated as living saints, but in addition, like the Cathar 'perfecti' before them,[63] they were called *boni homines* or *bons hommes* by their followers.[64] This seemingly harmless term, despite comments by some of the most distinguished scholars of heresy,[65] requires further interpretation. 'Good men' or 'good people' - these are exactly the terms which have been used for certain supernatural beings in the contemporary folk-belief: the 'good ladies' and the 'good men', the 'good people' were terms of great ambivalence, describing for instance fairy people or powerful good spirits in opposition to demonic beings. It was also a term for the deceased, who - according to popular belief - visited the houses of some people, who then were called 'the blessed' by others. And of course there was much ambivalence in a term like 'good people' or 'good men', it could even serve as a euphemism, since any powerful being could be dangerous, and harm as well as heal. All the inherent ambiguity should be noticed very well, when a Waldensian believer already in 1241 admits, that the *master* Petrus de Vallibus, who also served as a healer, was 'loved like an angel of God'.[66]

My conclusion is, that the identification of witchcraft and Waldensianism has not been the mere result of a labelling process, but rather that certain elements in the practice of Waldensianism made such a transformation plausible. As Peter Biller has demonstrated from the treatise *Cum dormirent homines*, its author did not invent his accounts on Waldensian religious practice, but rather exaggerated and distorted confessions from trial records. Beyond the 'heresy-topos', where Waldensians kissed devil-cats under their tails, the secrecy of the nocturnal gatherings could be associated with negatively connotated animals like bats or toads, and it could be linked with evil behaviour, sexual deviance, or the evil itself,[67] as is customary in popular ideas about witchcraft worldwide.[68] The custom of collecting money among the *credentes* could be linked with fantasies of hidden treasures of silver and gold, and again be related to encounters with the Devil, in order to enhance the plausibility of the story.[69] The important role of women in the movement - some *sisters* acted as equivalents to the brothers, and women frequently substituted the *magistri* during their absence - may have been associated with the importance of women in the magical arts. Some believers, like Galosna in Pinerolo, actually confessed, that magic was taught at Waldensian 'synagogues', and was exercised by women.[70] But finally, and most important, not only for inquisitors, but also for the Waldensian's neighbours, and maybe even for themselves, the holiness of the *masters*, their supernatural abilities, and above all the brethren's journeys to the 'other world', their shamanistic qualities, could have served as a *tertium comparationis* between Waldensians and witches.

The wealth of stories about visions, raptures, and regular journeys to the other world[71] opens up the possibility that some of the brethren had indeed developed a technique of 'ecstasies'. It is remarkable that Carlo Ginzburg in his *Storia Notturna*, focused on ecstasies and the prehistory of the cumulative crime of European witchcraft, and yet failed to associate the Waldensians' abilities with the witches' sabbath.[72] These similarities between the imagined abilities of Waldensian leaders and witches, however, do not yet explain why it should have been attractive to level the accusation of witchcraft against Waldensianism, not least because Waldensians could already be prosecuted for their heresy. Let us therefore take a microscopic view of the new crime's invention. This seems to be the appropriate method, since it emerged - as far as we know - within one generation in one particular European territory: the duchy of Savoy, by then a medium-sized territory in the process of state formation. A first hint is contained within a papal bull of Alexander V (ca. 1340–1410, r. 1409–1410) in 1409, which confirmed to the Franciscan inquisitor Ponce Fougeyron that innumerable Christians and Jews in a group of dioceses, roughly covering the region of the French Alps, and Savoy, constituted *novas sectas*, new sects, and performed and taught forbidden rites.[73] This is certainly a surprising claim, but there was no need to explain the character of the new heresy, since the decree had the form of a rescript. This means that the Inquisitor had formulated the text himself, and the papal chancellery only authorised it for his usage. Fougeyron was playing with older concepts of conspiracy, namely the Jewish conspiracy, which had been held responsible for the Black Death in that region.[74] Cohn and Ginzburg have rightly pointed to the fact that central terms of the witch stereotype, like the Sabbath, or the Synagogue, were a legacy of the earlier persecution of the Jews. The Jews and Christians in this strange new sect, however, were using sorcery, divination, and devil worship.[75] The bull was reissued to the same Franciscan inquisitor in the same region in 1418 by Pope Martin V (1368–1431, r. 1417–1431), and in 1434 by Pope Eugenius IV (ca. 1383–1447, r. 1431–1447).[76]

Within the next years, however, a decisive change occurred in the perception of the new sect; one is tempted to say, using the terminology of Thomas S. Kuhn, that there was a 'paradigm shift'.[77] Instead of mere sorcery, the new cumulative crime of European witchcraft was defined: a great conspiracy of the ultimate evil. A treatise called *Errores Gazariorum*, most likely written in 1435,[78] gave the first elaborate description of a witches' Sabbat,[79] and within five years the new sect was upgraded. In 1437 Pope Eugenius IV issued a general decree to all inquisitors about devil worshippers, who committed 'maleficia' by words, touch, or signs.[80] It was followed three years later by a papal bull 'ad perpetua rei memoriam', directed against the former duke Amadeus VIII of Savoy (1383–1451, r. 1416–1434), who had been elected by the Council of Basel as the counter-pope Felix V. (r. 1439–1449).[81] The bull connects this false pontificate with all the heresies in his duchy, devil-worshipping and sorcery, 'qui vulgari nomine *stregule* vel *stregones* seu *Waudenses* nuncupantur'.[82] This, finally, was the name of the new sect. They were neither Christians nor Jews; they were *Waldensian witches*. The papal bull used this terminology for the first time in 1440, explicitly maintaining that it was the popular terminology of a specific region, namely the duchy of Savoy.[83] In this territory, including the later Swiss dioceses of Geneva, Sion and Lausanne, the term *vauderie* or Waldensianism for witchcraft was in use early in the 15th century,[84] was predominant throughout the 16th century, and is still in use today.[85]

What was so peculiar about the duchy of Savoy, the cradle of our mega-conspiracy? As Robert Muchembled has pointed out, Savoy around 1400 was anything but a backward Alpine region: close to the Lombardic capital Milan, then Europe's largest town and the centre of early capitalism, with Alpine agriculture being integrated into a market economy. It was also close to Avignon, the pope's see and a major political centre. Duke Amadeus VIII made an attempt to forge his rather heterogeneous possessions between the Mediterranean Sea, and Switzerland, into a 'modern' state, an Alpine core state of Europe, at the crossroads of Italy, France, Spain, and the Holy Roman Empire. With his ambitious policy of state formation, symbolised for instance by the *Statuta Sabaudiae*, a general law introduced in 1430,[86] the duke felt strong enough to act as a European player, and indeed managed to be elected pope by the conciliarist party at the Council of Basel. His state, Savoy, served as a laboratory for religious reform movements, but it is not yet clear how political reforms and religious zeal fit together. Inquisitors were seemingly encouraged to persecute the Waldensian minority, and it is indeed in Savoy where we can find early evidence of a fusion of heresy and witchcraft.[87] The association of witchcraft and Waldensianism was promoted by local Franciscans,[88] and Dominican inquisitors. The soil may have been prepared by powerful preachers like the Dominican Vincent Ferrier (ca. 1350–1419, sanctified in 1458), whose apocalyptic sermons between 1399 and 1409 excited the region where the fusion took place.[89]

During the reign of Amadeus, Savoy was shaken by enormous waves of persecution. From the 1420s, the local Inquisitors, like the Dominican Uldry de Torrenté in the diocese of Lausanne (ca. 1420–1445),[90] stopped focusing on individuals, and began to try to execute hundreds of suspects. One can only guess at the practical requirements of such an enterprise in a world where hardly any proper prisons existed. These persecutions have not yet been explored systematically, and this is all the more regrettable, since they play a major role in our story. At least in some places these large-scale persecutions started with hunting Waldensians and ended up with burning witches.[91] The earliest report about these massive persecutions, written around 1431 by Johann Fründ (ca. 1400–1469), chronicler of the Swiss town of Luzern,[92] states explicitly that the new heresy of witchcraft, 'die ketzerye der hexsen', had emerged 'des ersten under den Walchen und darnach under den Tütschen', first among the Romance speaking, then among the 'Germans', referring of course to the Germanophone areas of Southern Switzerland alongside the language border.

After their pact with the Devil, the witches could fly through the air and visit wine cellars, banqueting and feasting whenever they wished, and could transform themselves into animals. Starting in 1428, more than a hundred men and women were burnt in Wallisian courts within just eighteen months, and on the other side of the mountain, where the persecution had begun earlier, even more were executed.[93] The Aosta valley, where Ponce Fougeyron had been working as an inquisitor, and where the witches were called *Gazzari*, meaning Waldensians, also witnessed a wave of persecution. All these valleys belonged to the duke of Savoy. The *Errores Gazariorum* was just one of a cluster of five lengthy reports about the new sect of witches written between 1430 and 1440,[94] all provoked by the witch-hunts in the duchy of Savoy, including some of the southern valleys of modern Switzerland, and in neighbouring Dauphiné. It was no longer the business of mendicant Inquisitors alone, since the Dauphiné employed a secular chief prosecutor, and in some Swiss valleys the responsibility was given to local courts. Witch-hunting, as in contemporary Africa, was a grass-roots movement, fuelled by popular demand.

Why did these persecutions start? If we compare Savoy to the South African case, we can see striking similarities: economic change, political stress, ideological pressure groups redefining the moral universe, and political actors conducting persecutions.[95] There are, however, three decisive questions that remain unresolved: Why were the systematic individual trials transformed into large-scale persecutions, why were they targeting Waldensians, and why were these heretics redefined as witches? The answer, I think, cannot be found in texts alone, although they may give us a clue. If we put the events in chronological order, it is clear that the large-scale persecutions in Savoy, the Dauphiné, the Valais, the Vaud and surrounding areas were triggered by a devastating mortality crisis in the region around 1427.[96] Mortality crises are not unusual in traditional societies, but may appear as 'unnatural' to contemporaries. As in so many other cases where witchcraft was suspected, 'unnatural events' played an important role, and only one generation after the shock waves of the Black Death had receded, new kinds of 'unnatural' hardships began to threaten subsistence in Alpine regions. An unprecedented number of rainy summers and extremely cold and long winters afflicted the Northern hemisphere. The winters of 1407–1408 and 1422–1423 where so severe that not only the major rivers, but even the Baltic sea was frozen, and Norwegian wolves were able to roam into Denmark.[97] In the 1430s the frequency of extreme winters increased, climaxing in 1431–1432, 1433–1434 and 1437–1438,[98] causing a series of Europe-wide famine years and mortality crises.[99] The climate was unfavourable for agriculture in general, and for Alpine life in particular. The 1430s have attracted some attention from economic historians and from historians of climate. Some scholars have seen in this the beginning of the 'Little Ice Age'.[100]

If the witchcraft persecutions succeeded the persecutions of the Jews, this was not only because the latter became less accessible as victims due to their expulsions from large parts of Western Europe, as Norman Cohn had suggested.[101] Another reason may well be that Jews had never been held responsible for the weather. European mythology attributed weather magic to *witchcraft*.[102] There was, however, a problem: since the earliest missionaries, Christian theology had denied the competing spiritual powers of sorcerers and diviners, and the efficacy of witchcraft in particular. As with the colonial law in Africa, medieval canon law did not punish witches, but those who believed in witchcraft.[103] The Roman church and the Christian states of Europe consequently suppressed any attempts at witch-hunting throughout the Middle Ages. This major impediment could only be overcome by means of constructing a new, unusual, and unprecedented crime, 'an ultimate conspiracy'. Only the language of heresy trials enabled secular and spiritual authorities to persecute witchcraft. Only by hunting Waldensians was it possible to persecute witches.

The fusion of Waldensianism and witchcraft, however, was only transitory. Savoyan Inquisitors and authors imagined witchcraft as the modernised version of Waldensianism ('modernorum hereticorum Waldensium'),[104] and the curial party used this particularity to label Savoy as a hothouse of new heresies and witchcraft, a political argument against the unwelcome Savoyan counter-pope. But although it was not implied in the contemporary papal bulls, nor in the first treatises about the new sect, its members were portrayed as predominantly female. And the illustrator of a manuscript of 'Le champion des Dames' clearly felt attracted by this interpretation of Waldensianism. He sketched witches riding through the air on sticks and broomsticks and decided to call them 'Vaudoises'.[105]

But this use of the term 'Vaudois' seems to have irritated and confused contemporaries. The chronicler Enguerrand de Monstrelet mentions that he could not explain why these witches were now called 'Vaudois'.[106] Even the papal bull of 1440 had to explain that these Waldensians were normally called 'stregule vel stregones' by the people, that means witches. The chief prosecutor of the Dauphine, Claude Tholosan, preferred to use the local term for sorcerers, 'faicturier' in his courts,[107] and the Swiss chronicler Fründ used the Latin term 'sortilei' or the local vernacular term 'Hexen', then almost unknown but later the general term for witches in German. The Council of Basel (1431–1449) provided the opportunity to discuss the new crime,[108] but if we examine the records of the council's theologians, the results are surprising. Despite many reflections about the new sort of witches, and their relation to Canon Law, only a few authors accepted the equation of witchcraft and Waldensianism. Among them was the Franciscan Ponce Fougeyron, possibly the author of the *Errores Gazariorum*,[109] and Jean Taincture (ca. 1400–1469) from Tournai, for whom the sect was more terrible than paganism, Islamic unbelief or even heresy, and implied the destruction of Christianity and the end of the world.[110] But most of the authors taking part in the debate, whether they accepted the reality of the new crime or not, preferred to avoid the identification of Waldensians and witches. Latin authors like John Nider preferred the neutral term Malefici,[111] and many used vernacular terms like bruxas, streghe, or Hexen.[112] Some famous theologians, such as Nicholas of Cusa (1401–1464), rejected the idea of a new sect on the basis of the *Canon Episcopi*, which had defined witchcraft as an illusion.[113] Others, including the Swiss Felix Malleolus (1389–1460), discussed the authority of Canon Law,[114] even if they were inclined to accept the change of paradigm, as were the Dominican cardinal Johannes a Turrecremata (1388–1468),[115] or the French Dominican inquisitors Jean Vineti (ca. 1400–ca. 1475) and Nicholas Jacquier (ca. 1400–14??).[116] Heinrich Kramer, the dominican Inquisitor and author of the *Malleus Maleficarum*, avoided the issue of Waldensianism altogether and defined witchcraft as the ultimate crime, the ultimate conspiracy.[117]

Detecting the ultimate conspiracy was a complex process, loaded with contingencies. It could hardly be portrayed as a necessary development, easily explainable by means of social scientific theory.[118] However, there are components that seem to allow a comparative perspective, and furthermore it is possible to identify intellectual traditions and historical events, which are helpful to explain the historical background. They enable us to understand - to use an old-fashioned but still useful term - why it was necessary for contemporaries to interpret 'why bad things happened to good people'. In their 'management of misfortune',[119] at least parts of the intellectual élites eventually accepted the popular concept that 'unnatural' hardship was caused by sorcery. To make it acceptable theologically, sorcery had to be recast as 'Vauderie'. Only afterwards could it be superseded by the new concept of a cumulative crime, consisting of apostasy and magic. Witchcraft, the crime of the Little Ice Age, was born. And in the following centuries, the Central European waves of persecution followed neatly the conjunctures of price movements, mirroring crop failure, malnutrition and 'unnatural' diseases, the immediate results of unfavourable weather in a traditional agrarian society.

Notes

1   I wish to thank Gabriel Audisio and Euan Cameron for exchanging some ideas, Peter Biller and Bill Sheils for having a look at an earlier draft of this paper, and Paul Brand (York) for checking the final version.

2   Isak Niehaus, Eliazaar Mohlala and Shokane Kally, *Witchcraft, Power and Politics. Exploring the Occult in the South African Lowveld* (London 2001).

3   Bronislaw Malinowski, *Magic, Science and Religion* (1925); *Magic, Science and Religion. And other Essays* (London 1948).

4   Carl F. Graumann and Serge Moscovici (eds.), *Changing Conceptions of Conspiracy* (Heidelberg and New York 1987).

5   Nicole Jacques-Chaquin, 'Demoniac conspiracy' in ibid., pp. 71–86.

6   Dieter Groh, 'The temptation of conspiracy theory, or: why do bad things happen to good people? Part I: preliminary draft of a theory of conspiracy theories', and 'Part II: case studies' in ibid., pp. 1–38.

7   Ibid., p. 17.

8   Ibid., pp. 17–20.

9   Norman Cohn, *Europe's Inner Demons: An Enquiry Inspired by the Great Witch-Hunt* (London 1975).

10 Gabriel Audisio, *Les Vaudois. Naissance, Vie et Mort d' une Dissidence (XIVe–XVIe siècle)* (Turin 1989); *Die Waldenser. Die Geschichte einer Religiösen Bewegung* (transl. by Elisabeth Hirschberger, München 1996); *The Waldensian Dissent. Persecution and Survival, ca.1170–ca.1570* (Cambridge 1999).

11 Euan Cameron, *The Reformation of the Heretics. The Waldenses of the Alps, 1480–1580* (Oxford 1984). Andreas Blauert, *Frühe Hexenverfolgungen. Ketzer-, Zauberei- und Hexenprozesse des 15. Jahrhunderts* (Hamburg 1989) , pp. 38ff., has already criticised this attitude.

12 Ignaz von Döllinger, *Beiträge zur Sektengeschichte des Mittelalters* (2 vols., München 1890. Reprint New York 1960); Herbert Grundmann, *Religiöse Bewegungen im Mittelalter. Untersuchungen über die Geschichtlichen Zusammenhänge Zwischen Ketzerei, den Bettelorden und der Religiösen Frauenbewegung im 12. und 13. Jahrhundert und über die Geschichtlichen Grundlagen der Deutschen Mystik* (Berlin 1935); *Verbesserte und Ergänzte Auflage, mit einem Anhang: Neue Beiträge zur Geschichte der Religiösen Bewegungen im Mittelalter* (Hildesheim 1961, translated as *Religious Movements in the Middle Ages* (London 1995); Gordon Leff, *Heresy in the Later Middle Ages. The Relation of Heterodoxy to Dissent, c.1250–c.1450* (2 vols., Manchester/New York 1967); Amadeo Molnar, *Die Waldenser. Geschichte und Europäisches Ausmaß einer Ketzerbewegung* [1973] (Freiburg/Br. 1993); Dietrich Kurze (ed.), *Quellen zur Ketzergeschichte Brandenburgs und Pommerns* (Berlin/New York 1975); Malcolm D. Lambert, *Medieval Heresy. Popular Movements from Bogomil to Hus* (New York 1977); 2nd edition: *Medieval Heresy. Popular Movements from the Gregorian Movement to the Reformation* (Oxford 1992); Grado G. Merlo, *Valdesi e Valdismi Medievali* (Torino 1984); Peter Biller, *The Waldenses, 1170–1530: Between a Religious Order and a Church* (Aldershot 2001).

13 For the history of witchcraft research, see Wolfgang Behringer, 'Zur Geschichte der Hexenforschung' in Sönke Lorenz (ed.), *Hexen und Hexenverfolgung im Deutschen Südwesten* (Ostfildern 1994), pp. 93–146.

14 Joseph Hansen, *Zauberwahn, Inquisition und Hexenprozeß im Mittelalter und die Entstehung der Großen Hexenverfolgung* (München 1900).

15 Howard S. Becker, *Outsiders. Studies in the Sociology of Deviance* (New York 1973).

16 Johannes Franck, 'Geschichte des Wortes "Hexe"', in Hansen, *Zauberwahn*, pp. 614–670, p. 615. We will not trace the question of sexual deviance further in this essay, although it would be tempting to explore either the 'labelling' of ascetic outsiders as sexual deviants, or the possibility of laxity among the Waldensians, comparable to the surprising behaviour of Cathar believers at Montaillou. The question of how 'heresy', and especially 'Vauderie' became a synonym for sexual deviance, and especially homosexuality, in some regions deserves future attention. Sodomy, however, was a capital crime, with death by burning the corpse to ashes thought to be the appropriate punishment. It would certainly not have been necessary to label sodomites additionally as witches. There is a short discussion in Audisio, *Les Vaudois*, p. 94f. See also E. William Monter, 'La sodomie a l'époque moderne en Suisse romande' in *Annales E. S. C.*, 29 (1974), pp. 1023–33.

17 Cohn, *Europe's Inner Demons*, pp. 32–59, 225–55; William Monter, *Witchcraft in France and Switzerland. The Borderlands during the Reformation* (Ithaca and London 1976), pp. 19–24; William Monter, 'Poursuites précoces. La sorcellerie en Suisse', in Robert Muchembled (ed.), *Magie et Sorcellerie en Europe du Moyen Age à Nos Jours* (Paris 1994), pp. 47–58; Blauert, *Frühe Hexenverfolgungen*, pp. 26–30.

18 'nec crediderit, maleficos iudicialiter posse occidi sine peccato ...' and 'respondit, quod crediderit ...', quoted in Kurze, *Quellen zur Ketzergeschichte Brandenburgs*, pp. 115, 120. One very self-confident believer, the forty year old Peter Beyer from Bärwalde, whose parents had also been Waldensians, claimed categorically in 1393 'Maleficos non crediderit occidi posse sine peccato., ibid., p. 173. The term 'maleficus' could mean evil-doers in general, those who had committed a capital crime, but in a narrower sense it meant sorcerers, and during the fifteenth century, for instance in Nider or the *Malleus Maleficarum*, it meant particularly 'witches'.

19 Heinrich Kramer (Institoris), *Malleus Maleficarum. Kommentierte Neuübersetzung* (ed. by. Günter Jerouschek/Wolfgang Behringer, Munich 2000), introduction.

20 Heinrich Institoris [Kramer], *Sancte Romane Ecclesiae Fidei Defensionis Clippeum Adversus Waldensium et Pickardorum Heresim* ... (Olomucz 1501), fol. 7 verso.

21 Cohn, *Europe's Inner Demons*, p. 38; Martin Erbstösser, *Ketzer im Mittelalter* (Leipzig 1984), p. 207f; Audisio, *Les Vaudois*, p. 51.

22 Examples in Blauert, *Frühe Hexenverfolgungen*, pp. 41ff.

23 Ferdinando Gabotto, 'Dissidents religieux à Genève, en Savoie et dans le Valais en 1428–1431 in *Bulletin de la Société d'Histoire Vaudoise*, 24 (1907); Maxime Reymond, 'La sorcellerie au Pays de Vaud au XVe siècle' in *Schweizerisches Archiv für Volkskunde*, 12 (1908), pp. 1–14; J.-B. Bertrand, 'Notes sur les procès d'hérésie et de sorcellerie en Valais' in *Annales Valaisannes*, 3 (1920–1), pp. 151–194; Grado G. Merlo, *Eretici e Inquisitori Nella Società Piemontese del Trecento* (Torino 1977), pp. 63–74, 114–20; Massimo Centini, *Streghe, Roghi e Diavoli. I Processi di Stregoneria in Piemonte* (Cuneo 1995).

24 Pierette Paravy, *De la Chrétienté Romaine à la Réforme en Dauphiné: Évêques, Fidèles et Déviants (vers 1340–vers 1530)* (2 vols., Rome 1993), Livre III, pp. 775–812 chapter 14 'La répression de la sorcellerie en Dauphiné'; pp. 813–907 chapter 15 'Autre procès dauphinois'; Livre IV, 'Une autre modèle de vie chrétienne: Les vaudois de Dauphiné', pp. 909–1178.

25 Emmanuel Le Roy Ladurie, *Montaillou. Village Occitain de 1294 à 1324* (Paris 1975); Matthias Benad, *Domus und Religion in Montaillou* (Tübingen 1990), pp. 32f., 60, 108, 110f. (spirits); pp. 32f., 37, 211, 224f. (magic); pp. 9, 29, 93, 150, 174, 212f., 222, 224, 245, 303, 329f., 331f. (sorcery).

26   Audisio, *Les Vaudois*, pp. 134 –73.

27   Kathrin Utz Tremp, 'Der Freiburger Waldenserprozeß von 1399 und seine bernische Vorgeschichte' in: *Freiburger Geschichtsblätter*, 68 (1991), pp. 57–85; *Waldenser, Wiedergänger, Hexen und Rebellen. Biographien zu den Waldenserprozessen in Freiburg im Üchtland (1399–1439)*, (Freiburg 1999); *Quellen zur Geschichte der Waldenser von Freiburg im Üchtland (1399–1439)* (München 2000).

28   Kathrin Utz-Tremp, 'Waldenser und Wiedergänger - Das Fegefeuer im Inquisitionsregister des Bischofs Jacques Fournier von Pamiers (1317–1326)' in Peter Jezler (ed.), *Himmel, Hölle Fegefeuer. Das Jenseits im Mittelalter*, Katalog des Schweizer Landesmuseums (Zürich 1994), pp. 125–34.

29   Claude Lecouteux, *Fantomes et Revenants au Moyen Age* (Paris 1986); *Geschichte der Gespenster und Wiedergänger im Mittelalter* (Köln/Wien 1987).

30   Jean Duvernoy (ed.), *Le Registre d' Inquisition de Jacques Fournier (1318–1325)* (3 vols., Toulouse 1965), vol. 1, pp. 533–5 (13. 3. 1320).

31   Keith Thomas, *Religion and the Decline of Magic. Studies in Popular Beliefs in Sixteenth and Seventeenth Century England* (London 1971), p. 713f.

32   Luisa Muraro, *La Signora del Gioco. Episodi della Caccia alle Streghe* (Mailand 1976).

33   Gui (1991) 444.

34   Wilhelm Wattenbach (ed.), *Monumenta Germaniae Historica, Scriptores*, vol. 9, 825–7; Margaret A. E. Nickson,'The pseudo- Reinerius treatise, the final stage of a thirteenth century work on heresy from the diocese of Passau' in *Archives d' Histoire Doctrinale et Littéraire du Moyen Age*, 34 (1967), pp. 255–314.

35   'Zwei von ihnen würden jedes Jahr in das Paradies eingehen und von Elias und Henoch die Binde- und Lösegewalt erhalten, die sie ihren Anhängern dann weiterverleihen können', Werner Maleczek, 'Die Ketzerverfolgungen im österreichischen Hoch- und Spätmittelalter' in: Erich Zöllner (ed.), *Wellen der Verfolgung in der österreichischen Geschichte* (Wien 1986), pp.18–39; the quotation is from p. 36.

36   Audisio, *Les Vaudois*, pp. 26f., 29, 31, 39, 52, 61.

37   Grado G. Merlo, *Eretici e Inquisitori Nella Società Piemontese del Trecento* (Torino 1977), pp. 43f., 48f; Audisio, *Les Vaudois*, pp.148, 169f.

38   Richard Kieckhefer, *The Repression of Heresy in Medieval Germany* (Liverpool 1979), p. 63.

39   Dietrich Kurze (ed.), *Quellen zur Ketzergeschichte Brandenburgs und Pommerns* (Berlin/New York 1975), p. 83–7.

40   Maleczek, 'Die Ketzerverfolgungen', p. 31f.

41   Audisio, *Les Vaudois*, p. 171.

42   Eduard Hoffmann-Krayer (ed.), 'Luzerner Akten zum Hexen- und Zauberwesen' in *Schweizerisches Archiv für Volkskunde*, 3 (1899), pp. 22–40, 81–122, 189–224, 291–329.

43   Giuseppe Bonomo, *Caccia Alle Streghe. La Credenza Nelle Streghe Dal Sec. XIII al XIX Con Particolare Riferimento all'Italia* (Palermo 1956, 1959; reprint 1971), pp. 74–84; Heide Dienst, 'Hexenprozesse im Landgericht Völs im ersten Jahrzehnt des 16. Jahrhunderts' in *Völs am Schlern 888–1988. Ein Gemeindebuch,* (1988) pp. 249–56.

44   Walter Niess, *Hexenprozesse in der Grafschaft Büdingen. Protokolle, Ursachen, Hintergründe* (Büdingen 1982).

45   Wolfgang Behringer, *Shaman of Oberstdorf. Chonrad Stoeckhlin and the Phantoms of the Night* (Translated by H.C. Erik Midelfort, Virginia University Press, Charlottesville 1998).

46   Eva Pócs, *Between the Living and the Dead. A Perspective on Witches and Seers in the Early Modern Age* (Budapest 1998).

47   Wolfgang Behringer, *Witchcraft Persecutions in Bavaria. Popular Magic, Religious Zealotry and Reason of State in Early Modern Europe* (Translated by J.C. Grayson and David Lederer, Cambridge University Press, Cambridge 1997).

48   Georg Luck (ed.), 'Totenvolk und Nachtschar' in *Rätische Alpensagen. Gestalten und Bilder aus der Sagenwelt Graubündens* (2nd ed., Chur 1935); Arnold Büchli, 'Wilde Jagd und Nachtvolk', in *Schweizer Volkskunde* 37 (1947), pp. 65–9; Klaus Beitl, 'Die Sage vom Nachtvolk. Untersuchung eines alpinen Sagentypus (mit Verbreitungskarte)' in Georgois A. Megas (ed.), *IV. International Congress of Folk-Narrative Research in Athens: Lectures and Reports* (Athens 1965), pp. 14–21; Josef Guntern, *Volkserzählungen aus dem Oberwallis* (Basel 1978).

49   Karl Ilg, *Die Walser in Vorarlberg* (2 vols., Dornbirn 1956).

50   Johannes Jegerlehner, *Was die Sennen Erzählen. Märchen aus dem Wallis. Aus dem Volksmund Gesammelt* (Bern 1916); Alois Senti, *Sagen aus dem Sarganserland* (Basel 1974).

51   Renward Cysat, *Collectanea Chronica und Denkwürdige Sachen pro Chronca Lucernensi et Helvetiae* (hgg. v. J. Schmid, Luzern 1969).

52   Joseph Hansen (ed.), *Quellen und Untersuchungen zur Geschichte des Hexenwahns und der Hexenverfolgung im Mittelalter* (Bonn 1901, reprint Hildesheim 1963), p. 414; Blauert, *Frühe Hexenverfolgungen* p. 20f.

53   Hansen, ed., *Quellen and Untersuchungen*, pp. 414, 546, 556, 569.

54   Audisio, *Les Vaudois*, pp. 92ff.

55   Peter Biller, 'Curate infirmos: the medieval Waldensian practice of medicine' in *Studies in Church History* 19 (1982), pp. 55–77; Audisio, *Les Vaudois*, pp. 162ff., 166, 172.

56   Peter Biller, 'Multum ieiunantes et se castigantes: medieval Waldensian asceticism' in *Studies in Church History,* 22 (1985), pp. 215–18.

57   Alexander Patschowsky and Kurt-Victor Selge (eds.), *Quellen zur Geschichte der Waldenser* (Gütersloh 1973) pp. 70–103, p. 73; 'The Passau Anonymous.' on the origins of heresy and the sect of the Waldensians in Edward Peters (ed.), *Heresy and Authority in Medieval Europe. Documents in Translation* (Philadelphia 1980), pp. 150–64, p. 152.

58   Merlo, *Eretico e Inquisitori*, pp. 48ff; Biller, 'Medieval Waldensian ascetism', p. 225f; Audisio, *Les Vaudois*, pp. 146, 169f.

59   Peter Brown, *The Rise and Function of the Holy Man in Late Antiquity* (1971; Peter Brown, *The Cult of the Saints: Its Rise and Function in Latin Christianity* (Chicago 1981); Donald Weinstein and Rudolph M. Bell, *Saints and Society* (Chicago 1982).

60   Ari Kiev (ed.), *Magic, Faith and Healing. Studies in Primitive Psychiatry Today* (2nd ed., New York. 1996); John Middleton (ed.), *Magic, Witchcraft and Curing* (Austin/London 1967).

61   Mircea Eliade, *Shamanism: Archaique Techniques of Ecstasy* (Princeton 1964); Gábor Klaniczay, 'Shamanistic elements in central European witchcraft' in Mihály Hoppál (ed.), *Shamanism in Eurasia* (Göttingen 1984), pp. 404–22.

62   Audisio, *Les Vaudois*, p. 172.

63   Arno Borst, *Die Katharer* (Stuttgart 1953), pp. 205, 240ff.

64   Merlo, *Eretico e Inquisitori* p. 48f.; Erbstösser (1984) 210ff; Audisio, *Les Vaudois*, pp. 24, 146, 170ff.

65   Grundmann, *Verbesserte und Ergänzte Auflage*, pp. 21ff., 65, 169, 209, 417, 423; Merlo, *Eretico e Inquisitori*, p. 48f.

66   'diligebat P. de vallibus Valdensem tanquam angelum Dei', Biller. 'The medieval practice of medicine', p. 66.

67   Biller, 'Medieval Waldensian asceticism', p. 223ff.

68   Wolfgang Behringer, *Witches and Witch Hunts* (Cambridge 2004).

69   Peter Biller, 'Thesaurus absconditus. The hidden treasure of the Waldensians' in: William J. Sheils and D. Wood (eds.), *The Church and Wealth* (Oxford 1987), pp. 139–54.

70   Döllinger, *Beitrager zur Sektengeschichte des Mittelalters*, vol. 2, p. 172; G. Boffito, 'Eretici in Piemonte al tempo del Gran Schisma (1378–1417)' in *Studi e Documenti di Storia e Diritto,*18 (1896), pp. 381–431; Cohn, *Europe's Inner Demons*, p. 37f; Blauert, *Frühe Hexenverfolgungen*, p. 28f.

71   Detailed evidence in Wolfgang Behringer, 'How Waldensians became Witches: Heretics and their Journey to the other World', in: Gábor Klaniczay and Eva Pós (eds.), *Demons, Spirits, Witches. Christian Demonology and Popular Mythology* (Budapest 2003) [forthcoming].

72   Carlo Ginzburg, *Storia Notturna. Una Decifrazione del Sabba* (Turin 1989); *Hexensabbat. Entzifferung einer Nächtlichen Geschichte.* (Aus dem Italienischen von Martina Kemper, Berlin 1990); *Ecstasies. Deciphering the Witches' Sabbath* (Transl. by Raymond Rosenthal, London 1990), pp. 78ff.

73   'quod nonnulli christiani et perfidi iudei infra eosdem terminos constituti *novas sectas* et prohibitos ritus eidem fidei repugnantes inveniunt, quos saltem in occulto dogmatizant, docent, praedicant et affirmant', Ernst Pitz, 'Diplomatische Studien zu den päpstlichen Erlassen über das Zauber- und Hexenwesen' in Peter Segl (ed.), Der *Hexenhammer. Entstehung und Umfeld des Malleus Maleficarum von 1487,* (Köln and Berlin 1988), pp. 23–70, p. 52.

74   Ginzburg, *Hexensabbat*, pp. 67–90; Ginzburg, *Ecstasies* pp. 63–88.

75   The text continues: 'suntque etiam infra eosdem terminos multi christiani et iudei sortilegi, divini, demonum invocatores, carminatores, coniuratores,superstitiosi, augures, utentes artibus nefariis et prohibitis', Hansen (ed.), *Quellen und Untersuchungen zur Geschichte des Hexenwahns,* pp. 16ff. See now the major study: Paravy, *De la Chrétienté Romaine à la Réforme en Dauphiné.*

76   Hansen, *Quellen und Untersuchungen* p. 16ff.

77   Thomas S. Kuhn, *The Structure of Scientific Revolutions* (Chicago 1962); 'Second thoughts on paradigms', in: Frederick Suppe (ed.), *The Structure of Scientific Theories,* (Urbana/Ill. 1974), pp. 459–82.

78   Errores Gazariorum, seu illorum qui scopam vel baculum equitare ', Basel, University library, ms. A II 34, f. 319 recto, 320 verso. Rome, Bibliotheca Apostolica Vaticana, Vat. lat. 456, fol. 205 verso – 206 recto. Its relation to the manuscript *Errores Valdensium* in the British Library, which also mentions maleficia and the witches' flights, still seems to be unexplored: Hansen, *Zauberwahn, Inquisition und Hexenprozeß*, p. 413.

79   Discussion of the term 'gazzari' by Martine Ostorero, Agostino Parvicini Bagliani, Kathrin Utz Tremp, and Catherine Chène (eds.), *L' Imaginaire du Sabbat. Edition critique des textes les plus anciens (1430 c. – 1440 c.)* (Lausanne 1999), pp. 301ff.

80   Hansen, *Quellen*, 17f.

81   Josef Stutz, 'Felix V', in *Zeitschrift für Schweizerische Kirchengeschichte*, 24 (1930), pp. 1–22, 1; Bernard Andenmatten and Agostino Paravicini-Bagliani (eds.), *Amédée VIII. - Felix V., Premier Duc de Savoie et Pape (1383–1451)* (Lausanne 1992).

82   Hansen, *Quellen* p. 18f. Joseph Hansen, 'Die Vauderie im 15. Jahrhundert' in Hansen, *Zauberwahn, Inquisition und Hexenprozeß*, pp. 408–15.

83   C. Lequin and J. Y. Mariotte, *La Savoye du Moyen Age* (Chambery 1970).

84   Martine Ostorero, *et al.*, eds., *L' Imaginaire du Sabbat.*

85   Edouard-L. de Kerdaniel, *Sorciers de Savoie* (Annecy 1900), pp. 17–32; Francois-Charles

Uginet, 'Frère Bérard Trémey (berardus Tremesii) o.f.m. et l' inquisition en Savoie au XVe siècle' in *Actes du VIIe Congrès de Société Savantes de la Savoie* (Conflans 1979), pp. 281–89. Monter, *Witchcraft in France and Switzerland*, p. 22f.

86   Robert Muchembled, *Le Roi et la Sorcière. L'Europe des Buchers XVe–XVIIIe Siècle* (Paris 1993).

87   Boffito, 'Eretici in Piemonte', pp. 381–43; Hansen, *Quellen*, p. 118–22. Cohn, *Europe's Inner Demons*, pp. 37ff; Blauer, *Frühe Hexenverfolgungen*, p. 28f; Paravy, *De la Chrétienté Romaine à la Réforme en Dauphiné*, p. 1054 (not mentioned in the 'index des personnes').

88   The Franciscan connections seem worth exploring. It was the Swiss friar Johannes of Winterthur, who reported the alleged devil-worship of the Waldensians in the mid-fourteenth century, the observant Bernardino of Siena, who first spread the news about the new sect in Italy in 1427, and John of Capestrano who tried to blend witchcraft with Jewishness: Cohn, *Europe's Inner Demons*, pp. 49ff.; Bernardino da Siena, *Prediche Volgari sul Campo di Siena 1427* (ed. C. Delcorno, 2 vols., Milano 1989).

89   Pierette Paravy, 'Remarques sur le passage de saint Vincent Ferrier dans les vellées vaudoises (1399–1403)' in *Bulletin de la Société d' Études des Hautes-Alpes* (1985/86), pp. 143–55. Paravy, *De la Chrétienté Romaine à la Réforme en Dauphiné*, pp. 343–54.

90   Bernard Andenmatten and Kathrin Utz-Tremp, 'De l'hérésie à la sorcellerie: L'inquisiteur Ulric de Torrenté OP (vers 1420–1445) et l'affermissement de l'inquisition en Suisse romande' in *Zeitschrift für Schweizerische Kirchengeschichte*, 86 (1992), pp. 69–119.

91   Gottlieb F. Ochsenbein, *Aus dem Schweizerischen Volksleben des XV. Jahrhunderts. Der Inquisitionsprozeß wider die Waldenser zu Freiburg im Üchtland im Jahre 1430* (Bern 1881); Gertrude Barnes Fiertz, 'An unusual trial under the inquisition at Fribourg, Switzerland, in 1399' in *Speculum*, 18 (1943), pp. 340–57; Blauert, *Frühe Hexenverfolgungen*, p. 40f.

92   Christian Immanuel Kind, *Die Chronik des Hans Fründ, Landschreiber zu Schwytz* (Chur 1875).

93   Hansen, *Quellen*, pp. 533ff.; Martine Ostorero, Agostino Parvicini Bagliani, Kathrin Utz Tremp, and Catherine Chène (eds.), *L' Imaginaire du Sabbat. Edition Critique des Textes les plus Anciens (1430 c. – 1440 c.)* (Lausanne 1999), pp. 23–98.

94   The texts of Johann Fründ, Johannes Nider, Claude Tholosan, Martin Le Franc, and the *Errores Gazariorum*, now edited in Ostero, *et al.*, eds., *L'imaginaire du Sabbat*.

95   Blauert, *Frühe Hexenverfolgungen*, p. 29f; Jacques Chiffoleau, 'Amédée VIII ou la Majesté impossible?' in Andenmatten and Paravicini-Bagliani, eds., *Amédée VIII. - Felix V*, pp. 19–49.

96   Gamba (1964) 287ff.

97   Lamb (1982) 187, 194f. Christian Pfister, G. Schwarz-Zanetti and M. Wegmann, 'Winter severity in Europe: the fourteenth century' in *Climatic Change*, 34 (1996), pp. 91–108.

98   Lamb (1989) 215ff.

99   Brian Fagan, *The Little Ice Age, 1300–1850* (New York 2001), p. 83f.

100 Wolfgang Behringer, 'Climatic change and witch-hunting: the impact of the Little Ice Age on mentalities', in: Christian Pfister, Rudolf Brazdil, and Rüdiger Glaser (eds.), *Climatic Variability in Sixteenth Century Europe and its Social Dimension* in *Climatic Change*, 43 (1999), Special Issue, September 1999, pp. 335–51.

101 Cohn, *Europe's Inner Demons*.

102 Valerie I.J. Flint, *The Rise of Magic in Early Medieval Europe* (Oxford 1991).

103 Dieter Harmening, *Superstitio. Überlieferungs - und Theoriegeschichtliche Untersuchungen zur Kirchlich-Theologischen Aberglaubensliteratur des Mittelalters* (Habilschrift 1971, Berlin 1979).

104   Martine Ostorero, *Folâtrer avec le Démon. Sabbat et Chasse aux Sorciers à Vevey (1448)* (Lausanne 1998), pp. 174, 274.

105   Martin Lefranc, 'Le champion des dames', written at Arras, ca. 1451, Bibliothèque Nationale, Ms. fr. 12476, fol. 105 verso; Hansen, *Zauberwahn, Inquisition und Hexenprozeß*, p 101.

106   Hansen, *Zauberwahn, Inquisition und Hexenprozeß*, p. 408.

107   Paravy (1979) 322–79. M. Osterero *et al.*, eds., *L'imaginaire du Sabbat*, pp. 355–438.

108   Monter, *Witchcraft in France and Switzerland*, p. 21; Blauert, *Frühe Hexenverfolgungen*, p. 30f.

109   Fougeyron was present at the Council until November 1433, then he went to the diocese of Aosta, the diocese of bishop George de Saluce, to start new inquisitorial trials. The earliest manuscript of the Errores Gazariorum was presumably written in the Aosta valley short before 1436, M. Osterero *et al.*, eds., *L'imaginaire du Sabbat*, p. 331ff.

110   Hansen, *Zauberwahn, Inquisition und Hexenprozeß* pp.184–8. Jean Tainecture, *Tractatus de secta Vaudensium*, ca. 1460; Hansen, *Quellen*, 133–195. Copies of the paintings are in Gustav Henningsen, *Fra Hekesjagd til Heksekult* (Kopenhagen 1984), p. 55.

111   F. Egger, *Beiträge zur Geschichte des Predigerordens. Die Reform des Basler Konvents 1429 und die Stellung des Ordens am Basler Konzil (1431–1449)* (Frankfurt/Main 1991); Werner Tschacher, *Der Formicarius des Johannes Nider von 1437/38. Studien zu den Anfängen der Europäischen Hexenverfolgungen im Mittelalter* (Diss. phil. Aachen 1998, Bielefeld 2001); Catherine Chène, 'Johannes Nider, Formicarius', in: M. Osterero *et al.*, eds., *L'imaginaire du Sabbat*, pp. 99–266.

112   Johannes Franck, 'Geschichte des Wortes "Hexe"' in Hansen, *Zauberwahn, Inquisition und Hexenprozeß*, pp. 614–70.

113   Nicolai Cusae Cardinalis Opera, II, Paris 1514, fol. 170 verso–172 recto; Wilhelm Baum, *Nicolaus Cusanus in Tirol. Das Wirken des Philosophen und Reformators als Fürstbischof von Brixen*, (Brixen 1983); Carlo Ginzburg, 'The Philosopher and the witches: An experiment in cultural history', in: Klaniczay and Pócs (1994) 283–93.

114   Hansen, *Zauberwahn, Inquisition und Hexenprozeß* pp. 109–12.

115   Ibid., pp. 112–18.

116   Ibid., pp. 124–30, 133–45.

117   Heinrich Kramer (Institoris), *Der Hexenhammer. Malleus Maleficarum* (Ed. by Günter Jerouschek and Wolfgang Behringer, München 2000).

118   Most scholars avoid this approach anyway, see e.g. Geoffrey Cubitt, *The Jesuit Myth. Conspiracy Theory and Politics in Nineteenth Century France* (Oxford 1993); Daniel Pipes, *Conspiracy. How the Paranoid Style Flourishes and Where it Comes From* (New York 1997); Mark Fenster, *Conspiracy Theories. Secrecy and Power in American Culture* (Minneapolis 1999); Timothy Melley, *Empire of Conspiracy. The Culture of Paranoia in Postwar America* (Ithaca and London 2000). Unfortunately, contemporary scholars no longer trace back modern conspiracies to the ultimate conspiracy of evil, witchcraft, although the African example demonstrates that this is not simply a problem of the past.

119   A nice phrase, borrowed from Niehaus *et al.*, *Witchcraft, Power and Politics*.

Chapter 3

Conspiracy and its Prosecution in Italy, 1500–1550: Violent Responses to Violent Solutions[*]

Kate Lowe

This chapter gives me the opportunity to review a number of well-known sixteenth-century Italian cases of conspiracy. By realigning some of their more salient aspects in order to highlight their political nature and their violent character, I hope to present them in a new formation and use them to emphasise both their particular peculiarities and the ordinariness of their violent procedures. The fact that conspiracies are perceived as political crimes should not deflect attention away from the violence, which permeated their course. The violence came from all sides. Not only did treasonable plots usually involve the use of violence to achieve their aims, but the authorities and individuals who had been targeted responded by using violence on the suspects and then often by executing or otherwise disposing of those deemed or pronounced guilty. Violent solutions spawned violent responses. I am using the words conspiracy and treason here to cover, in rather an old-fashioned way, acts of internal and external betrayal. Treason of course covers both, and includes conspiracy. One important distinguishing factor is that an individual can commit treason whereas conspiracy (or 'breathing together' of a plan) is by definition a group activity. I am not going to enter here more deeply into questions of definition.[1] All the examples examined were described in the sixteenth century as cases of treason or conspiracy.

My selection of cases of conspiracy dates from the period 1500 to 1550 and is both random and very partial, covering only a small fraction of the total number. The only criterion of selection used was that each case should include published source material, preferably either interrogation records or so-called confessions or later accounts of the case by those involved (in essence, therefore, material produced for public consumption); on occasion, a series of private or ambassadorial letters describing or discussing the case has been considered a sufficient basis for investigation. The insistence on documentation is deliberate because it lies at the heart of questions of conspiracy. All forms of documentation related to conspiracy are riven with bias, but that only increases the necessity of reexamining every piece of documentary evidence in the context of the whole conspiracy and in the context of other conspiracies of the time period. In effect, so-called trial records of conspiracies are merely intimidating interrogations where the prisoner (he is not formally accused) has no recourse to lawyers nor the possibility of mounting his own defence. For this reason, I shall refer throughout to interrogation or criminal records and not to trial records. It is very difficult to make straightforward comparisons between interrogation records and the statements released by the conspirators. Claims and counter-claims vied with each other for attention from differing political factions and regimes. Conspiracy accusations and justifications are in effect early forms of media or propaganda wars of versions of the truth. In addition, not only is disappearing (or perhaps never-existing) documentation a persistent theme but its opposite - invented documentation - is also very relevant and often mooted. It is as well to remember that conspiracy is often an anticipatory crime, something about to happen rather than something that has already happened, and that this has implications for the documentation. Often conspiracies only existed in the head, or passed their life at the planning stage and were 'discovered' when committed to paper, prior to being put into action. Another implication is that, conversely, spurious conspiracies could be conjured up with the greatest of ease, by planting words on the tongue through the use of torture, or by claiming to have intercepted treasonable letters. At least one and possibly three or four of the conspiracies I am going to look at fall into this category. This documentary doubt is compounded by the fact that because treason and conspiracy were considered political offences, there was a tendency to appoint special tribunals or special judges (one could also use here the word irregular) to deal with them.[2] These were then outside the mainstream of Italian documentary culture and their records (if any were kept) would have had no obvious home.

Even with this proviso, it is interesting to note just how few of the main criminal records of even very famous cases have been published. In some cases, of course, no formal interrogation was held and no documents ever existed. In most cases, though, no attempt seems to have been made to locate this material, even when the case went through the correct official channels and it is probable that material exists. Anyone who has looked at this type of criminal record in early sixteenth-century Italy will however be aware of the very limited objectives of interrogation in these cases. The questions asked always followed a set formula that started with the prisoner being asked if he knew why he was being interrogated. This fluidity with respect to the parameters of the crime left the prisoner at a distinct disadvantage, a disadvantage that deepened as the interrogation proceeded. The point of the questions was to ascertain the guilt of the prisoner. The procedural norms for conspiracy were sometimes laid down in the city statutes. The *podestà* or criminal judge could at his discretion order the use of appropriate and moderate torture in order to extract confessions.[3] If a prisoner refused to admit guilt, he was tortured, usually by means of the rope hoist, until he did (I have no examples of prisoners in conspiracy cases managing to maintain their innocence in the face of torture, although some managed to hold out for what seemed like heroic amounts of time).[4] Often the prisoner was aided in the formulation of his guilt by his interrogators suggesting 'storylines' and possible actors to take part in them. The main focus of the interrogation was to establish a narrative of guilt in which as many enemies of the then current regime as possible were embedded, and as many friends, relatives, servants and acquaintances of the prisoner were entrapped. In Giovanni Folchi's interrogation in the aftermath of the Boscoli conspiracy in Florence in 1513, questioning revolved around which friend of his had said what about various members of the Medici family and the previous Soderini regime. The aim was to force Folchi to admit that there had been criticism of the former and praise of the latter, but Folchi was wise to this obvious trap and tried to beat them at their own game, by reporting remarks to the effect that 'the Medici never harmed anybody'.[5] Filippo Strozzi wrote in his suicide note of 1538 that one of the reasons he had killed himself was to stop himself implicating innocent relatives and friends.[6]

Interrogations were normally repetitive and unhurried. Torture could be implemented at session after session if the prisoners were initially recalcitrant. These criminal records are not in general concerned with motive, as guilt is assured, but with establishing an often imaginary network of the guilty. For example, one of two primary objectives of the interrogations following the conspiracy planned by Pietro Fregoso in Genoa in 1534 was 'to reconstruct the network of relations between the accused and the environments generated by the phenomenon of exile'.[7] It is for all these reasons, and in particular because of the belief that violence would reveal a version that could be labelled 'the truth', that these records, while fascinating in their own right, must be read and understood with great delicacy and sensitivity.

Much more interest has focused on statements, of whatever sort, by the conspirators themselves than on the criminal records, although these statements can appear in a variety of formats which have markedly different histories of internal generation. I think greater attention was paid to this form of record in the past in the misguided belief that they represented the 'truth'. Now it is commonly acknowledged that all versions are clouded and that there is no one simple truth. All these statements are, in their own ways, driven, and they too have limitations. Confessions by the conspirators are shortened and tidied up versions of the narratives extracted from the prisoners under torture, authorised by the presence of a notary or by other official figures. There can be more than one draft of these. Given the circumstances of their production, they should be treated as a variant form of criminal record. Instead, statements by the conspirators produced in relative freedom and in happier circumstances outside the torture chamber are completely different in emphasis and structure from interrogation reports, although they too often follow set formulae. As for those convicted of other forms of treason, the tyrannicide Lorenzino de' Medici, guilty of treason against his cousin and ruler, afterwards wrote a justificatory *Apologia* which was later published,[8] and Antonio Grimani made a speech in his own defence at his trial in Venice in 1500, which is not published.[9]

But problems still remain. The conspirators' accounts are beautifully constructed rhetorical exercises full of self-justification and noble sentiment. Their authors are obsessed with explaining their motives, and their motives are always very noble and never fuelled by envy, jealousy or desire for political or financial gain. The writers rarely deign to mention the minor details and minor participants that are so important to the workings of a conspiracy. They tend to play down the role of their collaborators unless they are well-known and important people with strong ideological imperatives. Most of these statements come from the classically educated and are cast in a classical mould, although a few do not and are not. The perceived antithesis between classical and Christian culture means that most opt for classical rather than Christian role models - it is obviously easier on one's sense of self to conceive of oneself as aping noble Brutus rather than following reviled Judas. There are some exceptions to this type of statement, which actually are very helpful in understanding exactly what can be gleaned from the documentation. For example, an outsider, a third party, can write down his remembered version of conversations with a conspirator, and add his own gloss to the situation. This happened in the Boscoli conspiracy of 1513 in Florence when a friend of Boscoli's spent the night before his execution with him, and later left a written record of it. The friend was a humanist, but intensely Christian, and his beliefs permeate the whole account.[10]

The two other most common types of record for treason and conspiracies are letters and diaries, both of which, being essentially private or for family consumption only, have different aims.

I should like now to list in a very summary fashion the treason cases and conspiracies some of whose aspects I shall be considering. It will be obvious that I am considering cases from a wide variety of locations. I do not think it is realistic to pretend that there were not marked similarities between some (if not many) of the Italian regimes after the French invasion of the peninsula in 1494 - certainly the whole political scene polarised into a gigantic struggle between supporters of the French and supporters of the emperor. In some places, this struggle was intertwined with the older oppositions of local factions, struggles between different social groups vying for power or, especially in Florence and parts of Tuscany, home-grown oppositional ideologies. A large number of conspirators claimed to want a return to an older political status quo, preferably to a perceived golden age, either immediately before the arrival of the French shattered the delicate balance of power, or a more distant and glorious Latin past. In any case, symbolic distances between places on the Italian peninsula shrank during this period and connections between previously disparate cities and states multiplied. In order to include a couple of treason cases, my earliest chronological example dates from 1498. It is of course nonsense to use 1500 as a great dividing line in Italian history and I have done so only as a matter of convenience. In fact, 1494 makes much more sense in this context.

1. 1498 Venice, Antonio di Lando, treason (breaking official secrets)
2. 1500 Venice, Antonio Grimani, treason (incompetence in war)
3. 1512 Brescia, Nine Brescians, conspiracy to liberate their homeland (*patria*) from the French
4. 1513 Florence, Pietro Paolo Boscoli, conspiracy against the Medici
5. 1517 Rome, Five cardinals, spurious conspiracy against pope Leo X
6. 1522 Florence, number of youngish Florentines, conspiracy against Cardinal Giulio de' Medici
7. 1523 Sicily, the Imperatore brothers, conspiracy against the emperor, and Rome, Francesco Soderini, conspiracy (in fact external treason) against the pope
8. 1525 Milan, Girolamo Moroni, conspiracy against the imperialists
9. 1534 Genoa, Pietro Fregoso, conspiracy against the regime
10. 1535 Florence, Giovanbattista Cibo, conspiracy to kill Alessandro de' Medici

11. 1537 Florence, Lorenzino de' Medici murdered Duke Alessandro de' Medici, head of the regime in Florence
12. 1538 Florence, Filippo Strozzi, the leader of the Florentine exiles (*fuorusciti*), killed himself in prison after being repeatedly tortured
13. 1546 Lucca, Francesco Burlamacchi, conspiracy against Cosimo de' Medici
14. 1547 Genoa, Gian Luigi Fieschi, conspiracy against Andrea Doria
15. 1547 Piacenza, Ferrante Gonzaga, conspiracy against Pier Luigi Farnese, the duke of Piacenza and son of Pope Paul III

My intention in this analysis is to disrupt the flow of the established narratives of these individual conspiracies (which I have explained were established for the most part on the basis of critically flawed records). I want to use the material now in a compartmentalised and comparative fashion to address a series of questions, which I hope will provide enlightenment about the relationship between violence and the early modern political crime of conspiracy.

The first point of comparison concerns source material. Although most of the conspiracies and treason cases on the list are reasonably or very famous or infamous, in only a few instances has all the available source material been published or located, so the narratives or competing storylines are skewed. In the nineteenth century local historians carried out pioneering archival work, but only now at the end of the twentieth and beginning of the twenty-first are historians beginning to revisit these conspiracies with the intention of assembling a more complete picture. A good example of this is in fact contained in the excellent proceedings of the 1993 conference sponsored by the *École française de Rome* on *Complots et conjurations dans l'Europe moderne*, published in 1996. In the article by Arturo Pacini on Genoese conspiracies between 1528 and 1547, he adds significantly, for example, to the already burgeoning nineteenth-century documentation on the 1547 conspiracy of Gian Luigi Fieschi by inserting material from unpublished letters to Charles V in the *Archivio di stato* in Genoa.[11] The criminal proceedings against Gian Luigi Fieschi have never been published.[12] The only treason cases and conspiracies in my selection for which even partial criminal records have been published are: the sentences (*raspe*) pronounced by the *Avogaria di Comun* against some of the men implicated in the treason trial of Antonio Grimani in Venice in 1500;[13] interrogation records of some of the Brescian conspirators of 1512 and their circle;[14] the very short interrogation of Giovanni Folchi, one of the four main protagonists in the Boscoli conspiracy of 1513 in Florence;[15] the interrogation of one of the main witnesses, Marcantonio Nini, the *maggiordomo* of cardinal Petrucci, whose revelations formed the basis for the narrative of the 1517 spurious 'conspiracy' of five cardinals against pope Leo X in Rome in 1517;[16] Giovanbattista Cibo's official 'confession' of 1535 which he was forced to read out loud in the *Palazzo pubblico* in Florence;[17] and the incomplete but fascinating interrogation records of Francesco Burlamacchi in Lucca in 1546.[18] It should be clear from this that much more work needs to be done locating criminal records for famous conspiracies (or at least eliminating the possibility of their existence in obvious places), so that the narratives of the conspiracies can be recast. Without the inclusion of full interrogation records, however limited and biased, accounts of conspiracies make little sense. It is impossible to know what and whom the authorities most feared.

It is also important to know which magistracy or which officials carried out the interrogation or trial, and in whose name. Even this seemingly innocent question raises many problems and highlights the disputed and often irregular nature of procedure in cases of suspected treason. The prosecuting lawyer Nicolò Michiel successfully fought for the noble Antonio Grimani's trial for incompetence in war (which was a genuine trial in that there were prosecuting and defending lawyers and a vote was taken at the end to decide whether he was guilty or innocent) to be conducted in the Great Council, the *Consiglio maggiore*, in Venice, where a total of 1212 ballots were cast.[19] The Brescian interrogations of 1512 took place in front of the *podestà*, some captains and various other city officials.[20] Giovanni Folchi, one of the Boscoli accomplices in Florence, was interrogated by two of the *Otto di guardia* in 1513.[21] Marcantonio Nini was interrogated by Mario Peruschi, the procurator fiscal, Iacopo (or Giovaniacopo) Gamberana, the auditor of the criminal court of the governor of Rome, and Domenico Coletta, the vice-castellan of Castel Sant'Angelo; Giampietro Perracci, a copyist from the criminal court, took notes of the interrogation.[22] However, in an obviously two-tiered system with non-ecclesiastics being investigated by the secular authorities and cardinals by their peers, three further cardinals were appointed by the pope to investigate three of the accused cardinals. Unfortunately, the volume of 634 folios of the trial (or at least detailed investigation) of cardinals Petrucci, Sauli and Riario, last heard of in the possession of cardinal Lorenzo Pucci, has never been found, and almost certainly must have been deliberately suppressed. The case against a fourth cardinal, Castellesi, was with it, as is known from its notarial act of consignment.[23] The Sicilian conspirators were tried by the judges of the *Regia Gran Corti* in the presence of the advocator fiscal.[24] The Cibo confession (and therefore probably the prior interrogations) took place in front of the imperial ambassador, the captain of the Florentine militia, one of Alessandro de' Medici's counsellors, one of the *Otto di practica* (who happened to be

Francesco Guicciardini) and one of the *Otto di custode e balìa*.[25] The presence of
the imperial ambassador is worth noting. Finally, Francesco Burlamacchi was
interrogated by the three Lucchese judges of the Rota and the six 'respectable
citizens' elected by the *Consiglio Generale* of Lucca.

The hue of the interrogators or judges could be decisive in determining the
levels of violence used in these interrogations. Most secular courts authorised
the use of torture and it was admissible for certain crimes in ecclesiastical
courts, but status or class could play a part. Grimani was imprisoned under
appalling conditions and kept in leg irons for months but was not otherwise
tortured. Torture was employed in the Brescian interrogations, in the Boscoli
interrogations (where Machiavelli was amongst those tortured),[26] in the
interrogations into the 1517 conspiracy in Rome (where sleep and food
deprivation were employed against the elderly cardinal Riario, and the rope
hoist was used on cardinals Petrucci and Sauli, and repeatedly and for long
stretches of time on Nini), and Burlamacchi was also repeatedly tortured in
Lucca. It is not known whether Cibo was tortured but Florence did not have a
good track record of humanitarian treatment of prisoners, so it very likely that
he was. It is known from other sources that a high proportion of other
suspected conspirators were also tortured. The two plots that were successful
(Lorenzino de' Medici's assassination of Duke Alessandro de' Medici and
Ferrante Gonzaga's conspiracy arranging for the murder of Pier Luigi
Farnese) obviated the necessity for torture as the traitors were the victors, but
torture was used in the 1522 conspiracy in Florence against cardinal Giulio de'
Medici (at least against the French courier who was initially apprehended and
probably against others),[27] may have been used in the Sicilian conspiracy of
1523, and was the reason why Filippo Strozzi committed suicide, using a
sword left fortuitously in his Florentine cell in 1538, and splattering his suicide
note with his own blood.[28]

Reading these accounts of torture is rather ghastly. The accepted way of
transcribing screams and other expressions of intense pain was *ahimé* (alas! or
oh dear!), which is bad enough, but the voices of even those who were not
particularly articulate occasionally manage to interrupt notarial and court
formulae. The interrogators were much impressed by the blunt fortitude of
Marcantonio Nini who on 30 April 1517 was tortured on the rope hoist for
two hours without changing his story; the copyist recorded their 'admiration',
but also that they then moved on to a different type of torture to break him
down.[29] The cries of despair of the less robust but more verbally skilled are
chilling, and some, such as Francesco Burlamacchi, tortured not only with the
rope hoist but also with burning tongs on his feet,[30] plead for death as a
release.

Justificatory or explanatory statements by those accused or guilty of treason or conspiracy include: an account of the 1512 Brescia conspiracy by Giangiacomo Martinengo;[31] the cardinal conspirators' account of the conspiracy of 1517 in Rome;[32] Niccolò Martelli's account of the 1522 Florentine conspiracy against cardinal Giulio de' Medici;[33] Girolamo Moroni's account of his behaviour in 1525;[34] Lorenzino de' Medici's 'apology' for the events of 1537; Filippo Strozzi's suicide note of 1538; and Francesco Burlamacchi's handwritten declaration of 1546.[35] It should be noted, however, that some of these were prepared by the alleged conspirators in connection with their trials.

Taking in conjunction the views expressed in the interrogation records and in the justificatory statements, I should like now to look at the expressed aims and motives of various of the conspirators. Once again, they can profitably be placed in small groupings or sets, and the imperatives of conspiracy become clearer when examined through the lens of violence. At the same time, I should like to see, wherever possible, what type of violent action was envisaged by the conspirators in order for their plans to be put into practice. One can distinguish here between plans that involved military action to affect a change of government and those that required the death of an individual. This is the point at which it should be obvious that conspiratorial dreams, although sometimes planned and carried out by ideologically or politically charged and educated men with no past record of violent action, could not but be achieved through violent means. In pre-democratic societies, political change was only possible through force, and would-be conspirators persuaded themselves that violent means were legitimate if circumstances became intolerable. This seeming mismatch between violent action and normally non-violent men is what has produced so many rhetorically sophisticated *post facto* statements justifying acts of bloodshed.

One of the most potent and often cited reasons for launching a conspiracy was liberation from the existing, oppressive regime. Native Italians across the peninsula wanted to throw off the yoke of both French and imperial rule and return to the simpler, better past that had existed before their arrival. The nine Brescians in 1512 wanted to liberate their city from French control, and had hatched a plan whereby Venetian troops would be used to drive out the French. This constituted treason against the French king. Their plan, which involved violence at least for the soldiers in the respective armies, misfired and many civilians were caught up in the sack of the city by French forces under the duke of Nemours that resulted.[36] Military action was again the preferred means in the conspiracy planned by the Imperatore brothers in Palermo, whose aim was to drive out the imperialists and to make

Marcantonio Colonna king of Sicily under a French protectorate.[37] This was a complicated manoeuvre, which would have had repercussions across Italy, forcing the withdrawal of the imperial army from Lombardy, and leaving Milan at the mercy of the French king.[38] Girolamo Moroni was imprisoned in Milan in 1525 for conspiring with Francesco Sforza against the imperialists to effect a return to the status quo of pre-1494. The plot involved military manoeuvres and the participation of France and the Venetians.[39] Exact plans are not forthcoming for the 1534 conspiracy of Pietro Fregoso as the interrogation records are the main source, and we have seen that these were not in the main concerned with motive, but a return to French influence was the general idea. This conspiracy included an interesting role for a woman. Normally women in conspiracies only acted as catalysts (for example, Ricciarda Malaspina in the 1535 Cibo conspiracy mentioned below) but Suor Marta Fregoso, the prioress of the convent of S. Sebastiano, was much more active. Her convent became the fulcrum of the plot as it was used by pro-French sympathisers, who maintained contact with the exiles through Suor Marta's correspondence with her relatives.[40]

The 1547 conspiracy of Gian Luigi Fieschi had as its immediate aim the murder of the doge Andrea Doria, of his nephew and designated heir Giannettino, and of another of his closest associates, and the placing of Genoa under a French protectorate. In terms of local reordering of government, one of the conspirators who was later interrogated wanted a return to the practices of the past,[41] but there was also a large element that wanted an opening up of opportunity in government and the inclusion of more artisans. The plan was to kill the trio on a boat trip at night, but only the nephew was killed, while Andrea Doria managed to escape. The conspiracy in Piacenza in 1547 organised by Ferrante Gonzaga, the governor of Milan (with the permission and connivance of the emperor and the help of some Piacentine nobles), against Pier Luigi Farnese, the son of pope Paul III and the duke of the recently created duchy of Parma and Piacenza, was successful. Farnese was stabbed to death in his chamber in the citadel of Piacenza,[42] and his corpse was ritually mutilated and punished: it was castrated and hanged, then left to the mercy of dogs and crows.[43] At issue here were the ancient rights of the city and citizens of Piacenza;[44] the citizens were not pleased by the new arrangements and nor was Milan, which used to control the city.

A significant and well-known sub-set of conspiracies had the liberation of Florence from Medici control (or the removal by death of a prominent member of the Medici family) as their purported aim. Pietro Paolo Boscoli and Agostino Capponi were found guilty, according to the account written by Luca della Robbia, of 'having wanted to liberate the city and to kill Giuliano,

Lorenzo and Giulio de' Medici'.[45] They may have wanted to liberate their city, and have talked incautiously, but it does not appear as if any plan of action enabling them to achieve their goal had been formulated, so the subject of violence had not been broached. The five cardinals in 1517 were accused of plotting to kill pope Leo X by persuading a doctor to poison him whilst treating his anal fistula.[46] Although the common image of Italian assassins frequently painted them as poisoners, in practice poisoning was involved in a minority of conspiratorial or treasonable attempts.[47] The avowed aim of the 1522 conspiracy against cardinal Giulio de' Medici in Florence was to oust the Medici from office and to reinstate Piero Soderini to his office as *gonfaloniere a vita*. The mechanics of the restoration of the republican regime had been worked out in some detail, so this was no vague nostalgia for a golden past but a concrete blueprint for a different form of government. The conspirators planned to get rid of Giulio by poisoning him.[48]

Giovanbattista Cibo's motives in plotting to kill Alessandro de' Medici, the head of the regime in Florence, in 1535, are slightly unclear and appear to have no political element. He claimed to have been asked to commit the crime by his cousin, Hippolito de' Medici, and to have felt unable to refuse, because of the obligations of kinship and friendship that bound him.[49] However, it also seems probable that Cibo was willing to countenance the suggestion because his family honour was more directly at stake: Alessandro de' Medici was openly committing adultery with Ricciarda Malaspina, his sister-in-law. Cibo rather cleverly planned the murder to take place at the very spot where dishonour had been committed. Apparently Alessandro used to sit on a painted chest or strongbox (*cassone* or *forziere*) near to Ricciarda's bed in the Pazzi palace, and the plan was to fill a similar chest with explosives, swap it with the original and then explode it while Alessandro was sitting on it.[50] Early detection (the interception of a letter) meant that this daring and inventive assassination plan never reached fruition. Alessandro was successfully but brutally murdered two years later, in 1537, by his cousin, Lorenzino de' Medici, who stabbed him to death. Lorenzino's aim was straightforwardly to effect the removal of a tyrant, and thereby to liberate Florence.[51] This was a less complicated operation than many other acts of treason or conspiracy as it involved only him; with fewer potential breaking points, it had a greater chance of success. But it appears that Lorenzino had not thought through the consequences of his deed, because he admitted to being shocked that Cosimo had succeeded Alessandro and thus continued the line of oppression.[52] He refused to admit however that he was to blame if the *patria* was not liberated; he had tried his best and even risked his life and reputation. Anti-Medicean attacks did not stop with Alessandro's murder. Filippo Strozzi had opted for military action against Cosimo but with the rest of the exiles had suffered defeat at Montemurlo in 1537. His intention had been to inflict defeat and to chase the Medici out of Florence. Francesco Burlamacchi's conspiracy in Lucca in 1546 had as its aim to liberate Tuscany and to make a union within it, but he recognised that this could be alternatively described as 'the undertaking I have planned to carry out against the duke of Florence'.[53] He believed that ancient Tuscany, blessed with this sort of union, had been a better place. Burlamacchi was the elected head of government (*gonfaloniere*) at the time of his plot and his route to this rearrangement of power, he hoped, lay in his control of the Lucchese military forces and his carefully nurtured links with key office-holders in other Tuscan cities such as Pisa, Pescia, Pistoia and Barga. It is not clear how much resistance Burlamacchi thought he would encounter nor how much bloodshed he was prepared to countenance, but he certainly viewed the Medici as the enemy and the exiles as friends.

It is very striking how nearly all these conspiracies and acts of treason were in essence 'conservative', having as their main aim a return to the status quo of the past. None of them was radical or innovative (even Burlamacchi conceived of his Tuscan league as an ancient inspiration). Yet all were prepared to use violence and force to achieve their goals. This violent aspect was completely accepted even by men who had never committed any previous violent act. Only a few of the conspirators were routinely violent: the best example is Giovanbattista Cibo who in addition to the assassination attempt was involved in a serious brawl in Venice in 1527 and an attempted rape with violence on Murano in 1537.[54] Others carrying out murders were occasionally able to justify their actions by stating that their victims were themselves violent and deserved to die. Lorenzino claimed that Alessandro de' Medici was so despicable that he had even poisoned his own mother in an attempt to remove all trace of his ignoble ancestry.[55] Burlamacchi claimed that Cosimo de' Medici behaved so badly that his subjects were all discontented.[56] Some of the violent acts were planned by nobles or patricians with no history of violence but were to be carried out by men lower down the social scale who were more 'suited' to the task, as though between the act and its commission lay the social niceties of the class divide. It is also very noticeable how the justifications, which often relied so heavily on classical precedent, all came from the educated, who appeared to prefer classical values to Christian ones. Those who were paid to be violent (or merely employed as servants by conspirators and thereby caught up in the violence) did not feel the need or have the background to justify themselves. Instead, when faced with imminent death, they fell back upon the traditional comforts of religion.

The recourses to classical precedents are well-known, and are all from Tuscany, but they are still worth mentioning briefly, because they became an acceptable way of legitimating normally unacceptable behaviour. Many seeking change seemed to be so steeped in the classical world that it may have had more reality for them than their actual surroundings; as has been suggested, in some sense they may have been possessed by it.[57] Pietro Paolo Boscoli exclaimed most famously: 'Remove Brutus from my head so that I may make this step entirely as a Christian',[58] while Giovanni Folchi, one of his fellow conspirators, admitted during his interrogation to reading Aristotle's *Politics* with him. Lorenzino de' Medici compares his situation to that of Timoleon,[59] Filippo Strozzi to Cato.[60] Filippo Strozzi's Spanish warder commented in a letter to Charles V that Strozzi was a philosopher and had no shred of Christian morality.[61] Burlamacchi too drew inspiration from a reading of classical texts, in particular works of ancient history, and he mentions four lives of Plutarch - those of Timoleon, Pelopidas, Dion and Aratus - that convinced him that it was possible to achieve great things with only a few men. He was so fired up by these that he tried to persuade others to read them, but with little success.[62]

The Brescian conspiracy of 1512 had two oddities in this respect. First of all, the original nine members of the plot literally swore an oath of brotherhood on the consecrated stone of the altar of S. Domenico to liberate their homeland from occupation by a foreign army.[63] This Christian element amongst noble participants is unusual as is the fact that the enterprise was a group affair from the start. Usually one person claimed credit (or was given credit) for having the initial idea. But this is also the only conspiracy where the connection between danger and excitement is explicitly made. Luigi Avogadro, who was the tenth member of the group and who was later captured and executed, is said to have remarked: 'in important matters one cannot negotiate or run risks for great gain or great glory without great danger, and the magnitude of the danger is what makes the desire to do it praiseworthy and the execution of it glorious'.[64]

One last point about the conspirators is worthy of consideration - their age.[65] A swathe of conspirators were relatively young, so that they may have been motivated on two counts, because they were denied access to power and because they were still full of idealism. Pietro Paolo Boscoli was 35 in 1513[66] and the Florentine conspirators of 1522 were young, as was Giovanbattista Cibo who was 27 in 1535[67] and Gian Luigi Fieschi who was about 25 in 1547.[68] Their actions could therefore also be construed as rebellions against an established and hierarchical political reality that set much store on literal and metaphorical maturity. Other conspirators, such as Francesco Burlamacchi, were themselves mature (he was 47 or 48 in 1546)[69] and had enjoyed political power, so their actions should be considered less hot-headed.

The final section will consider the violent penalties inflicted on those found guilty of treason or conspiracy. The violence of the response and the barbarian nature of the punishments were in keeping with the violent solutions to political problems proposed by the conspirators. These official murders were both punitive and preventative, and only those with first-class connections (and often not even they) were able to escape them. Their circumstances and detail are often horrific. Let me mention here Antonio Lando, denounced for gossiping about official secrets in Venice in 1498, found guilty at a hastily convened meeting of the Council of Ten, and hanged that very night in the closed off Piazza di San Marco between the two columns. The haste and secrecy with which he was tried, convicted and hanged would in any case be bad as the denunciation appears to be unproveable, but the details provided by the diarist Sanuto make the scene truly pathetic. First, there was no rope, and as the shops were shut, someone was sent to the *Arsenale* for it. Then, in the course of being hanged, Lando fell and broke an arm before being definitively strung up.[70] The Brescians met a variety of unpleasant fates in 1512. Two were decapitated while a third was killed but then had his body hung from a gallows.[71] Luigi Avogadro was publicly beheaded and his severed head was taken on a lance to the top of the *Torre del popolo* where it was displayed; his body was quartered and posted at the place of execution.[72] The same ritualistic punishment was meted out to the bodies of some of the Sicilian conspirators of 1523: they were publicly beheaded (and their heads were then placed in lanterns made of iron and displayed) before their bodies were then quartered and displayed.[73] Boscoli and Capponi were beheaded in Florence in 1513,[74] Jacopo da Diaccetto and Luigi Alamanni were beheaded in Florence in 1522,[75] and Burlamacchi was beheaded in Milan in 1548,[76] but their bodies were not further defiled. Simple beheadings were the best, most honourable form of execution, although at least two methods of decapitation existed, the first using an axe and the second a mallet in combination with a primitive guillotine (*mannaia*).[77] Cardinal Petrucci was killed illegally (strangled in his cell) in 1517 and Marcantonio Nini, his majordomo, and Battista Vercelli, the surgeon who was supposed to have been going to be responsible for administering the poison, suffered the most, as they were publicly tortured as part of their punishment, with boiling pincers, hanged near Ponte Sant'Angelo, quartered, and the quarters publicly displayed.[78] Lorenzino the tyrannicide was himself killed by assassins in Venice in the late 1540s, so his violence spawned direct retaliation.

This opportunity to reexamine early modern Italian conspiracies in terms of their violence has shown that both their aims and the responses to them were indeed relentlessly violent. I think that modern perceptions of conspiracies in the past have been unduly swayed by the labelling of conspiracy as a political crime, and we have been taught to believe that political crimes, although they can be extremely violent and non-discriminatory in their targets, are somehow crimes with justificatory motivation. Hence there is a readiness or even desire to believe in the statements issued by conspirators, which deflects us away from a concentration on the violence towards higher and more ideological matters. It is also true that the continued advance of conspiracy theory has made us much more wary of the straightforward presentation of 'facts', so that we all feel comfortable not only with the notion that a conspiracy might have taken place when we are told that it has not (for example, Kennedy's death could have been masterminded by any number of interested parties) but also with the notion that what is declared a conspiracy by the authorities may have been nothing of the kind. But the inclusion of a certain number of spurious conspiracies (and/or of a number of embryonic and not fully fledged ones) in the overall total does not alter the central features of this crime. Given that political change was not forthcoming without force, conspiracy (or internal treason) was the only possibility and internal treason involved violence. Only men committed this crime because women were completely excluded from public participation in political life. In addition to being a masculine crime, often committed by younger men, conspiracy can also be seen as a masculinist one, where men attempted to carve out moments of personal glory and to impose their version of the world on their fellow citizens. The fact that this was usually a version that had already been tried, a return to the past, does not matter. By claiming to follow classical precedent, the more educated of them were able to legitimate their violent actions. And although only one conspirator in the selection articulated the link, I think it was precisely the excitement provided by danger that encouraged most conspirators in their attempts. If treason and conspiracy had not been so violent, they would not have been so dangerous, and if they had not been so dangerous, they would not have been so attractive. Even conspirators who genuinely believed in 'liberty' knew that the gains to be won were enormous, but the penalties for failure were terrifying. However, the mere fact that conspiracies kept on happening shows that the prospect of violent torture and dishonourable death was not in itself a sufficient deterrent. The violence inherent in the course of conspiracies must have mirrored too closely the random violence at large in early sixteenth-century Italy, and the lure of possible success was just too potent and seductive to ignore.

Notes

* Earlier versions of this chapter were presented at the *École française* de Rome in March 1999, and at the Renaissance Society of America's annual conference in Chicago in March 2001. I should like to thank audiences in Rome, Chicago and London for their comments. I should also like to acknowledge with gratitude the support of the Molly Cotton Foundation, which in 1982 awarded me a grant for the study of Roman conspiracies during the Renaissance. This article has developed out of that early work.

1   On this see S.H. Cuttler, *The Law of Treason and Treason Trials in Later Medieval France* (Cambridge, 1981), pp. 4–27 and Kate Lowe, 'The political crime of conspiracy in fifteenth- and sixteenth-century Rome', in Trevor Dean and K.J.P. Lowe, eds., *Crime, Society and the Law in Renaissance Italy* (Cambridge, 1994), pp. 184–7.

2   Cf. Barton Ingraham, *Political Crime in Europe* (Berkeley and Los Angeles, 1979), p. 30.

3   David Chambers and Trevor Dean, *Clean Hands and Rough Justice: An Investigating Magistrate in Renaissance Italy* (Ann Arbor, 1997), pp. 11–12.

4   However, the investigating magistrate Beltramino Cusadri in Mantua and Asolo in the 1470s and 1480s seems to have been less successful in using the rope hoist to extract confessions. See Chambers and Dean, *Clean Hands*, pp. 109, 116, 117, 118, 138.

5   John Stephens and Humfrey Butters, 'Notes and documents: new light on Machiavelli', *English Historical Review*, 97 (1982), p. 67: 'i Medici non feciono mai male a persona'.

6   Giorgio Spini, *Cosimo I e l'indipendenza del Principato Mediceo* (Florence, 1980), pp. 131–2: 'Per non venire più in potere dei miei inimici, ove … io sia costretto di nuovo, per violenza di tormenti, a dir cosa alcuna in pregiudicio dell'onor mio e degli innocenti parenti e amici miei … io … con le mie proprie mani finire la vita mia'.

7   Arturo Pacini, '"El ladrón de dentro casa": congiure e lotta politica a Genova dalla riforma del 1528 al tradimento di Gian Luigi Fieschi', in Yves-Marie Bercé and Elena Fasano Guarini eds., *Complots et Conjurations dans l'Europe Moderne* (Rome, 1996), p. 634: 'di ricostruire la rete delle relazioni tra gli imputati e gli ambienti del fuoruscitismo'.

8   Lorenzino de' Medici, *Aridosia, Apologia, Rime e Lettere*, ed. Federico Ravello (Turin, 1921), pp. 204–31.

9   Ester Zille, 'Il processo Grimani', *Archivio Veneto*, 5th series, 36–7 (1945), pp. 165–6. The diarists Marin Sanudo and Girolamo Priuli record aspects of his speech.

10   Luca della Robbia, 'Narrazione del caso di Pietro Paolo Boscoli e di Agostino Capponi (1513)', *Archivio Storico Italiano*, 1 (1842).

11   Pacini, '"El ladrón de dentro casa"', pp. 640–52.

12   *Dizionario Biografico degli Italiani*, 58 vols. so far (Rome, 1960–   ), XLVII, p. 464.

13   Zille, 'Il processo Grimani', pp. 186–94.

14   Federico Odorici, 'I congiurati bresciani del MDXII ed il processo inedito che li riguarda', in Giuseppe Müller, ed., *Raccolta di Cronisti e Documenti Storici Lombardi Inediti*, 2 vols. (Milan, 1856–7), II, pp. 36–115.

15   Stephens and Butters, 'Notes and documents', p. 67.

16 Alessandro Ferrajoli, *La Congiura dei Cardinali contro Leone X* (Rome, 1919: Miscellanea della reale Società romana di storia patria, 7), pp. 219–70.

17 John Stephens, 'Giovanbattista Cibo's confession', in Sergio Bertelli and Gloria Ramakus, eds., *Essays Presented to Myron P. Gilmore*, 2 vols. (Florence, 1978), I: History, pp. 263–8.

18 'Documenti' chosen and edited by Carlo Minutati, *Archivio Storico Italiano*, 10 (1847), pp. 146–62.

19 *I Diarii di Girolamo Priuli*, ed. Arturo Segre and Roberto Cessi, in *Rerum Italicarum Scriptores*, 24, part 3 (Bologna, 1912–38), I, p. 332.

20 Odorici, 'I congiurati bresciani', e.g. p. 45.

21 Stephens and Butters, 'Notes and documents', p. 67.

22 Ferrajoli, *La Congiura*, e.g. pp. 220–1, and *Archivio Segreto Vaticano*, AA. Arm. 1–XVIII, 5042, fol. 5r.

23 Ferrajoli, *La Congiura*, p. 137.

24 Giuseppe Salvo Cozzo, 'Transunto del processo contro i fratelli Imperatori', *Archivio Storico Siciliano*, n. s. 7 (1882), p. 350.

25 Stephens, 'Giovanbattista Cibo's confession', p. 263.

26 Roberto Ridolfi, *The Life of Niccolò Machiavelli* (London, 1963), p. 136: apparently Machiavelli bore six jerks on the rope hoist with great fortitude and 'thought the better of himself for it'.

27 Cesare Guasti, 'Documenti della congiura fatta contro il cardinale Giulio de' Medici', *Giornale Storico degli Archivi Toscani*, 3 (1859), p. 122.

28 Spini, *Cosimo I*, pp. 130–2.

29 Ferrajoli, *La Congiura*, p. 251: 'Qui ellevatus et pluries interrogatus perstetit ut supra; et cum vidissent eius duritiem, fortitudinem et persone robustitataem ac pertinaciam, iusserunt eum exquassari'. *Squassatio* is whipping with a rope.

30 Minutati, 'Documenti', pp. 161–2, esp. p. 162: 'Fatemi di gratia tagliar più presto la testa che tormentarmi tanto, ché io sono troppo stroppiato'.

31 Giangiacomo Martinengo, 'Della congiura dei Bresciani', ed. Giovanni Labus, in Rosmini, *Storie Milanesi*, IV, pp. 269–93.

32 *Archivio Segreto Vaticano*, AA. Arm. 1–XVIII, 5042, fols. 1r–13r. This document has now been published: see Kate Lowe, 'An alternative account of the alleged cardinals' conspiracy of 1517', *Roma Moderna e Contemporanea*, 11 (2003).

33 Guasti, 'Documenti', pp. 239–67.

34 Giuseppe Müller, 'Examen Hieronymi Moroni detenti in carceribus Marchionis Piscariae' in id., 'Documenti che concernono la vita pubblica di Girolamo Moroni', *Miscellanea di Storia Italiana*, III (Turin, 1865), pp. 474–97.

35 Leone del Prete, 'Dichiarazione autografa di Francesco Burlamacchi alla Signoria di Lucca intorno al suo trattato', *Giornale Storico degli Archivi Toscani*, 4 (1860), pp. 314–17.

36 Odorici, 'I congiurati Bresciani', pp. 17, 19, 32–4, 36–7.

37 On this conspiracy, see Salvo Cozzo, 'Transunto del processo contro i fratelli Imperatori', pp. 342–53. This is not however a transcript of the trial but an anonymous account. The original document is in Palermo, *Biblioteca comunale*, 4Qq D.47, fols. 169r–177v.

38 K.J.P. Lowe, *Church and Politics in Renaissance Italy: The Life and Career of Cardinal Francesco Soderini (1453–1524)* (Cambridge, 1993), pp. 132–4.

39 Müller, 'Examen Hieronymi Moroni', pp. 474–97.

40 Pacini, '"El ladrón de dentro casa"', pp. 633–4.

41 *Dizionario Biografico degli Italiani*, XLVII, p. 463.

42 Ludwig von Pastor, *The History of the Popes from the Close of the Middle Ages*, ed. Ralph Kerr, 3rd edn. (London and St. Louis, MO, 1950), XII, pp. 369–72.

43 See Denis Crouzet, *La Sagesse et le malheur: Michel de l'Hospital Chancelier de France* (Seyssel, 1998), pp. 27–30. I am grateful to Denis Crouzet for this reference.

44 *Dizionario Biografico degli Italiani*, XLV, p. 177.

45 Della Robbia, *Narrazione*, p. 283: 'aver voluto liberar la città e ammazzar Giuliano e Lorenzo e messer Giulio (de' Medici)'. The account continues: 'come il vero appare nelle loro examine'. These have not been published.

46 Ferrajoli, *La Congiura*, p. 265.

47 Marc Smith, 'Complots, révoltes et tempéraments nationaux: français et italiens au XVIe siècle', in Bercé and Fasano Guarini, eds., *Complots et conjurations*, pp. 95–9.

48 Guasti, 'Documenti', p. 242. For background to this conspiracy, see Lowe, Church and Politics, pp. 127–9.

49 Stephens, 'Giovanbattista Cibo's confession', p. 265: 'ero contento farlo, accioché fusse certo che li ero servitore, et che desideravo farli ogni piacere'.

50 Benedetto Varchi, *Storia Fiorentina*, ed. Gaetano Milanesi, 3 vols. (Florence, 1857–8), III, pp. 95–6.

51 Lorenzino de' Medici, *Aridosia, Apologia*, p. 221: 'Dico dunque che il fine mio era di liberare Firenze, e l'ammazzare Alessandro era il mezzo'.

52 Ibid., pp. 193 and 226.

53 Minutati, 'Documenti', pp. 147 and 159: 'l'impresa che io haveva ordinato fare contro la Excelentia del signor Duca di Fiorenza'.

54 *Dizionario Biografico degli Italiani*, XXV, pp. 248–9.

55 Lorenzino de' Medici, *Aridosia, Apologia*, p. 216. See on the question of Alessandro's racial ancestry: John K. Brackett, 'Race and rulership: Alessandro de' Medici, first Medici duke of Florence, 1529–37', in T.F. Earle and K.J.P. Lowe, eds., *Black Africans in Renaissance Europe*, forthcoming, Cambridge University Press, 2004.

56 Del Prete, 'Dichiarazione'. p. 317.

57 D. J. Gordon, 'Giannotti, Michelangelo and the cult of Brutus', in *Fritz Saxl (1890–1948): A Volume of Memorial Essays from his Friends in England* (London, 1957), p. 286.

58 Della Robbia, *Narrazione*, p. 290: 'Cavatemi della testa Bruto, acciò ch'io faccia questo passo interamente da cristiano'.

59 Ibid., pp. 218–19.

60 Spini, *Cosimo I*, p. 132.

61 Ibid.: 'El era philosopho y ninguna cosa tenía de cristiano'.

62 Minutati, 'Documenti', pp. 148, 153 and Del Prete, 'Dichiarazione', p. 315.

63 Odorici, 'I congiurati bresciani', pp. 15–16, 38 and 39. Unfortunately, the exact words of the oath are not recorded.

64 Ibid., p. 20: 'che nelle cose grandi non si puote negoziare nè arrischiarsi a gran guadagno e a gran gloria senza grande pericolo, e che la grandezza del pericolo è quella che fa l'ardire laudabile e l'eseguire glorioso'.

65 I should like to thank Ed Muir for this suggestion.

66 Della Robbia, *Narrazione*, p. 283.

67 *Dizionario Biografico degli Italiani*, XXV, p. 248.

68 *Dizionario Biografico degli Italiani*, XLVII, p. 462.

69 *Dizionario Biografico degli Italiani*, XV, p. 440.

70   *I Diarii di Marino Sanudo*, ed. R. Fulin *et al.* 58 vols. (Venice, 1879–1902), I, cols. 917–18, cited in D. Chambers and B. Pullan ed., *Venice: A Documentary History, 1450–1630* (Oxford, 1992), pp. 92–3.
71   Odorici, 'I congiurati bresciani', pp. 17–18.
72   Ibid., p. 20.
73   Salvo Cozzo, 'Transunto del processo contro i fratelli Imperatori', p. 351.
74   Della Robbia, *Narrazione*, p. 307.
75   Lowe, *Church and Politics*, p. 128.
76   *Dizionario Biografico degli Italiani*, XV, p. 445.
77   Chambers and Dean, *Clean Hands*, p. 12.
78   Ferrajoli, *La Congiura*, p. 111.

Chapter 4

Huguenot Conspiracies, Real and Imagined, in Sixteenth-Century France

Penny Roberts

At any time, in any place, but particularly in response to the effects of social or political instability, minority or marginal groups may become the target of conspiracy theories. Difference of religion, nationality, appearance or lifestyle become the source of fear, hostility and sometimes violence. The threat which such groups or individuals are believed to pose to the security or welfare of society make them the natural scapegoats for any misfortune. The medieval and early modern periods witnessed the ostracisation of several groups including Jews, lepers, witches, vagrants and heretics.[1] In some instances, the campaign against them was instigated or at least promoted by the authorities. However, those who governed did not always appear to share the anxieties of the ruled. In such circumstances, loyal subjects sought to warn their rulers of the dangers of toleration. Accusations of conspiracy, real or imagined, bolstered their petitions. Coexistence was alleged to be impossible. The religious ferment produced by the Reformation provided fertile ground for conspiracy theorists, intent on the removal of the confessional minority.[2] Such was the case in France, where the presence of native Protestants, or Huguenots, was portrayed as a threat to the security of the realm and to the welfare of the Catholic majority.

The association of Huguenots with conspiracy in sixteenth-century France was due to their peculiar status as a permitted religious minority combined with the fraught circumstances of civil war. The adoption of a faith contrary to that of their sovereign made them easy targets for accusations of treachery and subversion. 'Catholic propagandists were successful in fostering an image of Protestants as dangerous and treacherous agitators, enemies of the kingdom and of true religion'.[3] Such perceptions were only reinforced by audacious acts of rebellion against the incumbent regime attributed to the Huguenot leadership. In particular, it was believed to have masterminded the Tumult of Amboise of 1560, aimed at the removal of the influence at court of the Catholic Guise family; the Conspiracy or Surprise of Meaux of 1567, again an anti-Guise pre-emptive strike, this time attempting to kidnap King Charles IX and his mother, Catherine de Medici, which led directly to the outbreak of the second war; and the supposed conspiracy being hatched against the crown which precipitated the Saint Bartholomew's Day massacre of Huguenots in August 1572, the most infamous event of the wars.[4] Although there seems to have been no proof of a plot in this last instance, earlier attempts to seize the initiative made it seem plausible enough, and were used to justify the crown's subsequent actions in ordering the murder of the Huguenot leadership. The Surprise of Meaux, in particular, itself inspired by Huguenot fears of an international Catholic conspiracy, was believed to offer incontrovertible proof that the Huguenots had an agenda to seize the state.[5] Nevertheless, however justified the fears of their supposed targets, it seems fair to conclude that, at the national level at least, the Huguenots were dismal failures as conspirators. Despite their later association with theories of resistance to tyrannical rule, they were to achieve much more by the assertion of their influence at court and the flexing of military muscle than through desperate bids to seize power by force.

This essay will, therefore, be concerned less with the details of such conspiracies than with the frames of reference used to identify the Huguenots with subversive activities. Their treachery was couched by their opponents in political, religious, social and even economic terms, posing a threat to both the health and wealth of the body politic. The crown's decision to make peace with its Huguenot subjects, embodied in the so-called edicts of pacification, only increased anxieties about provincial and national security. Even when the Huguenots themselves were not believed to be plotting the downfall of Catholic France, their activities were said to expose chinks in the nation's armour by encouraging Protestant foreigners. Since the largest concentrations of Huguenot population were located in the towns of France, it was here that the danger was most keenly felt as a threat to the integrity of the urban community. Although local solutions were often sought, in representations to the crown the risks accompanying the presence of a belligerent religious minority were argued to carry national consequences. Huguenot betrayal of king and country was anticipated and demonstrable, the only uncertainty whether the attack would come from land or sea. Urban communities across France strove to prove their exceptional vulnerability to infiltration by hostile elements. Local points of entry, commercial considerations, and sources of dispute between the faiths, were relayed in detail to strengthen each case. It is a further demonstration of the provincial nature of a confessionally-divided country that the Huguenot menace was conceived in such terms.

As a result of this provincial character, accusations of seeking to undermine the crown and, therefore, the realm were not confined to the Huguenot leadership or to the court. Nevertheless, national events impinged on the consciousness of local authorities in their concern to deal with regional security. In the aftermath of the Tumult of Amboise, Claude de Tende, governor of Provence, was warned that many of those involved came from his province.[6] Reports of secret plotting involving Genevan ministers demoralised royal officials trying to deal with the growing unrest in Languedoc.[7] As confessional tensions developed into open warfare, so suspicion of Huguenot activities grew, and their identification as the enemy within became deeply entrenched in the Catholic mentality. In particular, the attempted or actual seizure of towns by their Huguenot inhabitants during the first war (1562–1563), a demonstration of betrayal which was not easily forgotten or forgiven, reinforced this image from an early stage. At Toulouse, the ill-fated coup was described in terms of 'invasion and treason'; at Angoulême, the Huguenots were cited as 'rebels and seditious'.[8] A decade later, the spreading of the Saint Bartholomew's Day massacre to the provinces over the ensuing six weeks should not be surprising in view of the suspicions harboured towards Huguenots in localities throughout France.[9] Even during the later stages of the wars, when the Catholic League posed the greater threat to monarchical authority, Huguenots continued to be viewed as suspect. As with the national leadership, such suspicions emanated from a mixture of actual incidents and unfounded rumour. Each account only served to reinforce the image of Huguenot treachery and recklessness, 'their audacity and temerity'.[10]

The use of provocative language was combined with accusations that the enemy within was in league with the enemy without. Throughout the wars, Huguenots were claimed to be conspiring with and inviting invasion by the representatives of foreign Protestant powers - England, Scotland, Geneva, the Empire and the Netherlands - and thus seeking to undermine the security of both the kingdom and the local community. Undoubtedly, the Huguenots sought foreign aid for their cause, as indeed did the crown and its Catholic commanders. However, in order to reinforce this association of Huguenots with 'the other', Catholics frequently tried to deny that most Huguenots were native to their locality, whilst Huguenots emphasised that, on the contrary, they were all from well-established local families.[11]

Furthermore, the blame for certain crimes commonly associated with outsiders and marginal groups, such as arson, was frequently levelled at Huguenots as enemies of the local community.[12] After the coups, attempted and successful, of the first war, urban communities continued to be vigilant regarding the (often rumoured) threat of surprise by Huguenot forces, during periods of both war *and* peace. This was reinforced by the sporadic nature (both chronologically and geographically) of the fighting, during which the Huguenot military seized strategic regional locations and diverted local resources. Nor did the edicts of pacification which punctuated the wars necessarily offer any respite for beleaguered Catholics. In 1581, those of Lectoure in Guyenne described how they were financing the occupation of their province by enemy (i.e. Huguenot) garrisons, as if they were 'nourishing a serpent in their bosom and paying for the knife which would cut their throats'.[13]

Provincial tensions provide us with telling insights into the way in which the Huguenot 'problem' was perceived and portrayed. The spectre of the (possibly internationally organised) Huguenot conspiracy appeared to be very real in the localities. In particular, the issue of regional security, and its attendant fear of foreign intervention, was of particular concern to coastal and frontier towns with their defensive and commercial priorities. The language they used expresses the degree of vulnerability, but also self importance, of such communities, charged as they were with the defence of the realm, acting as the barrier which kept the foreigner, the enemy, out. The usefulness of discrediting your perceived enemy through association with acts of conspiracy and betrayal, specifically of encouraging foreign invasion, is evident. Thus, a mixture of genuine fear and self-interest seems to have operated in border regions in their attempts to distance the Huguenot threat. As we will see, the organisation of Huguenot conspiracies might be locally, regionally, nationally or internationally based, and frontier communities were at the forefront of identifying and quashing them.

Frontier status was a highly valued commodity during the religious wars, especially during periods of peace and their attendant edicts of toleration. It allowed for exemption from Huguenot sites for worship, for example, as well as from the general directive to disarm and to erase fortifications established during the troubles. The buying and selling of weapons was prohibited in all but frontier towns, just as the carrying of arms was forbidden, 'except in frontier towns for use in case of necessity against invasion and incursion by the enemy, but not otherwise'.[14] Thus, the right of the inhabitants of the ports of Marseille and Toulon to retain their arms was upheld by the crown, in defence of the realm's 'maritime frontier'.[15] To live on a frontier was to face a permanent threat of infiltration, which could only be exacerbated by a period of civil strife. Borders were not only permeable to intruders, but also to the smuggling and dissemination to the enemy of important information via letters and other documents which might compromise national security. Such fears were openly expressed in a letter from Charles IX to Montmorency-

Damville, governor of Languedoc in December 1563, in which he urged that any such unauthorised activity be 'watched out for', and anyone found 'laden with letters, coming or going without my leave' be arrested and the king informed, paying particular attention to 'the frontier crossings'.[16]

Throughout the wars, there were regular reports of the interception of correspondence being carried by supposed foreign spies who were then questioned about their activities, including a man captured in Dieppe smuggling letters hidden under cheeses to England.[17] Suspect packages and home-grown plots were a major preoccupation of the authorities. Prior to the conflict, in autumn 1560, from Nantes and Angoulême came worrying reports of a conspiracy involving the bishop of St Brieuc and the poisoning of a local *sénéchal*. A suspect was interrogated about the carrying of suspicious packages and letters addressed to the bishop signed mysteriously 'he who knows'.[18] Only a couple of months before, the sieur de Burie requested permission 'to inspect the packages which pass through this town [Bordeaux] ... and are sent from one province to another' by which 'several things' might be 'discovered'.[19] Similarly, in 1568, the sieur de Barbezieux, reported the infiltration of secret Huguenot intelligence networks which would expose their 'bad intentions'.[20] In February 1563, the municipal authorities in Toulouse sought 'to uncover spies and those who roam the town like vagabonds', eject them, and plant their own spies outside suspects' houses.[21] Similar measures were taken in Lyon, 'to guard against surprises, plots, and machinations'.[22] Authorities were also vigilant with regard to subversive talk or straightforward insults aimed at the monarchy itself. For its part, the crown sought to have such matters referred back for investigation at the highest level in order to determine the seriousness of the threat. Any challenge to royal authority, even those of a much less dramatic nature such as resistance to the enforcement of justice, might indicate the existence of or willingness to support a conspiracy, internally or externally led. However, it was very much the physical threat of invasion by foreign and hostile elements 'by sea and by land' which preoccupied frontier communities and, thus, dominated their appeals to the crown.[23]

For claims to special treatment due to frontier status to be effective, the province concerned needed to present a case that its defence was not just vital for its own preservation, but for that of the realm as a whole. Therefore, a further strategy of frontier towns was to establish their superior credentials to others who might lay claim to similar status. Thus, Lyon reminded the king that it was 'the foremost frontier and the largest fortified town in the kingdom of its size', whose ruin therefore threatened that of France itself.[24] In Languedoc, Arles championed itself as the 'only boulevard of the province on the coast'.[25] The king himself referred to Marseille, as justification for its exemption from the provision of a site for Reformed worship, as 'one of the principal frontiers and key to our kingdom', a status which was repeatedly confirmed throughout the wars and beyond.[26] Likewise, Picardy's integrity was to be defended, 'because it is so important for the security and conservation of the frontier'.[27] The position of Bayonne and Dax in the far south west, on the border with Spain, was also judged to be dangerous, so that certain restrictions had to be imposed on local Huguenots. The town of Tussan in the diocese of Narbonne required special protection because of its situation on the frontier with Roussillon 'by which the enemy has always entered Languedoc during wartime'.[28] At Vienne, near Lyon, concerns were aroused in 1570 by the proximity and unsuitability of the most recently designated site for Reformed worship, since the bridge which linked them served as 'one of the main routes from Germany, Geneva, Bresse and Savoy in order to reach the Vivarais and Languedoc'.[29] In 1560, the authorities in Bordeaux expressed anxiety regarding the insufficient defence provided at Blaye which guarded river access to the town, 'where all foreign boats visit and the English leave their weapons when they disembark here'.[30] In 1563, it was again the threat from the English that most preoccupied them, citing 'intelligence between those of this region and the English', and endeavouring to investigate those with English connections in Bordeaux; in 1569, the Scots as well as the English were mentioned.[31] The province was described as lying on the frontier of the kingdoms of Spain, Navarre and England (the latter a hangover from medieval occupation), 'where the enemy could notoriously descend in six or seven hours, as experienced in recent days'.[32] It was requested, therefore, that loyal inhabitants and subjects be allowed to rearm themselves against the danger of such a surprise attack, and a local militia be appointed from among those who were 'not suspected of sedition' in order to search the town. It is important to note the use of language here - 'the enemy', 'loyal' inhabitants - clearly a confessional distinction during a period of supposed national peace.

Such loaded language was a commonplace of representations to the crown, reinforcing the loyalty of Catholic inhabitants in contrast to the 'enemy' and, therefore, conspiratorial disposition of local Huguenots. Thus, the Catholics of Lyon argued that it would be extremely difficult for good Christians (i.e. local Catholics) seeing their enemies (the Huguenots who had seized the town) at all hours going to their services nearby, not content at having enriched themselves with their possessions, but trying also to divert from the Christian faith the wives, children and domestic servants of good Christians in order to draw them to the new religion'.[33] They went on to classify their town as 'the primary head of the church in this kingdom', underlining its Catholic credentials, just as the inhabitants of other areas, notably the Burgundians, would lay stress on their Catholicity. Sometimes this could take the form of a blatant challenge to royal policy. The Catholics of Mâcon had a stark warning for the king, citing historical examples of the subversion of several empires and rulers as a result of a policy of toleration. They, in particular, were most painfully aware of the consequences of giving a free hand to the Huguenots who had seized their town during the first war, spreading 'their venom' and constructing a 'tower of Babel'.[34] On the whole though, most regions were seeking to curry favour with, rather than to antagonise, the crown; thus, an appeal on the grounds of Catholicity was proffered as a mark of loyalty to the integrity of the kingdom, thus undermining Huguenot protestations of obedience.

The crown was, in general, sympathetic to pleas on the grounds of frontier status, since it had an obvious interest in upholding the integrity of its borderlands, though the list of provinces able, and more than willing, to claim such privileges was long. In most instances, the validity of a region's claims to such status was self evident, even though some cases were considered more pressing than others. Yet, so attractive were the benefits of securing such a position that even a community well inland might try to assert its rights, as in the case of Le Mans. Here, royal privileges granted to the town in 1401 were cited in its defence, as a 'frontière de guerre', neighbour to the duchy of Normandy 'mostly held and occupied by the English, ancient enemies of the crown'.[35] There is no record of how the crown reacted to such a backdated claim, but Le Mans itself did manage to avoid being designated for Reformed worship, its Huguenots having to travel to Château-du-Loir, some distance to the south. The most successful claimant to the privileges which accompanied frontier status, however, was the region of Provence, including Marseille, the only province able to secure freedom from the imposition of official sites for Reformed worship at the end of the first war in 1563. Picardy in the north-east, probably the most frontline province when it came to security issues, also negotiated its own deal with the authorities, although a considerable Huguenot presence and the governorship of the Prince of Condé ensured that some provision was made as long as it was not seen to compromise provincial security. Likewise, in the fortress city of Metz, bulwark against the Empire, the presence of a considerable number of foreign mercenaries raised the possibility of services being conducted in German.[36] Conversely, in La Rochelle in 1563, 'the dangers of surprise by our old enemies the English' was used by local Huguenots to argue for their right to worship *within* the city walls.[37]

Compromises were also sought by less evidently strategically-placed areas, notably Brittany and Burgundy, two of the most vocal advocates of the privileges inherent in frontier status. In particular, such regions raised the spectre of their vulnerability to foreign invasion if the inhabitants were disarmed or the Huguenots were allowed to worship at strategic locations, such as major towns. The inhabitants of the province of Burgundy, the very identity of which, as Mack Holt has shown, was bound up with Catholicism ('la foy de Bourgogne' as it was termed), presented themselves as loyal defenders of a permeable eastern border.[38] They stressed that, unlike other frontier provinces, they were not afforded the natural protection of the sea or mountain ranges, and so it was much more important that their loyalty to the crown be retained through royal assurances that the faith of the region would be upheld and protected from the Protestant threat. The Burgundian town of Mâcon set out its vulnerable strategic position on the frontier of Bresse (the region adjoining Geneva), Switzerland, Savoy and Franche Comté, near where the Saône met the Loire en route to Orléans (a Huguenot stronghold).[39] On this basis, in 1563, the provincial governor, Tavannes, who was responsible for regional security, argued that the town should not be disarmed, otherwise it would give a considerable advantage to the province's hostile Protestant neighbours.[40] Dijon ('capital of the province') and Beaune argued the same case against disarmament on much the same basis, that it would be 'prejudicial to the king, the town ... and consequently to the whole realm'; a protest reiterated in 1568.[41]

However, it was the infiltration of 'estrangers', and other undesirable elements, especially as a result of the holding of Reformed services in the locality, which most exercised the authorities in Burgundy. In the 1560s, it was believed that an unprecedented influx of immigrant artisans, domestic servants, shop assistants and vagabonds posed 'the greatest peril' to the security of frontier towns, emphasising the inferior social status of (and overrepresentation of women among) such groups, designed again to denigrate the Huguenot cause.[42] There were fears, in particular, of the carrying of arms smuggled in from Geneva by these troublemakers, the possession of weapons underlining the threat which they posed. As a consequence, it was requested that the authorities be permitted to search out and expel suspects. In the summer and autumn of 1576, there were reports of 'armed strangers' attending services at Mâcon, despite the attendant risks of its position on a frontier.[43] This was unreasonable, it was argued, since sites for Reformed worship had been accorded throughout the realm, so there was no need for those from outside the region to seek out services elsewhere. From Bordeaux in 1563, governor d'Escars reported that due to fears about lapses of security at the city gates, the local inhabitants were afraid of having their throats cut by 'estrangers', and a number of Englishmen were languishing in prison with no clear directive on what should be done with them.[44] In contrast, a royal commissioner to the Protestant towns of Languedoc in 1563, reported that though there were strangers present, they were living peacefully and 'working at their trades'.[45]

In Brittany, similar concerns were expressed regarding the threat from foreign interlopers in the 1560s. In particular, ports such as Dinan, 'on the frontier with England', and Nantes, 'near which the English ordinarily surprise us and on seeing division between the people' could easily gain land (so representing both the revival of an old, and the posing of a fresh, threat), as well as the garrisons roundabout, were seen as especially vulnerable from invasion by land or sea.[46] In contrast to the views of Burgundians, Bretons saw the sea as rendering them more, not less, vulnerable to attack. As a result, the services at Dinan and Morlaix had been transferred to sites further inland, in accordance with the crown's directive to exclude 'his frontier towns, ... ports and harbours'.[47] The protestors at 'the most beautiful Breton port', Nantes, were not so fortunate, perhaps because their claim to frontier status was not sustained. It was declared that the town 'was not on a major frontier' and thus required only 'fifty men in the chateau' to defend it.[48] Instead the authorities concentrated their efforts on confining Huguenot inhabitants to the town's suburbs and reporting signs of seditious activity. In 1564, an accusation against the *sénéchal* that he 'wanted to sell the town to the Huguenots' was not upheld.[49] Nevertheless, the Nantais claimed that not only the English, but Flemings and Scots were being received by local Huguenots, as well as Protestants from the nearby 'heresy-infected' regions of Poitou and Anjou and others from outside the *sénéchaussée* (once again emphasising the importance of determining the non-native origins of the Huguenot problem).[50] Similarly, at Saint-Malo, the coming and going of English commerce was believed to be a cover for subversive Protestant activity, and the presence of 'the English and other strangers' at Reformed services a threat to local security.[51] Another prominent issue in Brittany was the potential disruption posed to commercial traffic, Spanish and Portuguese merchants allegedly having already been deterred from trading there due to armed gangs of Protestant gentlemen terrorising them as they went to and from Reformed services.[52] Huguenot attacks on Spaniards, in particular, was a commonly cited incident here, as elsewhere in France.[53]

Other frontier towns also expressed concern about commercial ruin and the deterrent to foreign merchants if services were allowed in their locality. The most important trading centre in France, Lyon, reported the threat to its all important commerce due to its proximity to Geneva, only twenty two leagues distant and easily reached via the river Rhône. But unlike Nantes and, indeed, Mâcon, the presence of 'estrangers' in Lyon was mostly seen as a boon rather than a threat. It was claimed that at least half of Lyon's inhabitants were foreigners from several nations on whom, along with its international fairs, the prosperity of the town depended. However, most of these residents were Catholics and the permitting of Huguenot worship would drive them away due to the prohibitions of their own rulers, King Philip of Spain, and the lords of Venice, Genoa, Florence, Lucca, and Milan, who 'on pain of death forbid them from frequenting, staying or trafficking in any town in the kingdom' where Reformed services were allowed. As at Nantes, the king was reminded that not only the town's prosperity but the royal coffers would suffer, as a result, in this case, of the removal of banking services, as well as the revenue from commerce, to the tune of 100,000 *écus* a year. Like Mâcon, Lyon made much of its sufferings as a result of the Huguenot takeover during the first war, for 'no town was more ruined'.[54] But in 1568, following the second war, the town was still having to argue the case for its exemption from Reformed worship in the interests of commerce and national security. For if they were allowed, the crown was warned, the best inhabitants would leave, and the fate of the town and the realm would be left in the hands of 'violent disrupters of the public peace', who would bring in soldiers from Germany and Geneva to threaten other provinces until they reached the very gates of Paris.[55] Elsewhere, as in Poitou during the third war when merchants from Orléans were the target, merchandise was seized by 'those who bear arms against the king, by which means they enrich themselves and finance the war'.[56] Whereas, in centres such as Dieppe, it was the Huguenots who complained about the impact of the wars on local trade.[57]

Finally, the nervousness with which both faiths viewed the status of frontier towns is reflected in the peace negotiations which took place in 1581 in the province of Dauphiné. The Huguenot deputies proved reluctant to cede a number of fortified sites and their attendant citadels, notably Gap and Livron. There was much dispute as to the frontier or other status of these towns, whether or not according to recent royal edicts the Huguenots were obliged to relinquish them, and the effect on local commerce if they did not. Catholic concerns included the supposed levying of German troops by Huguenot representatives in preparation for a renewed war.[58] For their part, the Huguenots were primarily concerned about the extent to which disarming of the faiths could be effectively synchronised so as not to render them vulnerable to attack. The arguments proffered by both sides centred around the upholding of the law as expressed in royal legislation, and thus which could prove themselves to be the most loyal subjects of the French crown. However, Catholic acceptance of the validity of Huguenot claims to uphold the law and serve the crown was not always forthcoming, and says much about the problems of integration for a religious minority. For instance, Catholics at various times expressed concern about the holding of judicial or other office by Huguenots, who apart from favouring their coreligionists, could not be expected to give the service to their community which was incumbent upon them. Since all authority was divinely instituted, it was their duty to act as God's representatives in service to a Catholic monarch and a Catholic people, which in the circumstances they could hardly do without being compromised by their faith. Their attendance at Reformed services, for instance, contravened royal legislation and set a bad example to the people. Therefore, it was argued, they should resign or be forcibly replaced. The presence of Huguenots in positions of local influence was seen to compromise local security and, ultimately, to provide an open invitation to conspiratorial activity. Two Burgundian officials, whose confessional sympathies were well known and whose activities were consequently watched closely by their opponents, were a clerk at Mâcon, Daulphin, 'a seditious and factious man', and the lieutenant-general of Dijon, Jean Morin.[59] The fortunes of such individuals fluctuated with the wars and subsequent shifts in royal policy, including the expulsion of their coreligionists from office with each outbreak of armed conflict. These variables, furthermore, were to prove crucial in determining the identification of Huguenots with conspiracy.

Yet, what can we know, at this distance, of the reality of Huguenot conspiratorial activity? For historians, their actions and statements, especially in the early years of the movement, suggest a radical potential that was never fully realised.[60] Yet many of the accusations examined here relied on hearsay evidence and the way in which Huguenot actions were construed. Although much feared, foreign incursions were rare, and consisted not of surprise attacks but broader military support at times of open warfare, such as that of John Casimir of the Palatinate during the 1560s and 1570s. Yet, subversion did not necessarily involve military initiatives or the use of spies. The infiltration of municipal posts through democratic means, as occurred at Toulouse with the election of sympathisers to the *capitoulat* in November 1561, prior to the insurrection of the following May, brought the Huguenots far closer to seizing lasting control of towns.[61] Furthermore, the tensions which were generated by the fear of conspiracy prompted some local authorities to defuse the situation by brokering oaths of mutual accord and peace.[62] Yet, these, like the efforts of the crown to establish official coexistence, mostly proved short-lived, as confessional strife escalated.

Huguenots were not universally dismissed as traitors, or for being in league with the enemy. For most Huguenots, a change of faith did not entail a rejection of king, nation or community, but rather the choice of a path which they hoped king, nation and community might soon be persuaded to follow. Their labelling as conspirators was the strategy by which the validity of their cause was undermined by those who opposed their recognition. But it was not just a cynical move on the part of those who argued that the Huguenot presence compromised local, regional and, ultimately, national security. Such a threat did indeed often seem very real; evidence of betrayal appeared to be forthcoming; and the whole issue was bound up with other broader concerns. Notably, it brought the question of the extent to which toleration of a religious minority compromised the security of early modern states boldly to the fore. Despite their protestations of loyalty, Huguenot efforts to gain recognition, and to secure protection and rights for their faith, as well as the threatening presence of a Protestant international with which they undoubtedly had links, reinforced Catholic distrust. Even without indulging in subversive activity, Huguenot differentiation from and rejection of the practices of the Catholic majority rendered them suspect, and this view was only strengthened by their engagement in armed resistance. Demonstrations of obedience and loyalty were not sufficient to expunge the taint of treachery which adherence to a different faith from that of their sovereign implied.[63] This was true even well after the Huguenots appeared to constitute a significant focus of opposition. Thus, despite their largely emasculated position in the seventeenth century, the ambivalence of their position within the French polity would continue to place them in the role of potential, if not actual, conspirators against king and country.

Notes

1   The classic study is R.I. Moore, *The Formation of a Persecuting Society: Power and Deviance in Western Europe, 950–1250* (Oxford, 1987). For the early modern period, see also C. Ginzburg and M. Gauchet, 'Le démon du soupçon', *Histoire*, 84 (1985), 48–56; D. Groh, 'La tentation des théories de conspiration', *Storia della Storiografia*, 14 (1988), 96–118.

2   Ole Peter Grell and Bob Scribner, eds., *Tolerance and Intolerance in the European Reformation* (Cambridge, 1996), esp. the essay by Scribner, 'Preconditions of tolerance and intolerance in sixteenth-century Germany', pp. 32–47.

3   Luc Racaut, 'The cultural obstacles to religious pluralism in the polemic of the French wars of religion', in K. Cameron *et al*, eds., *The Adventure of Religious Pluralism in Early Modern France*, (Bern, 2000), pp. 115–25 (quotation from p. 121).

4   For a recent overview of these incidents, see Robert J. Knecht, *The French Civil Wars, 1562–1598* (Harlow, 2000), pp. 66–70, 135–7, 163–6. More specifically on Amboise, see

most recently Corrado Vivanti, 'La congiura d'Amboise', in Yves-Marie Bercé and Elena Fasano Guarini, *Complots et Conjurations dans l'Europe Moderne* (Rome, 1996), pp. 439–50. I am grateful to Professor Mark Greengrass for this reference.

5   See R.J. Knecht, *Catherine de' Medici* (London and New York, 1998), pp. 114–17.

6   Bibliothèque Nationale, Paris, manuscrits français [hereafter BN, MS fr] 15871, fo. 146r (11 Sept. 1560). Vivanti, 'La congiura d'Amboise', p. 439, details the widespread provincial support expected to back up the Tumult.

7   BN, MS fr 15873, fo. 2r (13 Sept. 1560).

8   BN, MS fr 15876, fos. 117–22 (12 June 1562); 15877, fos. 68–72 (16 Sept. 1562). On events at Toulouse, see Mark Greengrass, 'The anatomy of a religious riot in Toulouse in May 1562', *Journal of Ecclesiastical History*, 34 (1983), 367–91.

9   Philip Benedict, 'The Saint Bartholomew's Massacres in the provinces', *Historical Journal*, 21 (1978), 205–25.

10   Quotation from Archives Municipales de [hereafter AM] Toulouse, BB107, fo. 178 (3 Feb. 1563).

11   For example, see Penny Roberts, 'Huguenot petitioning during the wars of religion', in Raymond A. Mentzer and Andrew Spicer, eds., *Society and Culture in the Huguenot World, 1559–1685* (Cambridge, 2002), p. 72.

12   For example, in Tours, BN, MS fr 15877, fo. 110. See also the examples cited in my 'Arson, conspiracy and rumour in early modern Europe', *Continuity and Change*, 12 (1997), 22.

13   BN, MS fr 15564, fos. 87–9r.

14   BN, MS fr 15880, fo. 228r, response of royal council to remonstrances of Catholics of Provence (12 Aug. 1564); also see 17832, fo. 71r (6 May 1564), regarding the arrest of a German merchant for selling weapons.

15   BN, MS fr 15879, fo. 134 (Mar. 1564).

16   BN, MS fr 3202, fo. 45r.

17   BN, MS fr 15551, fos. 272–7 (10 May 1570).

18   BN, MS fr 15871, fos. 46–50 (Nov. 1560).

19   BN, MS fr 15873, fo. 9r (14 Sept. 1560).

20   BN, MS fr 15548, fo. 43r (14 Sept. 1568).

21   AM Toulouse, BB107, fos. 178–9 (3 Feb. 1563); and on interception of letters, BB172 (1563), letter of *capitouls* to Charles IX.

22   AM Lyon, GG77, no. 5 (1563).

23   Quotation from the sieur de St Luc at Brouage, BN, MS fr 15562, fo. 233r (28 Mar. 1580).

24   AM Lyon, GG77, no. 11.

25   BN, MS fr 15564, fo. 112 (18 May 1581).

26   Archives Communales de [hereafter AC] Marseille, AA5, fos. 258–9r.

27   BN, MS fr 3187, fo. 12 (13 May 1562).

28   BN, MS fr 15871, fo. 33. On Bayonne, see BN, MS fr 15880, fos. 396r, 404v (1564); on Dax, 15878, fos. 86–7r (28 July 1563).

29   BN, MS fr 15552, fos. 266r, 268r, 270r, 272r (Sept. 1570).

30   BN, MS fr 15873, fos. 100–1r (11 Sept. 1560).

31   BN, MS fr 15878, fos. 88–90r (1 Aug. 1563); 15549, fos. 51, 55–6, 59r (28 and 29 Sept. 1569).

32   BN, MS fr 15878, fos. 294–5r (7 Dec. 1563); 15881, fos. 320–1 (1565).

33   AM Lyon, GG77, no. 11.

34   Archives Départementales de [hereafter AD] Saône et Loire, AC Mâcon, GG 122, no. 30
       (3 fos.).

35   AD la Sarthe, AC Le Mans, 987 (April 1563).

36   BN, MS fr 17832, fo. 72r. Cf. position at similarly strategically located Mézières, BN, MS
       fr 15548, fo. 32 (8 Sept. 1568).

37   BN, MS fr 15878, fo. 58r (24 June 1563).

38   Mack P. Holt, 'Burgundians into Frenchmen: Catholic identity in sixteenth-century
       Burgundy', in Michael Wolfe, ed., *Changing Identities in Early Modern France* (Durham and
       London, 1997), pp. 345–70.

39   AD Saône et Loire, AC Mâcon, BB38, fo. 145 (29 Oct. 1563); BN, MS fr 4635, fos. 13–
       14r (20 Oct. 1563).

40   BN, MS fr 4634, fo. 129 (20 Oct. 1563).

41   AM Dijon, D63 (1563); BN, MS fr 4048, fo. 77 (20 Sept. 1563); 4636, fos. 50–1 (30 Apr.
       1568).

42   BN, MS fr 4636, fos. 66–7 (11 Jan. 1567), 69r, 71r; AM Dijon, D63 (1563); BN, MS fr
       15881, fo. 339, on similar concerns in Nantes in 1565.

43   AD Saône et Loire, AC Mâcon, GG124, nos. 5 and 6.

44   BN, MS fr 15878, fo. 240r (3 Nov. 1563).

45   BN, MS fr 15878, fo. 120 (29 Aug. 1563).

46   AM Rennes, liasse 343 (10 Aug. 1563); BN, MS fr 15879, fo. 6r (8 Jan. 1563).

47   BN, MS fr 15881, fo. 336.

48   BN, MS fr 15875, fo. 268v, a position later challenged, see 15880, fo. 290 (23 Oct. 1564).

49   BN, MS 15879, fo. 58 (22 Feb. 1564); 15546, fo. 25 (8 May 1568).

50   BN, MS fr 15881, fo. 337.

51   BN, MS 15880, fo. 348 (1564); 15546, fos. 267–71, and 15547, fo. 12r (1568).

52   BN, MS fr 15881, fos. 409–10.

53   E.g. at Cluny in Burgundy, see BN, MS fr 4636, fos. 66–7 (11 Jan. 1567).

54   AM Lyon, GG77, no. 11.

55   AM Lyon, GG77, no. 12.

56   BN, MS 15548, fo. 101r (24 Oct.1568); 15551, fo. 220r (19 Apr.1570).

57   BN, MS 15548, fos. 175 and 177.

58   BN, MS 15564, fos. 20, 143; 15565, fo. 202r.

59   BN, MS 15546, fo. 53 (18 May, 1568), regarding the role of *greffier* Daulphin. AM Dijon,
       D63; B199, fo. 80r, B202, fo. 17v, on lieutenant-general Morin. On this issue in Orléans,
       see Christopher Stocker, 'The Parlement of Paris and confessional politics in the 1560s',
       Proceedings of the Annual Meeting of the Western Society for French History, 15 (1988), 38–47.

60   On the radical potential of the Huguenot movement, see Philip Benedict, 'The dynamics
       of Protestant militancy: France, 1555–1563', and Denis Crouzet, 'Calvinism and the uses
       of the political and the religious (France, ca. 1560–ca. 1572)', both in P. Benedict, G.
       Marnef, H. Van Nierop and M. Venard, eds., *Reformation, Revolt and Civil War in France and
       the Netherlands, 1555–1585* (Amsterdam, 1999), pp. 35–50, 99–113.

61   Greengrass, 'The anatomy of a religious riot'.

62   Notably at Caen, Lyon, Montélimar, Nyons, Orange, Orléans and Valence, see Olivier
       Christin, 'La coexistence confessionnelle, 1563–1567', *Bulletin de la Société de l'Histoire du
       Protestantisme Français* (1995), pp. 483–504.

63   For further discussion of the association between Calvinist 'heresy' and treachery in early
       modern France, see Charlotte Wells, 'Leeches on the body politic: xenophobia and

witchcraft in early modern political thought', *French Historical Studies*, 22 (1999), esp. pp. 359–60, 368–9, 377.

Chapter 5

Vengeance and Conspiracy during the French Wars of Religion

Stuart Carroll

'Vengeance is a sweet passion; whose impact is sweet and natural'

Those familiar with Montaigne's *Essays* may be surprised by the sentiments he expresses in 'On Diversion'. But we must remember that to our forefathers vengeance was not a blind passion undertaken in 'hot anger' but a legitimate means of defence. In particular, the honour code of the sixteenth-century French nobility demanded that satisfaction be sought for any infringement of honour. Though condemned by the Church and the monarchy, the right to private vengeance was claimed by nobles. Vengeance also figured among the most important themes of sixteenth-century French literature. Brantôme, for example, lamented those who refused to avenge the deaths of their fathers: they should 'die or be avenged, and not allow their arms to be sullied by their lack of resolution and a true blow'.[1] As David Quint has shown Montaigne's essays were, in part, an attempt to confront aristocratic mores and the bloody feuds they engendered. Vengeance was a sweet passion because it was based on reason and capable of being tamed. Montaigne proposes a counter ethics to the traditional model of heroic virtue, replacing it with the values of mercy, humility and yielding.[2]

Feuding was an integral part of kinship and noble relationships, and by its nature involved conspiratorial plotting. Vengeance killings had to be carefully planned, kinsmen and servants mobilised in defence of life and honour, and tactics and resources employed to manipulate royal officials and the legal system. Conspiracy is integral to faction politics. This paper will show how the interplay between vengeance and conspiracy shaped political events and created a dynamic paradigm which engendered political instability in the years leading up to the Massacre of Saint Bartholomew, and was a primary cause of the Massacre itself. First, I shall assess the relationship between religion and politics in the early 1560s. Calvinist militancy and conspiracy was essential to the creation of a politics of vengeance. The New Testament condemns vengeance but in tracts and pamphlets French Calvinists developed a new language of revenge. Secondly, I shall present a narrative outline of the Guise-Montmorency conflict between 1563 and 1566, a feud that dominates the political landscape. The third section will deal in more detail with the nature of Catholic conspiracy in the 1560s, which is poorly understood and has implications for our understanding of the mobilisation of both popular and aristocratic support. Finally, I shall conclude by showing how vengeance and conspiracy once again converged to unleash the Massacre of Saint Bartholomew.

Calvinism and Vengeance

The traditional historiography of French Calvinism, which stressed its moderation, is being replaced by a new scholarship which underlines the movement's militancy.[3] Calvin stressed the need to obey the duly constituted authorities. Far from being seditious, his ideas for reform and moral renewal promoted order; but Calvinists' belief in the righteousness of their cause and their antipathy for the abominations of Popery ran counter to this claim. Calvin personified the contradictory impulses of his teachings. While remaining aloof from the Conspiracy of Amboise in March 1560 he was implicated in an attempt to seize Lyon later that year. Moreover, Geneva was unable to temper the ardour of the faithful and control the rapidly expanding congregation, whose sense of righteousness and victimhood was reinforced by the psychology of Calvinism which saw the hand of Providence in events. The death of Henri II in July 1559 followed by his son François II in December 1560 was a sign of God's judgement on those who tried to suppress the Word. Calvin's chief lieutenant, Bèze, wrote the following poem at this time:

> Tool of bad men, Henri, thy thirst for blood
> it retribution found,
> From thy pierced eyeball gushed a purple flood
> Which crimsoned all the ground
>
> Following his father in thy mad career,
> François, unhappy youth,
> Thou felt'st God's arrow cleave thy guilty ear
> Fast closed against God's truth.[4]

Unequivocally condemned by the New Testament (Math., v, 38–9; 43–4), vengeance belongs to God alone (Romans, xii, 19–21), but the Old Testament is more ambiguous and individual acts were represented by Protestants as the just vengeance of God. If we follow Denis Crouzet religious violence is closely associated with proximity to Christ and we can see why individual Protestants were represented as instruments of God's will. Revenge for the burning of the Protestant councillor of the Parlement of Paris, Anne du Bourg, was swift. On December 17 1559, ten horsemen murdered Président Minard, a prominent supporter of repression in the Parlement. An informer, Julien Fermé, was also killed. The language of vengeance became a common convention of Protestant propaganda against the Guise-dominated régime of François II. Minard's murder was used the following year to threaten the second of the Guise brothers, Charles cardinal of Lorraine: 'Beware cardinal that you are not treated à la Minard by a Stuart'.[5] When civil war finally broke out in 1562 the Protestant commander, Condé, presented his cause as a 'vengeance publique'.[6]

The convergence of vengeance, human and divine, and conspiracy is first seen in the Protestant attempt to overthrow the Guise which ended beneath the walls of the château of Amboise in March 1560. The motivation of its leader, Jean du Barry, seigneur de La Renaudie, has recently been re-examined. He moved in the orbit of the Guise in the 1540s and it was probably through their favour that he escaped imprisonment for fraud and fled justice in 1546.[7] La Renaudie converted to Calvinism during exile in Switzerland and saw the Conspiracy of Amboise as an opportunity to defend the faith and recover his status in France. Above all he craved vengeance. In 1558 his brother-in-law, a leading member of the reform movement at Metz, had been summarily executed on the orders of the bishop, the cardinal of Lorraine.[8] La Renaudie's protectors had now become his persecutors.

The Protestant propaganda machine turned the bloody failure of the Conspiracy into a trial of the regime, and the martyrdom of those taken prisoner was depicted in a famous woodcut [fig.1]. The providential last words of the condemned man on the scaffold, Villemongis, were invoked to move the faithful: 'Lord, here is the blood of your children. You will have vengeance!'[9] This prophecy was fulfilled with the assassination of François de Guise in March 1563. The assassin, Poltrot de Méré, claimed to have delivered France from a tyrant but he also referred to his private motives: 'the indignity which the seigneur de Guise had perpetrated on the corpse of one who was his kinsman, and also another close kinsman at Amboise ... whom Guise had had killed in the dungeons. Since which time he had resolved to take vengeance for himself and for his *patrie*'.[10] No firm evidence exists to suggest that Méré was part of a wider conspiracy, but he implicated two leaders of the Protestant party: Soubise, a close friend of La Renaudie and one of the main

Lexecution d'Amboise, faitele 15. Mars. 1560.

A. Le Renaudie pendu ayant esté tué par le seul eur de Pardillan,
   auec vn escriteau disant la Renaudie dict la Forest chef descriel-
   les. Et depuis son corps fut mis en quatre cartiers & fut de suite
   bout d'vne lance dessus le pont d'Amboise.
B. Le Baron de Castelnau & ses compagnons decapitez.
C. Villemongis ayant trempé ses mains au sang de ses compagnōs

decapitez.
D. Sept pendus aux creneaux du Chasteau auec longues corde.
E. Trois teste arrachees pour memorial sur vne potence.
F. D'aultres mentau supliçe.
G. Chasteau d'Amboise.
H. Iardin du Roy dans ledit Chasteau.

Figure 1: *L'execution d'Amboise, faitele 15 Mars. 1560* (BL 1862d4) By permission of the British Library.

organisers of the Conspiracy of Amboise, and Admiral Coligny.[11]

For Guise's widow it was noted there 'is only one solace; that is to make sure that his friends will remember one day at the right time to avenge her injury'. [12] Family policy now developed along a typical dual strategy: in the public sphere they would mount armed demonstrations to pressure the crown into inditing the Admiral. At the same time they would conspire in private to undermine attempts by the Montmorency to protect Coligny, the favourite nephew of the Constable. Coligny and his supporters, Protestant and Catholic, would meet force with force and counter the Guise conspiracies by representing themselves in the public sphere as upholders of the monarchy and of peace.

'A Public Feud'[13]

Guise was a Catholic hero and his death shocked contemporaries. Paris staged a magnificent funeral procession for the corpse, in which people attended in their thousands with genuine enthusiasm. His martyrdom for the faith was memorialised in the large number of pamphlets printed in the months after his death.[14] Coligny hit back in the pamphlet war; though he denied complicity he did little to reduce the tension by his approval of the murder.[15] The Guise launched a private suit against Coligny (26 April 1563) supported by demonstrations of force in the capital. The conflict soon centred on who would conduct the judicial investigation. Coligny and his faction, increasingly ascendant on the royal council, arranged for the matter to be evoked to the *Grand Conseil*. The hope of the Guise lay in Paris and its Parlement, both hostile to heresy. In September the duke's widow, dressed in mourning and accompanied by her children, arrived in the city, and on the 30th she and 200 supporters presented themselves at the Parlement to press their suit. Tensions in the city ran high as the factions roamed the streets. The Guise were followed around by a large retinue and from mid-October each session of the Parlement was invaded by excited crowds. On 23 November the Admiral and his supporters arrived in the city in a magnificent show of force. The Venetian ambassador, estimating the numbers at 8–10,000 men, feared 'that any little accident might unleash a great scandal'.[16] The Guise retreated from the royal apartments in the Louvre to their own stronghold in the Marais.

Fearing the outbreak of civil war in the capital Catherine summoned the parties to the Louvre on 6 December to try and broker a peace settlement, but as so often during the Wars of Religion events on the streets ran out of the control of policy makers. Soon after the abortive peace conference Condé's chaplain was attacked by the members of the congregation of Saint Germain de L'Auxerrois and saved only by the intervention of Huguenot soldiers.[17] More seriously on 22 December a man attacked the priest of Saint-Séverin during Mass, wrestling him to the ground as he raised the Host. Reparation for this act took place eight days later when a procession wound its way through the streets from the Sainte-Chapelle to Saint-Séverin on the Left Bank led by the royal family, and in which the Venetian ambassador recorded the prominent role of the Guise family.[18] Along the route the people complied enthusiastically with orders to cover their houses with hangings and mount torches. Rumours of conspiracy fuelled the combustible atmosphere and these rumours were not without foundation: handbills were posted around the city which threatened the life of the Queen Mother and her chief councillors.[19]

Public enmities between the parties and their supporters were displayed day in day out through reciprocal taunts, challenges and insults. Many of these actions were ploys designed to attack the honour of the opposing group, and betray the imprint of conspiracy organised in the councils of the feuding parties.[20] The example of the Charry affair will suffice to adumbrate the tension gripping Paris over Christmas. Captain Charry was a Guise man retained among the royal guard. He quarrelled incessantly with Coligny's brother who, as colonel general of the infantry, was nominally his superior. Catherine found a threatening handbill in her apartments demanding that she remove Charry and other Ultra-Catholics from their commands. On New Years' Eve Charry was ambushed by three Protestant nobles, led by Chastelier Portaut, the Admiral's standard-bearer. Charry had apparently killed Portaut's brother in a duel fourteen years previously, and it seems likely that the Coligny brothers sanctioned the revenge killing.[21] To Catholics this was simply another example of Huguenot perfidy. Charry's body was given a magnificent funeral the following day and laid to rest in Notre Dame near the altar where the duke of Guise's heart was buried.

The Charry affair did nothing to stop the rising influence of the Protestants and the ascendancy of the Constable on the regency council, causing the Spanish ambassador to despair that 'the Guise and the Catholics act so meekly and defeatist, as if there was no remembrance of the death of M. de Guise nor of the Catholic Religion'.[22] Finally, on 5 January the king issued a decree, suspending judgement on the murder for three years. Several days later the Guise left court in pique.

The return of the cardinal of Lorraine from Trent soon after marked a shift in strategy. Now the family would attempt to build a wider, non-confessional, base of support by attracting their cousin Condé to their cause. The death of his wife in July severed his kinship ties to the Montmorency and removed a godly influence from his life. The cardinal now proposed that he marry a Guise princess: Anne d'Este or Mary Stuart. Assured of Condé's goodwill the Guise conspired to build on the popular support that the family had experienced in Paris during 1563, and hence further challenge and undermine the traditional Montmorency power base in Paris. To this end, the cardinal planned a triumphal entry into the city with his nephew. Fearing for his life, Lorraine was accompanied everywhere by an armed retinue of fifty men, even when he sang mass and preached in church; he ignored warnings from the governor, François de Montmorency, that arms were forbidden in the city thus making a showdown inevitable.[23] Several men were killed in the clash in the rue Saint Denis on 8 January 1565 and the cardinal and his nephew were forced to take ignominious refuge in a house nearby. At nightfall the cardinal stole across the river to the safety of the hôtel de Cluny on the Left Bank, where he was joined by his younger brother, the duke of Aumale. Humiliation for the Guise was compounded by their failure to rouse any popular support. Indeed, for the next two days the cardinal was trapped in his residence surrounded by hostile troops and Parisians threatening and poking fun at him.[24] Both sides began to gather forces in the vicinity of the city which cut across confessional lines: Montmorency was supported by Coligny; the Guise by Condé. A furious pamphlet war was unleashed in which both sides attempted to mobilise public opinion until the crown finally intervened to impose peace.

With support for the Guise waning the crown was able to impose a settlement at Moulins in January 1566.[25] Coligny swore publicly that he was not responsible for the murder of François de Guise, and then exchanged a kiss of peace with the cardinal. As so often in noble feuds peace was ephemeral. François's son, Henri, did not take part in the ceremony and in the following years refused to bow to pressure to sign an accommodation with his enemy.[26]

The Nature of Guise Conspiracy

As I have argued, Protestant conspiracy was integral to the outbreak of the Wars of Religion, and as late as March 1565 a Protestant was executed for plotting to overthrow the Valois and replace them with the Bourbon.[27] In 1567 the Protestant leadership plotted to seize the king at Meaux to forestall what it saw as an international conspiracy between France and Spain against the Reformed Religion. Initially, Catholic conspiracy shared many of the same characteristics because it too was intimately bound up with high politics.[28]

However, this began to change as order in the localities collapsed in the wake of the first civil war and Catholics in the provinces felt betrayed and abandoned by the crown. The formation of defence leagues in regions where royal authority was weak and Protestant insurgency most damaging inevitably involved conspiracy. Such leagues provided the organisation for those wishing to undermine the religious Peace of Amboise, which was particularly difficult to uphold in the Protestant heartlands of the South and West of the kingdom, where bands of soldiers continued to roam and where murder and violence, plots and conspiracies were common. The most significant of these sprang up in Languedoc and Guyenne in March 1563 and spread with the support of Catholic grandees, such as Blaise de Monluc lieutenant-general of Guyenne.[29]

Our most chilling evidence for Catholic conspiracy at this time comes from two documents in the archives at Chantilly.[30] Although these have now been published in both English and French, they have been left to speak for themselves and have remained largely unexamined. They deserve more attention:

> I the undersigned promise and swear by the living God to keep and maintain the association made by the captains, lords and knights of the order to avenge the death of Monsieur the duke of Guise, rendering service and fidelity to Messieurs his brothers, Madame his wife and Monsieur his son, as I promised to the said late duke of Guise, whom God absolve, for the recovery of the rights he had claimed without exception or reserve. I promise also to use all my strength up to the last breath to expel from this kingdom or kill those who have made peace without punishing the murder, and to inflict a shameful death on those who shared in the homicide, and I swear also to use all my strength in exterminating those of the new religion. In order to carry out the above, I promise to stand by to march on 27 October with my associates and those in my charge and to go wherever Monsieur de Monluc shall direct me to go for the accomplishment of the association. And as guarantee of the strict fulfilment of the above promises, I sign these present with my hand and seal them with my seal, 2 August 1563. Signed: Sansac, and sealed.

> I the undersigned promise and swear by the living God to render such obedience and loyal service to the duke of Guise, the cardinal his uncles, and to his mother, as I had promised to the late duke of Guise, for the recovery of his property as to avenge the death of the said duke up to the fourth generation of those who committed the said homicide or connived at it and of those who are yet defending the culprits. To this effect I am ready to march with my associates and company on 27 September next, promising to obey the orders of Monsieur de Monluc whom I recognize as lieutenant-general of the

enterprise in Guyenne. And as guarantee of the above I sign these presents with my hand and seal them with my arms, 16 August 1563. Signed: Guy de Daillon, and sealed.

They survive as copies made in early 1564 from originals signed the previous August, a time when both the Guise and the Montmorency were planning for confrontation.[31] The musters of their forces in September and October 1563 coincided with the Guise arrival at court and the presentation of a request for justice to Catherine de Medici. However, both documents refer not to an assembly of supporters at court but to an assembly of nobles in Guyenne where the local commander, Blaise de Monluc, was, on the one hand, under pressure from Catholics to resist the Peace of Amboise and, on the other hand, threatened by the policies of Jeanne d'Albret, whose establishment of Protestantism in Béarn was fanning the flames of confessional unrest.[32] Guise policy was thus to exploit Catholic resistance to the Peace in the West. Remarkable though these documents are, they are more ambiguous and more difficult to interpret than they seem at first glance. Two questions are particularly puzzling. First, what are these highly sensitive and incriminating documents doing in the papers of Condé at Chantilly? Secondly, why do they differ substantially in their content? In order to answer these questions and unravel the conspiracy we need to know more about the signatories.

The participation of Louis Prévost seigneur de Sansac, governor of the Angoumois, in a Guise conspiracy is especially curious, for he was a long-time confidant of the Constable de Montmorency.[33] They had once shared the same Ultra-Catholic prejudices and Sansac's zeal is redolent in his pledge to 'exterminate' heretics, but now their relationship was under strain as the Constable placed his family's traditional struggle against the Guise above religion; his interest dictated peace and the reintegration of his Protestant nephews into the royal council. Sansac's loyalties were soon put to the test as a commissioner for the implementation of the Peace edict in the Angoumois. He arrived to find a chaotic situation and a province dominated by armed Protestants. In June he sent a long memoir to the Queen Mother which paints a bleak picture of his impunity in the face of collapsing royal authority.[34] Anarchy seems to have been widespread elsewhere in the Western provinces from the Maine to Bordeaux.[35] Protestants remained in arms, harassing priests, stealing the tithe and plundering churches. In August 1563 the commissioners for the implementation of the peace in Bas Poitou warned Catherine that Catholics in the region would not endure Protestant contraventions of the edict for much longer.[36]

Nobles from both sides used religion as a pretext for brigandage and feuding. The commissioners urged that the governor of Poitou, Guy de Daillon, be given the resources to arrest the most dangerous culprits. We can surmise that Daillon's signature of the Guise conspiracy on 16 August suggests that he was unhappy about implementing the Peace with few resources in one of the strongest areas of Protestant activity. The Daillon were traditionally associated with service to the Valois and were to remain reliable royalists throughout the Wars of Religion. Guy was not a Guise man; indeed his arms were quartered with those of the Montmorency and this blood tie is reflected in other kinship links. Unlike Sansac he made no pledge in his oath to kill Protestants, which is hardly surprising as he was on good terms with the House of Bourbon-Vendôme and his younger brother, François, was a senior figure in the retinue of the young Henri prince of Navarre.[37]

So, I think then that these oaths tell us less about the Guise conspiracy against Coligny than the desperate choices faced by Catholic royal officers in the West trying to implement a Peace which they disliked. Presumably the Guise solicited many such oaths in the summer and autumn of 1563 and since the only surviving documents are found in the archives of the leader of the Protestant party, I shall infer that they were passed on by servants or associates of Sansac and Daillon who felt uncomfortable with a Guise alliance which undermined their traditional ties to the Montmorency, from which they and their masters had benefited.[38]

The mundane grumbling of royal officers at their lack of recognition had serious undertones in the South and West in 1563. Sansac and Daillon and the other Catholic governors offered their resignations, feeling that royal policy ignored their concerns and went too far in accommodating the Huguenots. It is therefore no surprise that they looked elsewhere for allies, as both a demonstration of Catholic solidarity and a reminder to the crown and the Montmorency that their services could not be taken for granted.[39] Importantly, each man tailored his oath to match his own needs which had little to do with events in Paris. Do these oaths demonstrate the strength of the Guise or paradoxically their weakness? Undoubtedly we are seeing signs of their influence in a region where their following was traditionally negligible. Yet this influence was contingent on local factors out of their control. As a significant figure in his own right Daillon had freedom to manoeuvre. His promise to support the Guise in their feud to the fourth generation echoes biblical convention and in no way limited his future political options.[40] The collapse of royal authority made for an uncertain political climate. Every clan cast around for allies for mutual protection. Factional fluidity forced the Montmorency to take the concerns of their supporters seriously: the

Constable now used his ascendant position at court to repair relations with former enemies and promote his allies and kinsmen in preparation for the inevitable showdown with the Guise.[41] Chilling though our two documents are they once again highlight the contingent nature of bonds between nobles in the sixteenth century and the complex and dynamic relationship between confessional and clientage loyalties.[42]

An appeal to confessional solidarity thus enabled conspirators to present family interests as a public cause and broaden their base of support. However the problem of mobilising effective support when religion was not at stake is illustrated by the Guise-Montmorency clash in Paris in 1565, when the abortive attempt to rekindle memories of Parisian solidarity for the Guise backfired, allowing Protestant pamphlets to demonstrate the shallowness of Guise influence among the people. After quitting the city, the duke of Aumale toured neighbouring provinces hurriedly trying to form an association. His letter to the youngest of the Guise brothers, the marquis of Elbeuf, intercepted and published by the Protestants, not only publicised the names of his co-conspirators but revealed his disillusion with conspiracy that relied on the Catholic populace: 'I find it good that the said lords wish to take heed leaving aside the towns, all the more since there is no assurance to be had in the people, as I have lately seen once again. But with the nobility, for my part I am firmly resolved and prepared'.[43] Once again, the Guise were trying to exploit local religious tensions unappeased by implementation of the Peace edict. Elbeuf was based in Touraine and had been in contact with possible allies in the Loire valley and Brittany. The bishop of Mans was accused of drawing up lists of suspected heretics in preparation for a new Sicilian vespers: 'of having taken part in mid-Lenten festivities by giving benedictions on horseback armed with a pistol; and following deliberations with the duke of Aumale, of having gone from house to house of the Papist gentlemen to make them enter into a public conspiracy, which he calls an association'.[44] While it may have disrupted pacification in Western France, the wider Guise conspiracy against Coligny foundered because of its dependence on men whose interest were largely local. In the South-West, Monluc remained aloof and informed the regent. After all, the Montmorency were ascendant at court and the crown now seemed disposed to interpret the Peace more favourably to Catholics. Support for the Guise was essentially fickle beyond its clientèle network and heartland of support in the North and East. With no substantial power base in the West they were reliant on men who had their own agendas. By the end of the year the cardinal of Lorraine had realised that the pursuit of Coligny would have to be abandoned if the family wanted to salvage any power at the centre.

Conclusion

Feuding and peace-making were an important, if largely overlooked, part of traditional faction politics.[45] Aristocratic vengeance was structured by cultural rather than emotional templates and thus intimately bound up with conspiracy: hidden plots, hired assassins, court coups, ambushes and public displays of enmity were all part of the politics of revenge. Politics however was changing in the 1560s as cheap print was used to mobilise the people for and against the Reformation. Public discourse was transformed by the righteous rage and religious zeal of Calvinism, which legitimised conspiracy and justified violence in the name of divine vengeance. Rumours of conspiracy heightened the sense of fear and insecurity. What distinguishes the Massacre of Saint Bartholomew from the events of the 1560s is the transformation of the Guise from being the main opponents of royal policy to being the instruments of a royal plot to eliminate the Protestant leadership. After the Peace of Saint Germain in 1570 the family had been excluded from power and Henri de Guise's unwillingness to reconcile his differences with Coligny was a running sore on the body politic. Lacking credit at court he once more looked to Paris, where hostility to Saint Germain and the Admiral was most bitter.[46] He conspired to exploit riots against the edict at the same time as his old adversary François de Montmorency was charged with restoring order. The Florentine ambassador reported 'that in Paris there are a growing number of gentlemen friends of the lords of Guise, and they have rented rooms in various quarters, plotting nightly something between them; and that they have come armed with certain weapons, such as small daggers and other concealable weapons, in order to strike quickly ... and that among the plans they have one of them will go and kill the Admiral in his lodgings'.[47] By now, however, the duke's room for manoeuvre was narrowing - popular support could not offset royal displeasure - and in May 1572 he finally signed and sealed the act which recognised the peace of Moulins and discharged Coligny. This allowed both men to appear at court in preparation for the marriage of Henri of Navarre and Marguerite de Valois in the summer. In a mutual display of enmity they refused to greet each other.[48]

Historians now largely agree that the conspiracy to murder Coligny and the rest of the Protestant leadership must be disassociated from the popular massacre which it sparked off.[49] Catherine wanted Coligny removed for fear that his intervention in the Low Countries would plunge France once more into civil war, so she sanctioned the Guise to pursue their vendetta. As in 1563, tensions in the city were high and exacerbated by the large numbers of nobles present for the marriage festivities. What had changed most in the intervening years was the royal council: gone was the steadying influence of the Constable whose conservatism on religious matters was balanced by his hostility to the Guise; gone was chancellor l'Hôpital the moral backbone of the regime and architect of the policy of religious toleration.

The role played by the mob and the role of the duke in the Massacre highlights the differences between popular religious violence and aristocratic notions of vengeance. Natalie Davis has interpreted the orgy of killing in the streets as enacting rites of violence which were didactic as well as vindictive, 'drawn from a store of punitive or purificatory traditions current in sixteenth-century France'.[50] The need for killers to forget that their victims are human beings is an enduring feature of the unconscious and the process of de-humanisation is completed by transforming the victim into 'vermin', 'beasts' and 'devils'. The gruesome fate of Coligny's corpse once it fell into the hands of the mob does not require elucidation here.

Guise's attitude to the corpse and the representation of his conduct have provoked less interest. However they are of crucial importance to our story. In his account of the murder, the Protestant, Simon Groulart, wished to equate the duke's conduct with that of the mob. After the Admiral's corpse was flung from his apartments into the courtyard, Guise is supposed to have wiped the blood from Coligny's face and then pushed it with his boot saying 'Venomous beast no longer will you spit your venom'.[51] But this does not fit with what anthropology tells us about the aristocratic feud in France. Feuds rarely evolved into endless bloody vendettas because they had limited political objectives: the promotion and protection of one's lineage. So it seems to me that our best account of the Massacre, written by Tomasso Sassetti, has it right when Guise told his men to fling the corpse out of the window so that he could recognise the victim, having done so he prevented them from plunging their daggers into the corpse, saying 'Enough, no more to the poor man'.[52] To the duke, vengeance was a dish best taken cold; once his debt of honour had been paid and his duty fulfilled he sought to distance himself from the orgy of killing: 'for the Admiral's death he was glad for he knew him to be his enemy, but for the rest the king had put to death such as might have done him very good service'.[53] This self-justificatory attempt to wash his hands of innocent blood is for others to judge, but it does seem that his emotionless response to the killing of Coligny and the general Massacre is, in its own way, as chilling as the gruesome street games played by the mob with Protestant corpses, and that this relationship between elite and popular violence is fundamental to understanding the Wars of Religion. It is no less true today that conspiratorial elites sanction ethnic and religious hatred for their own ends, legitimise murder and revenge in the name of religion and the public good and, whatever their protestations to the contrary, must be held accountable for the blood on the hands of their followers.

Notes

1   E. Forsyth, *La Tragedie Française de Jodelle à Corneille (1533–1640). La Thème de la Vengeance* (Paris, 1994), p. 38.
2   Revenge was to be bloodless and achieved by humiliating the opponent: D. Quint, *Montaigne and the Quality of Mercy: Ethical and Political Themes in the Essays* (Princeton, 1998).
3   P. Benedict, 'The dynamics of Calvinist militancy: France, 1555–1563' in P. Benedict, H. van Nierop and M. Venard, eds., *Reformation, Revolt and Civil War in France and the Netherlands, 1555–1585* (Amsterdam, 1999).
4   A. Duke, G. Lewis and A. Pettegree, eds., *Calvinism in Europe, 1540–1610: A Collection of Documents* (Manchester, 1992), p. 81.
5   D. Kelley, *The Beginning of Ideology: Conciousness and Society during the French Reformation* (Cambridge, 1981), p. 201, presumably this refers to Protestant captain, Stuart d'Aubigny.
6   D. Crouzet, *Les Guerriers de Dieu: La Violence au Temps des Troubles de Religion vers 1525 - vers 1610* (2 vols., Paris, 1990), i, p. 724.
7   Elizabeth A. R. Brown, 'La Renaudie se venge: l'autre face de la conjuration d'Amboise', in Y.-M. Bercé and E. Guarini, eds., *Complots et conjurations dans l'Europe moderne* (Rome, 1993).
8   This event is obscure and it surely could not have taken place without royal consent.
9   L. Regnier de la Planche, *Histoire de l'Estat de France sous le Règne de François II* (2 vols., 1836), i, p. 152.
10   J. Bonnet, ed., *Memoires de la vie de Jean de Parthenay-Larcheveque sieur de Soubise* (Paris, 1879), p.72.
11   A. de Ruble, *L'assassinat de François de Lorraine duc de Guise, 18 février 1563* (Paris, 1897), p. 77.
12   Ibid., p. 49. Soubise and Guise hated each other.
13   It is termed 'une querelle publique' in a contemporary document: *Responce a l'espitre de Charles de Vaudemont Cardinal de Lorraine, iadis prince imaginaire des Royaumes de Ierusalem, & de Naples, Duc, & Conte par fantasie d'Aniou, & de Provence, & maintenant gentilhomme de Hainault* (n. p., 1565)
14   D. El Kenz, 'La mort de François de Guise: entre l'art de mourir et l'art de subvertir' in J. Fouilleron *et al.* eds., *Société et Idéologies des Temps Modernes* (2 vols., Montpellier, 1996).
15   Ruble, *L'assassinat de François de Lorraine*, p. 93.
16   B[ibliothèque]N[ationale] MS Italiens 1725 fo. 46, 23 Nov 1563.
17   *Calendar of State Papers*, 1563, 7 December, p. 608: 'Peroceli was thrust in the thigh as he was walking in the streets. He that did it is thought to have slain him, and was conveyed away by his complices': BN MS Italien 2182 fo. 272.
18   See the reports of the papal Nuncio, Santa Croce: BN MS Italiens 2182, fos. 277v and 278v. The offender was burned alive on the same day: *Registres du bureau de la ville de Paris* ed. F. Bonnardot *et al.*, eds. (Paris, 1892), v, 1558–67, p. 342.
19   BN MS Italiens 2182, fo. 278v; *Lettres de Catherine de Médicis* H. de La Ferrière and comte Baguenault de Puchesse, eds. (9 vols, Paris, 1880–99), ii, p. 125. (1563).

20 In October the Constable de Montmorency and François de Guise's younger brother, the duc d'Aumale, quarrelled violently. The Constable pursued the issue with a public challenge, accusing a servant of Aumale's of conspiring to kill him; this challenge had to be met by counter-challenge and the offended party demanded satisfaction, though he knew a duel could not take place between men of unequal rank. As long as the counter-challenge remained in force it would continue to impugn the honour of the Constable until one of his men agreed to accept it: F. Decrue de Stoutz, *Anne de Montmorency* (2 vols, Paris, 1889), ii, p. 377.

21 Ruble, *L'Assassinat de François de Lorraine*, pp. 112–13.

22 *Mémoires de Condé ou Recueil pour servir à l'histoire de France* (6 vols., London, 1734), ii, p. 188.

23 For this and following: R. du Bouillé de Chariol, *Histoire des ducs de Guise* (4 vols., Paris, 1849–50), i, pp. 341–9.

24 Ruble, *L'Assassinat de François de Lorraine*, p. 249; A. Aubigné, *Histoire Universelle*, ed. A. de Ruble (9 vols., Paris, 1886–97), ii, p. 216.

25 Lorraine pressed in the royal council for Coligny's prosecution but he could count only on the support of his brother-in-law, the duke of Nemours: Ruble, *L'Assassinat de François de Lorraine* pp. 132–3.

26 Ibid., p. 124.

27 BN MS Italiens 2182 fo. 411v. The antipathy of the heir to the throne, Henri d'Anjou, for the prince de Condé must be seen in this light.

28 I am thinking here, of course, of the Catholic 'Triumvirate' formed during Easter 1561 by François de Guise and Anne de Montmorency to resist the advance of heresy.

29 J.W. Thompson, *The Wars of Religion in France, 1559–1576* (New York, 1909), pp. 216, 254; *Histoire Ecclésiastique des Églises Réformées au Royaume de France* (3 vols., Nieuwkoop, 1974), iii, pp. 60–5.

30 Archives de la Musée Condé. Papiers de Condé, Série L, vol xix, fo. 59. Printed in R. Knecht, *The French Wars of Religion, 1559–1598* (London, 1989), p. 107.

31 The queen mother wrote to both parties ordering them to demobilise: *Lettres de Catherine de Médicis:* ii, pp. 98, 101.

32 Monluc's uncharacteristic silence about his activities from 1563 to 1567 has been noted by a number of historians: P. Courteault, *Blaise de Monluc Historien* (Toulouse, 1908), pp. 471–7.

33 Sansac was a member of the Constable's retinue in August 1560, and the Constable was responsible for his entry into the privy council in April 1562: Decrue de Stoutz, *Anne de Montmorency*, pp. 275, 280.

34 A. Lublinskaya, *Mémoires pour servir à l'Histoire des Guerres Civiles en France (1561–63)*, (Moscow, 1962), pp. 257–60.

35 For a Protestant view of events in the Maine: *Adverstissement des crimes horribles commis par les seditieux Catoliques Romains au Pays & Conte du Maine depuis le mois de Juilliet 1564 jusques au mois d'Avril 1565* (n. p., 1565).

36 'Those of the Reformed Religion enjoy all the liberties that it has pleased you Madame and the king to grant them under the Edict without any contravention. Notwithstanding this, on their part they do not observe the Edict at all. There is not a single priest who is sure of his life ... there is not an incumbent who can freely enjoy his benefice': Lublinskaya, *Mémoires*, p. 298.

37   Le Père Ansèlme, *Histoire Généalogique et Chronologique de la Maison Royale de France, des Pairs, Grands Officiers de la Couronne & de la Maison du Roy: & des Anciens Barons du Royaume* (9 vols., Paris, 1726–33), viii, pp. 190–1.

38   John Bossy has taught us enough about sixteenth-century noble households and the moles, informers and spies who frequented them to give an indication of how this conspiracy was leaked: *Giordano Bruno and the Embassy Affair* (New Haven, 1991); *Under the Molehill: an Elizabethan Spy Story* (New Haven, 2001).

39   Sansac and Daillon's threat to resign their offices unless their resources were increased was undoubtedly a reflection of the difficulties they faced. But it was also a means of bullying the crown and of augmenting their credit at court. Other governors of the West, notably Jarnac and Biron, were playing the same game.

40   The Fourth Commandment employs this terminology which is repeated in Exodus, xxxiv, 7: 'The Lord ... will by no means clear the guilty, visiting the iniquity of the fathers upon the children and the children's children, to the third and fourth generation'.

41   Decrue de Stoutz, *Anne de Montmorency*, pp. 383–7. The reduction of Le Havre and the end of the war with England meant that the crown could now direct its full resources to implementing the Peace. Montmorency's second son Damville, perceived as a hardliner on matters of faith, arrived as governor of Languedoc in September 1563, providing local Catholics with a ducal focus for resistance and the hope that their concerns would be taken more seriously at court. He was careful to take Monluc with him when he toured the province and he made a point of meeting the other leaders of the Catholic League in the South West: *Lettres de Catherine de Médicis*, ii, p. 104, n. 1.

42   K. Neuschel, *Word of Honor: Interpreting Noble Culture in Sixteenth-Century France* (Ithaca, 1989).

43   Thompson, *The Wars of Religion in France*, p. 255.

44   *Adverstissement des crimes horribles commis par les sedtieux Catoliques Romains au Pays & Conte du Maine depuis le mois de Juilliet 1564 jusques au mois d'Avril 1565* (n . p., 1565).

45   S.M. Carroll. 'The peace in the feud in sixteenth and seventeenth-century France', *Past and Present*, forthcoming.

46   Guise looked in vain for allies. The Ultra-Catholic duke of Nevers understood his predicament but warned against killing: Ruble, *L'Assassinat de François de Lorraine*, p. 143.

47   A. Desjardins, ed., *Negociations de la France avec la Toscane* (6 vols., Paris, 1859–96), iii, p. 743.

48   Guise asked for king right to challenge Coligny to a duel or put the matter to arbitration by the marshals, thus challenging the legality of the 1566 accommodation: *Ruble L'Assassinat de François de Lorraine*, pp. 150–4.

49   B. Diefendorf, *Beneath the Cross: Catholic and Protestants in Sixteenth-Century Paris* (Oxford, 1991).

50   N.Z. Davis, 'The rites of violence' in *Society and Culture in Early Modern France* (Stanford, 1975), p. 186.

51   Bouillé de Chariol, *Histoire des Ducs de Guise*, ii, p. 505. XXX.

52   J. Tedeschi, 'Tomasso Sassetti's account of the St Bartholomew's Day Massacre', in A. Soman, ed., *The Massacre of Saint Bartholomew: Reappraisals and Documents* (The Hague, 1974), p. 137.

53   *Calendar of State Papers Foreign*, 1572–4, p. 185.

Chapter 6

'The Monarchical Republic of Elizabeth I' Revisited (by its Victims) as a Conspiracy

Peter Lake

I

A great deal of ink has been spilt of late on the prevalence, within the political culture of Elizabethan England, of certain strands of civic or classical republicanism. The influence of such 'neo-Roman' strains of thought and feeling has been pictured as pervasive throughout what Patrick Collinson has termed the 'monarchical republic of Elizabeth I', suffusing not only hitherto little known tracts about town government in Tewkesbury or the governance of Ireland, but also the thought and practice of men as central to the regime as William Cecil; men whose notions of counsel, good government, and political virtue and whose vision of England as some sort of mixed, if not polity, then certainly monarchy, are taken to be signs not only of the abiding effects of a classical, humanist education, but also of their membership of some sort of classical or civic republican tradition. Indeed, Markku Peltonen and Stephen Alford have argued that there was a positively republican ideological programme or set of assumptions underlying not only these plans but the wider agenda and mode of action of the privy council and its clients throughout the period from the mid 1560s until the late 1580s. Alford nicely sums up what is now an emergent orthodoxy on this subject when he claims that 'it is increasingly clear that England did experience republicanism in the middle of the sixteenth century - a republicanism on a classical model, in which Cicero and Quintillian's *vir civilis* could not only lead a *vita activa* by offering counsel and submitting advice but also involve himself in the legislative functions of parliament'. Alford goes on to quote Markku Peltonen's claim that this form of republicanism was not '"a constitutional goal", but "a theory of citizenship, public virtue and true nobility based essentially on the classical humanist and republican traditions"'.[1]

However, it is worth remembering that all this republican talk started with an article of 1987 by Patrick Collinson entitled 'the monarchical republic of

Elizabeth I', an article which was primarily concerned with a number of emergency plans put together by William Cecil and his clients in the early 1560s and then again more insistently in the 1580s, to allow the English Protestant state to perpetuate itself beyond the death of its head, Queen Elizabeth and, in effect, to choose or elect the next successor, thus staving off the threat of Mary Stuart and allowing the current religio-political dispensation to extend itself into the next reign. What started as a series of almost unthinkable expedients, forced on a regime confronting almost certain destruction if the ordinary course of dynastic politics and monarchical succession were allowed to run their course, has now become but the most spectacular expression of deeply held republican assumptions and aspirations that in fact held the Elizabethan regime together.[2]

In coining the term 'monarchical republic' Collinson was referring to the collective role of the privy council in guiding the course of Elizabethan politics often in directions not much wanted by the queen herself. In so doing, Collinson was building on a series of magisterial post revisionist articles by Simon Adams in which Adams had definitively overturned earlier faction-dominated versions of Elizabethan politics. On the old view, the queen manipulated the personal and ideological differences amongst her leading councillors to maintain both her own control over events and thus, in effect, political stability *tout court*. On Adams' account, the basic division within the regime was neither that between different groups or factions of councillors or courtiers, nor that between a unified government and an, often Puritan, parliamentary opposition, but rather one between a relatively united inner ring of advisers and the queen herself, as the council tried to push the queen into actions on a number of issues - the succession, marriage, Scotland and Mary Stuart, religious reform, popery, the Low Countries - which they took to be crucial for the security of the regime but which the queen did not. At crucial points, sometimes through the mechanism of parliament, sometimes not, the council and its agents or men of business invoked the support and opinions of an emergent Protestant political nation in an attempt to force or stay the queen's hand.[3]

Stephen Alford has recently extrapolated these insights backwards into the 1560s, while Ann McClaren has recently subjected them to a gendered interpretation. With Alford, she presents as central for Cecil and his associates a vision of the Elizabethan polity as somehow mixed rather than straightforwardly monarchical. On this view, counsel, to be given by both the council itself and in and by the parliament, was central to the prudent and legitimate exercise of royal power. McClaren sees that view, and the style of political manoeuvre and decision making that went with it, as predominantly a response to the problem of female rule. What we are dealing with here, she claims, was a series of mechanisms designed to rein in the queen and subject her to the calming advice of a group of reliably male (and increasingly Protestant) councillors.[4] As Adams, Collinson, Alford and McClaren all agree, in establishing itself this view of the polity lent heavily on a conspiracy theory involving a Catholic threat, both international and domestic, centred abroad on the Guisan faction in France and later on Spain (and the Catholic League), with its major pressure point in England and Scotland provided by the Catholic reversionary interest always already organising itself around Mary Stuart. On this view, 'the monarchical republic' becomes an essentially exclusionary set of mechanisms, designed to control a queen and place power in the hands of a male Protestant elite, excluding Catholics from the central decision-making processes and rendering the emergent Protestant regime capable of maintaining and reproducing itself in the face of the queen's vacillations and refusals and indeed even of her death.[5] This view of the polity was centred on the capacity of counsel to shape policy and (if not to constrain) then certainly to persuade the queen to do the right thing. Accordingly, the crucial mechanisms and relationships were those between monarch, council, and parliament whereby the queen could legitimately be counselled by those who bore rule under the crown and who had been called upon to counsel her. Necessarily this was a somewhat limited group. Most of the time it included only privy councillors and perhaps certain court office holders. When parliament was in session, the range of those actively involved in the process of counsel would be widened to include the whole nobility and the parliament men. Of course, more generous readings of the counsel-giving process might at times include what one might term the 'parliamentary classes' by which one might mean not merely the parliament men themselves - those lucky or unlucky enough to have been selected by their countrymen to represent them in parliament - but the wider group from which and by which the members of the parliament were habitually selected. Indeed one might widen the category still further to include not only those selected or likely to be selected, but all those involved in the various processes (public and private, ritual, and sometimes more openly 'political') of selection itself. In certain places and under certain (admittedly aberrant and exceptional) circumstances (for instance in county constituencies during contested or nearly contested elections) this might be quite a large and socially various group. Again, at moments of crisis or threatened or incipient crisis, the arena of at least potential participation might widen still further, to include, for instance, all those various sorts of person to whom the Bond of Association was, or - if monarchomach push had ever come to regicidal shove - might have been, tendered.[6] We might, indeed, imagine the political nation opening and closing, widening and narrowing again, as the air of political excitement or crisis was forced in and out of the bellows of both the local and national state. This, of course, was a process aided and abetted by central elements in the regime who intermittently, throughout the reign, turned to the wider political nation, assembled in parliament, but not only assembled in parliament, to put pressure back on the queen to take the sort of political or military action they deemed necessary to protect and perpetuate the Protestant regime in its confrontation with its popish enemies both at home and abroad.[7] On this basis, then, we should conceive of the monarchical republic as the ruling Protestant clique, and its agents and clients, or, more expansively, the emergent Protestant political nation, talking to itself and its queen.

II

For all that Collinson's earliest version of the monarchical republic was always set against the threat of Mary Stuart and of popery, his accounts of the phenomenon never discuss or indeed much mention, the activities or views of actual Catholics. On the face of it this is a rather striking omission, but it is all too typical of 'mainstream' writing on the period, which, for all the stress in recent revisionist accounts of the Reformation on the strength of conservative religious sentiment amongst 'English folk', and for all the emphasis placed in the last two or three decades on anti-popery as an animating force in the politics and culture of post Reformation England, still treats the doings of real life Catholics as a sideshow; the death throws of a small minority in the midst of a transition from being a Church to becoming a sect.[8] This, of course, will not do, and in the current paper I am going to examine what 'the monarchical republic of Elizabeth I' looked like to members of the group that that republic was more or less expressly designed to exclude from power - the Catholics. This inquiry is not primarily animated by a desire to rescue the losers from the condescension of posterity, nor even merely by the belief that it would be nice to know what Catholics thought (although, of course, it would). This is not an exercise in retrospective affirmative action for Catholics, but rather an enterprise shaped by the conviction that the inner dynamics and power relations of the Elizabethan regime are not best understood solely in terms of the view from the top down; that we should not simply take the winners and the rulers at their own evaluation of themselves and their actions. The view from the periphery might well have something important to tell us about the nature of the centre; the view from outside might well vouchsafe to us crucial truths about the nature of this regime that would otherwise be entirely lost to us if we restrict our researches, as most previous historians have, to listening to the regime talk to itself.

And this is especially so, since the fact that, throughout this period, the English state was a monarchy and no sort of republic meant that, with the queen unmarried and the succession unsettled, at any moment the losers might well become the winners and the winners losers. It was that prospect, after all, which so frightened some contemporaries and exhilarated others. The death of the present incumbent accompanied by a reversionary interest of the opposite ideological colouring to the ruling clique had produced the collapse overnight of the two previous religio-political establishments. Both perfectly viable and stable regimes, the one Protestant (Edward's), the other Catholic (Mary's), had simply imploded when confronted with the sudden unprovided-for death of the current monarch. This was what the fuss was all about, the situation, or rather the prospect, that, according to Collinson's initial account of the thing, produced 'the monarchical republic' in the first place.[9]

Not that the death of the monarch was the only means by which the political and religious dispensation might be changed. England being a personal monarchy, and Elizabeth being a woman, royal marriage (almost as much as royal death) offered the prospect of quite serious, indeed perhaps of fundamental, religio-political change. Accordingly, as a number of commentators have observed, the politics of Elizabeth's reign was, to a remarkable extent, a marital politics, or rather a politics of projected and failed matches, with contemporaries continually making their political and personal calculations and dispositions in the face of a number of hope- and terror-inducing what ifs concerning not merely the queen's health but also her marriage.[10] Of no group was this more true than the Catholics. In what follows I shall examine a Catholic text, *The Traetise of Treason* (1572), that subjected the inner workings of the Elizabethan regime to searching critique. The text in question was produced in the immediate aftermath of a failed marriage scheme - that between the duke of Norfolk and Mary Stuart - that Catholics hoped would substantially alter both the composition and ideological temper of the regime and the terms of allegiance on offer to Catholics. Moves and manoeuvres towards this match started within the inner circles of the regime. As Stephen Alford and Wallace MacCaffrey have both, in their different ways, pointed out, the match represented a dynastic means to achieve ends sought by all the major players. By integrating Mary Stuart into the English political elite, it offered the prospect of normalised relations with Scotland and something like a settled succession.[11]

But, on the way from means to end, the marriage also seemed to offer, or (depending on your perspective) threaten, the prospect of real political and religious change, both at the level of the structure and distribution of power in council and at court and of the conditions of political loyalty and favour on offer to English 'Catholics'. In short, the match threatened the nascent characteristics and structures of an emergent Protestant state (Collinson's 'monarchical republic') in England and Scotland. In the end, perhaps in part because of that and more certainly because the queen was having none of it, the marriage never happened. But not only did the projected match fail, that failure set in train a succession of events that ended with the more Catholic and Marian proponents of the project disgraced, discourted, dead, in prison or in exile. Thus, having wobbled, the hold on power exercised by the main players - and the dominant influence on policy making of the popish conspiracy - emerged not merely intact, but if anything strengthened, its basic premises and claims seemingly confirmed by the revolt of the northern earls, the pope's excommunication of the queen, and the Ridolfi plot. With their hopes dashed, their current circumstances worse now than they had been when these manoeuvres started, one of the would-be beneficiaries and present victims of this dynastic turning-point-that-refused-to-turn produced a retrospective analysis of what had gone wrong, of who had won and who had lost, and how and why that had happened.[12] There was more at stake here, however, than the production of retrospective and self-exculpatory explanations of failure. What was needed was an analysis of current circumstances, a calibration of the balance of political forces in court, country, and abroad, an outline of what to do next to limit the damage of this latest debacle: all designed to appeal to as many people as possible, not only to Catholics, but to all genuinely loyal Englishmen, that is to say to all Englishmen who were neither mad Puritans nor fully paid-up clients of the dominant (and treasonable) Cecilian (or, in a later version of the same analysis, Leicestrian) faction in Church and state. The result was an avowedly a-confessional, indeed a remarkably 'secular', account of the way politics worked at the Elizabethan court; a no holds barred analysis of the monarchical republic of Elizabethan I as both a conspiracy and tyranny.

III

In so characterising the regime *The Treatise* was, of course, seeking to replace one conspiracy theory with another. In fact, *The Treatise* was written in direct response to the deployment of the popish conspiracy theory in a series of tracts written by Thomas Norton and others between 1569 and 1571. These were designed not only to denounce and discourage the northern rebels, but also to turn opinion decisively against the duke of Norfolk and Mary Stuart. Indeed, these pamphlets represented the beginning of the campaign (backed, indeed probably instigated, by central members of the regime) to bring both the duke and the Scottish queen to the block; a campaign which culminated in the again officially orchestrated parliamentary agitation of 1572, in which, of course, Norton again played a leading role.[13]

The Treatise responded to these interpretations of the world in terms of a popish conspiracy with a very different sort of conspiracy, one centred on the inner circles of the regime. Interestingly, this conspiracy was not a particularly Protestant one. Rather, its main protagonists were presented not as convinced heretics or Protestants, but as politiques, malcontents, and machiavels, men motivated by personal ambition and greed, who were merely using religion and religious change as the pretext and occasion for a grab for political power. In *The Treatise* the villains of the piece were presented as Cecil and Bacon to whom the author of *The Treatise* referred throughout as the 'queen's two Catlilines' or these two 'English machiavels', thus adopting wholesale the terms of vituperation applied by Norton to the rebel earls of Northumberland and Westmoreland. He also compared Cecil and Bacon (just as Norton had compared papist apologists for the pope's bull) to Sinon, the crafty Greek, who, with Ulysses, had undermined proud Troy through the ruse of the wooden horse. According to *The Treatise*, Cecil and Bacon were now undermining the new Troy of Elizabethan England with their Trojan horse of religious innovation and alleged popish conspiracy.[14]

Cecil and Bacon were presented as having no 'substantial religion' but only 'certain imaginative opinions, which they alter with every time they live ... and do daily pass and change from one sect to another in such manner that now after xiiii years' end no man yet wotteth which sect shall prevail'.[15] The result was that in the Elizabethan regime we were confronted with 'a machiavellian state and religion, where religion is put behind in the second and last place whereby the civil policy, I mean, is preferred before it and not limited by any rules of religion but the religion framed to serve the time and policy'.[16] What was at stake here was not so much a positive link or affinity between Protestant doctrine and the political programme of the regime, so much as the occasion provided by religious change (of whatever doctrinal complexion) for political instability and innovation. It was because religious change provided them with both the opportunity and legitimation for their own rise to power that, at Elizabeth's accession, the two Sinons, Cecil and Bacon, had backed Protestant reform. For them, therefore, religious change had been a means to an end, not an end in itself. It had provided the pretext for political revolution, for the rise to power of 'that insolent and licentious brotherhood that, under pretense of a new religion, do call themselves a party Protestant', a group who might justly be compared in their 'subtlety, falsehood and lewd property' to the Greeks, while their dupes and victims, the blameless and honourable Catholics, invited comparison to the Trojans.[17]

Cecil, 'the chief of these two machiavellians, then of mean estate and out of credit, ... intruded himself' into Elizabeth's 'presence and service some few days before the death of her sister'. This new Sinon 'for baseness of parentage, for ambition of mind, for subtlety of wit, for smoothness of tongue, for shameless face, for little honesty and no conscience' was easily the equal of the Greek original. Once ensconced in the queen's favour he brought in his fellow conspirator - Bacon - 'by birth more base than himself, nearly yet allied with him and in heresy more fervent than he'. Together the pair turned the young and suggestible queen against 'the chief of her sister's council' and, by insinuating that Catholics were 'not satisfied in the question of her mother's marriage', persuaded her to back the Protestant cause. The result was 'the discrediting, the abasement and the impoverishing of all ... whom she found established in credit, authority and governance and likewise the advancement of the inferior and base sort to dominion and rule'; in short, 'the erection of a new party Protestant whereof themselves might be heads'.[18]

Their aim in sponsoring religious change was, therefore, to divide and rule; that is to say, by creating division and disorder, they sought to create a situation in which they alone could pose as the true servants and saviours of the queen and state. Catholics, both clerical and lay, were forced from the service of the crown by the triumph of heresy. This process provided both offices and perquisites with which the new men attached to Cecil and Bacon could be rewarded.[19] Amongst the first and most notable victims of this process had been the ancient nobility who had been systematically excluded from the counsels and favour of the crown. For the queen 'upon the first entry to her reign had committed the government of her affairs unto some few mean and base persons who forthwith used those few of the nobility (whom they reserved in appearance of credit) but as cyphers and signs'. On this score, the author's prize exhibit was the fate of the duke of Norfolk. Norfolk's only crime had been to be noble, popular, and opposed to the plots and practices of Sinon whom he had charged 'once at Greenwich ... with robbing the realm, dishonouring and endangering your queen to raise and maintain rebels abroad'.[20] 'Let this example, I say, joined unto the unjust captivity of the earls of Arundel, Worcester, and Southampton, of the lords Cobham and Lumley, the bishop of Ross ... be a pattern and precedent unto some others of the nobility now that yet think themselves full safe'. 'Can any man be found so blind, so popular and unnatural', our author asked, 'that seeth not and bewaileth not, with tears of blood, the wasting and consumption of your ancient nobility both in number, in wealth, in credit among your people and in authority with your prince? ... And who perceiveth not the great weakening of your prince's strength and state thereby? ... her surety must be presumed (by all common intendment) to consist more in the confidence of her ancient nobility, whose parents have been nourished under her progenitors, than upon a new nobility that accounteth the thanks of their advancement to be due rather to those that rule her and preferred them than unto herself whom they reckon to be but the hatchet in the workman's hands'.[21]

More generally, while at first they had promised not to oppress the consciences of the queen's Catholic subjects, as the first decade of the reign progressed, Cecil and his clique had gradually started to persecute the Catholics, squeezing them between their loyalty to God and to the queen.[22] Such conduct, of course, risked alienating by far the larger and richer portion of the population from the queen.[23] Abroad, the natural, indeed the inevitable, product of this course of action had been the excommunication of the queen by the pope, an act that 'hath set her Christian subjects free from obeying her for conscience's sake'. At home these policies of underhand persecution and provocation had institutionalised religious division and faction. All of this had been quite deliberate. 'These contrivers will not have the Catholic party so utterly extinct but that there should still remain a party of them to uphold and maintain the inward division, howsoever they oppress it and seek to make the other stronger'.[24]

Things had been no better in the arena of foreign relations where, under the tutelage of these two evil councillors, the queen had alienated her traditional allies - most notably the pope and the king of Spain - and sought alliances with the scum of Europe; 'with a Condie, an Orange, a Lodowick, a Murray, a Murton, and a French admiral'. Worse still, the regime had fished systematically in troubled waters, spreading rebellion and disorder throughout the neighbouring kingdoms by 'leagues with the French, Flemish and Scottish rebels'; by suborning 'great numbers of the noblest subjects of France, Flanders and Scotland severally to levy arms against their several and natural sovereigns and over that, without colour or cause, to violate the long continued amity with the house of Spain and to break the ancient league with the house of Burgundy by forcible taking of the king's money, by paying the same unto his own and other prince's rebels, by spoiling his good subjects, by succouring his rebels, by furnishing of pirates in infinite numbers to rob him and his people'.[25]

All these policies and more had been legitimated in terms of the peace and security of both the queen and state; what the author at one point referred to 'as the plausible shadow of your queen's security'. As the decade progressed, such claims were 'confirmed' by the imminence of a popish threat that had been largely brought into being by the extremity and ruthlessness of their own actions and thereafter, for their own malign ends, greatly exaggerated by the overheated rhetoric of the two Catilines and their clients. In response to this threat, the two Catilines assured the queen that their policies alone delivered 'all honour, security and quietness of reign, all amity abroad and all obedient affection at home'. But, in fact, they had achieved just the opposite; a surfeit, in fact, 'of passing dishonour, of decay of foreign friendship, of weakening obedience at home, of fear, of peril, of unsafety on all sides'. 'After fourteen years following the trade and steps of those men, instead of all quiet, security and prosperous reign, she never found herself less quiet, less secure, nor her estate more doubtful'. Rather Elizabeth had seen 'her honour touched, her security of state weakened, her assured friends in number diminished'.[26]

Despite the very considerable dangers that now threatened the realm, none of this was an accident. Rather, it was the result of a self-conscious plan. The conspiracy of these two Machiavellian Catilines fed off the very instability and sense of threat that their own policies had created. For, on the basis of the both foreign and domestic dangers that they themselves had provoked, the two men had been able to lure the queen into any number of illegal and oppressive acts at home and abroad; 'acts which being seduced and circumvented she hath been abused to think necessary for her own state and security'. They had been able to use her authority to destroy a whole series of men who stood in their way and to institute a virtual reign of terror in her name but in their interests.[27] Things had got so bad that men's 'mouths and tongues' were 'tied up from speaking, yea their very hearts and minds restrained from thinking (if it break out once) of any one sentence or syllable sounding toward the detection of this detestable enterprise or of any othere truth that the captains of this conjuration would have covered and concealed'. 'No man almost speaketh with other without tendering an account whereof they talk; yea whiles your queen, whom chiefly it importeth to know it, is by art and abusion deprived of all means that might bring her to understand it, whiles all books are forbidden, that would tell it, all letters kept from her that would show it and all access of those that would intimate it unto her is by one craft or other restrained and prohibited from her'. 'No letter almost goeth from friend to friend unopened; where no man's talk with other scant scapeth unexamined; where it is accounted treason, rebellion and sedition to have or to see, to send or to receive, to keep or to bear any letter, book or speech that might show you any part either of this conjuration or of the crafts and falsehoods used to bring it to pass. Yea when any just commendation of any nobleman among yourselves (whom these base fellows do envy or malign) is accounted a crime and derogation of your queen ... Can any man that hath wit or judgement see other therein than thraldom and slavery? Yea, what servitude can be greater? What governance can be further from clemency and mercy?'[28]

While the queen was being sequestered and lied to at court, the people were being systematically misled through an officially sponsored propaganda campaign using the full range of contemporary media - the press, performance, and rumour. Sinon and his allies regularly used a series of catspaws to address and misled 'the multitude' through the press. Under such circumstances, the author explained, the writer is 'rather but the cane or trunk through which some in authority do speak with whom the credit of the multitude commonly runneth.' Slanders were printed not only against Norfolk and Mary, but even against the king of Spain himself, 'whom by such forged devices they seek to defame and to bring in hatred likewise'. At one point the author listed 14 notorious lies about events in England, Scotland and in Europe recently 'published among you and given out some by print, some by great men's letters and some by lewd men's mouths sent abroad with them of purpose to fill your people's ears and move their affection as authority would have them'. 'There never wanteth in any common wealth any such petit odd fellows' - and elsewhere the author cited the lawyer and 'council man of business' Thomas Norton and the Puritan divine Sampson - 'that are ready always by words or by writing to blaze and set forth whatsoever any persons of authority would have for the time spread and believed among the vulgar sort, yea many times without the knowledge or consent of the chief prince or magistrate, as most of these are I verily believe'. This, combined with 'how long it is since the first of these libels have been in print commonly sold, how daily new and more do freshly come forth to confirm the former, how all come forth without name of maker, printer or privilege' surely confirmed that 'some of that authority were' the real authors and reporters of these rumours. For 'common practise hath testified that some of great credit are always setters of such botchers a work'.[29]

Nor were such official disinformation campaigns restricted to these 'unwonted libels published in print'. The author cited 'the books and libels, letters and songs, rhymes and talks at every table' designed to denounce Mary Stuart as 'an adulteress, a murderer, a papist, a competitor of your crown and whatsoever else could be thought on more odious'.[30] 'Behold the sundry smooth tales that ... have been publicly told both in the Star and Checker

Chambers, in the Guildhall and in other great presences', all of them designed to convict Norfolk and Mary Stuart in the court of public opinion of a series of absurd charges - 'of conspiring rebellions, of inducing strangers, of sacking London and of competing with your queen for her crown'.[31] Thus, the author triumphantly concluded, 'these two English Catilines' were 'the principal persecutors of these princes and the privy publishers of these pamphlets', desperate as they were to stir up a variety of 'false fears like flashes of lightening terribly thundered out unto you to abuse your queen, to blind your people and to deceive the world'.[32]

By playing on such fears of popish conspiracy had 'those two persons of mean parentage' been able, 'above their desert', to usurp 'the places of the noblest'. 'By false suggestion and crafty speeches' they had 'intruded themselves into her favour and credit that, with contempt and rejection of all the rest, she was wholly governed and ruled by them'. The greater the apparent political instability, the more imminent the danger, the closer had the bond become that bound the queen to her two low born heretic councillors.[33] The result was that between them the two Sinons, Cecil and Bacon, had come almost entirely to dominate the state. The author lamented 'your queen's delivery of herself, her realm and all her affairs' 'into the hands of her two Catilines'. At one point he denounced 'the tyranny of those two that reign by her name' and at another claimed that Elizabeth was 'a queen but in name', 'those rascals reigning indeed and effect over her and her realm'. There were, he lamented, 'two or three persons of mean birth and condition that, by false suggestions and crafty speeches, had so intruded themselves into her favour and credit that, with contempt and rejection of all the rest, she was wholly governed and ruled by them'.[34]

While they claimed to be preserving the public weal, the queen and her state from the plots of others, Bacon and Cecil were in fact using this language of the commonweal and the public safety to mask their ruthless pursuit of their own 'pestilent private purpose' and interests. Having displaced a series of public men, persons of ancient nobility, of 'place and credit', these lowborn evil councillors now systematically 'preferred their own private before the common profit of the prince and people'. They caused the queen's 'name, her credit and authority to be used and applied to serve other men's turns and private purposes'. All the policies undertaken by the regime were accordingly designed to further 'the private turns of those two machiavellians'; for the same 'private avarice and ambition of their own' they have 'circumvented your queen, endangered your state, stained her honour, oppressed her people, impoverished the realm and procured infinite perils to depend over the same'. Claiming to defend the queen and realm, these men in fact consistently preferred 'the present and the private before the remedy and provision for the common and perpetual'. Accordingly, they regularly perverted the course of justice; 'whatsoever impugneth their pestilent private purpose . . . must be taken and published for traitorous, seditious, slanderous, rebellious'.[35] The result was that quintessence of tyranny, the triumph of will over law, of private over public interest - except the tyranny in question was not that of the prince but of her two favourites.

On this basis, the author called upon the reader to judge whether, through these expedients and manoeuvres, the two Catilines' 'own private turns be thereby no better served than hers, nor their own avarice and ambition no better advanced than she, her crown or realm are strengthened.' 'Let the houses and possessions of these two Catilines be considered, let their furniture and building, let their daily purchases and ready ability to purchase still, let their offices and functions wherein they sit, their titles and styles claimed and used, let their places in council, let their authority over the nobility, let their linking in alliance with the same, let their access to the prince, let their power and credit with her, let this their present state, I say in all points (being open and unknown to no man) be compared with their base parentage and progeny (the one raised out of the robes and the other from a sheep reeves son)'. 'Behold at whose doors your nobility attendeth. Consider in whose chambers your council must sit and to whom for resolution they must resort. And let these things determine both what was the purpose indeed and hidden intention in that change of religion and who hath gathered the benefits of that mutation'. 'In their own hands, their friends and faction, remain all the offices of the realm, the charge of all the ports, the keeping of all the fortresses, the prince's treasure, armour and munition, together with the whole navy, which are the only walls and bulwarks of the land. And these points being laid and considered who seeth not that in their hands they have both the prince present, the succession to come and the whole realm to dispose at their will'.[36]

But this position of dominance, of preponderant power and wealth was far from being the limit of these men's ambitions. On the contrary, they wanted more; indeed, to adopt the language of the soap opera into which *The Treatise* was turning the high politics of the period, they wanted it all. For according to *The Treatise*, their ultimate aim was to divert the succession from the legitimate line altogether and to lodge it in the even more biddable hands of the Suffolk line 'unto which themselves are united and their children incorporated'. This explained their fervent efforts to prevent Elizabeth from marrying by 'often laying before her many crafty and false arguments and many false reasons ... to keep her in fear of her own state' as they sought to persuade her that 'there was none assured pillar for her to lean unto against all events but to keep herself free, to hold herself unmarried ... for by that only (said they) she should be able always to make her peace and to preserve her own state and to draw to her party what prince she would'. Having been desperate to dissuade her 'from marriage with the Catholic that every way was meetest for her, they neither can nor will since find any Protestant to supply the place'.

The same dynastic ambition also lay behind their no less fervent attempts to 'have made away the queen of Scotland, whose person and issue remained yet between them and their designment'.[37] For their master plan remained the rooting out of all the obvious legitimate claims to the English crown. They were desperate 'to extirp both the succession of her own line and of the family next her own in blood', the better to clear the way for their own ambitions[38] - hence their concerted and sustained campaign, conducted first in Scotland and latterly in England, against Mary Stuart, which 'plainly comprehendeth the alienation of the hearts and affections of the people and subjects from their heir apparent and prince in succession'. But such attempts to render the succession unsure were, in effect, an open invitation to civil war and foreign invasion. They thus represented the ultimate treason to the English commonwealth and monarchy. It was an age-old maxim that the best means to avoid 'civil division and sedition for the crown' was 'to make the succession known as foreseeing that no one thing in the world can so bring a realm into ruin as to leave the known heir in doubt'. 'To your commonwealth that never dieth what can be more odious, more dangerous and more unnatural then so to disfurnish it of a known heir as to have no mark of obedience nor allegiance left whereupon the people may fix their eyes'.[39]

Having thus rendered the succession entirely uncertain, having 'brought the cards to shuffling for the crown', the two English machiavel Catilines had taken good care to make 'themselves judges and arbitrators of the quarrel, to give the crown to whether party they list'. If it came to blows they were also in the best position to win the ensuing military struggle. For at that point their policy of divide and rule would surely prove its worth. The combination of religious division with dynastic rivalry was sure to divide the nation 'into factions that it may rent itself in pieces'. In such a situation, 'not only two but ten or twenty parties and factions may have colour each to resist and withstand the other' and in such circumstances of extreme 'civil sedition and intestine division' the two Catilines were in a perfect position to prevail.[40]

But if Mary Stuart and her supporters were a major block to such ambitions, behind them stood Elizabeth Tudor herself, and the author proceeded to present the campaign against Mary in Scotland and then in England as but the prelude or rehearsal for a similar move against Elizabeth.

In Scotland 'when the confederates could be permitted no longer by art to govern both prince and realm they forthwith by force deprived their queen and with plain violence usurped the regiment by strong hand and so do keep it to this day'. Similar anti-monarchical activity had taken place with English encouragement in Flanders and France. Why should not England be next? Similarly, the argument against female rule mobilised against Mary Stuart applied with equal force against Elizabeth. Just as in the recent past the usurpation of supreme power by Protector Somerset had been prepared for and presaged by the judicial murder of one Howard, so the final deposition of the last Tudor was being set up by the execution of another. 'Will they ... lack pretences to plead and object against her, when they see their time, that have found these pretences against her two cousins? Will they lack matter to defame her to the world and to bring her in hatred and obloquy to the people that have forged so many colourless slanders against these that are her nearest in blood?'[41]

Indeed, having deluded Elizabeth into multiple tyrannies and oppressions, the two Catilines had, in fact, left her even more vulnerable to deposition. 'These caitiffs will now have your queen to bear the burden of their cruelty. And because they feel themselves now in strength will bring her into hatred and obloquy to kindle in the hearts of her people a weariness of her subjection and a mislike of her regiment that they may be the readier and gladder to embrace the mutation that these men intend to attempt and to bear well whatsoever shall become of her, when these fellows shall think that time ripe by death or deposing to remove her'.[42] This, of course, was all of a piece with their driving the queen into open opposition to Spain and the pope. For now, isolated from her old allies abroad, and alienated from her Catholic, but not only her Catholic, subjects, she was at their mercy, to be disposed of when and how they saw fit.

Throughout Cecil and Bacon, their creatures and supporters had talked the language of the public interest and the commonweal, of the safety and security of queen and realm, but, all along, they had intended the very opposite. The queen's security was constantly 'talked of but nothing intended, the succession of her own line in short time desperate and she made the instrument to extinct the next'. Here lay the real treason of the day and it was 'the chief counselors and magistrates of your present government that are the capital contrivers of this treason now in hand.'[43]

IV

With this claim the argument of *The Treatise* reached full circle as it presented the reader with a full scale conspiracy theory to meet and match that underlying the policies and propaganda of the regime. The fit between the two was all but perfect. The Catholic vision of the nature of the regime as a conspiracy and a tyranny represented an almost perfect inversion of the Cecilian regime's civic humanist vision of itself. As Stephen Alford and others have pointed out, the protagonists and clients of the regime saw it as the epitome of the way in which a mixed polity or monarchy should work, with power distributed and coordinated between the different estates of the realm, at the head of which sat a virtuous prince, responding to the promptings of equally virtuous councillors; all of them united in their dedication to the commonweal and true religion. Cecil envisaged a group of good counselors advising and guiding the queen in the interests of the commonwealth, opening the conduits of counsel and communication at court, in council and in parliament, through which the queen could be informed about the condition and concerns of her subjects and the predicament and interests of her realm.[44]

The Catholic account simply inverted the moral polarities, turning praise into blame, the virtues claimed for itself by the regime and its denizens into the appropriate vices. Now instead of good we have evil counsel. Instead of the pursuit of the common good, we have the pursuit of private interest; law was being bent to serve the interests and will of private persons. The queen was being systematically misled; cut off from contact with her natural councillors the nobility, she remained at the mercy of a clique of evil councillors, who monopolised office and its fruits for themselves and their clients and dependents. Instead of peace and prosperity consequent upon the pursuit of the public good by virtuous rulers characteristic of good government, we have the division, the conflict, the oppression and persecution (of Catholics and the ancient nobility), the actual and potential revolt and foreign war (in Scotland, France and incipiently with Spain), typical of tyranny. Nor was this instability an accident, a by-product of the evil counsel of Cecil and his cronies. It was of the essence of their project; for only by creating instability, division and conflict, both in England and the surrounding countries, could this clique of lowborn machiavels hope to persuade the queen that she was in danger and that her only hope of security lay in their service and advice. Crucial to this manoeuvre was, of course, the spectre of a popish conspiracy against the queen and realm. This conspiracy was a mere figment, almost entirely invented by the ruling clique to scare the queen and people into doing what they wanted. Insofar as there were any elements in contemporary reality that appeared to confirm this scenario, they were themselves products of the machinations of the English machiavels; Catholic reactions, in self defence and moral outrage, to the provocations, aggressions, and persecutions perpetrated by these men in the queen's name. Over against the political and moral chaos created by these low born malcontents and traitors, *The Treatise* sketched a vision of traditional order and stability; a world in which God was in his heaven and the ancient nobility were on the Privy council; in which the old religion was restored and the traditional alliances with Spain and Burgundy were maintained and the succession was settled in its legitimate course.

From the early 1570s when this counter conspiracy theory was first developed and adumbrated in *The Treatise* until the final decade of the reign, these two different conspiracy theory centred versions of the Elizabethan regime continued to confront one another. When the Anjou match - the next dynastic turning point, in and through which certain English Catholics hoped to effect a material improvement in their circumstances and certain elements in the ancient nobility hoped to effect a return to the centre of power and influence - fell through, it was to precisely the same version of the regime as a conspiracy that at least some Catholics turned to explain that failure and to interpret and control their current predicament. They did so, of course, in the famous tract, *Leicester's Commonwealth*, which reproduced precisely the same account of the Elizabethan regime as that contained in the *The Treatise*, only now with Leicester not Cecil as the villain of the piece.[45] Again, after the outbreak of war with Spain, as the regime started to press down really hard on English Catholics, to justify what was for a few years a genuinely bloody repression, Cecil invoked once again an international Catholic conspiracy, centred now on Spain and the Catholic league, as well as on subversive elements amongst English Catholics. Confronted by such claims, Robert Parsons and his circle turned once again to precisely the same vision of the Elizabethan regime as conspiracy as that adumbrated in *The Treatise* and *Leicester's Commonwealth*. Again the regime was depicted as a conspiratorial clique of low born, atheistical, machiavellian evil councillors. Leicester having died in the interim, Cecil/Burghley was returned to centre stage, where he was presented as the sole surviving member of a five-man clique that, over thirty years, had systematically misled and sequestered the queen, highjacked the regime and tyrannised and exploited the realm. Having, for their own malign personal purposes and ambitions, prevented the queen from marrying, killed the only legitimate heir (Mary Stuart), and stopped the succession from being settled, Burghley and his associates were now seen to be facing the dreadful consequences of their ham-fisted machiavellianism, as the crisis, indeed the complete political breakdown and civil war, that Parsons confidently predicted would attend 'the next succession', approached.[46]

As a political myth, a narrative explanation of the recent course of English history, this version had at least as much going for it as the anti-popish conspiracy theory being propagated by central elements in the regime and their agents. Just like the anti-papal conspiracy theory, this view of the regime as a machiavellian conspiracy was able to incorporate a number of prominent aspects of contemporary political reality and recent history - combining 'facts' (like the prominence in/dominance of the Elizabethan regime by Cecil or that regime's involvement in rebellion in Scotland, France and the Low Countries or in the recent black propaganda campaign against Mary Stuart and Norfolk) with 'fictions' (like the imputation of the queen's refusal to marry to Cecil and his friends) - into a compellingly morally polarised and dynamic explanation of what had happened, was happening, and very likely would happen next. In that sense, in terms of the always already partial knowledge and *parti pris* perspectives of contemporaries, it was as 'true-to-life', that is to say as convincing and ideologically effective, as its hot Protestant, anti-papal alternative. It might also be taken to have adverted rather effectively to certain aspects of the Elizabethan regime (aka Collinson's and now Alford and Peltonen's 'monarchical republic') as an increasingly narrow, self serving, self perpetuating clique, to which (Protestant) historians working, as it were, from the inside out, have not always paid as much attention as they might.

We have here, then, two mutually exclusive conspiracy theories, each designed to falsify the other: to turn persons whose self presentation and image was that of good subjects, virtuous men, loyal and zealous servants of the queen, commonwealth and true religion, into their opposite - conspirators, traitors and machiavels. The evaluative terms, the positive (and negative) political and moral values and language in terms of which these claims and counter-claims were made, were equally 'republican' or 'neo Roman' and held entirely in common by both sides. This should not come as a shock; after all the participants in these exchanges were members of the same social and cultural groups, products of the same educational and social milieaux, carriers of the same bundle of (classicising) values, texts, authorities and apothegms in terms of which they all sought to interpret the world and explain and legitimate their own intentions and actions and excoriate those of their enemies. Theirs, then, was a struggle for possession of what we might term a unitary moral or linguistic terrain. The intensity of the resulting contest for those shared terms was in part a function of that very fact. But it was also a product of the logic of post Reformation confessional conflict. This was a world in which one person's heretic was another's true Christian; one person's rebel or heretic someone else's martyr; one man's virtuous councillor another's conspirator; one person's Christian prince another's persecuting tyrant. This, we might conclude, was a political and linguistic situation ripe for the production of conspiracy theory, as different groups struggled to maintain their view of themselves as good and of their opponents as bad, in a world in which the massive differences, indeed the complete moral polarities, separating the two sides were subject to sudden, vertiginous shifts, indeed to complete both con/ and in/version.[47]

By imputing to their enemies the lowest of motives, the deepest dyed villainy and cunning, the most ruthless methods, the most thorough-going deceit, both conspiracy theories allowed their propagators to indulge in thoroughly machiavellian analyses of what was really happening, to indulge in the most overtly a-moral exercises in 'policy' and political calculation, without letting the mask of virtue covering their own actions, intentions, and ambitions, slip for a moment. For 'policy' - barefaced, a-moral manoeuvre for political and personal advantage - was always something the other side did. It was just that in seeking to see through, explain, counter, and thus frustrate, the plots of the other side one had to understand from the inside, and thus to plumb the depths of, their methods and manoeuvres. As long as, in so doing, one was merely defending the commonwealth, the public interest, true religion, and the state from the purely private, a-moral and utterly illegitimate machinations of the other, one could indulge in orgies of such entirely secular a-moral political analysis and calculation and yet remain morally untouched by the pitch of machiavellian 'policy'. The conspiracies of one's enemies thus became the legitimating ground for one's own (more or less ruthless) and (more or less deceitful) manoeuvres for political (and, of course, personal) advantage. As the ultimate losers, the most privately disgruntled and publicly critical of contemporary observers, and also as a group anxious to avoid the thrust of the regime's Catholic centred conspiracy theories, certain Catholics exploited the dynamics of this situation to produce almost entirely secular, disenchanted, indeed a-moral readings of the workings of the political system, under the guise of laying bare the conspiracy of machiavellian evil counsel currently afflicting the Elizabethan state, the English people and, of course, their own political fortunes. They did so, moreover, twenty years or so, before the current account of the emergence of such a sceptical, Tacitean rendering of politics would have us believe was possible.

We are also seeing here what was to be the abiding relationship set up between what we might term conspiracy theory and a politics of the public sphere; a relationship that was to remain in place for the remainder of the reign, indeed arguably for the remainder of the early modern period. That is to say, in a monarchical system centred on the court and the council, with even parliament an intermittent presence in (rather than a structural feature of) the polity, the process of counsel giving was supposed to remain private. Taking politics to the people, canvassing positions and policies in public, through the press, circulating manuscript, the pulpit, or rumour was a deviant and potentially dangerous act, legitimation for which came most readily from some species of conspiracy theory.

For 'ins', that is for members of what became over the course of the 1570s and 1580s an increasingly homogeneous Protestant inner circle, their clients and supporters, the pressing danger presented to the realm came from without, from both foreign and domestic Catholic conspiracy. This, combined with the queen's rooted disinclination to act decisively against this threat, created a situation in which recourse had to be had to opinion outside the inner counsel-giving circle in order to persuade (or constrain) Elizabeth, if not always to do the right thing, then, at the very least, not to do the wrong one. In practice, of course, this often meant opposing the policy preferences and predilections of the queen, all the while expressing complete personal loyalty and obedience to her person and state. This, of course, was precisely what elements within the regime were doing in and through the pamphlets and performances of Norton and Fleetwood as they sought to bounce the queen into taking definitive actions against both Norfolk and Mary Stuart. As a number of historians have pointed out, undertaking such manoeuvres could be a ticklish business, often best accomplished through the good offices of third parties, persons (like Thomas Norton) dubbed by Michael Graves 'council men of business' and by others cultural and political facilitators to the Elizabethan great and the good.[48]

For 'outs', that is, as it turned out most frequently in Elizabethan England, for Catholics, this meant that, with the means of normal political communication and counsel-giving having been clogged by the activities of evil heretic and atheistical councillors, recourse would have to be had to wider bodies of opinion. In theory, such an expedient was designed to remove the blockages that were inhibiting the proper functioning of the polity by lobbing truth bombs over the wall of lies and disinformation with which the likes of Cecil and Bacon or Leicester had surrounded the queen; hence the stress placed in *The Treatise* on the concerted, pseudo-official nature of the disinformation campaign launched against Norfolk and Mary Stuart. Only thus could the scales be removed from the eyes of the monarch and evil be replaced with virtuous counsel. While that might be the legitimating theory, in practice, of course, such manoeuvres were designed to stir up considerable trouble for and opposition to the ruling clique, all the while leaving those doing the stirring free to express their total dedication and loyalty to the person of the monarch.

When, in the face of express royal displeasure, those other 'outs', the more radical denizens of the Elizabethan puritan movement, wanted to excuse their own continued public agitation for further Reformation they posited a similar conspiracy of evil counsel, this time emanating from the bishops and their mostly clerical hangers on. Their own pleas, petitions and polemics were intended, ostensibly at least, to force a way into a royal ear otherwise blocked by the misinformation and lies put about by this self interested clerical interest group. John Field, at least, acknowledged in private that the resulting campaigns were in fact designed to take the issue to the people and thus to exert pressure back on the bearers of power in Church and state to give way to puritan demands for change. In turn, from the 1570s on, these puritan activities provoked their own reaction, a reaction which by the late 1580s was hardening into something like a third (anti-Puritan) conspiracy theory, with which certain conformist, Catholic and 'royalist' observers and polemicists could interpret central features of the contemporary political scene in proto-absolutist terms that were entirely at odds with the internal workings and wider world view of the 'monarchical republic'.[49]

Either way, the result was that, throughout the reign, the supposedly intimate and confidential circles within which counsel was supposed to be given and politics conducted were intermittently and yet consistently breached and broadened, by a variety of groups, each claiming to be responding to a conspiracy of one sort of another which had prevented the normal channels of counsel and communication from working properly. Of course, all such actions represented emergency arguments and expedients, one-off reactions to the most pressing of threats and conspiracies. The popular politics of the public sphere, the orgies of tale and truth-telling, the exercises in a-moral, machiavellian Christian policy, being envisaged here, were only legitimate because there was a conspiracy by corrupt, genuinely machiavellian and heretical or popish elements to mislead the prince, take over the polity, and reform/ruin the Church. Once the emergency had passed, once the conspiracy had been frustrated, things could go back to 'normal' and the various 'publics' thus created and appealed to could be closed down; natural rulers and councillors could go back to ruling the commonwealth and counselling the prince and ordinary Christians and subjects could go back to being ruled. However, the religious divisions of the Reformation and the subsequent processes of confessionalisation and (geo-)political conflict ensured that 'normality' took an unconscionably long time to return. In the English case, of course, these pan-European religio-political forces were over-determined by other, local, circumstances. The gender and peculiar marital status of the monarch and the consequent dynastic circumstances of the kingdom ensured that Collinson's 'Elizabethan exclusion crisis' lasted at least from the early 1560s until the execution of Mary Stuart, and arguably until the fall of Essex and the inception of the secret correspondence between Robert Cecil and James VI. The accession of James I may have briefly appeared to offer a return to (patriarchal) normality but by then, after forty or so years of this sort of conspiracy-centred political tale-spinning and public posing, the style of political analysis and public pitch making produced by 'the crisis' had become so entrenched in the political culture of the nation that it was by no means clear what a 'normal' monarchical politics might look like. After all, by the close of Elizabeth's reign the three central conspiracy theories - the anti-papal, the anti-puritan, and the 'republican' or 'commonwealth' critique of evil counsel and court corruption - in terms of which English politics was to be conducted for the bulk of the seventeenth century, were all in place. And so, too, was the mode of public politicking in and through which those same conspiracy theories would be used to broaden the base of political involvement and participation. But that, thankfully, is another story.

Notes

1   Markku Peltonen, *Classical Humanism and Republicanism in English Political Thought 1570–1640* (Cambridge, 1995); idem, 'Citizenship and republicanism in Elizabethan England' in Martin van Gelderin and Quentin Skinner, eds., *Republicanism, a Shared European Heritage* (Cambridge, 2002), vol. 1; Stephen Alford, *The Early Elizabethan Polity: William Cecil and the British Succession Crisis, 1558–1569* (Cambridge, 1998), quote at p. 116. On the wider cultural context for these claims see P. Mack, *Elizabethan Rhetoric* (Cambridge, 2002), especially chapters 6, 7, 8.

2   Patrick Collinson, 'The monarchical republic of Elizabeth I' an article first published in *The Bulletin of the John Rylands Library* in 1987 and subsequently reprinted in Collinson's *Elizabethan Essays* (London, 1994). For a further development of the same case see Collinson's Raleigh lecture, 'The Elizabethan exclusion crisis and the Elizabethan polity' *Proceedings of the British Academy*, 84, 1995.

3   See Simon Adams, *Leicester and the Court: Essays on Elizabethan Politics* (Manchester, 2002) part I, especially chapters 1–4.

4   A. MacClaren, *Political Culture in the Reign of Elizabeth I: Queen and Commonwealth, 1558–1585* (Cambridge, 1999); also see her 'The quest for a king: gender, marriage and the succession in Elizabethan England', *Journal of British Studies*, 41, (2002) and 'Gender, religion and early modern nationalism; Elizabeth I, Mary Queen of Scots and the genesis of English anti-Catholicism', *American Historical Review*, 107, 2002.

5   The *locus classicus* for this view is, of course, Simon Adams unpublished 1973 Oxford D.Phil. thesis 'The Protestant cause: religious alliance with the western European Calvinist communities as a political issue in England, 1585–1629'. For Collinson see materials cited

in note. 2 and for MacClaren those cited in note 4. In his *Early Elizabethan Polity*, Alford essentially extrapolates Collinson's and Adams' views backwards into the 1560s, producing, in the process, a picture of William Cecil as a more determinedly Protestant and more avowedly anti-Catholic figure than many previous accounts have allowed. Also see Michael Graves, *Thomas Norton, the Parliament Man* (Oxford, 1994), especially chapter 6 The roots of English anti-Catholicism stretch, of course, back into Edward's reign for which see C. Davies, *A Religion of the Word: the Defence of the Reformation in the reign of Edward VI* (Manchester, 2002), especially chapter I and D. McCulloch, *Tudor Church Militant: Edward VI and the Protestant Reformation* (London, 1999). For other more general discussions of Elizabethan anti-popery see R. Bauchkam, *Tudor Apocalpyse* (Abingdon, 1978); P. Lake, 'The significance of the Elizabethan identification of the pope as Antichcist', *Journal of Ecclesiastical History,* 31, (1980); C.Z. Wiener, 'The beleagured isle: a study of Elizabethan and early Jacobean anti-Catholicism', *Past and Present*, 51, (1971).

6   For the notion of parliamentary selection see M. Kishlansky, *Parliamentary Selection* (Cambridge, 1986); on the Bond of Association see Collinson, 'Elizabethan exclusion crisis' and D. Cressy, 'Binding the nation: the bonds of association 1584 and 1696' in De Lloyd Guth and J.W. McKenna, eds., *Tudor Rule and Revolution* (Cambridge, 1982).

7   I intend to expand on these remarks in an essay to be published in a forthcoming book of essays on the public sphere in early modern England.

8   I refer, of course, to the work of, amongst others, Eamon Duffy, Christopher Haigh and J.J. Scarisbrick. The conceit, of course, is Christopher Haigh's, see his 'From monopoly to minority: Catholicism in early modern England', *Transactions of the Royal Historical Society*, 5th Series, 31 (1981).

9   This, of course, is the paradox at the heart of Collinson's typically subtle analysis in 'The monarchical republic of Elizabeth I' and 'The Elizabethan exclusion crisis'.

10   Susan Doran, *Monarchy and Matrimony. The Courtships of Elizabeth I* (London, 1996) and idem, 'Religion and politics at the court if Elizabeth I: the Hapsburg marriage negotiations of 1559–1567, *English Historical Review*, 104, (1989). Also see Alford, *Early Elizabethan Polity*.

11   Wallace MacCaffrey, *The Shaping of the Elizabethan Regime* (Princeton, 1969), part V and Alford, *Early Elizabethan Polity*, chapters 7 and 8.

12   *The Treatise* is conventionally attributed, on the basis of a number of internal hints dropped about the author's foreign nationality, political affiliations and range of knowledge, to John Leslie, Bishop of Ross, Mary's ambassador in England. This is not an implausible reading but it should be noted that the only extended scholarly discussion of the tract's authorship by T.H. Clancy does not plump unequivocally for Ross's authorship. Instead Clancy concludes that while 'the evidence is hardly conclusive', 'the best working hypothesis seems to be that our pamphlet was compounded of "inside dope" and educated guesses current in the conservative, anti-Cecil and pro-Stuart, atmostphere at the Inns of Court and the circle of Catholic refugees at Louvain'. Clancy also opines that Part Two of *The Treatise* might have been written earlier, 'perhaps in the 1568–9 period', with the preface to the English reader and the First Part (which replies to the government pamphlet *Salutem in Christo*, point for point) being added later in Flanders. See T.H. Clancy, 'A political pamphlet: *The Treatise of Treasons*, 1572' in G.J. Eberle, ed., *Loyola Studies in the Humanities* (New Orleans, 1962).

13   For this see the pamphlets collected together in *All Such Treatises as Have Lately Been Published by Thomas Norton* (London, 1571*);* also see William Fleetwood, *The Effect of the Declaration made in the Guildhall by M. Recorder of London, Concerning the Late Attempts of the*

Queen's Evil, Seditious and Disobedient Subjects (London, 1571) and R.G., *Salutem in Christo* (London, 1571). Graves, *Thomas Norton,* chapter 6 and idem, 'The management of the Elizabethan House of Commons: the Council's "men of business"', *Parliamentary History,* 2, (1983).

14 *The Treatise of Treasons (1572),* p. 102a for two Catilines; pp. 84a–5, 42a, for Machiavel epithet; preface sig. E3r.f for Sinon and Ulysses parallel.

15 Ibid., p. 139; also see p. 97a for their religious tergiversations through the Tudor period.

16 Ibid., Preface to the English reader, quote at sigs. A5r.–v.

17 Ibid., Preface to the English reader, sig. E6r.

18 Ibid., Preface to the English reader sig. Iv; pp. 86a–90, 93.

19 Ibid., p. 92.

20 Ibid., pp. 27a, 153; for Norfolk see 44, 52a–3, 123.

21 Ibid., pp. 123, 101a–102a.

22 Ibid., Preface to the English reader sigs. E7r.–v.; pp. 137a–8, 92–3.

23 Ibid., p. 101a.

24 Ibid., 93a, 103a, 168a4.

25 Ibid., pp. 96, 104a, 28a–9; for more on Scotland, France and Spain see pp. 160–2.

26 Ibid., Preface to the English reader, sigs. E7v.; pp. 169a–170a.

27 Ibid., pp. 18, 120.

28 Ibid., Preface to the English reader, sigs. A8r.–v.; pp. 162a–3.

29 Ibid., Preface to the English reader, sig. E2r.; pp. 62–a, 70a–74a. For Norton and Sampson as the sort of catspaws as were always to be found amongst the clergy and the lawyers see p. 124.

30 Ibid., pp. 80, 117a.

31 Ibid., pp. 79, 80. The passage refers to the instructions given to the London authorities by the Council and the subsequent speech to leading Londoners by the recorder Fleetwood at the Guildhall and the pamphlet account of it by Fleetwood, cited in note. 13.

32 Ibid., pp. 83a–4.

33 Ibid., Preface to the English reader, sig. I 3v.; pp. 31; 93a–4.

34 Ibid., pp. 149a; Preface to the English reader, sig. I 5r.; pp. 29a, 31.

35 Ibid., Preface to the English reader, sigs. A8r., I 4r.; pp. 84–5, 134.

36 Ibid., pp. 96–7, 106.

37 Ibid., pp. 106a–109a.

38 Ibid., preface, sigs. I 4r., A3v.

39 Ibid., pp. 15–19, quote at 19, 69, 111–22.

40 Ibid., pp. 167–a, 111–a, 166–7.

41 Ibid., pp. 156a, 157–a, 165, 166–a.

42 Ibid., pp.163a.

43 Ibid., 173, 124.

44 Alford, *Early Elizabethan polity,* chapters 1 and 4.

45 *Leicester's Commonwealth: the Copy of a Letter Lately Written by a Master of Art of Cambridge (1584),* ed. D.C. Peck (Athens, Ohio, 1985).

46 Robert Parsons, *Elizabethae Angliae Reginae Haeresim Calvinianum Propugnantis, saevissmum in Catholicos sui regni edictum . . . cum responsione as singula capita . . . per D. Andream Philopatrum* (1592); Richard Verstegan, *A Declaration of the True Causes of the Great Troubles Presupposed to be Intended Against the Realm of England* (1592); *An Advertisement Written to M.L. Treasurer of England* (1592); also see, *The Copy of a Letter Lately Written by a Spanish Gentleman* (1589) and *News from Spain and Holland* (Antwerp, 1593). This last item is a trailer for Parsons' next

great tract *A Conference About the Next Succession* of 1594/5. On these tract see Victor Houliston, 'The Lord Treasurer and the Jesuit: Robert Person's satirical *responsio* to the 1591 proclamation', *Sixteenth Century Journal*, 32, (2001).

47   Some sense of the hall-of-mirrors quality of much post Reformation polemic and perception can be gleaned from Brad Gregory's *Salvation at Stake: Christian Martyrdom in Early Modern Europe* (Cambridge, Mss., 1999) On the inversionary potential of conversion in an age of confessional polarisation see M.C. Questier, *Conversion, Politics and Religion in England, 1580–1625* (Cambridge, 1996). For the rhetorical forms appropriate to such exchanges see Quentin Skinner, 'Moral ambiguity and the art of persuasion in the renaissance' in S. Marchand and E. Lunbeck, eds., *Proof and Persuasion: Essays on Authority, Objectivity and Evidence* (Brepols, 1996).

48   On men of business see Graves, *Thomas Norton* and 'The management of the Elizabethan House of Commons' and P. Collinson, 'Puritans, men of business and Elizabethan parliaments', *Parliamentary History*, 7, (1988).

49   See P. Collinson, 'John Field and Elizabethan Puritanism', reprinted in his *Godly People* (London, 1983), the crucial quotation is at p. 367. On anti-Puritanism see P. Lake, *Anglicans and Puritans? English Conformist Thought from Whitgift to Hooker* (London, 1988) and P. Lake and M. Questier, *The Antichrist's Lewd Hat: Protestants, Papists and Players in Post Reformation England* (London, 2002), part IV. Also see J.A. Guy, 'The 1590s: the second reign of Elizabeth I?' and 'The Elizabethan establishment and the ecclesiastical polity', the introduction and chapter 6 of Guy, ed., *The reign of Elizabeth I: Court and Culture in the Last Decade* (Cambridge, 1995). Guy's break between the first and second reigns is arguably a tad too stark; crucial here was the appointment of Whitgift to Canterbury and his anti-puritan crackdown of 1583/4, which can itself be seen, in part, as a response to the 'popular' and 'puritan' agitation over the Anjou match, and then as the trigger for the rebirth of a newly energised and radicalised Elizabethan Puritan movement, which, of course, in turn, provoked the anti-Puritan, anti-populist, proto-absolutist reaction of the late 1580s and early 1590s. See P. Collinson, *The Elizabethan Puritan Movement* (London, 1967), parts 5, 6 and 8.

Chapter 7

The Paranoid Prelate: Archbishop Laud and the Puritan Plot

Jason Peacey

The seventeenth century provided fertile ground for the nurturing of conspiracy theories, far beyond the obvious fear of an international Catholic campaign against Protestantism: the 'Popish plot'. Scholars recognise that during the 1620s and 1630s concern also existed regarding a nationwide, and indeed international, Puritan plot to undermine the Church and the monarchy in England, and action taken against a range of opponents was underpinned by the perception of a dangerous 'godly' conspiracy.[1] The treatment of Puritanism during the reign of Charles I revealed that the king and Laud were fearful of the threat to uniformity and to obedience. For Laud, the godly plot sought to undermine uniformity in the Church, and by extension the security of the civil government. In 1626, John Cosin talked of Puritans as the 'domestic enemies', who were 'dangerous to church and monarchy', because 'so little do they care for authority'.[2] The Feoffees for the Purchase of Impropriations were considered to be 'the main instruments for the Puritan faction to undo the church'.[3] Most important, however, was the Puritan press, and the activities of authors such as Alexander Leighton, Henry Burton, John Bastwick, and William Prynne. Not everyone saw in Prynne's early works, and particularly *Histriomastix*, the piece of dangerous sedition which Laud recognised, but the works of Burton, Bastwick, and Prynne in the later 1630s were more clearly radical, and the authorities feared that their impact would be to 'stir up sedition among the people', in terms of undermining their allegiance, and to incite the Scots to rebellion.[4] Laud said that 'tis not we only, that is the bishops, that are struck at, but through our sides, your majesty, your honour, your safety, your religion, is impeached'.[5] The trial of Burton, Bastwick, and Prynne in 1637 demonstrated not merely Laud's 'narrow-minded obsession with uniformity', but also revealed the extent to which he had 'gradually come to think - with some show of reason - that he and his order were in imminent danger'.[6] In August 1637, he told Sir Thomas

Wentworth that 'these men do but begin with the church, that they might after have the freer access to the state', although he also worried about his personal safety in the light of the mass of libels which appeared in and around London and Westminster.[7]

The aim of this paper is to advance our understanding of the way in which this Puritan plot was understood by the government of Charles I. It is not strictly concerned with William Laud, so much as with the system with which he was associated, and this is not the place to enter the debate about Laudianism and the Caroline 'captivity' of the Church.[8] Although it is concerned with 'paranoia', it does not offer a psycho-historical account of Laud, although his 'paranoia' regarding the activities of the Puritans has frequently been commented upon.[9] Charles Carlton suggested that 'throughout his life Laud constantly felt that he was threatened by enemies, whom he often vaguely defined, and sometimes named... Psychologically he needed a bogeyman lurking in the shadows to do him harm, for this would enable him in good faith to wage the fights which he abhorred, and yet relished'.[10] Hugh Trevor-Roper described Laud as the 'frightened bishop', while Patrick Collinson wrote of the 'near paranoia' of the leading Arminian clerics, and more recently Tom Cogswell talked of Laud being 'self possessed'.[11] The problem with labelling Laud a 'paranoiac' is the implication that he perceived something which did not exist, when it is possible that Laud's fears were entirely justified. Demonstrating this would require assessing the nature of the Puritan threat, in terms of the aims and strength of the Puritan faction in England in the early seventeenth century, and indeed Laud's 'paranoia' is usually studied in terms of whether or not he was correct.[12] A great deal of attention has been paid to the literary underground and its techniques, and studies of the Personal Rule and the prosecution of dissent during Laud's archbishopric tend to focus on the obvious 'martyrs' – Alexander Leighton, William Prynne, John Bastwick, and Henry Burton – all of whom were deemed guilty of sedition, of undermining allegiance, and of endangering uniformity. Historians have explicitly addressed the extent to which the activities of such men constituted 'a real threat to the existing order in church and state', and have analysed the strengths and weaknesses of the interpretation of Puritan activities and motivation made by the authorities. It has been suggested that Prynne was 'too much the individualist ever to be involved in a conspiracy'; that the government failed to develop a 'realistic picture' from the evidence presented to them; and that Laud was ignorant of the details regarding the circulation of Puritan works. Worried for his personal safety, and by the apparent erosion of established authority, Laud took stern measures against such men on the basis of misreading evidence, and miscalculating and exaggerating the threat posed by Puritan propaganda. Nevertheless, scholars have been keen to stress that, however much the authorities 'mistook particular details', they 'assessed their overall danger correctly'. Stephen Foster concluded, therefore, that although there was no 'conspiracy', nevertheless these Puritan authors 'brought the government into disrepute and incited the kind of insurrection which became a reality only a few years later'. The Puritan martyrs, in other words, have been perceived as laying the foundations for the Covenanter rebellion, and for the challenge to royal and episcopal authority in the early 1640s, and it is certainly valid to question the importance of the treatment of the Puritan martyrs for the creation of crisis in England. By seeking to crush a 'phantom conspiracy', Laud helped to discredit episcopacy, and 'turned his victims into real conspirators'.[13] Such attention to the nature of the Puritan threat, however, has been at the expense of analysis of Laud's state of mind. Rather than scrutinising his paranoia in terms of the reality of a 'Puritan plot' against Church and crown in the 1630s, this paper explores his thought patterns and his interpretation of evidence. It seeks to recover from his actions the ideas and attitudes which underpinned his fear of the Puritans.

The aim is to demonstrate that there was more to Laud's fear of the Puritans than merely the ideas which they espoused. It is certainly true that, for Laud, the godly plot involved undermining ecclesiastical and civil government by threatening uniformity. It was the overwhelming desire for uniformity which underpinned a notion that those who found it difficult to conform posed a threat, and both Laud and Charles saw enemies where they found critics.[14] Laud also ran together personal opposition to him and opposition to the institution he headed. Laud operated with an extremely broad notion of what it was to be a conspirator, and defined conspiracy not just in terms of sedition but also mere combination. He employed a concept of conspiracy with which we are familiar - the engagement of one or more individuals in illegal or subversive activities - as well as an archaic definition, according to which conspiracy involved harmonious action or 'combination' for an agreed end or purpose, which was not necessarily seditious. Both definitions were employed at once, since collaboration was crucial to the success of seditious activity, and Laud may not always have recognised the distinction, although there is evidence that the two were sometimes separable in Laud's mind, since measures were taken against collaboration irrespective of its intended outcome.

I

To the extent that the threat came from Puritan thought, efforts to undermine Puritanism required attacking the vehicles - printed books - by which such ideas spread. However, the Puritan threat was perceived to consist in more than merely the threat posed by those writing Puritan pamphlets, and the danger that their ideas would incite people to disobedience and non-conformity. Puritans were not merely targeted for the danger inherent in their thought, but also for the way in which they operated. Scholars have drawn attention to the fear of 'popularity' which fed into anti-puritanism in the early seventeenth century, and this is related to the perception that leading Puritans were merely the most visible element in, and the ringleaders of, a widespread conspiratorial network of grandees, clerics, and merchants.[15] Laud's paranoia lay not so much in perceiving a threat from Puritan ideas, as in his understanding of the collaborative nature of the Puritan movement. Laud felt threatened by collaborative projects because they were 'popular', and because they did not originate in established authority. The conspiracy was, as Judge Richardson claimed, 'to set up the Puritan or separatist faction', and to create a Puritan 'community' within the country. Laud's paranoia is revealed most clearly in his attitude to members of a Puritan community which was law-abiding, if non-conformist, and which was not necessarily involved in anything which could realistically be labelled as a plot to undermine the Church or government. The perceived need for uniformity underlay the fear of those who worked together towards goals with which Laud could not approve, but who did nothing overtly to endanger the established system and authority, and it is in observing the lengths to which Laud was prepared to go to root out 'conspirators' that it is possible to gain an appreciation of his paranoia.[16] Laud sought, in other words, to demonstrate that Puritan authors stood at the head of a larger faction, rather than being lone madmen. Offering a convincing picture of the danger posed by the Puritans obviously necessitated demonstrations of numerical strength, but in doing so, and in seeking to punish members of the Puritan community, Laud treated Puritan sympathisers as collaborators, and in the process defined conspiracy as combination.[17]

That combination was something instinctively feared by the authorities is evident from the frequent notice taken of collaborative godly ventures which betrayed evidence of organisation and collegiality. Laud arguably feared Puritan lectureships because they were funded by public contributions and donations, and as much as this was disturbing because such lecturers lay outside Church control, they also revealed evidence of 'combination'.[18]

Combination lectures too were opposed by Laud and the Arminians so long as they betrayed evidence of popularity, and were beyond the control of those authorities which could guarantee orthodoxy.[19] The Feoffees project was inherently collaborative, as was the Puritan press. In September 1640, therefore, Laud was informed of a combination of thirty individuals in London who had joined forces in order to maintain a press for printing Puritan works.[20] Bishop Juxon's 1640 visitation articles, furthermore, included a specific question relating to collaborative planning within the Church: 'doth any priests or ministers... meet together in any private house or elsewhere to consult upon any course to be taken by them or by any other... which may any way tend to the impeaching or depraving of the Church of England'. In the same year, notice was also taken of the meetings held at John Downham's house regarding the planning of an entirely legal petition against the 'etcetera' oath.[21] Such instances reveal concerns regarding the possibility of combination and collaboration being used in order to foster dissent and the expression of discontent. However, it is important to recognise that collaboration could be investigated even in the absence of any obvious connection with disobedience. The four ministers (William Gouge, John Davenport, Richard Sibbes and John Taylor) who composed a letter which urged the collection of money to offer aid to distressed Protestant ministers in the Palatinate were reprimanded, and in June 1640 and investigation was launched into a private academy in London.[22] Examinations were taken of Bullen Reymes, a scholar under Alexander Calendrin, who kept a school in Leathersellers' Hall, having previously taught in a succession of private houses in the City. Reymes was asked to name the other scholars and to list the works studied, which evidently included Horace, Virgil, Homer, and Cicero, as well as more modern authors, such as John Rainolds. That Calendrin's loyalty was doubted is evident from Reymes' denial that religion could be used in order to justify subjects taking up arms against their prince.[23] Furthermore, it is also evident that the collegiality of the Puritan community was considered noteworthy, and undesirable, even when it was recognised that individual Puritans were benign. In June 1640, therefore, in his well known analysis of the Puritan faction, Conway investigated the nature of the Puritan movement while being forced to concede that its leaders had no harmful intentions. He told Laud that the earl of Warwick was the temporal head, and the earl of Holland the spiritual head of the Puritans, but he went on to say that neither man meant to do either good or hurt, and that they were motivated instead by the desire to be the principal pillar of the 'cabal'.[24]

To some extent, therefore, the problem with Puritans was perceived to lie in the collegiality and 'popularity', and the voluntaristic and combined efforts to achieved shared goals, even when those goals were legal. This can be observed in a number of ways with reference to the Puritan martyrs. Part of the concern regarding Puritan pamphleteering involved recognition that the dissenting press was collaborative in nature, both in terms of authorship and publication. The interrogation of Edmund Peacham in 1615 had centred on his 'helpers and confederates', and on his possible knowledge of a conspiracy.[25] Alexander Leighton was likewise considered to have worked with confederates, although at his Star Chamber trial little precise information was available regarding the identity of his associates, either in prayer meetings or in publishing. Leighton acknowledged their existence, and the fact that he had written *Sion's Plea* at their request, but refused to reveal their identity.[26] Part of the fear underlying the prosecution of Prynne for *Histriomastix* - a work which not all considered seditious, and which had been granted an official licence - involved the presumption that it had been the work of more than one hand.[27] According to Prynne, Laud frequently suggested, both in private and in the Star Chamber, 'that my *Histriomastix* was compiled by combination… it being impossible for any man of what profession soever, though sixty years old, to peruse or read all those authorities quoted in it'.[28] Richardson too said that 'there were many heads and hands therein', besides Prynne's own.[29]

Furthermore, during preparations for the 1637 trial of Burton, Bastwick, and Prynne, Laud arranged for extracts to be made from Burton's works, in order to substantiate his conjecture that Prynne had been involved in their composition.[30] In part, such collaboration was implied by evidence of Burton's visits to Prynne in the Tower, and it could be substantiated by evidence regarding Prynne's role in writing the appendix to Bastwick's *Flagellum* in 1635, and by the collaborative nature of *The Divine Tragedy*.[31] But while collaboration between the three martyrs was not difficult to demonstrate in 1637, it is interesting that Laud and the authorities went to such lengths to find, and draw attention to, such evidence, to the point of over-stretching their case. It was not simply necessary to demonstrate the danger inherent in the ideas of such men, but also to prove that they had been working together; that they were conspirators. According to Foster, 'Laud spent his time fruitlessly scanning Burton's sermons and *Newes from Ipswich* for internal evidence of Prynne's authorship when the Star Chamber information could simply have included the four works Prynne definitely did compose in 1636'.[32] Laud and the authorities overstretched the evidence in their determination to secure a conviction of conspiracy as well as sedition. Moreover, there is evidence that Laud sought to extend the conspiracy beyond the members of the triumvirate. He told Wentworth: 'I cannot prove it but I have strong conjecture that the Lord Bishop of Lincoln hath more hands than beseems him in this business'.[33] Such emphasis on unproveable conjectures may help explain Laud's reputation as a paranoiac.

However, there is more to Laud's understanding of the Puritan conspiracy than the collaboration between authors such as Burton, Bastwick, and Prynne. The most often neglected aspect of the 1637 Star Chamber trial is that the authorities also targeted those involved in the processes of printing and publication.[34] The information brought into court by the attorney general contained charges not just against Burton, Bastwick, and Prynne, but also against the printers Robert Raworth and John Crouch, while the High Commission also presented articles against the stationers Thomas Purslowe, Gregory Dexter, and William Taylor, who were charged with attempting to bring out Prynne's *Instructions for Churchwardens*, and with collaborating in the production of the *Divine Tragedy*.[35] Dexter and Taylor both admitted being commissioned to print the epistle to a work which they had never seen, and revealed the number of copies produced, and the price paid by Prynne, as well as the fact that they had burnt the manuscript according to Prynne's directions.[36] Furthermore, the desire not just to silence Puritan 'leaders' such as Burton, Bastwick, and Prynne, but also to dismantle their network of friends and allies, also explains the trial of John Lilburne in 1638, who was accused of procuring the printing of 10-12,000 copies of Puritan tracts in Delft.[37] Indeed, it also explains the investigation of the smuggling of such works into England by Puritan clerics such as Jeremiah Burroughes and William Bridge.[38] It also provoked vigorous attempts to use diplomatic pressure in order to undermine such printing on the Continent, and with the help of a network of spies Sir William Boswell was able to secure a court order in Amsterdam for the condemnation of John Canne for printing *A Brief Relation* (of which 10,000 copies had been printed in English, and 3,000 in Dutch), and for the trial of Willem Christaensz, who had translated and printed *News from Ipswich*.[39] This formed but one part of a more general attempt to investigate and undermine the printing of Puritan books, and English Puritan communities in general, in the Low Countries.[40]

In addition to charging members of the publishing industry who ought properly to have been regarded as mere accessories to the 'crimes' committed by the 'conspirators', the investigation of the printing of Puritan tracts in the 1630s reveals important evidence relating to the way in which Laud and the authorities interpreted the 'plot'. The authorities were arguably not very adept at employing typographical evidence as a method of detecting the work of anonymous publishers and printers.[41] Nevertheless, that they were interested in printing techniques is evident from the case brought against Purslowe,

Dexter, and Taylor, which had all the hallmarks of a classic conspiracy theory involving secret meetings and illicit packages around which elaborate theories could be developed. Evidence was presented, therefore, that Prynne's servant, Nathaniel Wickens, had visited the printers, and that covert meetings had been held at Wickens' house in Newgate Market, in order to deliver page-proofs. Most importantly, Wickens was reported to have delivered to the stationers a printing block to be used for the initial letter of the *Divine Tragedy*, which was 'very curiously cut in boxwood and sealed up close in paper'. Part of the purpose of such surreptitious activity was that this particular device 'was a new letter, not known amongst any of the printers here in London, but was cut of purpose for his use'. What was concluded on the basis of this, however, was bizarre, for it was said that this printing block contained hidden images. It was 'a very complete letter as ever you saw, for to look upon it the usual way it seemed a complete and perfect C, but turn one side of it and it appeared a pope's head, and then turn it another way and there appeared an army of men and soldiers'.[42] Dexter admitted using this new letter 'C', but denied knowledge of hidden images, and scrutiny of the letter in question reveals that the authorities' interpretation of the evidence appears to have been more than a little hysterical.[43]

II

Laud's fear of mere combination is evident, however, in more than just his treatment of those directly involved in writing and publishing Puritan tracts. It emerges from the way in which he tracked down, and prosecuted, men who could not be accused of actively seeking to undermine the Church or government. He targeted 'accessories after the fact', those guilty by association, and those who had merely read seditious literature, and who were sympathetic to Puritan ideas. As he investigated the 'plot', however, Laud unravelled deeper and deeper levels of involvement, and every new 'participant' led him to the discovery of many more. Laud explored such avenues of inquiry *ad nauseam*. He feared, expected to find, and detected evidence of, a massive network of people opposed to him, and he read conspiracy into opposition. This can be observed in the way in which Laud's attempt to undermine the Puritan threat involved unravelling not just the connections between authors, and their dealings with printers, but also the mechanisms by which works were distributed. In 1629, Matthew Wren oversaw examinations of seventeen individuals in Cambridge regarding the distribution of Prynne's recent works, which revealed how they had been purchased by prominent godly members of the university, including Thomas Ball, Dr Anthony Tuckney, William Bridge, Dr Samuel Ward, Dr John Arrowsmith, Thomas Goodwin, and Stephen Marshall.[44] Prynne's 1634 trial was followed by an attempt to call in copies of *Histriomastix*, which involved discovering his distribution network, and the names of those who had purchased copies.[45] Such endeavours also explain why the charge brought before Star Chamber in 1637 named a whole raft of ministers and merchants from London and the provinces, who were accused of assisting in the dispersal of seditious literature.[46] In addition, Prynne's servant, Nathaniel Wickens, was commited to prison, where he remained until 1640, while the stationer John Bartlet was imprisoned for buying and selling the martyrs' books.[47]

However, the zeal with which the authorities sought to understand the distribution of Puritan tracts, track down copies, and take action against those responsible, is most clear from the investigation launched into the activities of the Somerset clothier, John Ashe, who was 'well known' to be a 'very precise man and full of zeal', and who was labelled by one contemporary as 'a strict Puritan'.[48] Ashe, it transpired, received 200 copies of one work, which he either sold or lent to friends. As copies were traced, however, it emerged that the books had been passed extensively around the county, and each person examined revealed yet further men who had read the work and who too needed to be called in for questioning. In November 1636, therefore, the authorities examined John Rosewell, the vicar of Doulting, who admitted receiving a copy from his son, Anthony, one of Ashe's apprentices. The latter confirmed that Ashe had given him a dozen copies to sell, and that he had lent copies to James Dugdale and John Strode. These two men were questioned in turn, as were other local men, such as Richard Cooper of Bruton and Thomas Parsons of Batcombe.[49] Strode was found to have lent the book to Peter Higgins, and while William Bord of Batcombe refused to say from where he had received his copy, he nevertheless admitted that Ashe was 'the original from whence these books came'.[50] Ashe was also found to have sent a copy to Richard Bernard, rector of Batcombe, and the latter admitted lending it to Edmund Morgan, rector of Pill, who too was questioned.[51] Ashe confirmed that he had received 200 copies from London which were to be sold for 8d. each, and that the money was to have been returned to Henry Burton.[52]

What this case reveals is Laud's willingness to pursue tenaciously the trail of evidence, as enquiries and examinations revealed an ever more complex web of men who were at least interested in, if not sympathetic towards, Puritan literature. It probably also served to confirm his suspicion that there was an extensive network of dissent, and indeed conspirators, in the country at large. The 1637 trial, therefore, was not just about the triumverate of Burton, Bastwick, and Prynne, nor even about the possibility of their having worked in a collaborative fashion. It was about their role as the centrepiece of a larger network and a wider conspiracy. The trial was about the entire group, and about a confederacy who had 'long envied and maligned your majesty's happy government and the good discipline of the church', and who had 'by confederacy, among themselves, out of some schismatical and factious humours', sought to villify the Church, and who had produced books to incite the people for the achievement of their factious ends.[53]

III

However, it is also possible to extend this analysis in order to demonstrate that attempts were made to target individuals far beyond those who could reasonably be argued to have conspired in order to produce and distribute dangerous Puritan tracts, or in order to advance seditious, non-conformist, and disloyal ends. It is then possible to suggest what the targeting of certain individuals reveals about Laud's mentality, and his understanding of the Puritan plot.

Laud was clearly disturbed by the reaction to the 1637 trial and punishment of Burton, Bastwick, and Prynne, and the 1638 trial of Lilburne. He complained to Thomas Wentworth that the martyrs' words on the pillory had been noted down by the audience, before being copied and spread throughout the City.[54] Concern regarding Lilburne's behaviour on the pillory prompted an investigation in April 1638 into his address to the crowd, and his distribution of seditious literature.[55] This reflected a more general concern regarding the men with whom the martyrs associated. The investigation of Lilburne's case in 1638 involved not just detecting what Lilburne had himself done, but those with whom he was known to have consorted. His trial saw discussion, therefore, of his association with servants of John Wharton – who was suspected of playing a prominent role in the activities of the triumvirate – and a concern to find out where he lived, and with whom he was associating.[56] After Lilburne's conviction, furthermore, records were kept of those who visited him in prison, just as information had been gathered on Prynne's visitors.[57] In addition to exploring the friends and associates of the martyrs, the authorities demonstrated concern regarding those who expressed sympathy and support for their plight and cause, and a number of legal cases were instigated. In 1634, William Brearcliffe, vicar of North Cave, near Hull, had faced legal proceedings for uttering approving comments on Prynne's *Histriomastix*, and such cases became more common in later years.[58] After the 1637 trial, therefore, articles were drawn up against Henry Tailer of Hardingham in Norfolk, for speeches reported to have been made against Laud regarding his speech at the sentencing in Star Chamber.[59] Information was also presented in High Commission against George Catesby, for speaking in favour of Prynne and Burton, while evidence was also submitted to two Middlesex JPs in January 1638 regarding Joseph Hutchinson, beadle of the new corporation, who had been overheard in the Castle Tavern in St Clement's saying that they were 'as honest and as good subjects as any the king has'.[60] The desire to suppress support for the prisoners was also evident from the case of two men who were imprisoned upon delivering a petition from Burton's parishioners, and from the notice taken in 1639 of Mr Maunsell, Prynne's chamber fellow at Lincoln's Inn, who had expressed confidence that when Prynne was punished he took it patiently and joyfully, whereas his adversaries might have had quaking hearts.[61]

Indeed, there is also evidence that possessing copies of the three men's works was regarding as being incriminating.[62] In February 1639, therefore, it was recorded that the library of a minister called Mr Knowles contained an account of the proceedings against the martyrs, while in the same month the London woodturner, Nehemiah Wallington, was in trouble before the Star Chamber, where his ownership of *The Divine Tragedie, Newes From Ipswich*, and Burton's *Apology*, formed part of the charge.[63] Under examination, George Stevenson admitted that he had a copy of one of Bastwick's books two years earlier, 'but knoweth not from whom he had it, nor where it is at this time'.[64] In 1643, meanwhile, William Flower, a London citizen and grocer, petitioned Parliament to complain that he had been imprisoned for nine months for possessing a copy of *News From Ipswich*.[65] Criminalising the ownership of undesirable books could have led to the arrest of leading members of the aristocracy in the late 1630s, and perhaps the earl of Suffolk had cause to be grateful that it was not widely known that he had purchased four books by Prynne in September 1639.[66] Fear of being found to be in possession of such works led some men to hand their copies over to the authorities. Thomas Martin, therefore, an attorney at Barnard's Inn, sent to the attorney general a borrowed copy of *Histriomastix* in November 1637, once he realised that it was by Prynne, and after having kept it locked away for fear of the harm it might do.[67]

More obviously, concern was expressed at the large crowds who attended Burton, Bastwick, and Prynne on their journeys from London to their various prisons in 1637, which Laud professed to be something which was 'strange should be suffered in any well-ordered state'.[68] An investigation was launched in September 1637 into those who had met, conversed with, and entertained Prynne, and who had given him gifts, 'or other remarkable expressions of courtesy or encouragement'.[69] While Laud may have been disturbed to learn that Henry Burton was met by the Puritan legend John Dod, greatest attention was paid to those who met Prynne.[70] One John Maynard, who had been employed to convey Prynne to Carnarvon Castle, recorded that twenty men had dined with him at Barnet, though none had had private conference with the prisoner, and that he met six men at St Albans. Prynne's reception at Coventry, where he met Alderman Clarke, was felt to merit further investigation, and the borough only avoided forfeiting its charter when the aldermen paid fines of £100 each.[71] Information was also brought against Miles Burkitt, on the grounds that when Burton and Prynne passed through his parish, he preached that though the faithful were molested, persecuted, and cropped, yet they would continue faithful still. Burkitt was also reported to have been present at a fast, held at Marston St Lawrence, which called for the prisoners' deliverance.[72]

The most thorough investigation, however, was launched into the case of those Puritans who had met and entertained Prynne at Chester. It was as a result of the behaviour of these 'notorious characters', according to Trevor-Roper, that Laud, 'the frightened bishop, was driven to ferocity'.[73] The bishop of Chester, John Bridgeman, complained to Richard Neile, Archbishop of York, of 'four factious citizens' who entertained Prynne: Sheriff Calvin Bruen; Alderman John Aldersey; a hosier called Robert Ince; and the latter's brother Peter Ince, the local stationer. He also drew attention to a local Gray's Inn lawyer called John Bostock, who was 'more inward with Prynne than any other'. Pleading that he lacked the authority to punish them, Bridgeman suggested that they should be prosecuted at the High Commission in York; saying that 'it may do good for example to others of that strain'.[74] As a result, the 'Chester men' faced prosecution in York, based upon evidence provided by Bridgeman.[75] Calvin Bruen was styled 'a silly but a very seditious fellow', and was accused of visiting Prynne outside Chester, of praying with him, and of entertaining him to dinner. He was also accused of procuring a picture to be drawn of Prynne, and for copies of it to be made. He was also accused of having acquired a copy of Leighton's *Sion's Plea*, which he apparently displayed in his shop. Having been arrested, Bruen was forced to make more than one appearance at the High Commission, and to appear before the privy council in Whitehall. He was eventually fined £500.[76] The two Ince brothers were accused of accompanying Prynne to St John's church, and to Thomas Aldersey's house. Peter Ince and his wife were both arrested, and he was eventually fined £300 plus £50 costs.[77] A local grocer called Peter Leigh, a gentleman called Richard Goldbourne, and one Mr Trafford were also summoned to York, and after being kept there for a month, were fined £200, £300, and £150 respectively. When they refused to acknowledge their error, however, they were forced to flee abroad, leaving wives and children, trades and professions. Intimidation of their families in their absence led to one wife having a miscarriage.[78] Little wonder, then, that the city of Chester sent a letter to the archbishop of York complaining of the harassment of many innocent men, or that Prynne would later style such punishments 'vexatious and most exorbitant'.[79]

The thoroughness of the investigation into the activities of the 'Chester men', and the severity of their punishments, obviously provides evidence for those who argue that the authorities over-reacted to the incident of Prynne's reception. In effectively treating such men as collaborators and co-conspirators, despite their having done nothing illegal or proscribed, they may have displayed something approaching paranoia.[80] Indeed, the affair took one further bizarre twist which would support this interpretation, in relation to the decision to stage a public burning of the pictures of Prynne which had been circulating in Chester. That the authorities proceeded with such a ceremony (at Chester High Cross on 12 December 1637) in spite of the fact that the pictures had already been destroyed, leaving them with only the empty frames, is a testament to their fear of Prynne's influence, and to their zeal 'to put a stop to any hero-worship of the condemned author'. This 'rather ludicrous ceremony' once again speaks volumes about the state of mind of Prynne's prosecutors.[81]

IV

However, there exists evidence regarding Laud's treatment of his enemies which is of even greater significance. The prosecutions which followed the 1637 trial, and which reflect upon Laud's treatment of the Puritan plot, reveals how he found evidence which enabled him to make connections between different aspects of the conspiracy, and its different historical phases. Laud not only operated with a profound sense of the identity of the 'usual suspects', and proved anxious to demonstrate collusion between them. Those against whom he was fighting were also recognised to be the heirs of earlier Puritan pressure, and to have been carrying the torch from earlier battles. His zeal for action against Puritan opponents was probably informed, in other words, by his recognition of the power of family traditions of non-conformity, godly communities, and Puritan patronage networks.[82] On more than one occasion, therefore, it seems clear that Laud was targeting those men and women with the purest Puritan pedigrees. The most interesting aspect of Laud's interpretation of the Puritan plot, therefore, is his understanding of the 'continuity of Puritanism', and his detection of the persistence of the Puritan conspiracy. While this paper is not concerned with testing the extent of the Puritan threat, it is concerned with recognising contemporary perceptions regarding the nature of that threat, and about suggesting that this provides an important consideration in understanding the nature of early Stuart political and religious tensions prior to 1642.

In terms of connecting different Puritan incidents, it is possible to look not just to the fact that Laud detected that English and Scottish Puritans were in league from an early stage, but also to the case of John Ashe.[83] Ashe was not just a random figure on whom to devote such attention. His appearance in papers relating to the investigation into Puritan publications in 1636 and 1637 almost certainly triggered alarm bells in Laud's mind. Ashe was one of the usual suspects, having played a central role in an earlier Puritan cause célèbre; the so-called 'Beckington riots' against Laudian altar policy. The mention of his name in relation to Prynne probably explains the rigour with which his role in distributing Puritan literature was investigated. Furthermore, this investigation quickly revealed the involvement of other men long associated with Puritanism in Somerset, such as Bernard, rector of Batcombe since 1613. He had been presented for refusing to bow at the name of Jesus on more than one occasion, but more famously was involved in resisting the new altar policy in the early 1630s, for which he was eventually jailed.[84] Well might Sir Robert Phelips, in his often quoted comment to Laud, have made a connection between those 'odd lunatics Prynne, Bastwick, and Burton', and the 'rioters of Beckington'.[85]

More significant, however, is evidence regarding the connections which Laud recognised between the 'plots' in the 1630s and earlier Puritan pressure. Laud was almost certainly aware, for example, of the Puritan pedigrees of the personnel behind the scheme for the purchase of impropriations, and that William Gouge was not only a friend of Henry Burton, but also a former assistant to Stephen Egerton at the Puritan hot spot of St Anne's Blackfriars, having been recommended to the post by Arthur Hildersham. Indeed, Laud would have been aware that Gouge embodied the persistence of a Puritan stronghold in the parish which dated back to the 1580s.[86] Laud was probably also aware that another of the Feoffees, Rowland Heylyn, had been involved in Puritan circles since at least the time when he was one of the overseers of the famous will of Sarah Venables.[87] We do not know Laud's reaction to the reappearance in 1640 of 'advice tending to reformation', the document at the centre of Puritan petitioning campaigns in 1603-4.[88] And it is unclear whether or not Laud understood that two of the stationers prosecuted in 1637, Dexter and Taylor, had their own professional Puritan pedigree, having been apprenticed to the firm of widow Aldee, one of printers of *Histriomastix*.[89] But he certainly understood that there was a connection between Bastwick and Leighton which dated back as far as 1617.[90] The archbishop sought not merely to smear Bastwick and his friends by associating them with Leighton, but also to develop a picture of their involvement in a conspiracy.[91] In 1634, as Foster noted, 'Laud scented a conspiracy behind the composition of so long a work as *Histriomastix*, as he had in the authorship of *Sions Plea*, and he may possibly have thought it the same conspiracy in both cases'.[92] Subsequently the attempt was also made to link the three Puritan authors to Leighton, although the 'paucity of evidence genuinely linking Leighton to the triumverate reduced propagandists to employing vague language to explain their association. All four were at least the same *sort* of men and very likely of the same "sect" or "brotherhood"… The shadowy and apparently undiscoverable nature of the links between Burton, the author of the "Ipswich libel", and Leighton had finally become proof positive of the sinister intentions of their presumed organisation'.[93]

Furthermore, it is also possible to suggest that the heavy-handed treatment of the 'Chester men' was explicable in the light of the way in which Laud recognised the continuity of Puritanism, and the Puritan pedigrees of his opponents. The prosecution of Bruen was partly about the need to undermine those associating with Prynne, and about dismantling his network of friends and fellow 'conspirators'. But it was also about Bruen himself, whose name probably raised fears in Laud's mind. In part this was because of the Puritanism with which the Chester men were themselves connected. Bridgeman claimed that Robert Ince had been punished for schismatical speeches years before, and that Peter Ince was responsible for securing for the town supplies of Puritan books.[94] Bishop Bridgeman claimed that Bostock had long been one of the most active Puritans in the area, saying: 'I verily believe there hath been no libellous or scandalous pamphlets published either from beyond sea, or printed in England for diverse years, but he hath gotten it and dispersed it'. More importantly, 'he hath been a great conventicator (as his neighbours affirm) and (if report be true) of long acquaintance with Prynne when he wrote his libels'.[95] From interviews with the wife of Peter Ince, Bridgeman also discovered another longstanding contact of Prynne's, who visited him in the Tower of London following his censure for *Histriomastix*.[96] The will of a local Puritan matriarch, Martha Bate, also revealed the links between Bruen, William Trafford, and Richard Goldbourne, all of whom were involved in Prynne's reception.[97]

More important still was the association which Laud would almost certainly have been able to make to a long tradition of Puritanism in the Chester area. Specifically, Bruen's name would have conjoured fears because of his father, John Bruen. The latter had been converted to Calvinism in the late 1580s (after which he named his children Calvin and Beza), and became a leading member of the godly gentry in the area, and 'the model of a reforming Puritan gentleman'.[98] Bruen emerges from the pages of his biography (published in 1641) as the head of a godly household dominated by the Bible, and as the patron of godly ministers such as Sabbath Clark.[99] Moreover, he played an active role in the removal of images and stained glass from churches, opposed the practice of wakes, and burnt playing cards and dice. Most importantly, he grew 'famous' for his godliness, and his memorial would speak of someone 'whose virtues fair through all our coasts do sound'.[100] His work was commended by the Puritan patriarch, William Perkins, and he corresponded with other Puritan grandees such as Sir Robert Harley. Indeed, his house became a focal point for the education of local and national gentry figures. Bruen came to play a role in the education of local children, including Sir Richard Grosvenor, and in playing host to 'many gentlemen of the best rank in the country', who 'desired and made much great suit, some for their children, and some for themselves, and some for their friends, to sojourn with him'.[101] Such visitors included Lady Egerton, the daughter-in-law of Lord Chancellor Egerton, and it was claimed that Bruen's house 'was the common inn, or constant harbour of the church, and of God's children'.[102] Members of Bruen's immediate family were in trouble as early as 1608 for not kneeling for communion, and were noted patrons of Puritan ministers including William Hinde and Thomas Paget.[103] Bruen also appears to have been a friend of Nicholas Wentworth, son of the notorious Elizabethan Puritan, Peter Wentworth.[104]

Bruen was not only a prominent local Puritan, nor even just a member of the godly gentry whose influence and fame extended beyond his local community. In his patronage of William Hinde (his biographer, and brother-in-law), he was associated with a Puritan cleric and author of national importance. Hinde's numerous works of biblical scholarship and commentary, published in the early years of the seventeenth century, were dedicated to men at the heart of the Banbury Puritan circle, such as Sir Erasmus Driden, Sir Anthony Cope, Sir William Cope, and William Fiennes, 1st viscount Saye, and they revealed his friendship with leading Puritan divines such as John Dod and Robert Cleaver.[105] Hinde also edited the sermons of John Rainolds, which were dedicated to another Puritan divine, Henry Airay, provost of Queen's College, Oxford.[106] To Laud, therefore, Calvin Bruen's involvement with

Prynne probably offered disturbing testimony to the existence of family traditions of godliness, and of the persistence of Puritan pressure.

V

Without wishing to pass judgement on Laud's 'paranoia', therefore, it is possible to observe certain aspects of his reaction to the Puritan 'threat', and to gain an understanding of the nature of the Puritan conspiracy. Laud's response was famously heavy-handed, but it was not so much the severity which is interesting as the targets. It is now clear that Laud was intent not just to pursue the 'odd lunatics' with whose trials we are so familiar. He also sought to attack their friends, employees, and agents; recognising, perhaps, that the key to the shape and substance of Puritanism under the early Stuarts was provided by money and organisation as much as by ideology.[107] However, Laud also targeted their associates, sympathisers, and readers, including those who were doing nothing illegal or explicitly proscribed. Laud, admittedly motivated by the desire to make examples of people in order to dissuade others, nevertheless appears to have been unable to differentiate between sympathy for Puritanism and opposition to Laudian innovations on the one hand, and seditious attempts to undermine the Church of England and the monarchy on the other. Moreover, he expected to find evidence of the involvement of the 'usual suspects' in undesirable behaviour, and explicitly sought to demonstrate links between different celebrated incidents of dissent and non-conformity, both in order to develop a picture of a web of Puritan intrigue in the 1630s, and to demonstrate the continuity of the Puritan threat. Laud detected evidence, therefore, of what historians such as Nicholas Tyacke call a 'radical Puritan continuum'. Tyacke has sought to stress that the existence of such a tradition does not imply the 'inevitable rise and triumph of Puritanism' of Whig historiography, since it was the rise of Arminianism which jolted men with Puritan inclinations to reassess their attitudes towards the Church, and which rejuvenated their campaign for 'further reformation'.[108] However, having explored the thought patterns of Laud and his allies in the 1630s, and having exposed their acute fear of the existence of a large-scale Puritan plot, it is possible to suggest that Puritanism and Laudianism existed in at least a symbiotic relationship, and that the rise of Laudianism was based in part upon a reaction to a perceived persistent threat. Rather than label Laud as a paranoiac, perhaps we ought to recognise in him a post-revisionist *avant la lettre*.

Notes

1   L.J. Reeve, *Charles I and the Road to Personal Rule* (Cambridge, 1989), p. 67.

2   *The Correspondence of John Cosin* (Surtees Society, 52, 1869), pp. 93, 102.

3   W. Laud, *The Works* (ed. J.H. Parker, 8 vols, Oxford, 1847–60), iii. 216–17.

4   W. Prynne, *A New Discovery of the Prelates Tyranny* (London, 1641), p. 9; P[ublic] R[ecord] O[ffice], PC 2/47, fo. 148; C[alendar of] S[tate] P[apers] D[omestic] *1636–7*, p. 565; Laud, *Works*, vi. 44; Laud, *Works*, vii. 300–2, 329.

5   Laud, *Works*, vi. 38

6   S. Foster, *Notes from the Caroline Underground* (Springfield, Ohio, 1978), p. 56.

7   Laud, *Works*, vi. 500; Laud, *Works*, iii. 228–9, 235, 237.

8   N. Tyacke, *Anti-Calvinists* (Oxford, 1987); P. White, *Predestination, Policy and Polemic* (Cambridge, 1992); J. Davies, *The Caroline Captivity of the Church* (Oxford, 1992). See also: K. Fincham, ed., *The Early Stuart Church, 1603–1642* (Basingstoke, 1993).

9   C. Carlton, *William Laud, 1573–1645* (London, 1987), p. 127. For Laud, see: N. Tyacke, 'Archbishop Laud', in Fincham, ed., *Early Stuart Church*, pp. 51–70.

10   Carlton, *Laud*, p. 151; C. Carlton, 'The dream life of Archbishop Laud', *History Today* (December 1986), pp. 9–15.

11   H. Trevor-Roper, *Archbishop Laud, 1573–1645* (3rd ed., London, 1988), p. 323; P. Collinson, 'Lectures by combination. Structures and characteristics of church life in seventeenth century England', in *Godly People* (London, 1983), p. 491; T. Cogswell, 'Underground verse and the transformation of early Stuart political culture', in S.D. Amussen and M.A. Kishlansky, eds., *Political Culture and Cultural Politics in Early Modern England* (Manchester, 1995), p. 277.

12   See: W. Haller, *The Rise of Puritanism* (New York, 1957).

13   Foster, *Caroline Underground*, pp. 41, 45, 58, 62. See: K. Sharpe, *The Personal Rule of Charles I* (New Haven, 1992), pp. 758–65.

14   P. Lake, 'The Laudian style: order, uniformity and the pursuit of the beauty of holiness in the 1630s', in Fincham, ed., *Early Stuart Church*, pp. 161–85; P. Lake, 'The Laudians and the argument from authority', in B.Y. Kunze and D.D. Brautigam, eds., *Court, Country and Culture* (Rochester, NY, 1992).

15   R. Cust, 'Anti-Puritanism and urban politics: Charles I and Great Yarmouth', *Historical Journal* 35 (1992); Collinson, 'Lectures by combination', p. 492; R. Cust, 'Charles I and popularity', in T. Cogswell, R. Cust and P. Lake, eds., *Politics, Religion and Popularity in Early Stuart Britain* (Cambridge, 2002).

16   Foster, *Caroline Underground*, p. 45; J. Rusworth, *Historical Collections* (8 volumes, London, 1721), ii. 237.

17   The sense of Puritans being a conspiratorial party emerges clearly from Heylyn: P. Heylyn, *Cyprianus Anglicus* (London, 1671).

18   Cust, 'Anti-Puritanism'. See also: P. Seaver, *The Puritan Lectureships* (Stanford, 1970), pp. 240–66.

19   Collinson, 'Lectures by combination'.

20   *CSPD 1640–1*, p. 40.

21   Seaver, *Puritan Lectureships*, p. 264.

22   Seaver, *Puritan Lectureships*, p. 248.

23   PRO, SP 16/457, fos. 129, 131.

24   *CSPD 1640*, p. 278.

25   T.B. Howell, ed., *A Complete Collection of State Trials* (33 vols, London, 1811–26), ii. 869–71;
       J. Spedding, ed., *The Letters and Life of Francis Bacon* (7 vols, London, 1861–74), v. 93–4;
       CSPD 1611–18, p. 306.

26   Foster, *Caroline Underground*, p. 34; S.R. Gardiner, 'Speech of Sir Robert Heath', in *Camden
       Miscellany* 7 (Camden Society, new series, 14, 1875), p. 10.

27   Foster, *Caroline Underground*, pp. 42–3.

28   S.R. Gardiner, ed., *Documents Relating to the Proceedings Against William Prynne* (Camden
       Society, new series, 18, 1877), pp. 34–5.

29   Foster, *Caroline Underground*, p. 44; Gardiner, ed., *Documents*, p. 18; Rushworth, *Historical
       Collections*, ii. 234–5.

30   *CSPD 1637*, p. 48.

31   M.J. Condick, 'The life and works of John Bastwick (1595–1654)' (University of London
       PhD thesis, 1983), pp. 104, 109; Trevor-Roper, *Archbishop Laud*, p. 318; Longleat House,
       Whitelocke Papers vii, fo. 213; Bodl[eian Library, Oxford] MS Bankes 18, fo. 41.

32   Foster, *Caroline Underground*, p. 54; PRO, SP 16/354, fos. 357–9v.

33   Trevor-Roper, *Archbishop Laud*, p. 325; Laud, *Works*, vii. 355.

34   Trevor Roper, *Archbishop Laud*, pp. 319–20; Bodl. MS Bankes 18, fos. 41–3.

35   *CSPD 1637*, pp. 49, 174–5; Foster, *Caroline Underground*, p. 62; PRO, SP 16/357, fos.
       307v–9v; SP 16/371, fo. 179.

36   *CSPD 1637*, pp. 175, 543.

37   PRO, PC 2/48, fo. 229v; *State Trials*, iii. 1317–18. For the printing of Prynne on the
       continent, see: K. Sprunger, *Trumpets from the Tower. English Puritan Printing in the Netherlands,
       1600–1640* (Leiden, 1994), pp. 98–101, 102–6, 200–4, 206, 211; A.F. Johnson, 'The
       'Cloppenburg' press, 1640, 1641', *The Library* 5th series, 13 (1958), pp. 280–2.

38   Foster, *Caroline Underground*, p. 49; Bodl. MS Tanner 68, fos. 9v, 10v, 283v; B[ritish]
       L[ibrary], Harleian MS 390, fo. 455; T. Webster, *Godly Clergy in Early Stuart England*
       (Cambridge, 1997), p. 87.

39   Sprunger, *Trumpets from the Tower*, pp. 119–24, 144–55, 153, 158–9, 163, 215–17; PRO, SP
       84/152, fos. 219–20; SP 84/154, fos. 151v–2; SP 16/387, fo. 148v.

40   PRO, SP 16/387, fo. 148v; H. Carter, 'Archbishop Laud and scandalous books from
       Holland', in *Studia Bibliographica in Honorem Herman De La Fontaine Verwey* (Amsterdam, 1966),
       pp. 43–55; K. Sprunger, 'Archbishop Laud's campaign against Puritanism at The Hague',
       Church History 44 (1975), pp. 308–20.

41   Foster, *Caroline Underground*, p. 63; S.K. Jones and J.R. Harris, *The Pilgrim Press* (Cambridge,
       1922); see also: *CSPD 1623–5*, p. 163.

42   *CSPD 1637*, pp. 174–5; Bodl. MS Bankes 18, fos. 41–3.

43   *CSPD 1637*, p. 175; *A Divine Tragedie Lately Acted* ([London], 1636), sig. A2. Initial letters
       were a key means of identifying printers, and in 1572, Matthew Parker can be shown to
       have been involved in casting a new initial printing letter, at a cost of 40 marks, in order
       to avoid detection of his propaganda: J. Bruce and T.T. Perowne, eds, *Correspondence of
       Matthew Parker* (Parker Society, Cambridge, 1853), pp. 411–12.

44   PRO, SP 14/144, fos. 12–13v. See: *CSPD 1628–9*, pp. 525, 538, 563, 569; Webster, *Godly
       Clergy*, pp. 87, 243.

45   Trevor-Roper, *Archbishop Laud*, p. 164; Gardiner, ed., *Documents*, p. 58.

46   *CSPD 1637*, p. 49. The men were: William Wakelyn, John Ashe, the grocer William
       Bankes, a silenced minister from Coleman Street called Rice Boys, a button seller called
       George Kendall, a merchant called Edward Manning, Randall Boracy, Harmon Sheath, a

bodymaker called Samuel Richardson, Peter Wetherick, a butcher from Cheapside called Richard Rogers, a gunsmith called William Watson, a pewterer from Old Jewry called Thomas Jackson, Edmund Chillenden, and the ironmonger William Chaverton, as well as Robert Reeve, a silkman in Friday Street and churchwarden of Burton's parish. See: Foster, *Caroline Underground*, p. 53; T. Birch, ed., *The Court and Times of Charles I* (2 vols, London, 1848), ii. 273; T. C. Dale, *Members of City Companies in 1641* (London, 1934), pp. 96, 140, 144, 181; PRO, PC 2/48, fos. 179, 226. Rogers was accused of sending a copy to Nicholas Trye, a shopkeeper in Knightsbridge, in the diocese of Exeter, as was James Ouldham, a turner in Westminster Hall: Longleat, Whitelocke Papers vii, fos. 90v–2; *State Trials*, iii. 1324.

47   *CSPD 1639*, pp. 220, 358–9; *CSPD 1639–40*, p. 216; PRO, PC 2/50, fos. 189, 201; *CSPD 1637–8*, pp. 26–7.

48   Birch, ed., *Court and Times*, ii. 274; Somerset Record Office, DD/PH 221/25–6.

49   H[istorical] M[anuscripts] C[ommission], *Third Report* (Nendeln, 1979), p. 191; Longleat, Whitelocke Papers vii, fos. 86, 90. For Dugdale, Cooper, and Parsons, see: Longleat, Whitelocke Papers vii, fos. 90v–92.

50   Longleat, Whitelocke Papers vii, fos. 86, 87v.

51   Longleat, Whitelocke Papers vii, fos. 87, 88–88v.

52   Longleat, Whitelocke Papers vii, fos. 86, 89r–v, 90; HMC, *Third Report*, p. 191. He claimed, as others had done, that he had burnt perhaps 100 copies after he heard it was dangerous, and that he also forwarded a copy to Laud: *CSPD 1636–7*, pp. 393–4.

53   *CSPD 1637*, p. 49.

54   Laud, *Works*, vi. 497.

55   Bodl. MS Bankes 13, fo. 18; Bodl. MS Bankes 18, fo. 33.

56   *State Trials*, iii. 1315, 1317–18.

57   PRO, PC 2/49, fos. 55v, 56–56v; Longleat, Whitelocke Papers vii, fo. 213.

58   R.A. Marchant, *The Puritans and the Church Courts in the Diocese of York 1560–1642* (London, 1960), pp. 102–5, 232–3; Borthwick Institute, York, CP.H. 2046.

59   *CSPD 1637*, p. 582.

60   *CSPD 1637–8*, pp. 64, 139, 142. For support for the three Puritans in the godly community, see: J. Fielding, 'Opposition to the personal rule of Charles I: the diary of Robert Woodford, 1637–1641', in P. Gaunt, ed., *The English Civil War* (Oxford, 2000), pp. 115, 118.

61   E.W. Kirby, *William Prynne* (Cambridge, Mass., 1931), p. 38; W. Knowler, ed., *The Earl of Strafforde's Letters* (2 vols, London, 1739), ii. 57; *CSPD 1638–9*, pp. 586–7.

62   *CSPD 1639–40*, p. 566.

63   *CSPD 1638–9*, p. 499; N. Wallington, *Historical Notices of Events Occurring Chiefly in the Reign of Charles I* (2 vols, London, 1869), i. xxxvii–xlvi.

64   PRO, SP 16/448, fos. 93–4.

65   HMC, *Fifth Report* (Nendeln, 1979), p. 91; L[ords] J[ournals] vi. 97; C[ommons] J[ournals] ii. 158; *CJ* iii. 94; *LJ* v. 447.

66   Cambridge University Library, Dd.VIII.33, fo. 75v. I owe this reference to Patrick Little. In September 1638 Sir Archibald Johnston recorded reading Prynne's *Unbishoping of Timothy and Titus*. G.M. Paul, ed., *Diary of Sir Archibald Johnston of Wariston 1632–1639* (Scottish History Society, 61, 1911), p. 378.

67   Bodl. MS Bankes 63, fo. 42.

68   Laud, *Works*, vi. 497; Laud, *Works*, vii. 372–4.

69   PRO, PC 2/48, fo. 102v; HMC, *Twelfth Report II* (London, 1888), p. 167; *CSPD 1637*, p. 44; PRO, SP 16/367, fo. 129; Gardiner, ed., *Proceedings*, pp. 66–7.

70   Condick, 'Bastwick', p. 138.

71   *CSPD 1637*, pp. 433–4; PRO, SP 16/368, fos. 24r–v; PRO, PC 2/48, fo. 180; Trevor-Roper, *Archbishop Laud*, p. 323; Prynne, *New Discovery*, p. 92.

72   *CSPD 1638–9*, pp. 214–15. See also: *CSPD 1637*, p. 209; Webster, *Godly Clergy*, p. 231.

73   Trevor-Roper, *Archbishop Laud*, p. 323; *CSPD 1637*, p. 403; Knowler, ed., *Strafforde's Letters*, ii. 115. See: M. Aston, 'Puritans and iconoclasm, 1560–1660', in C. Durston and J. Eales, eds., *The Culture of English Puritanism, 1560–1700* (London, 1996), p. 110; BL, Harleian MS 165, fos. 21–3. See also: Prynne, *New Discovery*, pp. 91–109; Lambeth Palace Library, MS 943, p. 559.

74   *Cheshire Sheaf* 3 (1883), pp. 9, 13, 32–3; Prynne, *New Discovery*, pp. 218–20, 222. For Bostock: *The Register of Admissions to Gray's Inn* (2 vols, London, 1889), i. 196; R.J. Fletcher, ed., *The Pension Book of Gray's Inn* (2 vols, London, 1901–10), i. 327.

75   Borthwick Institute, HC.CP. 1637/4; *CSPD 1638–9*, p. 220; Marchant, *Puritans and the Church Courts*, p. 54n; Lambeth Palace Library, MS 943, p. 554; *Cheshire Sheaf* 3, pp. 32–3. See also: Chester Archives, Assembly Book (AB) 2, fo. 42v. For Bridgeman's letters, see: Prynne, *New Discovery*, pp. 94–5, 218–26.

76   *Cheshire Sheaf* 3, p. 9; J.S. Burn, *The High Commission* (London, 1865), p. 65; PRO, PC 2/48, fo. 142. For the pictures, see: Bridgeman's letter to the archbishop of York in November 1637: *Cheshire Sheaf* 3, p. 13.

77   *Cheshire Sheaf* 3, pp. 32–3; Prynne, *New Discovery*, p. 224; *CSPD 1637*, p. 492; Burn, *High Commission*, pp. 64–5. For Ince, see: D. Nuttall, *The Book Trade in Cheshire to 1850* (Liverpool Bibliographical Society, 1992), p. 22.

78   Burn, *High Comission*, pp. 63–4; Prynne, *New Discovery*, p. 102.

79   *Cheshire Sheaf* 1 (1878), pp. 20–1; W. Prynne, *The Antipathie of the English Lordly Prelacie* (2 vols, London, 1641), i. 223.

80   On the fact that the Chester men had defied no known laws or orders: Prynne, *Antipathie*, ii. 290–1; Prynne, *New Discovery*, pp. 91–3.

81   Aston, 'Puritans and iconoclasm', p. 110. See: Prynne, *New Discovery*, pp. 103–7; Prynne, *Antipathie*, ii. 290–1.

82   For family traditions see: J. Eales, 'A road to revolution: the continuity of Puritanism', in Durston and Eales, eds, *Culture of English Puritanism*, pp. 200–1.

83   Laud, *Works*, iii. 230, 299–300.

84   M. Stieg, *Laud's Laboratory* (London, 1982), pp. 106, 297–302; Somerset RO, DD/PH 221/25–6; Lambeth Palace Library, MS 943, pp. 481, 485–510. See: T.G. Barnes, 'County politics and a Puritan cause célèbre: Somerset church ales, 1633', *Transactions of the Royal Historical Society*, fifth series 9 (1959), pp. 103–22.

85   Somerset RO, DD/PH 221/20.

86   N. Tyacke, *The Fortunes of English Puritanism, 1603–1640* (London, 1990), pp. 8, 14; Longleat, Whitelocke Papers vii, fo. 213.

87   Tyacke, *Fortunes*, pp. 8, 14.

88   *CSPD 1640–1*, p. 210.

89   Foster, *Caroline Underground*, p. 63.

90   Condick, 'Bastwick', pp. 50–1, 53.

91   Condick, 'Bastwick', pp. 54–61.

92   Foster, *Caroline Underground*, pp. 42–3.

93   Foster, *Caroline Underground*, p. 57.

94   *Cheshire Sheaf* 3, p. 9.

95   *Cheshire Sheaf* 3, p. 13.

96   *Cheshire Sheaf* 3, pp. 32–3; Prynne, *New Discovery*, p. 224.

97   R.C. Richardson, *Puritanism in North-West England* (Manchester, 1972), p. 137.

98   Aston, 'Puritans and iconoclasm', p. 100. See: BL, Harleian MS 6607 ('A godly profitable collection of divers sentences out of Holy scripture… by that deare and faithfull servant of God, John Bruen').

99   For Clarke see: Richardson, *Puritanism*, pp. 122, 187.

100   Aston, 'Puritans and iconoclasm', p. 100; S. Hindle, *The State and Social Change in Early Modern England, 1550–1640* (Basingstoke, 2002), pp. 66–7.

101   W. Hinde, *A Faithfull Remonstrance of the Holy Life and Happy Death of John Bruen* (London, 1641), p. 113; J. Eales, *Puritans and Roundheads* (Cambridge, 1990), pp. 54, 78; BL, Additional MS 70002, fo. 134; Hindle, *State and Social Change*, p. 201.

102   Hinde, *Faithfull Remonstrance*, p. 185.

103   Richardson, *Puritanism*, pp. 95, 137.

104   R. Steward-Brown, ed., *Cheshire Inquisitions Post Morten… 1603–1660* (Record Society of Lancashire and Chesire, 84, 1934), pp. 92–5.

105   W. Hinde, *A Plaine and Familiar Exposition of the Fifteenth, Sixteenth and Seventeenth Chapters* (London, 1611), sig. A2; W. Hinde, *A Plaine and Familiar Exposition of the Eighteenth, Nineteenth and Twentieth Chapters* (London, 1611), sig. ¶3; W. Hinde, *A Plaine and Familiar Exposition of the Ninth and Tenth Chapters of the Proverbs of Salomon* (London, 1612), sigs. A3, A3v; W. Hinde, *A Plaine and Familiar Exposition of the Eleventh and Twelfth Chapters of the Proverbs of Salomon* (London, 1612), sigs. A3, A3v; W. Hinde, *A Plaine and Familiar Exposition* (London, 1615), sig. A2; W. Hinde, *The Office and Use of the Morall Law of God* (London, 1622), sig. B; W. Hinde, *A Path to Pietie* (Oxford, 1613), sig. *2. In 1614 Dod and Hinde published *Bathshebaes Instructions*, which was also dedicated to Saye: *Bathshebaes Instructions* (London, 1614), sig. A3. For the Banbury circle, see: C. Durston and J. Eales, 'Introduction', in Durston and Eales, eds. *Culture of English Puritanism*, p. 29; Collinson, 'Lectures by combination', p. 484.

106   J. Reinolds, *The Prophecie of Obadiah* (Oxford, 1613), sig A2; Dr. I.R of Queen's College, *The Discovery of the Man of Sinne* (Oxford, 1614), sig. ¶2.

107   Tyacke, *Fortunes*, p. 21.

108   Tyacke, *Fortunes*, p. 20; N. Tyacke, 'The rise of Puritanism and the legalising of dissent, 1571–1719', in O.P. Grell, J.I. Israel and N. Tyacke, eds, *From Persecution to Toleration* (Oxford, 1991), p. 27.

Chapter 8

The Closest Bond: Conspiracy in Seventeenth-Century French Tragedy

Malina Stefanovska

Aujourd'hui l'on s'assemble, aujourd'hui l'on conspire
Corneille[1]

With the exception of Machiavel and of the libertine thinkers inspired by his thought, the political philosophy of the early modern period did not provide many critical insights into the issue of the bond between ruler and subjects. Contemplating the monarchy as an immutable divine construct, it elaborated an ideal in which the king was defined as the father of his people, with identical interests.[2] It was from this perspective that thinkers sought to define notions of sovereignty or reason of state, referred to the fundamental laws of the Kingdom and gave moral precepts for the art of ruling.[3] One notable exception in which the subjects' relationship to the ruler came to the fore was the entitlement to fight or depose a heretical prince, a usurper, or a tyrant, affirmed by the sixteenth-century 'monarchomachs', whether Protestant or extreme Catholics, and sometimes supported by representatives of the Catholic Church in its conflict with Protestantism (as was the case with the Jesuit authors Mariana, Molina and Suarez).[4] The vertical and horizontal bonds that constituted a political community were represented and problematised on stage, particularly in the conspiracy tragedies, popular in the early seventeenth century.[5]

No doubt, theatrical fashion was rooted in historical reality: a reign such as Louis XIII's, framed on the one side by Henry IV's assassination and on the other by the Fronde, and rocked by numerous plots against Richelieu or the king himself[6] would privilege literary interest in faction politics and conjuring. That conspiring was a preoccupation if not an outright obsession is testified to by the sheer number of French nouns, accompanied by related verbs and adjectives, today largely forgotten, belonging to that lexical field: conjuration, *conspiration, complot, ligue, brigue, cabale, faction, parti, intrigue, machination, menée, sédition*.[7] Any opposition to the prince, whether in theory or in practice, was termed conspiring. Indeed, taken in its broader sense as a concerted and secret group effort to advance one's interests, faction making designated a courtier's everyday activity. In certain cases, the term 'sedition' was even used metaphorically for the inner turmoil of passions central to seventeenth-century views of the self.[8] Literary testimonies of real or fictional plots abound in aristocratic memoirs, theatre, history writing, and in the emerging historical novel. But the relationship to theory is no less compelling. If 'conspiracy tragedies' constituted an important subcategory within classical plays it is no doubt because their subject matter enabled the staging of some crucial questions for early modern political thought: the legitimacy of power, the balance between sovereignty and individual rights or between expediency (and secrecy) and the law, the quality of the political bonds in the community and the related distinction between public and private interests. The theory of Divine right monarchy which rested on an entirely idealised figure of the Prince needed a theme and a figure for representing the practical problems of political action and political bonds. And that theme was conspiracy.

I will examine here three French tragedies written in the mid-seventeenth century and constructed around conspiracy: Corneille's *Cinna* (1640–1641), Tristan L'Hermite's *Seneca's Death* (1644), and Cyrano de Bergerac's *The Death of Agrippina* (1654). The conspiracy motif enables each playwright to explore such notions as political legitimacy and the conflict between public and private interests.[9] Corneille uses it to stage the birth of an idealised absolutist prince and State, while the two libertine writers question (Tristan L'Hermite) or entirely delegitimise (Cyrano de Bergerac) the public, political sphere. It is not insignificant that, chronologically speaking, these three plays span the period of the Fronde in which such issues were at the forefront of public preoccupations.

Corneille's *Cinna or the Clemency of Caesar-Augustus*, premiered in 1640–1641 by the already established author of *Le Cid*, and *Horace*, was Corneille's greatest success and one of the most successful plays of the entire century. As its title suggests, the play has a double focus. Its two heroes, the plotting subject (Cinna) and the Emperor-usurper (Octavius-Caesar-Augustus), as well as its symmetrical repetition of the conspiracy motif give it a dual structure. The play also stages a duel of a sort, won by Augustus over Cinna through his clemency which, in a critic's terms, derives from more than simple generosity or politics, it 'is the very defining feature of the king and the State'.[10]

In this tragedy Corneille emphasises the political, public scope of the conspiracy planned against the emperor Augustus by Emilia (his adoptive daughter), Cinna (his favourite and her lover) and Maximus (another favourite of the emperor and an undeclared suitor to Emilia). From the outset, as a

Corneille scholar notes, the theatrical figure that Corneille decides to stage points to issues of legitimacy: 'The emperor, unlike the king, is not a dynastic, hereditary figure but one whose political powers inhere in his sole person. The imperial system ... repeatedly calls into question the legitimacy of the one who rules, for every successive emperor must justify his rise'.[11] This questioning is amplified when we learn that Augustus himself has come to power through repeated violence and represents a usurper figure commonly dramatised in the period's plays, including the two discussed below. Cinna and Emilia both act out of a wish to avenge her father's and his relatives' assassinations by Augustus. However, their motives soon appear less clear-cut than at first. Corneille's originality consists in presenting the Emperor at a moment of a political and personal crisis: his legitimacy is called into question not only by the conjurors, but by himself as well. Haunted by the torrents of blood spilled in order to acquire power, he wishes to relinquish it and shares his intent with Cinna and Maximus. When asked for their advice, the two favourites take opposite stands, demonstrating the inextricable mixture of private and public interests: Maximus argues in favour of Caesar's decision, but out of private, egotistical motives. He wants to gain Emilia's love by any means and believes (wrongly) that she will be satisfied by an abdication. Later, the same private passion will make him betray the other conjurors. Cinna on the other hand advises Augustus to stay in power so as to prevent the nobility's recurrent squabbling and their 'bloody alliances'. But he does so with a devious intent as well: he wishes to avenge both Rome and Emilia, and Augustus' abdication would make his plot pointless. For him as well, the public is enmeshed with the private since his conspiracy, while planned for the good of Rome, would also bring him personal glory and Emilia's hand.

Let us examine the characters' motives a little closer: conjuring against a tyrant could be justified by the public good, but in this case, each particular combination of interests is played against the entirely public stance eventually taken by Augustus as he overcomes his private passions. Cinna is not completely unjustified, since Augustus himself had initially seized the throne violently, in transgression of the law, thus earning the name of a usurper and a tyrant. However, Cinna's reasons for plotting are mixed, value and interest driven, since he is fighting both for the freedom of Rome and for Emilia's hand. Although the conspiracy involves many Romans, he is aware that its moral and political justification hinges upon success:

> Demain j'attends la haine ou la faveur des hommes,
> Le nom de parricide ou de libérateur,
> César celui de prince ou d'un usurpateur.
> Tomorrow I shall win men's hate or favour,

> The name of monster or deliverer,
> Caesar the name of great prince or usurper. (250–2)

Cinna shows an awareness that his acts will be reinterpreted, thus giving primacy to historical change over intemporal ethics.[12] His motives, predominantly political at the outset, turn increasingly personal as the play progresses, a fact which makes him less and less justifiable. The impure mixture is connoted by the double meaning of the 'vows' - matrimonial and conspiratorial - exchanged between the two young people.

Emilia, for her part, is driven by the filial duty of avenging her father's murder. This familial duty is of a higher ethical order than a personal interest such as ambition.[13] Moreover, resentments such as hers can have a political impact when they multiply, as Emilia's confidante remarks when advising her mistress to let others act for her: 'He who lives hated by all, cannot live for long' (Qui vit hai de tous ne saurait longtemps vivre, 89–94). Still, her motives are mixed: they rest on the feudal values of reciprocity and revenge, criticized by Corneille a few years earlier, in *Le Cid*. Moreover, her wish for personal glory intrudes into the feeling of duty:

> Joignons à la douceur de venger nos parents,
> La gloire qu'on remporte à punir les tyrans,
> Et faisons publier par toute l'Italie,
> 'La liberté de Rome, est l'oeuvre d'Emilie'
> (Let us unite the pleasure of a parent's
> Avengement with the glory that one gains
> By punishing a tyrant. Let us cause it
> To be proclaimed throughout all Italy:
> 'Emilia hath achieved Rome's liberty'. (107–10)

A further intrusion of the private in the political plot demonstrates Emilia's inability to rise up to public considerations: being a woman, she must entrust Cinna with the physical act of assassination in exchange for which she promises to marry him. However, by doing so, she involves personal interest in an act of moral revenge. Her rightfulness is further put into doubt by her particular status as an adoptive daughter to Augustus after her father's murder. She justifies her lack of attachment to him by the call of blood, for being moved by kindness is 'to sell one's flesh and blood' (84). Emilia is thus contemplating what would be considered a double parricide - of her ruler and her father - an act for which she makes herself into a prize. This does not leave her relationship to Cinna intact: they have now entered into a mercantile exchange, one which duplicates the relationship of passion but might kill it too. The seeds of their disunion become more visible as Cinna, moved by Augustus' wish to give up power, hesitates to commit the murder while Emilia relentlessly pushes on.

Finally, as we have seen, Maximus' double betrayal is motivated by the basest kind of self-interest, concupiscence. If a conspiracy can be justified by satisfying public interest and strengthening a political alliance against a tyrant, then this one fails on both accounts.

Neither is it justifiable, for that matter, by Augustus' actual governance. Although his ascent to power is rooted in violence, he strove to rule justly since. In the argument set forth to convince him to remain in power, Cinna draws the distinction between a usurper and a tyrant, valid in political theory at large and established through historical practice:

> ... et tous les conquérants
> Pour être usurpateurs, ne sont pas des tyrans
> Quand ils ont sous leurs lois asservi des provinces,
> Gouvernant justement, ils s'en font justes princes
> Thy arms have conquered Rome, and not all conquerors
> Are tyrants merely by usurping power.
> When they reduce a country to obedience
> And govern justly, they are hence true princes. (423–6)

Though less pressing in Corneille's times since the French dynasty was stable and based on the 'fundamental laws of the kingdom', the figure of the usurper harked back to the earlier religious wars and was central in all early modern political debates.[14] Linked and sometimes conflated with it was the 'tyrant' whose deposition it was legitimate to plot according to the Huguenot thinkers mentioned above. Thus in French political thought, the 'tyran d'Etablissement' was such by unlawfully establishing his power. As Cinna's assertion shows, he could continue being viewed as a tyrant or earn the title of a rightful prince depending on how he ruled.[15] In that respect, as pointed out previously, the Roman Emperor had an exemplary status. More broadly, the usurper could also be taken for the very figure of Machiavelli's 'new prince' who came to power or founded a State, rather than inheriting it. This type of prince in particular had to display the traits recommended by Machiavelli and the theorists of the 'Reason of state'[16] in order to stay in power and successfully govern his newly acquired State: dissimulation, simulation, secrecy, discerning the right moment, understanding political conjunctures, putting himself above the common law, in other terms all the characteristics needed in contemporary politics. To that extent, he could be more efficient than a simple heir to the throne for his State's welfare and stability. In fact, in

Pascal's view, this figure would actually stand for any ruler including the rightful king since all political power stems from an initial usurpation.[17]

For Corneille, however, Augustus' initial usurpation placed him at the mercy of an endless cycle of familial and political revenge, infighting and murder. In his first famous tragedy, *Le Cid*, Don Fernando, the king, explained to his nobility that a royal art of ruling consisted in overcoming such a feudal honour code in order to spare his subjects' lives. But Don Fernando was not directly involved in the familial vendetta acted out by Don Rodrigo and his beloved Chimena. Here, on the other hand, Corneille first placed the usurper-emperor in the midst of the revenge cycle, then proceeded to set him above it. His initial coming to power bears an uncanny resemblance to this conspiracy so that the entire tragedy can be viewed as framed by two plots of which the latter intends to neutralise the former, yet uses the same means: secrecy, lawlessness, murder. The double bind in which Augustus' plea for advice places the two conjurors is only matched by his own, since he is a usurper who comes to question his own legitimacy. After gradually learning that he has been betrayed by all those he considered closest to him, Augustus is finally the one who unties the Gordian knot of revenge, self-interest and moral remorse plaguing all the protagonists, and who thus gives legitimacy to his political power. In a famous monologue in which he sheds his private self (Octavius) for the public figure of Augustus, the Emperor decides to rise above the logic of revenge and show kingly clemency. Instead of punishing the conjurors, he forgives them and showers them with favours: Cinna with the consulate, Emilia with the permission to marry him, Maximus with a governorship. His astounding generosity has immense consequences. Firstly, it sways the conjurors and creates new bonds of love and respect towards him. The broader political implications are spelled out by the Empress Livia in the form of a prophecy announced to her by the Gods. Indeed, Augustus' overcoming of his justifiable human passions (indignation and thirst for revenge) will represent the mythical birth of the rightful ruler in the usurper and potential tyrant and the final eradication of all conspiracies:

> Oyez ce que les Dieux vous font savoir par moi,
> De votre heureux destin c'est l'immuable loi.
> Après cette action vous n'avez rien à craindre:
> On portera le joug désormais sans se plaindre,
> ... Jamais plus d'assassins ni de conspirateurs,
> Vous avez trouvé l'art d'être maître des coeurs,
> Rome, avec une joie et sensible et profonde,
> Se démet en vos mains de l'empire du monde.
> ... Elle n'a plus de voeux que pour la monarchie

... Hear what the gods
Would have thee know through me. Thus they decree
Unalterably thy happy destiny:
After this, thou hast nothing more to fear.
Without complaining, men will wear thy yoke,
And the most stubborn will renounce all plots
And think it glorious to die thy subjects.
No shameful purpose, no ungrateful envy,
Will e'er assail so fair a life. Henceforward
There shall be no assassins nor conspirers,
For thou hast learned the way to rule men's hearts.
Rome with a joy both keen and deep consigns
Unto thy hands the empire of the world.
... Her mind from ancient error wholly free,
She now desireth naught but monarchy. (1755–1770)

The happy end also represents the erasure of the conspiracy around which the play was built. Corneille creates, as critics have remarked, a founding figure who uncannily resembles the absolutist king by reconciling the rightfulness of his governance with his status as 'ab-solutus', i.e. independent from the law. Giving up private revenge makes Augustus similar to the idealised construct of the absolutist King whose interests were deemed necessarily identical to those of his people.[18]

It is interesting to note here that Augustus's generosity prevents him from falling into another trap which would delegitimise his rule and which, tellingly, is advocated by Maximus, Cinna's co-conspirator and counterfoil. Advising Augustus to keep the Empire, Maximus defines it as his private possession:

Rome est à vous, Seigneur, l'empire est votre bien,
Chacun en liberté peut disposer du sien,
Il le peut à son choix garder ou s'en défaire,
Vous seul ne pourriez pas ce que peut le vulgaire.
Rome is thine, sire; the empire
Is thy possession. Everyone can freely
Dispose of his own property. As he chooses,
He can retain it or be rid of it.
Couldst thou not do as private persons can? (451–4)

The French term Seigneur (Lord, rather than sire) that he uses, although entirely appropriate to address a prince as well, connotes more precisely the option that he presents to Augustus: to rule as an ordinary, private individual [le vulgaire] over his possessions [votre bien]. Such a government was defined in 1613 by the Loyseau who draws a parallel between the public 'Seigneurie' where the Prince holds an *imperium* or *dominatio* over his subjects, and the private one where the Lord holds *dominium*, or *sieurie*, over his slaves, i.e. human beings considered as his property.[19] This legal theorist contrasts them with the office of a sovereign prince. In distinction to the unlimited right of a private master over his property, the latter is limited by the fundamental laws of the kingdom, which means that the Sovereign Prince is a keeper and not the owner of the Crown and that he cannot bequeath it at his personal will. As we can see from the terms used by Maximus, he considers the Empire Augustus' private property and thus - although it is unclear how he stands in Roman jurisprudence - he goes directly against the French early modern understanding of kingship and sovereignty. While he might appear as taking sides against conspiracy, his advice would have led Augustus to pattern his acts after private interests, like the conspirators. He would in fact have become identical to Maximus himself, perfectly fitting the Aristotelian definition of the term 'despotes': the ruler of a private household.

Augustus, however, chooses complete publicness over private status and methods, and thus turns from a usurper into a just prince. His transformation, or rather his true coming into being instantly strengthens the bonds between him and the conjurors, who will henceforth dedicate themselves either to the private sphere (marriage) or to public affairs, but in a regulated and contained manner (one year of consulate). Their own, horizontal, ties have also improved because they understand and forgive each other, though they are now subordinated to their faithfulness towards Augustus. Sparing his subjects' lives (a freed slave who led Maximus to treason is the only one to die in this tragedy), will enable Augustus to keep a well populated Empire and to successfully rule over it: through his clemency, and by overcoming his private self, Augustus ensures his grip over the hearts and the communion of two orders: the order of persons (Cinna, Emilia, Maximus) and the order of the State.[20] Livia's prophecy explicitly relates his victory to Rome's willingness to bear his 'yoke'. Her apparent slip of tongue when she refers to 'monarchy' instead of Empire shows that Corneille had in mind the legitimacy of the French absolutist monarchy as much as that of the Roman Empire represented on stage.

In this symbolic birth of the prince, conspiracy acts as a matrix of a kind: Augustus' illegal founding moment was a *coup d'état*, likened to conspiracy in early modern political theory.[21] Another, apparently similar scheming against him will enable Corneille to bring to light their respective differences and to better define the limits of the Prince's action: critics have noted that in his theatre symmetry functions as a ruse and serves 'to obfuscate an original dissymmetry that is the mainspring of all absolutist political theory'.[22] It is not surprising that in such a fictional staging of origins, Augustus' founding conspiracy would be instantaneously legitimated and erased from memory by its quasi re-enactment by Cinna. And in this play in which everyone was continuously looking back, the past can finally be laid to rest and the future permitted, as Livia states (le futur est permis). After all, as John Lyons reminds us, the war on the past was a part of absolutist thought in early modern Europe.[23] As well as the mythical phoenix to whom he was likened, the absolutist ruler had no ancestry and no past. He was born by an ultimate act of will.

It goes without saying that *Cinna* is one of Corneille's most optimistic political plays and perfectly sums up the fragile ideological balance of its time. In his tragedy *Les Horaces*, written a couple of years earlier, the birth of Rome out of two inimical factions, Alba and Rome, foregrounds the literary creation of a national unity based on absolutist politics.[24] In this other founding drama a similar motif - political conspiracy - serves to stage the absolutist political sphere and to delineate the limits of its action. It also makes possible a representation of the political bond that grounds the State. *Cinna* has been related by scholars to the unusual and short lived equilibrium of the time when it was composed, for the year 1640 constitutes for France the end point of a relative period of stability.[25] That stability, seemingly sustained by Richelieu's monetary reforms, the calm of the nobility and the recent occupation of Savoy and Turin, was soon to be disrupted by news of Cromwell's revolution, and by the conspiracy and execution of Cinq Mars. Corneille's later conspiracy plays, *La Mort de Pompée*, *Nicomède*, or *Suréna*, will not provide any acceptable model of legitimacy. His views of the political sphere will move closer to the authors examined below.[26]

Seneca's Death, written by Tristan L'Hermite, was the first play premiered by Molière's Illustrious Theater in 1644.[27] The libertine poet and playwright followed Tacitus' recently translated account of a plot against Nero and its brutal suppression. The story is well known: after discovering the broad conspiracy led by Roman notables, the Emperor sentenced to death his former tutor Seneca accused of participating in it. Nero had already revealed his moral monstrosity: he had come to power by plotting against the lawful heir to the throne, Britannicus, whom he poisoned.[28] He later had his own mother, Agrippina, murdered. As well as his predecessor, Corneille, Tristan L'Hermite uses conspiracy to stage issues of political legitimacy and action. Relying on the Roman historian's account, however, he transforms his pessimistic stance into an entirely Manichean perspective: Nero and Sabina Poppea are presented as pure monsters, while Seneca and his wife are given irreproachable moral values (unlike Tacitus, he clears Seneca of the suspicion of conjuring). From the outset, Nero is called a usurper and a tyrant who keeps Rome in fear of his violence. His repeated description as 'odious tyrant' and 'parricidal tyrant' (1226) seems well deserved. Nero himself asserts that he is 'firmly seated in the usurped throne' (Je suis bien affermi dans le Trône usurpé, 8). As opposed to Augustus, there are no intimations that he might have gained any legitimacy during his reign. The conspiracy is planned by Nero's favourite, the senator Sejanus, as well as a large number of prominent figures, such as Lucanus. Though illegitimate as a form of action, it is justified by Nero's immorality and by the large number of Romans involved. Several other factors emphasised by the author contribute to it: it is mentioned that Nero uses foreign soldiers against the Roman 'citizens' thus endangering the national community itself; the conspiracy is said to be carried out for the 'public good' (salut public, 644); to put Seneca to death, the emperor decides to use an 'oblique way', namely poison, for fear of having to face public hatred (se charger de la haine publique, 138); he voices his fears that the Senate would 'prompt the Romans to conspire for his fall' (ne pousse les Romains à conspirer ma perte, 150). In fact, in an extended exposition of his fears, Nero seems to develop the entire theoretical situation described by the monarchomachs as justifying the deposition of a usurper. So does another conjuror who, alluding to Caesar's assassination, states that sometimes Gods use Humans in order to punish Tyrants (pour punir les Tyran, les Dieux ... se sont servis des hommes, 617). These, in fact, are the exact terms used by the Huguenot resistance theorists mentioned above. Nero speaks fearfully of the people of Rome:

> Ce farouche animal, sujet au changement
> Commence a s'ennuyer de mon gouvernement
> Et pourrait essayer de se mettre en franchise,
> Si mes déportements lui donnaient quelque prise.
> This savage beast, prone to change
> Is starting to be bothered by my rule
> And it could try to free itself from me
> If my conduct gives it a valid reason. (140)[29]

Through such details the usurper Nero is presented as occupying a precarious, unstable position which forces him to act covertly. He thus remains close to a conjuror in his strategy and never acquires the prominent stature and public character necessary for ruling the Empire. To the contrary of Corneille's Augustus, he has no room for issues of legitimacy, only for those of efficiency. Sabina Poppea's advice to him - 'To ensure a throne, one must be ready to/ Confound at times the innocent and the guilty' (Pour s'assurer d'un throne, il faut être capable/ De confondre par fois innocent et coupable, 37) - seems a direct echo of Machiavelli's or Naudé's reflections on the expediency of political action. He is easily convinced to strike defensively and to condemn Seneca upon unfounded suspicion. One can see how his lack of legitimacy breeds an endless cycle of fear and defence of which this conspiracy is only one manifestation.

The leader and soul of the plot against Nero is a woman, Epicaris, who remains defiant until the end. This is where Tristan L'Hermite parts most significantly from his source, since he presents Epicaris in an entirely positive light, while Tacitus wrote that she was a liberated slave who, in his words, 'had not had a single decent thought until then.' Indeed, in spite of the play's title, Epicaris seems to dispute the central role accorded to Seneca: while he appears in only two scenes, she is present in six and demonstrates undisputed civic values to which she subordinates everything else. Thus, for instance, in act II, scene 3, she refuses Lucanus's advances and reprimands him explicitly:

Aussi toute l'amour qu'il faut que l'on s'explique,
Doit avoir pour objet la liberté publique
C'est ce qui des grands coeurs eschauffe les desirs,
Et qui doit t'obliger a pousser des soûpirs.
For any love that one would want to voice,
Must have one goal, solely public freedom
Great men's desires are solely 'roused by it,
And it alone should cause all of your sighs. (549–52)

Epicaris' motives for conjuring are entirely selfless, and she describes in details all the emperor's misdeeds which justify her act. Her lines have the form of complete public speeches addressed to the city, the people, the women of Rome, the sacred values of Rome, the entire world. The only character to be physically tortured at the end of the play, she reveals nothing and even keeps enough strength to defy Nero and insult Sabina Poppea. Epicaris is likened to a goddess of freedom sent from elsewhere to inspire and bring together the conjurors. Although described as an illustrious beauty, she is also presented as free from any personal bonds that could dampen her courage and influence her acts. It is not unlikely that her role owes less to Tacitus than to the early modern idealization of strong women and to the perception that they were a socializing factor in the community. This is strongly reinforced by the epithet that Pison attaches to her, that of a 'Généreuse Amazone' whose usage was particularly inflected in seventeenth-century France.[30] Epicaris helps view this conspiracy as a means to reinforce ties between the citizens who oppose a tyrant. Such bonds, however, are not all presented as unproblematic: unlike Epicaris, other conjurors realise that the planned assassination creates a conflict between their public and private selves. Aware that their plot needs public legitimation, Sejanus, one of the conjurors, thus suggests to murder Nero in front of the theatre, 'and take a public revenge for a public insult' (Et venger en public une injure publique, 458). But the main hero Seneca unsuccessfully pleads to be allowed to retire to a private status and life and, though aware of Nero's evil character, refuses to plot against his former pupil because of the private attachment he still feels toward him. Pison, another would-be conjuror, refuses to carry on as well for fear that Nero would take revenge on his wife. He complains to Rufus: 'Do you wish that my audacity/ Bring death to my wife and all my progeny?' (Veux-tu que mon audace/Face périr ma femme avec toute ma race?, 1239–40). Finally, Lucanus confirms that he loves the Republic, but yearns for Epicaris as well (553). When the conjurors discover that Nero suspects them, they demonstrate different levels of civic fortitude: some show fear, others become traitors, others yet, like Epicaris, remain constant. Seneca accepts his death sentence with clearheadedness and stoicism. In this play, conspiracy is presented in a positive light, as can be seen from the following question addressed by one conjuror to another:

> Auquel des deux partis vois-tu plus d'asseurance,
> Et lequel est le plus digne de confiance,
> Te semble plus traitable et paroist plus humain,
> Du Tiran parricide, ou du Peuple Romain?
> Which of the parties do you deem the surest,
> And which is more deserving of your trust,
> Which seems to you more sensible and human,
> The tyrant parricide, or the Roman people? (1223–6)

And yet, plotting is also a heuristic device to test the integrity of the participants' political commitment. Seneca's role and speech indeed show its limits and the superiority of the private self over politics. Unlike Augustus in *Cinna*, he puts his personal reputation above the ruin of his country and does not want to be considered ungrateful, as is the tyrant who accuses him. Indeed, when he refuses to participate in the plot, Seneca covertly alludes to his new interest in Christian doctrine. This political drama thus closes on the criticism of imperial politics and its subordination to higher moral and personal values. On the eve of the Fronde, it stages the moral victory of a strong hero in the face of an unjust State.

In comparison with the above plays, in his *La mort d'Agrippine*,[31] Cyrano de Bergerac adopts an entirely bleak perspective. He constructs a political universe of generalised mistrust, lying and dissimulation, in which all players plot against each other at the same time as they conspire to assassinate the emperor Tiberius. Here is the main plot: Agrippina, the widow of Germanicus, Tiberius' nephew whom he had been forced to adopt and whom he later had murdered, conjures to assassinate the Emperor with Sejanus, a Roman senator and Tiberius' favourite, to whom she promised her hand. Sejanus needs Agrippina to become a legitimate pretender to the throne, since she is of royal blood. She, however, knows that Sejanus is guilty of poisoning Germanicus upon Tiberius' orders and intends to have him killed as well if the plot succeeds. Sejanus has also promised marriage to Livilla, Agrippina's sister in law, in exchange for her help in the conspiracy, and with no intention of honouring it. Livilla, who has already killed her own husband for Sejanus, now wants to remove Agrippina for fear of her revenge. Finally, Tiberius as well intends to have Agrippina murdered fearing that she might conspire against him, and entrusts Sejanus with it. At the end of the play Livilla, enraged by Sejanus' betrayal, ends up betraying to Tiberius the generalized conspiracy in which she participated as well. Thus each character plots against all the others simultaneously. Allies turn out to be enemies and make promises that they do not intend to honour. Dissimulation and simulation, practised by each towards all the others give this play a 'jack-in-the-box' structure, where one conspiracy constantly pops out of another. The reader is constantly surprised by new twists and gets dizzy trying to disentangle them. The dramatic plot is thus also carried out against the implied spectator. Often words uttered by a character can (and get to) be interpreted in two completely opposite ways and the play's tension rests on that ambiguity. For instance, in act III, scene ii, Agrippina whom Tiberius overheard threatening him, justifies herself saying that she was simply narrating her dream. She then uses another example to convince the emperor that words can be misleading when taken out of context:

> Et cependant, Cesar, un fourbe, un lasche, un traistre
> Pour gagner en flateur l'oreille de son Maistre,
> Peut te dire aujourd'hui ... Sejanus te trahit.
> Yet, Caesar, a liar, a coward, a traitor
> Who wishes to flatter his Master's ears,
> Can tell you today... Sejanus betrayed you. (813–15)

As it happens, Sejanus enters the stage in the very space of her caesura, overhears the second half of the line, and thinks that he is being betrayed. He immediately admits to his conspiracy, thus forcing Agrippina to invent a new frame for interpreting this confession:

> On peut te dire pis encor de luy, de moy:
> Mais à de tels rapports il est d'un Prince sage,
> De ne pas ecouter un foible tesmoignage.
> People can tell you worse about him, about me
> But a wise Prince faced with such reports
> Ought not to listen to weak testimonies. (823–5)

Such reversals and double entendres are so common that Tiberius appropriately sums up the entire dramatic plot by exclaiming to his confidant: 'Hear us all compete in feigning' (Mais escoute nous feindre à qui feindra le mieux, 432).

While not directly influenced by the events of the Fronde, *La mort d'Agrippine* successfully depicts a complete breakdown of the political and social bonds that hold together a State. The characters cannot even maintain ties and positions that are in their own interest. Even though Agrippina has serious reasons to plot against Tiberius, she refuses his offer to hand over his political power to her because she interprets it as a lure, and prefers revenge to settlement. Likewise, Tiberius refuses Agrippina's submission while at the same time planning to accuse her of conspiracy. Livilla reveals herself by revealing the plot. There is no moral, political, or even logical justification to the behaviour of the conjurors, who in fact coincide with all of the characters. The tragedy gives a grim picture of the political sphere and shows that it is governed by greed, lies and evil, but offers neither a way out of it, nor a redeeming set of private moral values. The constant discursive and linguistic equivocation on which it rests is also an implicit commentary on the impossibility of any effective personal communication. For instance, immediately after Sejanus's confession discussed above, Agrippina helps him convince Tiberius that it was all a misunderstanding, playing on the term's linguistic ambiguity: to the Emperor who exclaims 'Yet Sejanus himself has conjured, he admits it...!' (Mais enfin, Sejanus luy-mesme a conjuré,/ Il l'advoue...), she replies: 'I have conjured your deep wisdom a hundred times/ Not to listen to these cowardly enemies'(J'ay conjuré cent fois ta profonde sagesse, De ne point escouter ces lasches ennemis, 828–30).

There are no heroes, only villains, in this tragedy, and the generalised conspiracy is the dramatic device which asserts their interchangeability. Cyrano de Bergerac's libertine bent asserted in a lengthy defence of a materialist view of death might explain his refusal of any hierarchy crowned by royal power. Yet, in *La Mort d'Agrippine*, this grants no more positive value on the conspiratorial bonds formed against Tiberius. While some plots may be justified by the wish to free the State from a tyrant, in this case the values professed by the conjurors consist solely of ambition, fear or lust for revenge. Generally, a conspiracy at least tests the bonds of secrecy and faithfulness between those involved, but here there are no bonds so to speak, since they are all fake. That is not to say that the tragedy legitimises political power, or claims that accepting a tyrant might at least avoid civil war, which would amount to stressing the vertical bond between the ruler and the ruled over the horizontal ties between the subjects. The final punishment of the conjurors could be interpreted that way, but since Tiberius who has usurped power and acts as a tyrant (he is repeatedly called both) is not presented as any better or more lucid than the others, it is hard to grant him the status of a hero. The outcome of the plot thus does not legitimate its intended victim any more than its perpetrators, if by the end it is clear who belongs to which category. Indeed, according to the editor's introduction, in spite of the tragedy's title, it is not even certain whether Agrippina or Livilla is the one who dies at the end. Conspiracy, no longer used to define a particular form of power or question the political bonds it entails, turns into a *perpetuum mobile*, a permanent machine gone awry in a hell-like universe. Rather than classical tragedy,[32] this play thus comes to resemble the Sartrian afterlife in No Exit (*Huis Clos*) where each character is doomed to keep betraying all the others. The free thinking Cyrano de Bergerac who wrote his play in the turmoil of the civil war in France used the conspiracy motif to represent the downfall of the entire political sphere and of any legitimacy it might carry.

Notes

1   'Today we gather, today we plot', Pierre Corneille, *Cinna ou la Clémence d'Auguste*, verse 139. Quotations in English from *The Chief Plays of Corneille*, transl. by Lacy Lockert (Princeton, 1952), slightly modified.

2   Bossuet can be taken as the mouthpiece of absolutist theory in this respect. See his *Politique tirée des Propres Paroles de l'Ecriture Sainte*, in *Œuvres* (Paris, 1847), vol. 1. Most official or legal texts carried such formulations.

3   See Etienne Thuau, *Raison d'Etat et Pensée Politique à l'époque de Richelieu* (Paris, 1966).

4   Among the *huguenots* who wrote on the subjects' rights to oppose their rulers the best known are Hotman with his *Franco-Gallia* written in 1573, shortly after the Saint Bartholomew's Day massacre of the Protestants in Paris. Théodore de Bèze composed his treatise *Du Droit des Magistrats* that same year in Latin and had it translated into French the following year, and Duplessis-Mornay who in 1579 composed under the pseudonym of Junius Brutus, his *Vindiciae Contra Tyrannos*. The common thread that runs through these three works is their constitutionalist bent, for even according to these radical Protestant authors the right to oppose kings in certain circumstances belongs solely to

magistrates or to persons in official positions, and never to subjects in their private capacity. Their differences lie in the precise definition of such officials. Hotman attributes that right to the Estates General but not to the Parliaments, de Bèze extends it to lower ranks of officers such as hereditary high nobility and to elected magistrates who governed cities, Duplessis-Mornay especially favours the lowest ranks of officials.

5   Bénédicte Louvat, *Poétique de la Tragédie Classique* (Paris, 1997), p. 150 and Georges Couton, *Corneille et la Tragédie Politique* (Paris, 1984). See also a special issue of *Vives Lettres* on 'Complots et coups d'État sur la scène de théâtre, XVIe – XVIIIe siècles', edited by François-Xavier Cuche (4, 1997). Other conspiracy plays include *La Mort de César* by Scudéry, *La Mort de Brute et de Porcie ou La Vengeance de la Mort de César* by Guérin de Bouscal, *Le Grand et Dernier Solyman ou La mort de Mustapha* by Mairet, Racine's *Britannicus*, and *Bajazet* and several of Corneille's later plays such as *La Mort de Pompée, Suréna* etc.

6   Jean-Marie Constant, *Les Conjurateurs. Le Premier Libéralisme Politique sous Richelieu* (Paris, 1987). Arlette Jouanna, *Le Devoir de Révolte: la Noblesse Française et la Gestation de l'Etat Moderne, 1559–1661* (Paris, 1989).

7   *Le Dictionnaire de Furetière* (1690), *le Dictionnaire de l'Académie* (1694).

8   As in Corneille's *Polyeucte*, where the heroine describes her inner turmoil as a tyranny of her passions over her reason: 'And though the outside be without emotions/ The inside is but trouble and sedition' (*Et quoique le dehors soit sans émotion/ le dedans n'est que trouble et que sédition*, v. 503–4, my translation).

9   On this distinction in the seventeenth century thought, as well as on the libertine position, see N.O. Keohane, *Philosophy and the State in France. The Renaissance to the Enlightenment* (Princeton, 1980).

10   Bernard Dort, *Corneille Dramaturge. Essai* (Paris, 1957), p. 60.

11   John Lyons, *The Tragedy of Origins. Pierre Corneille and Historical Perspectives* (Stanford, 1996), p. 74.

12   In his reading of *Horace*, John Lyons calls this position 'historical relativism'. We shall see that it is directly opposed to the unchanging (and positive) moral value attributed to conspiracy in Tristan L'Hermite's play.

13   Revenge as well as the rage which motivates it has a public, political aspect. According to Aristotle, anger does not limit itself to what we call today psychology but is part of a coherent set of public values. On that topic, see the special issue of *Paragraphes* on *La Vengeance dans la Littérature d'Ancien Régime*, ed. Eric Méchoulan (Montréal, 2000).

14   The parallels and differences between the concepts of despot, tyrant and usurper preoccupied many early modern thinkers, from Machiavelli and Naudé, to the Huguenot constitutionalists and Hobbes. See Thuau and Jacques Rancière, *Les Mots de l'Histoire. Essai de Poétique du Savoir* (Paris, 1992), p. 44.

15   The distinction between a tyrant and an absolute king was as subtle as it was crucial: the latter, though above the law, obeyed those of reason, of God and the fundamental laws of the Kingdom. Hence his conduct was predictable to an extent, unlike that of the tyrant or despot who respected no laws and ruled at whim.

16   See Michel Senellart, *Les Arts de Gouverner. Du* Regimen *Médiéval au Concept de Gouvernement* (Paris, 1995), and *Machiavélisme et Raison d'Etat* (Paris, 1989).

17   For Pascal, whose conservative political thought was influenced by Augustine, this made the prince's worldly rule no less legitimate. In his opinion, such worldly matters were not to be addressed by Christians.

18   Such formulations can be commonly found in absolutist spokesmen such as Silhon (quoted in Thuau) or Bossuet.

19   Charles Loyseau, *Traité des Seigneuries*, in *Cinq Livres du Droit des Offices* (Cologne, 1613), p. 11 and below.

20   Michel Prigent, *Le héros et l'Etat dans la Tragédie de Pierre Corneille* (Paris, 1986), p. 67.

21   The general parallel between a plot and a *coup d'Etat*, a highly advised form of action for the prince, is stressed in Gabriel Naudé's *Considérations Politiques sur les Coups d'Etats* (1639).

22   Mitchell Greenberg, *Corneille, Classicism and the Ruses of Symmetry* (Cambridge and London, 1986), p. 10

23   Lyons, p. 75.

24   Ibid.

25   Dort, p. 63.

26   Michel Prigent, (p. 26), sees Corneilles dramatic trajectory as an evolution from 'a providential complementarity between the hero and the State to their fundamental incompatibility'. He relates it to the historical episodes of the aristocratic domination, the Fronde, and Louis XIV's personal rule.

27   Tristan L'Hermite, *La Mort de Seneque*, first published in 1646. Quoted here from *Théâtre du XVIIe siècle*, vol. II, ed. Jacques Truchet (Paris, 1986), my translation.

28   Racine's *Britannicus* (1669), which I will not discuss here, takes up the same story, but with a different focus.

29   I want to note here the positive connotation of the French term *'franchise'*, from which derived the name of Franks, the free Germanic tribe considered to be the ancestors of the French nobility, whereas the Gauls were deemed to be the (bonded) ancestry of the popular classes.

30   This nickname, borrowed from characters depicted in baroque novels, was claimed by Mlle de Montpensier, Louis XIV's cousin and a famous Fronde rebel, in her *Memoirs*.

31   Savinien Cyrano de Bergerac, *La Mort d'Agrippine*, ed. C.J. Gossip (Exeter, 1982), my translation. First published in 1654, the play probably circulated in manuscript form during the Fronde. According to the editor, a *Sejanus* by Ben Johnson was staged in 1603 by Shakespeare's company, but he thinks it unlikely that Cyrano de Bergerac read it. Another *Séjanus* by Jean Magnon was published in France in 1647.

32   Dominique Montcond'huy in 'La tragédie de la conjuration et ses enjeux au XVIIe siècle' *Lettres Vives*, 4, (1997), pp. 65–89 calls this play 'an anti-tragedy of conspiracy'.

Chapter 9

Faults on Both Sides:
The Conspiracies of Party Politics under the Later Stuarts

Mark Knights

In Swift's *Gulliver's Travels* the King of Brobdignag summarises seventeenth century British history as 'only a heap of conspiracies'.[1] Modern commentators have tended to agree and a number of studies have highlighted the way in which plots fostered and reflected a conspiratorial outlook throughout the century.[2] Attention has focused on real or imagined religious conspiracies, with popery or Puritanism (and later, Dissent) playing the role of seditious villain. This conspiratorial mentality continued well into the eighteenth century and, according to Bernard Bailyn and Gordon Wood, was crucial in explaining the American Revolution.[3] But the factors shaping the conspiratorial mindset in the eighteenth century are seen by both Bailyn and Wood as different to those prevailing in the preceding era. Religious conflict was now less important. Rather, Bailyn and Wood studied a fear of corruption and of an authoritarian state power, anxieties that stemmed from 'old Whig' or 'commonwealth' concerns about the decline of virtue and the erosion of independence.[4] The language of old Whiggery and classical republicanism thus articulated a conspiratorial mentality.[5] How, then, should we explain this apparent shift in emphasis and discourse?

Wood offered some very suggestive thoughts in an article specifically about conspiracy in the later seventeenth and early eighteenth century.[6] He claimed that 'more than any other period of English history, the century or so following the restoration [of 1660] was the great era of conspiratorial fears and imagined intrigues'.[7] Wood observed that 'all manner of people in the eighteenth century resorted steadily to conspiratorial modes of explanation and habitually saw plots by dissembling men behind patterns of events'.[8] He suggested that this reflected the attribution of a greater role to individual human agency: everything was seen as the product of will and intention, the concerted design of individuals rather than of directly divine or social and economic forces. Yet, Wood argued, at the same time the political world was becoming both larger (as a politically aware public grew) and more complex (as the fiscal-military state expanded). As a result of this mismatch, 'masquerades and hidden designs formed the grammar and vocabulary for much of the thought of the age …This in turn encouraged an opposition politics dedicated to the unmasking of hypocrisy'. The idea of deception thus closed the gap between men's proclaimed intentions and their contrary actions. It offered a rational explanation at a time when the political world was 'expanding and changing faster than its available rational modes of explanation could handle'.[9] If, then, the clue to an evolving discourse of conspiracy lay in the political world, what was it about that world that was important?

This chapter seeks to answer this by relating conspiracy not so much to republican discourse or fear of popery/Puritanism but to the rage of party after the Revolution of 1689 and to extend Wood's analysis of a dissimulating political culture by focusing on party polemic. This is not to deny the enduring force of both a Puritan/popery or republican model; but rather to emphasis a dimension that has been overlooked. The chapter will thus examine the bitter, publicly contested, conflict between Whig and Tory in the later Stuart period, rather than the Country ideology pursued by Pocock and others. I argue that a language of conspiracy can be found inherent in party political contest, in civic conflict as much as civic humanism and in party polemic as much as republican theory. The conflict between Whig and Tory divided nearly every borough and county, and thus offered a readily accessible framework and shaping discourse.[10] The practice of publicly contested politics was thus important in embedding and developing a conspiratorial mindset. This party-based language of conspiracy did embrace some of the religious rhetoric of the early and mid seventeenth century, not least because Whig and Tory drew on earlier stereotypes of popery and dissent. But the language of party also developed beyond these roots. The public nature of the party contest produced an innovating political culture. Public discourse, particularly when linked to frequent elections, heightened fears that the people were being misled by unscrupulous parties (or at least by their leaders and polemicists). Frequently asked to make choices at elections, the public were now the key target of politicians of both sides of the political divide; and each side came to believe that the public discourse of the other was intrinsically insincere, misrepresentative and manipulative.[11] Once partisan politics are added to Wood's analysis, the political culture he described is more easily explicable and understandable.

I want to make three main points. First, party could be (and often was) conceptualised in conspiratorial terms. The first earl of Halifax famously observed that 'the best party is but a kind of a conspiracy against the rest of the nation'.[12] Those who argued for the illegitimacy of party politics wished for the recovery of a mythical unity, the undermining of which could be explained in terms of a conspiracy. Whilst some of this analysis drew on a Country tradition, as Pocock suggests, Whig and Tory also saw *each other* in terms of conspiratorial groupings. Each party criticised its rival for acting in a conspiratorial manner. Whigs saw Tories as intent on a set of sinister designs (to advance tyranny and/or priestcraft, at home and abroad); and Tories saw Whigs as equally seditious (aiming to destroy the Church, justify resistance against legal authority, and advance their own monied men). Yet such accusations were also part of the political game. In an age of publicly competitive politics, the language of conspiracy was also a tool, a rhetorical ploy that delegitimised a rival party and legitimised one's own claims. This was very important if political allegiances, so necessary in an age of frequent elections, were to be fostered and maintained. There was thus a degree of intentionality about the deployment of such accusations. Separating how far the language shaped outlooks and how far calculation was involved in the choice of language is often a difficult task. But the accusation of conspiracy could certainly be a political weapon as much as a mindset. So Tories and Whigs shared a language of conspiracy with those who rejected party altogether.

This forces us, second, to examine a linguistic struggle and to suggest that language itself might have been contributing to the anxiety about conspiracy. The nature of public discourse, in an age of frequent elections and appeals to the public as umpire, heightened anxiety that language was being misused for partisan purposes. Each party believed the other to be abusing words in order to deceive readers and hence manipulate their allegiances and choices. In a context of frequent elections after the passage of the Triennial Act in 1694, and the lapse of the licensing laws in 1695, each party's writers could (and must) appeal to the people. But each side believed the other to be spinning lies and misrepresentations in order to mislead the people and hence win their votes or weaken their allegiance. In such circumstances words could not be taken at face value. This destabilisation of meaning both reflected and exacerbated a conspiratorial mindset; no meaning was straightforward because of the arts of partisan rhetoricians; but the dissimulation of words in turn heightened a sense of conspiracy, particularly when they appeared to have private or 'cant' meaning. Words, under the pressure of publicly contested politics, had ambiguous and dissimulating meanings. Moreover, if these were not deconstructed for readers, the outcome might be truly serious. For all but five years between 1689 and 1713, England was at war with one of the greatest powers Europe had seen, Louis XIV's France. The parties stood for very different programmes, not only in terms of the war, but also in relation to the nature of the state, the role of the people and Church, and the succession.[13] In these circumstances failure to make the right choice because of being misled by the language of party could be, quite literally, disastrous. So the misrepresentations of print in turn encouraged more use of the press to disabuse the public, creating another vicious spiral of suspicion.

Third, the language of conspiracy had a cultural impact. The anxiety about the power of words to mislead derived from viewing the Civil War as the outcome of mistaking words for things, for Puritan rhetoric and popish flattery of the king had both deluded the people and their governors. Both sides could see the Civil War as clear proof of what happened when men abused language to cover their true design. Such a view of how language could be used conspiratorially was thus to shape the way in which 'the people' were conceptualised and how men ought ideally to converse with one another. Anxiety about conspiracy thus heightened concerns about the public's inability to discern what was true and hence about popular irrationality and susceptibility to manipulation. The public was depicted as too irrational, too dependent and corrupted by partisan feuding, to see through the lies pedalled by their opponents. For the Whigs, the huge outpouring of public support for the High Church Dr Henry Sacheverell in 1710 and the riots of 1715–1716 against the Hanoverian succession seemed proof that the people had been corrupted by the misleading slogans of the Jacobites and High Churchmen. The social and political paternalism of the Hanoverian Whigs was thus in part a reaction to a fear and the language of conspiracy. And reason and rationality seemed to offer one way to cut through and avoid the dangers of excessive partisan passion.

This chapter will develop the first and second of these points more fully than the last, which will be discussed more fully elsewhere.[14] A general argument will be sketched about the conspiratorial nature of partisan politics; and a case study of an extended pamphlet debate in 1710 will attempt to illustrate the argument and illuminate issues to do with the dissimulation, hypocrisy and political lying associated with the conspiracy of party.

The Conspiracy of Party

The backdrop against which all discussion of conspiracy took place in the later Stuart period was the Civil War. Those hostile to party therefore warned of the consequence of division by invoking the memory of intestine war. Thus in 1710 a tract which attacked both parties gave a potted history of the causes of the Civil War because, its author explained:

> It is my intent to shew that from the beginning of our contests to this very time, the zeal and affections of the people have always been kept up by both parties with fair and specious pretences to the publick good, till the heads and leaders of either side could get themselves into the saddle, and then they have driven on their own interests, and left the poor people to shift for themselves till they should have no further occasion to make use of their credulity.[15]

But the memory of the Civil War also shaped how each of the parties viewed the other. The Tories in particular repeatedly claimed that the ancestry of the Whigs lay with the rebels of 1641–1642. For writers sympathetic to the royalist cause the war had been a conspiracy of ambitious, scheming politicians who used the cloak of religion to cover their designs and lure the nation into war. For writers sympathetic to the parliamentarians, on the other hand, the war had equally been the result of a conspiracy, but one located at the early Stuart Court and concerning monarchs and their favourites who sought arbitrary power and the introduction of popery. As Swift put it when speaking for the Tories in *The Examiner* in 1710, 'We charge the [Whigs] with a design of destroying the establish'd church and introducing fanaticism and freethinking in its stead. We accuse them as enemies to Monarchy; as endeavouring to undermine the present form of government and to build a commonwealth, or some new scheme of their own, upon its ruins. On the other side, their clamors against us, may be summed up in those three formidable words, popery, arbitrary power and the pretender'.[16]

This bipartisan sense of conspiracy owed much to interpretations of the causes of the Civil War. But what else was it about party that seemed so conspiratorial? Here we should return to the analysis of George Savile, marquis of Halifax, who recorded some thoughts about party in the early years of William III's reign. Halifax's first concern was with rationality, for, he alleged, party debased rational argument. Party encouraged boldness rather than wisdom and fostered a party opinion rather than a rationally construed private opinion. Party 'leaves no liberty of private opinion', he complained, since men had to follow their leaders. Party thus 'maketh a man thrust his understanding into a corner and confine it till by degrees he destroys it'. Halifax even referred to his as 'an unreasonable age' in which reason only provoked, rather than cured, passions. Party left the fool following the knave.

Thus 'the mixture of fool and knave maketh up the parti-coloured creatures that make all the bustle in the world'. And the knaves, he said, all clung together, in 'a kind of corporation', united in their restless selfishness even if divided among themselves on other grounds.[17]

Another of Halifax's worries was that party politics involved an appeal to the people, an art of popularity. This only increased the number of fools and expanded the scope for knavery. The art of popularity necessitated lies, rumours and half-truths. And, Halifax thought, party made for unnecessarily bitter exchanges and thus cut 'off one half of the world from the other, so that the mutual improvement of men's understanding by conversing &c is lost and men are half undone'.[18] Party thus undermined the one tool, civil conversation, that spread rationality; the result was that 'the use of talking is almost lost in the world by the habit of lying'.[19] Worse still, Halifax thought, party gained adherents through the manipulation of empty slogans. 'The world hath of late years never been without some extraordinary word to furnish the coffee-houses and fill the pamphlets. Sometimes it is a new one invented and sometimes an old one revived. They are usually fitted to some present purpose, with intentions as differing as the various designs several parties may have, either to delude the people, or to expose their adversaries'.[20] Party names thus caused men to mistake words for things: 'Names to men of sense are no more than fig-leaves; [but] to the generality they are thick coverings that hide the nature of things from them. Fools turn good-sense upon its head, they take names for things and things only for names'.[21] Party labels, Halifax suggested, were themselves the clearest example of this:

> Amongst all the engines of dissention, there hath been none more powerful in all times, than the fixing names upon one another of contumely and reproach, and the reason is plain, in respect of the people, who tho generally they are uncapable of making a syllogism or forming an argument, yet they can pronounce a word; and that serveth their turn to throw it with all their dull malice at the head of those they do not like; such things ever begin in jest, and end in blood.[22]

Halifax rejected the concept of party, hankering after an ideal world of rational unity. Party was a conspiracy because by definition it divided rather than united, and it did so through the abuse of reason and language.

Yet Halifax was himself calling something 'conspiracy' which others might see merely as dishonesty, deception, or even the practice of politics. Conspiracy was a real fear but it was also a way of talking, a way of delegitimising an alternative viewpoint. Thus we can find the most partisan politicians (and some thought Halifax nowhere near as impartial as he liked to claim)[23] attacking rival partisan politicians as self-seeking conspirators against the public interest. The Whig leader Charles Montagu (who ironically took the title of Halifax on his peerage in 1700 but cultivated party almost as assiduously as Savile had repudiated it) could thus attack the Tories in a tract of 1701 as selfish knaves who worked against the public interest by manipulating language and promoting the designs of France.[24] 'I would fain have the world rightly informed,' he wrote, 'that they may distinguish the true patriots of England from the false ones'.[25] Against such a set of conspirators, he claimed, only the Whigs could be trusted. A Tory pamphlet in turn attacked Montagu and his fellow Whigs by talking the same language. Its author endeavoured 'to disabuse the nation, and recover the people from the false notions and prejudicate prepossessions, imposed on them by a turbulent malcontented and seditious party, who would lead them blindfold into dangerous errors, set them at variance with their representatives and put them out of love with parliaments, that their own faction might rule and rifle us again at pleasures'.[26] Both sides thus saw the other as conspiratorial, or at least talked as if they did. And the two Halifaxes, together with the Tory pamphleteer, all saw the misrepresentations of the other to be part of the problem they were facing. No doubt Montagu hated the Tories with a passion; but he was also sufficiently a master of rhetoric to know that the language of conspiracy was not only appropriate but could also do considerable damage to the Tories when read, heard or discussed by a publicly-minded public.[27] Montagu's Tory critic attacked him for his 'base and sorded arts, in mis-representing men and things'.[28] Montagu was said to have summoned 'all his powers of malice and Billings-gate rhetorick, to bespatter those that he thinks have detected and supplanted him' and thus his poisoned words required 'an antidote'.[29] In short, Montagu used his skills with the pen to deceive the public; and public print was necessary to counter-act the evil. Conspiracy was thus a way of undermining a rival standpoint, a way of talking; but the way in which conspiracy worked and might be remedied was also perceived to be through language. In order to examine this conundrum more carefully we need to return again to explanations of the Civil War.

One of the features of post-Restoration accounts of the war was to pin a good deal of the blame for the bloodshed on the abuse of language and to claim that the Civil War had produced a confusion of tongues akin to Babel.[30] A linguistic account of the origins of the war was enshrined in law, for the 1660 Act for the Safety and Preservation of His Majesties Person asserted that 'the growth and increase of the late troubles and disorders did in a very great measure proceed from a multitude of seditious sermons pamphlets and speeches dayly preached printed and published with a transcendant boldness defaming the person and government of your Majestie and your royall father'.[31] Fears about the consequences of uncontrolled public discourse were clearly evident during the Restoration period (as they had been before it). But the emergence of party politics added a new twist to the way in which language could be used for conspiratorial purposes, for each side accused the other of creating - or indeed of being little more than - lie machines. 'Nothing is more remarkable in the Whigs' remarked High Church Tory Joseph Trapp, 'than their unparallel'd impudence in lying. They will positively affirm the most unheard of absurdities in reason, and the most notorious falshoods in fact'.[32] The Whigs responded by accusing the Tory of maintaining his argument by 'an abominable jargon of hard words, with which he amazes and deludes the ignorant, and confounds the understandings of the wise'.[33] Party thus created a polemically warped contest in which language was part of the conspiracy and the means by which private ends might be pursued against the public interest.

Polemical Dispute in 1710

A printed exchange that took place in 1710 in the wake of the trial of the High Church cleric Dr Henry Sacheverell reveals this abuse of language more fully and shows how polemic was conceived to work as part of the conspiracy of party. [34] The printed debates highlight concerns about real identity, private interest, and the wilful use of political lies to hoodwink the public. Sacheverell had preached an inflammatory sermon against 'revolution principles' and thereby whipped up High Church and anti-Whig fervour. The trial had produced sustained ideological warfare between the two parties and a series of tracts suggested that the parties were not what they appeared to be, that words no longer matched things, and that language was being used for conspiratorial purposes to delude the people.

The printed debate was initiated by *Some Thoughts of an Honest Tory upon the present proceedings of that party* (1710).[35] This title was highly misleading. Purporting to come from an 'honest Tory', the work was in fact that of Benjamin Hoadly, a Whig cleric who preached Lockean doctrine and epitomised everything an 'honest Tory' abhorred.[36] Hoadly's tract was thus a deliberate fabrication of opinion, a fictionalising of views which he imagined or hoped might be held by moderate Tories disgusted by the extremities of their own side.[37] Hoadly was not the only one, however, to have assumed a fictional, false identity. A reply, *The Thoughts of an honest Whig*, was written by a Tory - though one reader also suspected he might be a Jacobite, noting that 'the bent of this mans discourse shows him to be disaffected to the government'.[38] *Faults on Both Sides*, which ostensibly was of no party and sought in some measure to adjudicate between them, was also the product of a fictional character. It claimed on the title page to have been written by 'Richard Harley'. The real author was probably Simon Clement; but other hands were also thought to have been involved and it is quite possible that the mention of Harley in the title was deliberate, since the appeal to moderate opinion on both sides of the party divide was entirely in line with the policy of Robert Harley.[39] Each of these tracts were thus not what they seemed; each was charged with a partisan viewpoint, even when that viewpoint (as in the case of Harley) was antagonistic to extreme party divisions. The pamphlets raised questions about the true identity of their own and their opponents' parties and it is no surprise that the exchange prompted Charles Davenant to resurrect his fictional cross-dealing, self-interested character, Tom Double, who had earlier been used successfully to pillory those Whigs (like Montagu) who appeared to be men on the make. This concern about double identities is important because it stressed how intrinsic dissimulation, deception and personal ambition were thought to be to partisan politics.

Another tract therefore sought to expose the deception. *Most Faults on One Side* claimed that once you stripped away the plausible veneer of the *Faults'* pretence of moderation, you found 'much of the Republican... a zealous friend to the Dissenters and a bitter enemy to the Church and Clergy'.[40] But *Most Faults* was itself highly partisan, belonging squarely in the High Church Tory camp. There was an unrefuted allegation that Sacheverell himself had been involved in its production, since he had given it 'gilded and neatly cover'd to several members of Parliament'. The tract is, however, generally attributed to Sacheverell's friend, Joseph Trapp, who was both a professor of poetry and ardent High Churchman.[41] Moreover, *A True History of the Honest Whigs*, written to answer Hoadly, was in fact the work of Tory Ned Ward, who had in any case already previously published his piece under a different title and who also fictionalised his politics.[42] The exchange thus took on the appearance of a debate between hidden identities by writers who indulged in fictionalising politics.

The obvious question lying behind much of the 1710 debate about misleading identities was, if the parties were not true to their original character, why was it that the people could not see this and act accordingly? Why did 1710 lead to a Tory landslide at the general election if Sacheverell and his allies were no more than frauds? Or (from a Tory perspective) why had the Whigs clung on to power for so long, exhausted the nation through a long war-effort but got rich? One explanation was that there were 'faults on both sides' because in each party private ambition successfully conspired against the public good. Cunning, self-interested leaders misled the nation through tricks and artifice. The subtitle of the *Faults* was thus 'an essay upon the original cause, progress and mischievous consequences of the factions in this nation. Shewing that the heads and leaders on both sides have always imposed upon the credulity of their respective parties, in order to compass their own selfish designs, at the expense of the peace and tranquility of the nation'. Its stated aim was thus to depict a kind of conspiracy against the nation by a pack of self-seeking men who pursued their own, rather than the nation's interest. Men were, it argued, being kept from agreeing by:

> Designing men in both parties, who have each in their turns artfully contrived to keep open the breach and ventilate the heats and animosities of ignorant people; that by the strength of their respective factions, they may be enabled to promote their own sinister designs, which generally have been to engross the places and profits of the government into their own hands, to raise vast estates to themselves by purloining all they can from the publick, and to establish such an interest as may always support them from being call'd to account for their misdemeanours.[43]

What is interesting, however, is that such a view was shared across the political and religious spectrum. Conspiracy theory was not confined to the moderate, Country Whigs but was subscribed to by Court Whigs, moderate Tories and Court Tories. Moreover, it was a conspiracy theory that related both to the substance of ideological dispute and to the manner in which such a difference was maintained among the people.

The betrayal of honesty was thus the central claim made by each pamphleteer. *Some Thoughts*, the first tract in the series, suggested that the Tories had proselytised through 'artifice ... lyes and calumnies, by personal undeserved praises and undeserved abuses'. The leaders of the Tories were, it was claimed, thus deliberately misleading the public, and were merely making use of Sacheverell whom they paid 'as they would do a fidler, that plays the tune that is call'd for, and helps forward a country dance'. The tract thus suggested that the deliberate manipulation of the passions of the people had been made more important than an appeal to reason and argument. Sacherverell fever was thus depicted as little more than a trick, employed by unscrupulous leaders for political ends. Indeed, the trick rested on 'that numerous train of lyes and calumnies, which our agents, with applause, scatter abroad through the whole country'.[44] This conspiratorial view of politics suggested that lies and misrepresentations were being spread, quite deliberately, by party leaders. But the tract was itself an attempt to highlight the dishonesty of the Tories in order to destabilise the loyalty of their supporters, at election time.

Simon Clement's *Faults on Both Sides* pursued the theme of dishonesty, though this time with the intention of appealing to moderate men to join together behind Robert Harley, who sought to construct a party of the 'third way'. The pamphlet therefore attacked both sides for the disparity between their words and their deeds. Clement alleged that when the Whigs prevailed in the 1690s 'they were no sooner got into power but their former zeal for the publick turn'd all into words and professions, when in deeds they greedily pursued their own private Interests, and fell on the readiest ways to enrich themselves at the nation's cost, prostituting their principle to their profit'.[45] There was thus a mismatch between Whig words and deeds. Indeed, Clement said, they spread lies against men like Harley, whose actions had shown him 'much more a true patriot and a true Whig than his adversaries; it was their deserting the true interest of their country and running into and supporting all the mismanagements of their late reign, that made him join with those that were call'd Tories ... to rescue the nation from the rapine of that corrupt ministry'.[46] *Most Faults on One Side* agreed. The Whigs promoted 'falshoods in fact and fallacies in reasoning'.[47] Indeed, the Whigs were, on this reading, incapable of political honesty: 'with relation to the government or our constitution in church and state they are upon principle dishonest and not fit to be trusted in the administration of either'.[48]

But if the Whigs were guilty, so were the High Church Tories. *Some Thoughts of an Honest Tory* lamented that 'we used to complain of the methods and arts of the whigs; and we are now combatting them with more infamous weapons than they ever in my memory used against us. We are lamenting the profaneness of others; what greater profaneness is there than to be wicked for the Church? We are crying out upon Hypocrisy: What greater hypocrisy is there, than to make an extravagant noise about obedience the cloak for turbulency?'[49] *Faults on Both Sides* developed this argument further. The 'generality of the Tories' were said 'to consist mostly of a looser and less thoughtful sort of people, who look no further than the outside of things and take up with notions they don't understand, condemning the very same thing in others which they have practised themselves; they are mightily influenced by the High-flying clergy and dance after their pipe in every thing; and we see what madness they are run into for the silencing an incendiary: what a noise do they make with their nonsensical addresses and furious insolent sermons?' Such men had contended so long about 'the shadow, that they seem to have lost the virtue, power and substance of it'. Worse, they were hypocrites, for the fiercest contenders for religion seldom showed any piety in their lives and fiery ministers filled 'their sermons with reviling, slander and invective, to stir up men's minds to wrath and discord'.[50] Religion was thus used as a cloak for villainy to trick the gullible. *Faults on Both Sides: Part the Second* was almost entirely devoted, as its subtitle explained, to 'shewing that the clergy, of whatsoever denomination, have always been the ring-leaders and beginners of the disturbances in every state; imposing upon the credulity of the laity, for no other end than the accomplishing their own selfish designs at the expense of the peace and tranquility of the nation'.

Each participant thus accused the other of political dishonesty and the deliberate use of lies. Whig, Tory and moderate all claimed that things were not as they seemed. In such circumstances it was perhaps inevitable that they each accused the other of a deceitful use of language. *Some Thoughts* suggested that the Tories had deliberately reversed or confused meaning: 'When we are forced to explain ourselves upon absolute non-resistance or hereditary right; we have the absurdity to own, that by absolute non-resistance we mean a non resistance which is not absolute and that by hereditary right we mean the same with the Whigs Parliamentary right. And yet we have the conscience to raise the spirits of the poor people against them by the deceitful use of these words and by clamours about a difference where we cannot maintain any'.[51] This abuse of language was not a side issue. Rather it was central to the politico-religious problems, largely because each side thought the practice of labelling - without which a pluralistic discourse could hardly take place - led to serious misrepresentations of their true positions. The misrepresentation of standpoints through incorrect labels was a central argument for Simon Clement, who thought that the way in which contemporaries used Whig and Tory led to their misunderstanding each other:

> It may be very material also to observe to you, that as these names of distinction are taken from words signifying parties differing in their religious sentiments; the world has been led into, and still persists in a mistake, as if the one sort were altogether dissenters and the other included all that were true church of England men, whereas there has always been a great number of the Whig party, even of the clergy as well as the laiety, who are zealous for the episcopal church government as the Tories themselves; so that they are indeed more truly to be accounted factions in the state than in the church.[52]

Words did thus not represent things. The parties were no longer true to their original principles, having deserted them for private gain, and that hence the party labels had themselves become misleading for the public. *Faults on Both Sides* claimed that the parties had shifted their identities. Thus the Court Whigs, by their sacrifice of the public for private advantage, had become

Tories: they 'were in their actions really turn'd Tories, though they still affected to be counted as good Whigs as ever'.[53] And many 'Tories themselves became Whigs in practice', joining with 'old staunch Whigs' who had never abandoned their principles.[54] Party labels had, it was suggested, become part of the conspiracy against the public, who were being fooled that Whig and Tory represented something they did not. In a similar vein, *Some Thoughts* argued that the Tories had abandoned their principles of passive obedience and thus were no longer really Tories.[55] *Faults on Both Sides* argued that if labels were set aside the honest men of each party would find themselves much closer than they thought and might unite for the public good.

Yet the High Church Tory response, *Most Faults on One Side*, balked at the terminology employed by Clement and claimed that it was the Whigs (for the allegedly impartial, Harleyite Clement was termed a Whig) who were playing with words: they loved to put 'interpretations ... upon the words and actions of those they don't love'.[56] The claims made by *Faults on Both Sides* were thus themselves mere sophistry, not only because Whig and Tory were 'really as distinct and opposite as East and West' but because to amalgamate them itself required an act of mislabelling.[57] Indeed, Clement's whole appeal to 'moderation' was exposed as a verbal device: 'Whatever they talk about they entrench themselves in the words Unity, Peace, Forbearance and the like; and then they think they are safe; because by vertue of those sounds they can throw dust into people's eyes and darken their understandings'. 'The truth is', the tract continued, 'the great fundamental principle of the whigs is confusion; not only in government both of church and state, but also of reasoning and thinking; they hate all order, clearness and regularity; they are for huddling and jumbling ideas and things, as much as possible, and for destroying distinction, even that of good and evil, of truth and falshood'.[58] This developed into a full-scale assault on the Whigs' artful and highly misleading reliance on the word 'moderate'. Only Tory moderation - stout defence of the church - was real moderation; 'all besides it, is Cant and Delusion'.[59] Indeed, Trapp alleged that it was 'a jest to say that all the difference lies in party-names: Those words, no doubt, are us'd in a very loose signification, and are often apply'd to persons that don't deserve them. But still there is a real and visible distinction in men's principles and practices, whatever names are put upon them or whether they have any names put on them or no'.[60]

The debates over whether or not words represented things and were being used correctly encouraged authors to see each other's arguments as literary as well as political pieces. Thus Joseph Trapp accused the author of the *Supplement to the Faults on Both Sides* of 'false English' and in turn *A Vindication of the Faults on Both Sides* attacked Trapp's work for the standard of its English, by which 'he discovers the meanness of his own talent, and shews that he is but (what some call) a Haberdasher of small-wares'.[61] Trapp was thus termed 'Mr Critic', because he was both politico-religious and literary critic (as High Church professor poetry his two functions were almost interdependent).[62] In this vein, argument and true wit had, it was claimed, been abandoned for scurrilous railing or dullness.[63] As critics of each other, the pamphleteers professed shock at the abusive language employed in partisan rivalry. The Tory *Thoughts of an Honest Whig* claimed that the whigs' 'violent heats and indiscretion' had made their position weaker rather than stronger: 'hot headed men never did good to any cause'.[64] *A Vindication of the Faults on Both Sides* responded to the rabidly Tory *Faults on One Side* by suggesting that 'he that can entertain himself with rant, railing, begging the question and miserable trifling, instead of argument, may find enough in it … I bear his contempt with patience'.[65]

A refined style of writing was important because the conspiracy of party could be exposed if it could be shown to be a lie or mere railing. An exposed lie or piece of sophistry or railing could thus become proof of conspiratorial design, placing an emphasis on a discourse of evidence, reason and rationality. This became pertinent after *Most Faults on One Side* claimed that dissenters had, after the Sacheverell trial, participated in destroying their own meeting houses.[66] *The Vindication of the Faults on Both Sides* refuted this as an attempt to 'bid defiance to truth' and then devoted a number of pages to presenting an alternative and very detailed account of what had really happened so as to put it 'out of doubt'.[67] In other words, unless an argument was backed by carefully argued proof, it failed to convince, and the design could be exposed. Similarly *Faults in the Fault-finder* attacked *Faults on Both Sides* for being 'erroneous' and offered 'a small collection of proofs from undeniable evidence'.[68] Truth could therefore only be established by evidence and reason; yet partisan conviction undermined readiness to accept the proof offered by the other side. A passionate partisan thus failed to discern the designs of his own party. *Faults on no Side* (1710) argued that 'tho both sides have their errors, neither will own them'.[69] Men thus took on the title of honest when they were rogues, the author argued. 'In short, men and women, of whatsoever degree and perswasion, delude themselves with a pretended innocence'.[70] Party locked men into an inability to discern when they were being misled and even to misinterpreting evil design as good. Thus 'back-biting and slandering men of loyalty and affection to the throne [passed] for a care of its welfare'. Yet the irony of the pamphlet is that while it highlighted the inability to discern fault, all the examples of hypocrisy were ascribed to dissenters and Whigs. The Tory author was thus guilty of precisely the type of refusal to acknowledge the faults of his party of which he accused others.

The 'Faults' controversy raised important questions. The tracts repeatedly accused each other of telling lies and deliberately misleading the public through public discourse, in sermons and the press. This was what Joseph Trapp called 'the most impudent lying and slander or villainous falsehoods in fact, positively affirm'd without the least pretence of proof'.[71] Central to the process of political lying was the press. *Faults on Both Sides* thus castigated the 'Rehearsals, Reviews, Observators, Pamphlets on both sides, all stuffed with fit matter to keep out the ferment and no care taken to suppress them'.[72] Political lying went hand in hand with the abuse of words. Lying, misrepresentation and verbal artifice were all seen as deliberate tools in an armoury of self-interested partisans who conspired against the public good. All sides felt that the public was thus being misled by schemers; but they all saw each other as the culprits. The language of conspiracy was thus flexible enough to be appropriated by all, and to provide a point of intersection with other discourses, of religion, of interest or of the commonwealth.

Yet a conspiracy based on a manipulative public discourse could only work if the people lacked virtue, rationality or judgement. The temptation was thus to ascribe a reversal of political fortune to the public's failure to see through attempts to mislead them. As the whiggish *A Supplement to Faults in the Fault-finder* (1710) put it, when trying to explain the success of Tory lies and slanders, 'Strange! Have the common people no judgment? Are they a meer mobile? .... every scandalous story is taken upon trust and as readily believ'd as if the quality of lying were not in nature'.[73] The public nature of politics therefore created a dilemma. Were the people the bulwark against conspiracy or the irrational tools of plotters and those who abused language to achieve their wicked ends? The more vitriolic the dialogue became, the more the formal representative process at the polls relied on the judgement of a public informed by a series of misrepresentations, labels, stereotypes, defamations, slanders, libels, distortions, rumours, half-truths and lies. The language of conspiracy undermined confidence that the public could see through this misinformation and one remedy was to remove the perceived motor of much of the conspiratorial manipulation of the people: frequent elections. And to justify a Septennial rather than a Triennial Act the Court Whigs spoke the language of public interest, patriotism and virtue, a discourse that rejected anything that was conspiratorial.

The language of conspiracy and the conspiracy of language thus helped shape public policy and had important consequences for the structure of politics and for social and cultural attitudes. Between 1689 and 1714 oppositional politics could not simply be fought on the grounds of a struggle between liberty and power because power kept shifting hands, to the Tories in the early 1690s, early 1700s and 1710–1714 and to the Whigs in the mid 1690s, mid 1700s and after 1714. These shifts, and corresponding shifts in public opinion, were explained in terms of a conspiracy, not just of self-interested men but also of men who used manipulative rhetorical techniques to manipulate public discourse. The language of party thus articulated and shaped conspiratorial fears. This discourse certainly overlapped with the oppositional, republican or civic humanist critique; but fear of corruption went much wider, penetrating the party struggle and becoming a tool of that party struggle. In turn the language of conspiracy was an important factor in pushing the Whigs into repealing the Triennial Act in 1716 and into espousing an ideal of a politer, more rational, though inherently less inclusive form of politics.

Notes

1   *Gulliver's Travels* (1726), Voyage to Brobdignag, chapter vi.
2   For secondary literature on the fear of a Catholic conspiracy see: P. Lake, 'Anti-popery: the structure of a prejudice', in R. Cust and A. Hughes, eds., *Conflict in Early Stuart England* (1989); C. Hibberd, *Charles I and the Popish Plot* (Chapel Hill, 1983); R. Clifton, 'Fear of popery' in C. Russell, ed., *The Origins of the English Civil War* (Basingstoke, 1973); I. Thackray, 'Zion undermined: the Protestant belief in the popish plot during the English Interregnum', *History Workshop Journal* 18 (1984); J. Miller, *Popery and Politics in England 1660–1688* (Cambridge, 1983). For secondary literature on contemporary perceptions of a Puritan or dissenting plot see P. Lake, *The Antichrist's Lewd Hat: Protestants, papists and players in post-Reformation England* (New Haven, 2002); Lake, *Anglicans and Puritans?: Presbyterianism and English Conformist thought from Whitgift to Hooker* (1988); T. Harris, *London Crowds in the Reign of Charles II* (Cambridge, 1987); M. Finlayson, *Historians, Puritanism, and the English Revolution: the Religious Factor in English Politics Before and After the Interregnum* (Toronto, 1983); R. MacGillivray, *Restoration Historians and the English Civil War* (The Hague, 1974). For works on individual plots after the Restoration see also R. Greaves, *Deliver Us From Evil: the Radical Underground in Britain, 1660–1663* (Oxford, 1986); Greaves, *Enemies Under His Feet: Radicals and Nonconformists in Britain, 1664–1677* (Stanford, Calif., 1990); Greaves, *Secrets of the Kingdom: British Radicals from the Popish Plot to the Revolution of 1688–1689* (Stanford, Calif., 1992); J.P. Kenyon, *The Popish Plot* (1972); R. Ashcraft, *Revolutionary Politics and Locke's Two Treatises of Government* (Princeton, 1986); J. Garrett, *The Triumphs of Providence: the Assassination Plot, 1696* (Cambridge, 1980). For an overview of how some of these fears overlapped see T. Corns, J. Downie and W. Speck, 'Archetypal mystification: polemic and reality in English political literature 1640–1750', *Eighteenth Century Life* 7 (1982), 1–27. For a synthesis of historical and literary plots see also R. Braverman, *Plots and Counterplots: Sexual Politics and the Body Politic in English Literature, 1660–1730* (Cambridge, 1993).

3   B. Bailyn, *The Ideological Origins of the American Revolution* (Cambridge, Mass., 1967); G. Wood, *The Creation of the American Republic, 1776–1787* (Chapel Hill, 1969).

4   The 'old Whig' critique of the new commercial and centralised state has been mapped out in J.G.A. Pocock's *The Machiavellian Moment: Florentine Political Thought and the Atlantic Republican Tradition* (Princeton, 1975) and *Virtue, Commerce, and History : Essays on Political Thought and History, Chiefly in the Eighteenth Century* (Cambridge, 1985). The vision of state authority as based on self-governing communities and dispersed power has now become the model for understanding the early modern state. Much of this literature is synthesised in M. Braddick, *State Formation in Early Modern England c.1550–1700* (Cambridge, 2000).

5   Such a language also drew on the concept of an 'ancient constitution'. For discussions of these see G.J.A. Pocock, *The Ancient Constitution and the Feudal Law: a Study of English Historical Thought in the Seventeenth Century* (New York, 1967); G. Burgess, *The Politics of the Ancient Constitution: an Introduction to English Political Thought, 1603–1642* (Basingstoke, 1992); M. Zook, *Radical Whigs and Conspiratorial Politics in Late Stuart England* (Pennsylvania, 1999); J. Greenberg, *The Radical Face of the Ancient Constitution: St. Edward's 'Laws' in Early Modern Political Thought* (Cambridge, 2001).

6   G. Wood, 'Conspiracy and the paranoid style: The American-Revolution as a psychological phenomenon. Causality and deceit in the eighteenth century', *William and Mary Quarterly* 39 (1982), pp. 401–41.

7   Wood, 'Conspiracy', p. 407.

8   Wood, 'Conspiracy', p. 408.

9   Wood, 'Conspiracy', quotations at pp. 422–3, 429.

10 For surveys of the local dimension of the party struggle see W. Speck, *Tory and Whig: the Struggle in the Constituencies, 1701–1715* (1970); P. Halliday, *Dismembering the Body Politic: Partisan Politics in England's Towns, 1650–1730* (Cambridge, 1998); and E. Cruickshanks, S. Handley and D.W. Hayton, eds., *The House of Commons 1690–1715* (Cambridge, 2002), 5 vols, esp. vols 1 and II.

11 For a fuller discussion see my *Representation and Misrepresentation: Politics and Language in Later Stuart England* (Oxford), forthcoming.

12 W. Raleigh, ed., *The Complete Works of George Savile, First Marquess of Halifax* (Oxford, 1912), p. 225. Halifax was here drawing on Hobbes [R. Ruck, ed., *Leviathan* (Cambridge, 1996), pp. 163–4].

13 For excellent surveys of what divided the parties see G. Holmes, *The Making of a Great Power: Late Stuart and Early Georgian Britain 1660–1722* (1993) and T. Harris, *Politics under the Later Stuarts: Party Conflict in a Divided Society 1660–1715* (1993).

14 See note 11.

15 *Faults on both sides: or an essay upon the original cause, progress and mischievous consequences of the factions in this nation* (1710), in *A Fourth collection of scarce and valuable tracts, on the most interesting and entertaining subjects* (1752) [known as the *Somers Tracts*], vol, 3 p. 295. The author was probably Simon Clement.

16 *The Examiner*, 3 May 1711.

17 *Complete Works*, p. 233.

18 Ibid., p. 225.

19 Ibid., p. 253.

20 Ibid., p. 104.

21 Ibid., p. 253.

22 Ibid., p. 47–8.

23   For Halifax's political position see H. Foxcroft, *A Character of the Trimmer: Being a Short Life of the First Marquis of Halifax* (Cambridge, 1946); M. Knights, *Politics and Opinion in Crisis 1678–1681* (Cambridge 1994; M. Brown, *The Works of George Savile Marquis of Halifax* (Oxford, 1989), 3 vols, introduction to volume 1.

24   *The Present Dispositions of England Considered. The Second Edition with the addition of a preface occasioned by a late pamphlet intituled England's Enemies Exposed* (1701).

25   *The Present Dispositions of England Considered* (1701), p. 16.

26   *England's Enemies Exposed* (1701), dedication.

27   Montagu had risen to public notice through his skills as a poet. For his biography see Cruickshanks *et al, The House of Commons 1690–1715*, iv. 850–80.

28   *England's Enemies Exposed*, p. 11.

29   Ibid., pp. 18–19, 20.

30   S. Achinstein, 'The Politics of Babel in the English Revolution' in J. Holstun (ed) *Pamphlet Wars: prose in the English Revolution* (1992).

31   13 Car. 11 cap 1.

32   *The character and principles of the present set of Whigs* (1711), p. 24.

33   *The Character of a Modern Tory in a letter to a friend by which it is most evident that he is the most unnatural and destructive monster (both in religion and politicks) that hath yet appear'd in any community in the world* (1713).

34   The debate ran to 35 titles, the most important of which are: Benjamin Hoadly, *Some Thoughts of an Honest Tory upon the present proceedings of that party* (1710); Simon Clement, *Faults on Both Sides … By way of answer to the Thoughts of an Honest Tory* (1710); *A True History of the Honest Whigs. A Poem. In Answer to the Thoughts of an honest Tory* (1710); *Faults on Both Sides: part the second* (1710); Joseph Trapp, *Most Faults on One Side* (1710); *Faults in the Fault Finder* (1710); *Faults on no Side* (1710); *A Supplement to the Faults on both Sides: containing the compleat history of the proceedings of a party since the Revolution* (1710); *An Answer to that part of the pamphlet entitul'd, Faults on Both Sides, which relates tot he deficiency of the English army in Spain* (1710); *The Thoughts of an honest Whig upon the present proceedings of that party* (1710) - dated as the 'latter end' of August on the National Library of Scotland copy; S. Clement, *A Vindication of the Faults on Both Sides* (1710); *The Tatler's ecclesiastical thermometer or weather glasss exemplifying Faults on Both Sides* (1710) - a broadside listed in W.T. Morgan, *Bibliography of British History* (Bloomington, Indiana, 1937), vol. ii, p. 182 but not traceable on ESTC; *A Supplement to Faults in the Fault-finder. in Answer to the Vindication of Faults on Both Sides* (1711); Daniel Defoe?, *R-s on both sides* (1711). The controversy might also be said to include Charles Davenant's *Sir Thomas Double at Court* (1710), to which *A Supplement to the Faults on both Sides* was also an answer. For bibliographical information about the Faults controversy see William Morley, *Queen Anne Pamphlets. An Annotated Bibliographical Catalogue* (Kingston, Ontario, 1987), appendix A.

35   *Faults in the Fault-finder* p. 3 claimed *Faults On Both Sides* was 'a favourite with the publick' while *Most Faults* thought it had been extolled 'to the Skies' by Whigs [p. 3]. *Faults on Both Sides* went through at least four editions in 1710 and was translated into French and Dutch.

36   An effigy of Hoadly and his books were burnt in March 1710 [Strathmore mss at Glamis Castle, box 75, bundle 6, newsletter 30 Mar. 1710].

37   A similar fictional pretence was present in *A supplement to the faults on both sides: containing the compleat history*, which was presented in the form of a dialogue between 'Steddy' (an old whig) and 'turn-around' who had been seduced into toryism for a short while before

abandoning them.
38   Manuscript note on Cambridge University Library Syn.7.70.28/1.
39   *Faults on both Sides* was 'supposed to be written by Ld Pet[erboroug]h and the accurate Mr
      Fletcher' [BL Trumbull mss LIV, 25 Oct 1710, Bridges to Trumbull]. But for the
      identification of Clement as the author see *Philological Quarterly* vol. lvi (1977), 266–71; J.
      Downie, *Robert Harley and the Press: Propaganda and Public Opinion in the Age of Swift and Defoe*
      (Cambridge, 1979), p. 121. For Clement's career see also P. Gauci, *Politics of Trade. The
      Overseas Merchant in State and Society* (Oxford, 2001), 189.
40   *Most Faults on One Side* (1710), p. 5.
41   Trapp was a poet, playwright, professor of poetry at Oxford 1708–1718, and friend of Dr
      Sacheverell, whom he succeeded at Newington lectureship. Swift called him a 'coxcomb'
      [*The Prose Works of Jonathan Swift*, ed. H. Davis (13 vols, 1939–68), iii. 11–12] and 'second-
      rate' [ii. 140] but also fostered his appointment as chaplain to Lord Bolingbroke in July
      1712. Trapp is alleged to have had a hand in writing *The Examiner* [Kennett, *The Wisdom of
      Looking Backward* (1715), p. 168].
42   H.W. Troyer, *Ned Ward of Grub Street: a Study of Sub-Literary London in the Eighteenth Century*
      (1968).
43   *Somers Tracts*, 4th collection, iii, 291–2.
44   Ibid., p. 285.
45   Ibid., p. 300.
46   Ibid., p. 308.
47   *Most Faults on One Side* (1710). The quotes come from the full title of the tract.
48   *Most Faults*, p. 18.
49   Somers Tracts, 4th collection, iii, 288.
50   Ibid., p. 323.
51   Ibid., p. 289.
52   Ibid., p. 297 cf. Ibid., p. 367.
53   Ibid., p. 304.
54   Ibid., p. 305.
55   Ibid., p. 285.
56   *Most Faults on One Side* (1710), p. 36.
57   Ibid., p. 21.
58   Ibid., p. 23.
59   Ibid., pp. 23–4.
60   Ibid., p. 21.
61   *Postscript to Most Faults*, p. 55; *Somers Tracts* 4th collection, iii, 367.
62   Ibid., p. 369.
63   Pope most famously used dullness against the Whigs, but it is clear that he was building
      on a longer satire of polemical dullness.
64   *Thoughts of an Honest Whig*, p. 3.
65   *Somers Tracts*, 4th collection, iii, 374.
66   *Faults on One Side*, pp. 36–8.
67   Somers Tracts, 4th collection, iii, 367, 372–3.
68   *Faults in the Fault-Finder*, p. 3.
69   *Faults on No Side*, p. 2.
70   Ibid., p. 4.
71   *Most Faults*, p. 55.

72   *Somers Tracts*, 4th collection, iii, 306 cf. *A Supplement to the Faults on Both Sides* (1710), pp. 51–2. The *Thoughts of an Honest Whig* (1710), p. 6, reflected on the use made by the Whigs of the *Observator* and *Review*.

73   *Supplement to Faults in the Fault-Finder*, p. 25.

Chapter 10

'Popery at St. James's': The Conspiracy Theses of William Payne, Thomas Hollis, and Lord George Gordon

Colin Haydon

Introduction and Background

'Though sometimes amusing', John Roberts once observed, 'it is always disturbing when intelligent people seriously talk nonsense'.[1] Often, of course, the cranks' fulminations are inconsequential. When Lord Grange opposed the Witchcraft Act's repeal in 1736, he was treated with scorn.[2] The nonsense propagated by two of this essay's subjects, William Payne and Thomas Hollis, did not prove - at least immediately - dangerous. But sometimes the nonsense espoused by intelligent men is not only disturbing but also produces terrifying results. One thinks of the monks who concocted Europe's intellectual witchcraft mythology.[3] Or of Maximilien Robespierre and his discourse of 'complots', 'fripons', 'scélérats', and 'faux patriotes'.[4] The conspiracy thesis of Lord George Gordon, this essay's third subject, was one facet of the 'No Popery' hysteria that produced the catastrophic riots of '80. That 'the Hobgoblin' of Popery,[5] in Defoe's phrase, could unleash such tumults seems today astonishing. But, as Roberts stated, it is vital to eschew the 'anachronistic incredulity which we bring to anything which does not rest on our own intellectual assumptions'.[6]

In eighteenth-century England, the fear of disguised enemies was remarkably widespread and protean. In his volcanic sermon of 1709, *The Perils of False Brethren*, Dr Sacheverell maintained that rationalists, the heterodox, and Whigs, despite their professed friendship to the Church of England, sought its ruin.[7] The Methodists, their enemies claimed, were clandestine subversives - secret Jacobites or Jacobins, disguised Papists or Levellers reborn.[8] One Hampshire clergyman, writing to a friend in the 1750s, expressed concern about the infiltration of the Church by unorthodox men:[9] Bishop Lavington of Exeter, 'in his youthful Days', he noted, 'thought very freely'.[10] In political circles, Jacobite entryism was feared. In 1752, accusations of Jacobitism were made against three close associates of the duke of Newcastle - Bishop Johnson of Gloucester, William Murray, later lord Mansfield, and Andrew Stone, sub-governor of the Prince of Wales. Before it was dropped, the claim was discussed in both the privy council and parliament.[11] Burke's picture of the 'King's Friends', in *Thoughts on the Cause of the Present Discontents* (1770), was another variation of the theme of surreptitious subversion.[12]

The dread of papist entryism was very strong in post-Reformation England. Thus, plain-clothes Jesuits seemed especially sinister and dangerous. William Prynne popularised the belief that Papists had masterminded the Civil Wars and Charles I's execution. The notion was common that sectaries were 'Papists in disguise' in the seventeenth century.[13] It is unsurprising that entryism seemed a favoured papist tactic: that staple figure of much Protestant polemic, Antichrist, was the archetype of the clandestine subversive, perverting and wrecking the Church from within. Of course, Popery's response to Protestantism was flexible, dependent on circumstances. In Catholic states, or where warfare was viable, force was employed: the rack, the stake, and the sword. But in stable Protestant states, subtle, ingenious tactics were needed. Hence Thomas Macro, preaching in 1731, juxtaposed the two threats from Papists - '*open* Invasion upon ... Religious and Civil' liberties and, alternatively, '*secret* Villainy'.[14] One document, among the Cholmondeley (Houghton) manuscripts, is a distillation of Protestant fears. 'The Measures propos'd and resolv'd on for introducing Popery at K James's Accession' recognized that 'the Protestant Religion hath ... obtained a firme beliefe in the mindes of ye Generallity'.[15] None the less, Catholic growth was achievable by 'insensibly filling all places military and Civil, and the Dignities of the Church and of the Universities with wise Couragious and well-tempered Roman Catholicks, or such Loyall Protestants as are desireous of an accommodation betwixt the two Churches'.[16] Between 1689 and 1746, Catholic Jacobites wanted armed insurrection. After Culloden (1746) and Quiberon Bay (1759), that proved impossible. Under George III, therefore, vigilant Protestants confidently awaited telltale signs of popish entryism. Soon, they were sure they had detected them, and they accordingly formulated a conspiracy thesis which provided, in their eyes, a convincing explanation of political events.

What alarmed 'true Protestants' were the political élite's changing attitudes towards Catholics and policies consequent on these. From the 1760s to the 1780s, élite attitudes towards Catholics softened considerably.[17] Since the Reformation, Protestants had feared that the English Papists' allegiance lay principally with the Pope, not the Crown, and, from 1689, Catholic support for Jacobitism enraged, and alarmed, politicians. But with the increasing weakness of the Papacy in the eighteenth century, and the demise of Jacobitism, the political threat posed by Catholicism withered. After 'James III''s death in 1766, the Vatican recognised George III's title and English Catholics henceforth prayed for him. Between 1772 and 1774, Pope Clement XIV hospitably received members of George's family. Rockingham thought that the Catholics now constituted 'a very dutiful and loyal part of the King's subjects',[18] and, in 1769, Blackstone argued that

> if a time should ever arrive, and perhaps it is not very distant, when all fears of a pretender shall have vanished, and the power and influence of the pope shall become feeble, ridiculous, and despicable, not only in England, but in every kingdom of Europe, it probably would not then be amiss to review and soften [the anti-Catholic laws].[19]

One leading Catholic nobleman, the ninth Lord Petre, enjoyed George III's friendship, and, in 1778, entertained the king and queen at his home, Thorndon Hall in Essex.[20] In 1785, the Prince of Wales secretly married the Catholic Maria Fitzherbert. Lord Mansfield had a circle of Catholic friends. The *rapprochement* between the Catholics and the political establishment seemed solid.

Imperial needs also impelled the politicians' reappraisal of Catholicism. Largely quiescent in the earlier eighteenth century, Ireland was becoming, from the 1760s, a most distressful country. Her economic, social, and religious problems exercised politicians in London. The Whiteboy disturbances and, later, the Volunteer movement, a powerful force for change, further dismayed them. The American war proved disastrous to Ireland's economy, producing widespread unemployment. Reform respecting trade and landholding was urgently needed; conciliation of the Catholic majority was essential. Besides Ireland's age-old problems, ministers faced new colonial problems from 1763. By the Peace of Paris, France ceded Quebec to Britain. In this extensive territory, the French population, numbering some 70,000, prized its French laws and its Catholic faith. The treaty promised that Catholic Canadians could 'profess the worship of their religion ... as far as the laws of Great Britain permit'.[21] But, for Britain to retain the province, generous concessions seemed necessary - especially given the American troubles. In Grenada, another gain of 1763, it was also necessary to reconcile the Catholics to British rule.

More generally, Enlightenment thinking sanctioned pragmatic policies. Religious persecution was decried as one loathsome attribute of 'the former age' or contemporary popish states. Enlightenment writers detested Popery, irrational and obscurantist, but argued that the proper weapon against it was education, not force. Protestants should eschew coercion since they deplored persecution in Catholic Europe. Tolerance was praiseworthy on principle and, practically, because confessional discord enervated a polity. Progressive, 'rational' clergymen propagated such ideas from the established Church's pulpits. Did 'popish doctrines appear ten thousand times more absurd than they do', John Hey stated in 1774:

> I would not, for the world, interrupt the weakest devotee of that sect, even in the performance of the most frivolous ceremony: his most childish relique should not be more sacred to him on a religious account, than it should be to me from a reverence to the Liberties of Mankind.[22]

Political change and enlightened thinking yielded significant benefits for England's Catholics. The authorities ceased to prosecute Papists. Increasingly regarding the anti-Papist laws, dating from Elizabethan and Jacobean times, as redundant, they did not wish to harass peaceable subjects. Mansfield, as lord chief justice, determined to block prosecutions. As he now maintained, the penal laws 'were not meant to be enforced except at proper seasons, when there is a necessity for it; or, more properly speaking, they were not meant to be enforced at all, but were merely made *in terrorem*'.[23] In 1772, parliament itself passed a private Act to rescue a Catholic, Anne Fenwick, 'from the injustice of its own statutes'.[24] Using the penal laws, her brother-in-law hoped to secure her property, but the Act made her a pleasing settlement.[25] Then, in 1778, the first Catholic Relief Act was passed. In return for taking an oath of allegiance, Catholics could, in future, purchase land legally. Catholic priests and schoolmasters, if apprehended, were no longer liable to life imprisonment. Rewards for priest-catchers were ended.[26] The Act's provisions were limited: they merely legalized the *de facto* practice of magistrates in the later eighteenth century. They did not give Catholics freedom of worship - that was not granted until 1791. None the less, the Act's resonance was considerable - unsurprisingly: this was the first major law to benefit Catholics since the Elizabethan settlement.

The 1778 Relief Act was, in part, passed because North's government hoped to employ Catholic troops in the American war and, in consequence, needed Catholic goodwill.[27] That was also cultivated in the colonies and Ireland. In 1774, Parliament passed the Quebec Act. It initiated a nominated legislative council - not an elected assembly - to govern the colony and gave Catholics places on it. It perpetuated the French legal system in civil cases. An oath of allegiance, containing nothing objectionable to the Catholics' faith, was carefully drafted. Furthermore, the Act instituted a system of endowments for the Roman Catholic clergy, who were permitted to hold land and take tithes from their flocks.[28] The measure was momentous. Despite Britain's Protestant constitution, it made 'the Catholic religion ... the established religion of ... [a] vast continent'.[29] Respecting Grenada, Catholic participation in its council and assembly was sanctioned.[30] North's ministry oversaw various reforms in Ireland. In 1774, foreshadowing the penal code's revision, an oath of allegiance was devised which Catholics could take.[31] In 1778, Luke Gardiner's Relief Act removed the restrictions imposed in 1704 on Catholics holding and inheriting land, and allowed Catholics to lease land.[32] For the Catholic majority, this constituted 'a great victory over the prejudices of those who called themselves true protestants' in the country.[33]

Pragmatic politicians, and an educated, enlightened élite, largely approved these pro-Catholic measures. For George III, the Quebec Act was 'founded on the clearest principles of justice and humanity'.[34] It was a monument, Lord Lyttelton told the Lords, to the age's 'charity and universal benevolence' - 'the gloomy reign of persecution and priestcraft ... [was] at an end ... [and] science ... had ... enlightened the human mind'.[35] But this benevolence was not universal. As Burke observed, 'the whole Nation ... [had] for a long time' ingested 'the poison, which under the Name of antidotes against Popery ... [had] been circulated from ... [the] Pulpits, and from ... [the] presses'.[36] Locke, as Gordon recalled, had argued against toleration for Papists as their 'allegiance and service ... [were to] another prince'.[37] John Wesley deplored the Relief Act, since it encouraged Papists to spread 'their intolerant, Persecuting Principles'.[38] And for Payne, Hollis, and Gordon, the measures greeted by George III as just and humane were really proofs of a 'dark secret', a sinister conspiracy.

William Payne

William Payne, the first case study, was a carpenter by trade, who lived at Bell Yard in London. He was profoundly anti-Catholic, and had puritanical disposition. His rank and his outlook partly explain the rôle for which he became notorious. In later-seventeenth and early-eighteenth-century England, tradesmen and craftsmen played an important part in the Reformation of Manners campaign; and it is likely that this continued in the later eighteenth century. Payne possibly had links with petty Reformation of Manners societies and the early Methodists. Moreover, the lesser middling sort commonly provided 'reforming' or 'informing' constables; and, from c. 1760 to 1782, Payne was an informing constable in the City of London. These men aimed to check vice; they arrested vagrants and prostitutes, and brought prosecutions for swearing and Sunday trading.[39] Payne, who keenly prosecuted beggars and Sunday street traders,[40] additionally waged war on Popery.

William III's Act against Popery (1700) detailed procedures for anti-Catholic prosecutions and promised a reward of £100 for the apprehension and conviction of priests.[41] While the Act remained on the statute book, persecution remained a possibility - despite the hostility of an increasingly enlightened élite. Payne appreciated this, and between 1767 and 1771, he instituted many anti-Catholic prosecutions: they were, Eamon Duffy observes, 'on a scale unknown since the Popish Plot'.[42] Masquerading as a possible convert, Payne visited a number of Roman Catholic chapels in the City and the East End and collected the evidence he needed. He began by indicting two laymen, a bricklayer and a victualler, for hearing mass. In 1767, at the Surrey assizes, he prosecuted one John Baptist Malony for exercising his functions as a priest. Malony was found guilty and sentenced to life imprisonment, as the Act of 1700 prescribed (he was pardoned in 1771). Four London mass-houses were temporarily closed. Greatly encouraged, Payne charged at least another fifteen priests - including Bishop Challoner and his coadjutor, James Talbot - and nine Catholic schoolmasters. But Payne was thwarted. Lawyers sometimes overawed prosecution witnesses, and juries did not convict. The lord mayor of London declined to proceed against Papists. The judiciary, led by lord Mansfield, defused prosecutions. No conviction, it was argued, was possible without incontestable proof that a defendant was a priest. Or that he had said mass. Was there evidence of ordination? Had Payne witnessed mass? The mass was celebrated in Latin; and he knew no Latin. Payne's character was blackened: his chief motive, it was maintained, was the priest-catcher's reward.[43]

By 1771, Payne's campaign was in ruins. But from the outset, Payne knew he was pitted against a hostile establishment. In 1767, he published a pamphlet, *Cry Aloud, and Spare Not; or, an Alarm to All the Protestants of Great Britain and Ireland*. The text, Isaiah 58:1, was well chosen: Payne, like an Old-Testament prophet, aimed to inveigh boldly against evil (the verse continues, 'lift up thy voice like a trumpet, and shew my people their transgression ...'). The author was, the title-page stated, 'a True-Born Englishman, Or, the Little English Carpenter'. This was cleverly worded. It linked Payne's endeavours to traditional English liberties. It linked patriotism and anti-Catholicism.[44] 'Little' suggested his battle with massive, malevolent enemies; 'carpenter' possibly evoked Christ. The pamphlet was '[h]umbly addressed' to the Church of England's clergy - probably ironically, given that, to men like Payne, its anti-Catholicism seemed tepid.

Most of Payne's pamphlet was a tirade against Popery, derived partly from a Protestant martyrology, Matthew Taylor's *England's Bloody Tribunal.*[45] *Cry Aloud* castigated 'the cursed religion of ... [the] diabolical church of antichrist',[46] examining its theology and history; the warning 'Beware of Popery' punctuated the diatribe. The 'devil was the founder of' Popery;[47] its adherents were 'the deluded sons of the scarlet whore', 'falsely called christians'.[48] The Catholics were cruel persecutors: Payne recalled the Marian burnings under Bonner, 'one of the prime ministers of hell, a faithful servant to the devil's viceregent the pope'.[49] Payne was sure that 'Popery is just the same as ever it was, where it dare to shew its tyranical spirit.'[50] 'O bloody Papists', he added, 'let us never be afraid to expose their hellish deeds ...'.[51]

Payne believed that there was a conspiracy to expose, or rather several. The first conspiracy was the work of Catholic states - Payne characterized France and Spain as 'our old, inveterate savage and blood-thirsty enemies'.[52] The governments of Portugal and France had expelled the Jesuits in 1759 and 1764 respectively; Spain did so in 1767. Consequently, Payne noted, 'swarms of Jesuits' had come to England and Ireland; but he doubted the authenticity of 'the seeming quarrel' between the rulers and the Society.[53] '[F]or my part', he declared, 'I cannot at present think [it] to be as represented by the popish powers, a thing real'.[54] 'Are not the Jesuit [sic] papists as well as others?', he asked. 'Are not their principles of religion the same?' The 'quarrel', he feared, was fraudulent, part of a plot: instead of a genuine rift, '[i]s it not rather a scheme, in order to strengthen the popish party now among us?'[55] The Catholics also wanted to strike at the British in the New World. In America, Payne alleged, popish missionaries taught the Indians 'to extirpate the English, because they cruelly murthered the Saviour of mankind'.[56]

The second conspiracy was domestic and involved, Payne hinted, men of influence. Of course, a man of his station knew little of politics and lacked access to politicians. None the less, in 1767, 'si monumentum requiris, circumspice'. Popery, Payne contended, was 'over-spreading the land'.[57] Mass-houses had 'opened round the town ... [with] great numbers flocking to them day after day, in open defiance of the good laws now in being'.[58] Catholics worshipped publicly in 'their great cathedral by Lincoln-inn-fields' (the Sardinian embassy chapel).[59] Certain priests, though indicted, still conducted illegal services.[60] Popish missioners, moreover, were making converts among 'the lower sort of people'.[61] The threat to 'our priviledges [sic], as Englishmen and Protestants', Payne thought, was obvious.[62] Although his piece included loyal rhetoric, his charge was clear: parts of the establishment were conniving at Popery's growth. One judge, it was said, was 'a friend to popery';[63] Payne, with heavy irony, dismissed the suggestion, since 'no honest man can take or receive a sallery from the government' and encourage Popery.[64] Was not the powerful's 'secret ... [that] we [are] going to have a popish Government once more in England'?[65]

Thirdly, Payne believed that there was a conspiracy involving the press. Its aim, he contended, was to stifle a free discussion of Popery. In 1766–1767, there was frenzied discussion about 'the growth of Popery' in print; and, eventually, the *Gazetteer*'s printer determined to cease publishing material about it. '[W]e have', the *Gazetteer* announced cryptically, 'very particular reasons for rejecting (for the future) every thing relative to popery'.[66] Payne was horrified and, in a letter, told the printer 'immediately to publish those reasons, or else it will appear ... your reasons are very ill grounded, and such reasons as will appear at this time (when Popery is over-spreading the land) to be very unreasonable'.[67] Keith Thomas has observed that some belief systems 'possess a resilience which makes them virtually immune to external argument'. Once the 'initial premises are accepted, no subsequent discovery will shake the believer's faith, for he can explain it away in terms of the existing system'.[68] This is true of conspiracy theories with a vengeance. '[N]o man with his eyes open can ever turn from the Protestant interest, to that of Popery', Payne declared, 'unless for some devilish view'.[69] He demanded that the printer publish his letter. If he did not, Payne maintained, 'it will be thought, (and that upon very good ground) you have been influenced by the Popish party, or that you are become a proselite to their idol worship';[70] no 'true Protestant' would deliberately suppress discussion of Popery.

> Now sir I am clearly convinced you was not in a dream, as I before thought, unless your mature deliberations and writings are all a dream: if your [sic] are turned Papist, it's plain you are in a dream, for I am well persuaded from reason and scripture that every one who turns papist, must be totally blind ...[71]

However, the printer unsurprisingly determined not to publish the letter,[72] doubtless confirming the fears which Payne had expressed earlier.

Were Payne's prosecutions and his thesis important? Seemingly not. Payne disgusted the élite. '[T]his Payne', said Mansfield, unfairly, 'is a very illiterate man'.[73] His ideas, and those of others like him, were scorned. In 1767, one 'S.R.' published *A Letter to a Member of Parliament: Concerning the Effects of the Growth of Popery, on the Price of Provisions; By a Journeyman Shoemaker*. This through-the-looking-glass pamphlet turned Payne on his head: employing ludicrous arguments and grotesque logic, 'S.R.' postulated that Protestants should *welcome* Popery's growth. In the preface, he mockingly 'vindicated' the humble's competence to discuss religion and politics. Then, he argued that 'we should encourage papists among us, because ... [with their many fasts] they eat less than protestants'.[74] His 'Cobler's Calculations' showed that a 'Roman Catholic consumes about two thirds of the provision that a protestant does, so that we may say, he is a third part a better subject in times of scarcity'.[75] Other deductions followed. Britain's success in war was explained: 'forty thousand protestants, especially *Englishmen*, have as much specific flesh and blood in them, as sixty thousand *Frenchmen*, and so are a fair match for them in the nature and reason of things ...'.[76] And so on. Nor was Payne's campaign just an object of ridicule: it was also counter-productive. In 1778, Shelburne cited it as proof that that the law needed amendment when the Lords debated the Catholic Relief bill. Payne was, he said, 'the lowest and most despicable of mankind, a common informing constable of the city of London'.[77] Shelburne, despite his 'anti-Papistical sentiments',[78] with the rest of Chatham's ministry, had deplored Malony's prosecution and sentence: they were disgraceful in a land of liberty and in an enlightened age. With characteristic self-importance, Shelburne proclaimed how he, 'with his colleagues in office, were so perfectly persuaded of the impolicy and inhumanity of the law, that they ventured to give ... [Malony] his liberty at every hazard'.[79] The 1778 Act froze the legislation which had permitted Payne's prosecution of the Catholic priests and schoolmasters.[80] Even after the Gordon riots, a sop was not given to 'Protestant' opinion. A bill *'for securing the Protestant Religion'* - by prohibiting Catholics from teaching Protestant children - was passed in the Commons, but lost in the Lords.[81]

Thomas Hollis

Unlike Payne, Thomas Hollis was, of course, a man of rank and substance. Born in 1720, he inherited considerable wealth, which allowed him to indulge his many interests. He was educated in England and in Amsterdam, entered Lincoln's Inn, and, from 1748 to 1753, toured Europe. Proficient, seemingly, in Dutch, French, and Italian, besides Latin and Greek, he read and bought books prodigiously. His education made him a republican and imbued him with an 'ardent love of liberty'.[82] Hollis venerated republican Rome and English republicans and Whigs: on reaching his majority, he began purchasing land in Dorset, and named the farms Harrington, Locke, Marvell, Milton (his great hero), Russell, Sydney, and so forth.[83] Detesting corruption, he chose not to enter Parliament, but to foster privately the cause of liberty. He purchased, and sometimes reprinted, books extolling liberty and republicanism. He sent such works to private individuals, to libraries in Berne and Italy, to Christ's College, Cambridge, and, above all, to Harvard. In addition, Hollis patronised print engravers and bookbinders. Boswell, when on the Grand Tour, found Hollis' gifts in various libraries, 'bound in red Morocco, and adorned with gilded Stamps of the Cap of Liberty, Pitch-forks, [and] Swords'.[84] Hollis' interests highlighted his eccentricity; but, regarding Popery, he was positively paranoid. In his later years in London (he lived in Dorset from 1770), he believed that Catholic agents watched him continuously, that they tampered with his mail, and that they infiltrated his household. He thought they planned to injure, or even kill, him.[85]

Hollis' loathing of Popery is nicely captured in his inscription in Harvard's copy of Samuel Morland's *The History of the Evangelical Churches of the Valleys of Piemont* (1658):

> Reader, Whomsoever thou mayest be that shalt peruse these lines, whether Pagan or Jew, Christian or Mohammedan or Sceptic, consider well the Doctrines, Practices, Massacres of the Papists; and, so long as the arm of Popery is uplifted against thee, so long be thine uplifted against Popery, in justice to thyself and to Mankind.[86]

Hollis' friends thought similarly. The most like-minded was Francis Blackburne, the crypto-Socinian archdeacon of Cleveland, who, in 1780, published the massive, two-volume *Memoirs of Thomas Hollis*. Others in the coterie included the Socinian Caleb Fleming, the West Country minister and historian William Harris, and Theophilus Lindsey, rector of Catterick from 1763 to 1773, who abandoned Anglicanism for Unitarianism. Hollis' family were Dissenters, but his own faith was private, complex, and obscure.[87] However, his links with Blackburne, Fleming, and Lindsey, and with members of the largely heterodox Club of Honest Whigs, proclaim his own religious heterodoxy.[88] Unlike Payne, Hollis and his sophisticated associates saw 'Popery' as more than just the Roman church's tenets, practices, and government. They tended to use 'Popery' as a Humpty-Dumpty word, meaning what they chose. 'Popery' was 'that foulest hydra',[89] with many heads. It meant ecclesiastical tyranny, the imposition of unscriptural, unprovable dogma, and the unwarrantable stifling of ideas.[90] Consequently, established Churches - including the Church of England - might well display 'Popery'. 'Popery' also entailed the crushing of civil liberties. Unsurprisingly, in the 1760s and 1770s, events at home, and in America, convinced Hollis' circle that the court, and its favoured politicians, were 'popishly inclined'.

None the less, as his inscription in Morland's *History* indicates, Hollis above all detested the Popery of the Church of Rome. Rome was the heart of darkness, the centre of international conspiracies. Tactics altered, but Popery's objectives were constant and change was impossible.[91] For Blackburne, in the

Memoirs of Thomas Hollis, the pontificate of Clement XIV (1769–1774) was clinching proof of this. Clement's dissolution of the Society of Jesus in 1773 seemed the prelude to sweeping reforms, exciting much interest in England. But a reactionary hierarchy apparently thwarted further change. In 1774, Clement died, and his body's rapid decomposition fuelled suspicions of poison. 'Of this murder', Blackburne observed in the *Memoirs*, 'the jesuits were brought in guilty, by the common suffrage of Europe, for

> Who finds the heifer dead and bleeding fresh,
> And sees fast by a butcher with an axe,
> But will suspect, 'twas he that made the slaughter?'[92]

Even a pontiff could not shift the Vatican's age-old policies; no individual could combat the vast, sinister organisation of Popery. 'The abolition of the order of jesuits', Blackburne declared sadly, 'was an act of heroism which could be undertaken and accomplished only by a man who valued his life less than his duty'.[93] Moreover, the Jesuits adroitly turned the dissolution to their advantage. Soon, ex-Jesuits were coming to England, and exercising their functions there.[94]

At home, Hollis maintained, there was a rapid 'growth of Popery'. The evidence for this appeared abundant:

> the absurd custom of sending the children of professed protestants to foreign popish seminaries for education, the permission of popish schools in this kingdom, the pompous glare and mummery of public masses, not only in ambassadors [sic] chapels, but celebrated in almost every city and market town in the land, together with the influence of every popish lord and gentleman in his own neighbourhood, the multitudes of protestant servants retained in popish families, and married to popish wives and husbands; [given all this,] the man who should affirm, that there is no increase of papists among us, or that such increase is not ... inimical to every principle of civil and religious liberty ... must either have his senses bound up in some thick cloud upon the brain, or have such senses as have never been exercised to discern good and evil.[95]

Furthermore, Hollis believed that ecclesiastics of a Laudian complexion were infiltrating the Church of England's hierarchy,[96] and were conniving at this growth. Admittedly, some inferior clerics 'stepped forth against ... popery ... [but this was of] little public benefit, being unsupported by their leaders, and to sure detriment in their fortunes'.[97] The government was complicit too. The lenity to Catholics seemed especially sinister since it contrasted sharply with the Church's, and politicians', apparent hostility to Dissent.[98] To counter the conspiracy, Hollis, Fleming, Harris, and Lindsey bombarded the press, and particularly *The London Chronicle*, with innumerable pieces about Popery.[99] Hollis reprinted an anti-Papist classic from 1674, Thomas Staveley's *The Romish Horseleech*, and secured favourable comment for it in *The Monthly Review*.[100] One priest, he claimed, bragged that he had converted 1,500 people.[101] In September 1768, Hollis published in *The London Chronicle* his 'Plan for preventing the growth of popery in England', advocating a new set of anti-Papist laws.[102]

In 1767, in order to calm the outcry, the bishops organised a census of Papists.[103] The returns demonstrated convincingly that the alarm was unjustified. 69,376 Papists were listed for England and Wales;[104] in 1765, one newspaper had claimed that London and its environs contained some 200,000.[105] But Hollis and his circle were unconvinced. Indeed, they assimilated the results into their self-confirming conspiracy thesis. Archdeacon Blackburne was soon writing of a cover-up: 'I am informed that the lists about London are very superficially taken and that management has been used to sink and suppress discoveries'.[106] The *Memoirs of Thomas Hollis* pronounced that the clergy compiled the returns 'in a superficial, and, in some instances, in a partial and unfaithful manner'.[107] Dr Harris later wrote of 'the reasonable alarm we were under from ... [Popery's] increase from 1744 to 1767'.[108]

The colonial policies of different governments, Hollis and Blackburne maintained, further revealed the conspiracy. The Rockingham ministry acknowledged the Catholic Bishop Briand as 'Superintendent of Clergy' in Quebec, and permitted his consecration in France.[109] On learning that Briand had gone to Canada with the government's connivance, Hollis was outraged at 'so daring an insult upon the constitution'.[110] Archbishop Secker seemed especially culpable: had he really known nothing of the arrangement until the last moment, as he claimed?[111] Hollis, dying on 1 January 1774, did not witness the Quebec Act's passage. But he doubtless spoke from the grave in the *Memoirs*. In Blackburne's words, his

> reflections upon our ministerial and ecclesiastical connivances at popery, would probably have been thought severe had they been made public in 1763; but the Quebec bill put an end to all surmises, and gave a full view of the effects of a spirit of popery actuating the carcase of a Protestant government.[112]

How influential were Hollis' ideas? It appears that, as propagandists, Hollis and his coterie were so prolific that they very appreciably swelled the 'No Popery' debates in the pages of the metropolitan press.[113] The alarm about the 'growth of Popery' became general, as Parson Cole noted;[114] and this resulted in the decision to take the 1767 census. Moreover, the fiercest attack on the Quebec bill was launched by Chatham, Hollis' most important friend. Hollis' home in Dorset was near Chatham's; in his last years, Hollis attempted to find a house for himself in Lyme Regis and another for Chatham.[115] Chatham's speech in the Lords echoed Hollis' conviction that pro-Catholic measures were violations of the constitution.

> He deduced the whole series of laws from the supremacy first revindicated under Henry the 8th down to this day, as fundamentals constituting a clear compact that all establishments by law are to be Protestant; which compact ought not to be altered, but by the consent of the collective body of the people.[116]

In the Commons, Colonel Barré denounced the bill, and interestingly employed the language of Catholic conspiracy. The measure, he said,

> had originated with the Lords, who were the Romish priests that would give his Majesty absolution for breaking his promise given by the royal proclamation in 1763 ... [Lord North] might go on and support that or any sinful affair, as he was sure of getting absolution for all at last. He was certain, by the noble lord and his dependants' proceedings, that after their death people might say as they did after the death of king Charles, 'that by papers found in their closets, they appeared to have died in the Roman Catholic belief'.[117]

Lord George Gordon

Lord George Gordon was a controversial figure in his lifetime, and has remained one for some historians. For Horace Walpole, he was 'the lunatic apostle'.[118] Charles Turner MP, himself a notable eccentric, observed that the 'noble lord had got a twist in his head, a certain whirligig which ran away with him if anything relative to religion was mentioned'.[119] But when, in 1779, Gordon visited Scotland, he was elected President of the Protestant Association and fêted.[120] John Wesley, who visited him when imprisoned in the Tower after the riots, thought him sincere.[121] And Gordon was included in Paul Wright's *New and Complete Book of Martyrs* (1785?), an updated version of Foxe's *Actes and Monuments*.[122] Past historians tended to treat Gordon disdainfully. Eugene Charlton Black saw '[t]his gaunt, hawk-faced young man' as 'erratic, if not insane'.[123] George Rudé, interested in the riots not the individual, thought him 'a man of limited political capacity' and condemned his 'immoderate language'.[124] Recently, however, two scholars have viewed

Gordon more sympathetically. Douglas Hay praises his stand against capital punishment;[125] and Iain McCalman describes him, approvingly, as a 'modern revolutionary figure'.[126] The present writer, none the less, maintains that Gordon was 'unbalanced, irresponsible, and dangerous'.[127] Like the other George Gordon, Lord Byron, he was 'mad, bad, and dangerous to know'.

Gordon's demand for the 1778 Act's repeal can probably be explained by his earlier life, as well as by his eccentricity. Born in 1751, he was sent in 1758 to Eton, where he remained until 1765. After his schooling, he entered the navy, where the 'No Popery' tradition was strong,[128] becoming a lieutenant in 1772. When, therefore, he became MP for Ludgershall in 1774, his experience was limited to two regulated, confining institutions; he had no knowledge of affairs or political realities in England. Gordon himself was conscious of this. 'A young man, between twenty and thirty', he later wrote, 'was, to be sure, a very uncommon and unseemly sort of a President for the Protestant Associations of Great Britain to make choice of'.[129] Moreover, he did not grasp how circumscribed were the Relief Act's provisions. In his biography of Gordon, his friend Robert Watson erroneously called the measure 'the Bill for repealing the penal statutes in force against' the Papists; and this was seemingly Lord George's perception too.[130] Gordon failed to appreciate the day-to-day toleration increasingly enjoyed by the English Catholics in the 1760s and '70s, and polite society's approval of it. And, perhaps, he had a ghost to lay. Henry Sacheverell's High Churchmanship was partly a reaction against his family's Puritanism/Dissent (his paternal grandfather was imprisoned for Nonconformity in the 1660s and died in gaol).[131] Comparably, with Catholic and Jacobite forbears, no wonder Gordon protested too much.

Gordon's fullest exposition of his conspiracy thesis was a two-part pamphlet,[132] *Innocence Vindicated, and the Intrigues of Popery and its Abettors Displayed*. It was published in 1783, though Gordon apparently wrote most of it for his defence counsel prior to his trial for high treason in February 1781.[133] Unsurprisingly, it presents Gordon and his actions very favourably, emphasising his loyalty to the King, his integrity, and his impeccable manners.

Gordon maintained that 'dangerous incendiaries and malignants' had 'divided the King from the people, separated the Protestant Colonies from the Crown …, [and] sowed the seeds of civil war in Great Britain and Ireland'. These men had 'brought the true public liberty, safety, and peace of these kingdoms … into the utmost peril'.[134] Furthermore, Gordon argued, this was clearly a popish conspiracy: 'Popish Innovations' constituted 'the foul nest of the … grievous abominations, and evil things of this reign'.[135] The passing of the Quebec and Catholic Relief Acts showed that.[136] Like Payne and Hollis, Gordon thought that Popery was always the same. He believed that the

Catholics were still largely Jacobites, and that Catholic oaths were worthless. Following Locke and Wesley, he maintained that 'no government, not Roman Catholic, ought to tolerate Popery'.[137] Protestantism was incompatible with 'the toleration and encouragement of Idolatry'.[138]

Gordon believed that the conspiracy was at the heart of government. At an audience in May 1780, he told George III that he needed to 'clear away all the suspicions of Popery from his government and counsels'.[139] '[S]ome honorable and timely method of quieting the minds of the Protestants', was required, he continued, 'before the suspicion of Popery at St. James's should prevail generally throughout the three kingdoms'.[140] The king - a pitiable 'ill-educated Elector of Hanover' - was egregiously misled by his 'evil Counsellors'.[141] Gordon accepted testimony that the earl of Bute was 'a bigotted Papist';[142] Lord North ignored the Protestant petitions against the Relief Act.[143] Indeed, with the exception of Lord George Germain, the king's 'courtiers and confidential servants, to a man … shewed every appearance of hatred and evil dispositions towards … [Gordon], and the Petitions of the Protestants'.[144] Worst of all, the 'evil Counsellors' had approved the Relief Act 'for the diabolical purpose of arming the Papists against the Protestant Colonies in America'.[145] Meanwhile, some English Catholics boasted that their religion was *particularly well thought of by the rulers of the nation*.[146]

But the ruler of the nation? Gordon had doubts about George's Protestantism: when the king told him, '*I am myself a Protestant* … [and] *a friend to Toleration*', Gordon apparently replied that it gave him 'pleasure to hear him say he was himself a Protestant'![147] The king told Gordon that he taken no part in the negotiations preceding the Relief Act.[148] But when Gordon pressed him on specifics, he became evasive.[149] His suspicions heightened, Lord George 'determined to find out, and ascertain, the king's own real inclinations, if possible, with respect to Popery'.[150] George was plainly uninterested in the Protestant petitions, and refused to recommend them for North's consideration.[151] More minor circumstances were disturbing too. The king had accepted the hospitality of the Catholic Lord Petre.[152] A 'Papist Tradesman' was employed at court (trifles light as air were confirmations strong as proofs of holy writ).[153] At St James's, Gordon claimed, servants who had signed the Protestant Association's petition fearfully anticipated dismissal. Some even wanted, and had, their signatures erased from it.[154] When recounting these circumstances, Gordon brazenly described the comptroller of the household as 'the King's Inquisitor'; and denounced 'the King and his Popish Counsellors'.[155]

Innocence Vindicated was effectively written. It emphasised the 'intricacy, the perplexity, and the mysteriousness' of the conspiracy - a conspiracy which,

Gordon claimed, was 'too obscure for ... [his] understanding to compass'.[156] The Relief Act's origins in the plan to use Papists in the American war was the government's 'dark secret'.[157] Lord George promised that his pamphlet would lay before the public 'mysterious and obscure subjects' and 'open up to the world a very dark series of transactions'.[158] The title-page stated that it described 'Transactions, hitherto unknown'. But if the details were new, Gordon had propagated the thesis' central tenet before the riots. Indeed, his speeches in 1779 and 1780 were blunter than his later writing. In the debate on the king's speech in 1779, he claimed that the Scots were 'convinced in their own minds that the King is a papist'.[159] In March 1780, 'he told the House he had 160,000 men in Scotland at his command, and that if the King did not keep his coronation oath ... they were determined to cut off his head'.[160] The following month, he informed the Commons that his followers 'had not yet determined to murder the King and put him to death: they only considered they were absolved from their allegiance'.[161] The imputation was, perhaps, that the Pope had absolved the Catholic king from his coronation oath to uphold Protestantism.

The Gordon Riots

Were Gordon's ideas important? Charles Turner saw Lord George as 'a laughing stock, and ... the make game of the whole House'.[162] '[T]his man is so mad ...', Horace Walpole ejaculated in January 1780.[163] It was perfectly possible to deplore the Relief Act - on sober religious grounds, for instance - while discounting Gordon's rantings. But there were others besides Gordon who propagated the flatulent thesis that there was 'Popery at St. James's'.

The *Appeal from the Protestant Association to the People of Great Britain* was published on 5 November 1779. It maintained that something 'is necessary to be done, to assure the nation in general ... that it is not the intention of the Legislature, to encourage the growth of Popery'.[164] The next year, in June, the appalling Gordon riots erupted. A subversive paper, *The Thunderer*, declared, at the tumult's height, that it 'has long been the design both of the court and ministry to establish arbitrary power, and the Roman Catholic religion in England'.[165] It particularly scorned 'the *Romish* complexion of *Pious* the *third* our *Protestant* king'.[166] The 'pot house politicians', another writer claimed, 'are instructed to accuse his Majesty of a predilection for Popery'.[167] One print depicted George as a tonsured monk, with a picture of the Pope in his rooms and the Protestant petitions strewn in the privy.[168] Unsurprisingly, an attack on St James's was expected during the riots.[169]

Similar nonsense was heard on the London streets during the disturbances. Some claimed, Samuel Romilly recorded, that the king was a Catholic and privately heard mass; his confessor supposedly directed his political actions.[170] It was said that Lord Mansfield 'had advised the dragoons to ride over the Protestants that He is a Roman Catholic & Had made the King one'.[171] When a mob destroyed his house in Bloomsbury, one rioter rejoiced that his wealth would no longer pay for popish masses.[172] Nor were the rumours confined to the metropolis. Around Alton in Hampshire, 'the lower class of the people seem'd inclineable to join ... [the commotions] on a mistaken notion of universal popery being to be established amongs us'.[173] Near Lord Dartmouth's home at Woodsome in the West Riding, demonstrators, convinced that North had fled there, maintained that he had 'encouraged popery'.[174] Lord George Gordon's conspiracy theory had a remarkable - and remarkably dangerous - currency.

Conclusion

In a short essay, it is impossible to investigate fully a complex subject's many facets and nuances. The language of both Payne and Gordon was sometimes guarded or evasive; the meaning of broad hints is usually clear, but veiled innuendo is occasionally susceptible of more than one interpretation. Brisk summaries of the pamphlets unavoidably obscure this. The theses' schizophrenic qualities merit sustained examination - for instance, the depiction of George III first as the Papists' victim, then as a crypto-Papist. Above all, the separate analyses of three publications from 1767, 1780, and 1783 hide the wider, underlying continuities of 'No Popery' thinking during the period. In 1780, the radical journalist William Moore denounced Popery in *The Thunderer*.[175] During the previous decade, in *The Whisperer*, he had alleged that Papists planned to kill the king and, in 1770, had fired Portsmouth dockyard.[176] After the Gordon riots, the government forbade meetings on Sundays - the usual day - of religious debating societies: it believed they had encouraged the tumults.[177] But in the 1770s, if not before, such bodies had, unobtrusively, promoted 'No Popery' feeling in the capital.[178] The Gordon riots themselves had an ominous precursor. On 22 June 1774, George III had gone to Westminster, to give the Quebec bill the royal assent. In the streets, crowds shouted 'Remember Charles I!', 'Remember James II!', and 'No Popery!'. Seditious papers attacking George were posted on churches and in other public places.[179]

In 1767, 'S.R.' had ridiculed William Payne and his kind: '[t]he near connexion between Popery and the price of provisions', he sneered, 'when once mentioned - will be so apparent to a considerate mind - that he will wonder how he neglected or missed it'.[180] But during the Gordon riots, Payne, like a malevolent Wagnerian dwarf, re-emerged, exhorting the crowds 'to have the Bill repealed ... [and] declaring that their forefathers had been persecuted and massacred by Papists, and [he] hoped it would not happen again'.[181] If 'S.R.' witnessed the riots, one presumes he recognised, belatedly, that the nonsense Payne talked was not amusing, but deeply disturbing.

Notes

1   J.M. Roberts, *The Mythology of the Secret Societies*, 2nd edn (St Albans, 1974), p. 15.

2   Keith Thomas, *Religion and the Decline of Magic* (London, 1971), p. 581.

3   H.R. Trevor-Roper, *The European Witch-Craze of the 16th and 17th Centuries* (Harmondsworth, 1969), pp. 40–54.

4   Geoffrey Cubitt, 'Robespierre and conspiracy theories', *Robespierre*, ed. Colin Haydon and William Doyle (Cambridge, 1999), pp. 75–91.

5   [Daniel Defoe], *The Great Law of Subordination Consider'd* (London, 1724), p. 20.

6   Roberts, *Mythology*, p. 15.

7   Henry Sacheverell, *The Perils of False Brethren* (London, 1709).

8   John Walsh discussed this subject in his 1987 Birkbeck Lectures.

9   Hampshire R[ecord] O[ffice], Photocopy 605, 46, 52, 68.

10 Ibid., 42.

11 J.C.D. Clark, ed., *The Memoirs and Speeches of James, 2nd Earl Waldegrave 1742–1763* (Cambridge, 1988), p. 59; Stephen Taylor, '"The fac totum in ecclesiastic affairs"? The duke of Newcastle and the crown's ecclesiastical patronage', *Albion* xxiv (1992), pp. 430–1.

12 Paul Langford, ed., *The Writings and Speeches of Edmund Burke. Volume II: Party, Parliament, and the American Crisis 1766–1774* (Oxford, 1981), pp. 241–323.

13 John Miller, *Popery and Politics in England 1660–1688* (Cambridge, 1973, repr. 1978), pp. 85–6; Barry Reay, *The Quakers and the English Revolution* (London, 1985), pp. 59–60, 65, 96.

14 Thomas Macro, *Charity of Temper* (London, 1732), p. 25. My italics.

15 Cambridge University Library, Cholmondeley (Houghton) MS 72/18/1, unfoliated.

16 Ibid.

17 Colin Haydon, *Anti-Catholicism in Eighteenth-Century England, c. 1714–80* (Manchester, 1994), pp. 164–203.

18 William Cobbett, *The Parliamentary History of England, from the Earliest Period to the Year 1803*, XIX (London, 1814), col. 1,144.

19 William Blackstone, *Commentaries on the Laws of England*, IV (Oxford, 1769), p. 57.

20 M.D. Petre, *The Ninth Lord Petre* (London, 1928), pp. 39–48.

21 Reginald Coupland, *The Quebec Act* (London, 1925, repr. 1968), p. 21.

22 John Hey, *A Sermon Preached before the University of Cambridge, on Saturday, November 5, 1774* (Cambridge, 1774), p. 17.

23   John, Lord Campbell, *The Lives of the Chief Justices of England*, 3rd edn, III (London, 1874), p. 401.

24   W.M. Elofson with John A. Woods, eds., *The Writings and Speeches of Edmund Burke. Volume III: Party, Parliament, and the American War 1774–1780* (Oxford, 1996), p. 643.

25   12 Geo. III, c. 122.

26   18 Geo. III, c. 60.

27   Robert Kent Donovan, 'The military origins of the Roman Catholic relief programme of 1778', *Historical Journal* xxviii (1985), pp. 79–102.

28   14 Geo. III, c. 83.

29   Cobbett, *Parliamentary History*, XVII (London, 1813), col. 1,403.

30   Vincent Harlow, 'The new imperial system 1783–1815', *The Cambridge History of the British Empire. Volume II: The Growth of the New Empire 1783–1870*, ed. J. Holland Rose, A.P. Newton, and E.A. Benians (Cambridge, 1940, repr. 1961), pp. 151–2.

31   Nigel Abercrombie, 'The first Relief Act', *Challoner and his Church*, ed. Eamon Duffy (London, 1981), p. 175.

32   R.B. McDowell, *Ireland in the Age of Imperialism and Revolution 1760–1801* (Oxford, 1979), p. 189.

33   Ibid., p. 190.

34   *Annual Register* xvii (1774), 'The History of Europe', p. 78.

35   Cobbett, *Parliamentary History*, XVII, cols 1,405–6.

36   Elofson with Woods, eds., *Writings of Burke. III*, p. 614.

37   John Locke, *Epistola de Tolerantia/A Letter on Toleration*, ed. Raymond Klibansky and J.W. Gough (Oxford, 1968), p. 133; [Lord George Gordon], *Innocence Vindicated, and the Intrigues of Popery and its Abettors Displayed*, 2 parts, continuous pagination, 2nd edn (London, 1783), p. 16.

38   *A Letter from the Rev. Mr. John Wesley, A.M. To the Printer of the Public Advertiser* (n.p., 1780).

39   Joanna Innes, 'Politics and morals: The Reformation of Manners movement in later eighteenth-century England', *The Transformation of Political Culture: England and Germany in the Late Eighteenth Century*, ed. Eckhart Hellmuth (Oxford, 1990), pp. 112–14.

40   Eamon Duffy, 'Richard Challoner 1691–1781: A Memoir', *Challoner and his Church*, ed. Duffy, p. 22.

41   11 and 12 Will. III, c. 4.

42   Duffy, 'Challoner', p. 22.

43   Haydon, *Anti-Catholicism*, pp. 172–3; Duffy, 'Challoner', p. 22.

44   Cf. Linda Colley, *Britons: Forging the Nation 1707–1837* (New Haven and London, 1992), pp. 11–54; Colin Haydon, '"I love my king and my country, but a Roman Catholic I hate": anti-Catholicism, xenophobia, and national identity in eighteenth-century England', *Protestantism and National Identity: Britain and Ireland c. 1650–c. 1850*, ed. Tony Claydon and Ian McBride (Cambridge, 1998), pp. 33–52.

45   Advertised in volumes or in parts on the back of Payne's pamphlet.

46   [William Payne], *Cry Aloud, and Spare Not* (London, 1767), p. 17.

47   Ibid., p. 29.

48   Ibid., pp. 11, 13.

49   Ibid., p. 10.

50   Ibid., p. 28.

51   Ibid., p. 27.

52   Ibid., p. 23.

53   Ibid.
54   Ibid., pp. 23–4.
55   Ibid., p. 24.
56   Ibid., p. 29.
57   Ibid., p. 26.
58   Ibid., p. 24.
59   Ibid., p. 30.
60   Ibid., p. 28.
61   Ibid.
62   Ibid., p. 27.
63   Ibid., p. 25.
64   Ibid.
65   Ibid., p. 26.
66   Ibid., p. 25.
67   Ibid., pp. 25–6.
68   Thomas, *Religion and the Decline of Magic*, p. 641.
69   [Payne], *Cry Aloud*, p. 26.
70   Ibid.
71   Ibid.
72   Ibid., p. 27.
73   Edwin H. Burton, *The Life and Times of Bishop Challoner (1691–1781)*, II (London, 1909, repr. Farnborough, 1970), p. 94.
74   'S.R.', *A Letter to a Member of Parliament: Concerning the Effects of the Growth of Popery, on the Price of Provisions; By a Journeyman Shoemaker* (London, 1767), p. 23.
75   Ibid., p. 22.
76   Ibid., pp. 27–8. As a constable, Payne policed markets and, in 1772, presented to the Lords a scheme for lowering many provisions' prices. I am grateful to Joanna Innes for this information and for showing me her entry on Payne in the *Oxford D[ictionbary of] N[ational] B[iograpy]*, ed. Colin Matthew and Brian Harrison (forthcoming).
77   Cobbett, *Parliamentary History*, XIX, col. 1,145.
78   Lord Edmond Fitzmaurice, *Life of William, Earl of Shelburne ... With Extracts from his Papers and Correspondence*, III (London, 1876), p. 84.
79   Cobbett, *Parliamentary History*, XIX, col. 1,145.
80   18 Geo. III, c. 60.
81   Cobbett, *Parliamentary History*, XXI (London, 1814), cols 714–26, 754–66.
82   [Francis Blackburne, ed.], *Memoirs of Thomas Hollis*, I (London, 1780), p. 5.
83   W.H. Bond, *Thomas Hollis of Lincoln's Inn: A Whig and his Books* (Cambridge, 1990), pp. 10, 32.
84   J.C.D. Clark, *English Society 1660–1832* (Cambridge, 2000), p. 362.
85   Bond, *Hollis*, p. 30. On Hollis' life, see Caroline Robbins, *The Eighteenth-Century Commonwealthman* (Cambridge, Mass, 1959), *passim*; Robbins, 'The strenuous Whig, Thomas Hollis of Lincoln's Inn', *William and Mary Quarterly*, 3rd Series, vii (1950), pp. 406–53; Bond, *Hollis, passim*.
86   Bond, *Hollis*, pp. 9–10.
87   Ibid., pp. 3, 6.

88   G.M. Ditchfield, 'The changing nature of English anticlericalism c. 1750–c. 1800', *Anticlericalism in Britain c. 1500–1914*, ed. Nigel Aston and Matthew Cragoe (Stroud, 2000), p. 102; Clark, *English Society*, p. 362.

89   [Blackburne, ed.], *Memoirs of Hollis*, I, p. 214.

90   Cf. Andrew C. Thompson, 'Popery, politics, and private judgement in early Hanoverian Britain', *Historical Journal* xlv (2002), pp. 333–56.

91   [Blackburne, ed.], *Memoirs of Hollis*, I, p. 395.

92   Ibid., I, p. 460.

93   Ibid.

94   Ibid.

95   Ibid., I, p. 352.

96   Ibid., I, p. 431.

97   Ibid., I, p. 214.

98   In particular, in 1772 and 1773, Parliament refused to relieve Dissenting ministers and schoolmasters of the registration requirement of subscription to the Anglican doctrinal articles.

99   Haydon, *Anti-Catholicism*, p. 185.

100   Thomas Staveley, *The Romish Horseleech*, 2nd edn (London, 1769); *Monthly Review* xlii (1770), pp. 34–6; [Blackburne, ed.], *Memoirs of Hollis*, I, p. 420.

101   [Blackburne, ed.], *Memoirs of Hollis*, I, p. 252.

102   Ibid., I, pp. 359–61, II (London, 1780), pp. 706–8; *The London Chronicle*, 22–4 September 1768.

103   *Annual Register* x (1767), 'Chronicle', p. 109.

104   John Bossy, *The English Catholic Community 1570–1850* (London, 1975), p. 184.

105   Martin H. Fitzpatrick, 'Rational Dissent in Late Eighteenth-Century England, with Particular Reference to the Growth of Toleration', University of Wales PhD thesis, 1982, pp. 158–9.

106   Ibid., p. 161.

107   [Blackburne, ed.], *Memoirs of Hollis*, I, p. 351.

108   Bodleian Library, Oxford, Vet. A5 e.1,117.

109   P. Langford, *The First Rockingham Administration 1765–1766* (London, 1973), p. 254.

110   [Blackburne, ed.], *Memoirs of Hollis*, I, p. 317.

111   Ibid.

112   Ibid., I, p. 215.

113   J.P. Thomas, 'The British Empire and the Press 1763–1774', University of Oxford DPhil thesis, 1982, pp. 329–61.

114   British Library, Add. MS 5,811, fols 132v–5v.

115   Bond, *Hollis*, pp. 10, 31.

116   Cobbett, *Parliamentary History*, XVII, cols 1,403–4.

117   Ibid., cols 1,393–4.

118   J.A. Cannon, 'Gordon, Lord George (1751–93)', *The House of Commons 1754–1790*, ed. Sir Lewis Namier and John Brooke, II (London, 1964), p. 514, col. 1.

119   Ibid.

120   Robert Kent Donovan, *No Popery and Radicalism: Opposition to Roman Catholic Relief in Scotland 1778–1782* (New York and London, 1987), pp. 36–7.

121   Nehemiah Curnock, ed., *The Journal of the Rev. John Wesley, A.M.*, VI (London, 1938), p. 301.

122 Paul Wright, ed., *The New and Complete Book of Martyrs* (London, 1785?), pp. 816–18.

123 Eugene Charlton Black, *The Association: British Extraparliamentary Political Organization 1769–1793* (Cambridge, Mass, 1963), pp. 147–8, 132.

124 George Rudé, *Hanoverian London 1714–1808* (London, 1971), p. 220; Rudé, 'The Gordon Riots: A study of the rioters and their victims', *Transactions of the Royal Historical Society*, 5th Series, vi (1956), p. 102.

125 Douglas Hay, 'The laws of God and the laws of man: Lord George Gordon and the death penalty', *Protest and Survival: Essays for E. P. Thompson*, ed. John Rule and Robert Malcolmson (London, 1993), pp. 60–111.

126 Iain McCalman, 'Mad Lord George and Madame La Motte: riot and sexuality in the genesis of Burke's *Reflections on the Revolution in France*', *Journal of British Studies* xxxv (1996), p. 366.

127 Colin Haydon, *Oxford DNB* (forthcoming).

128 Haydon, '"I love my king and my country"', pp. 44, 48–9. See, too, Sydney Smith's satire on this: 'Peter Plymley', *Letters on the Subject of the Catholics*, 6th edn (London, 1808), pp. 39–40.

129 [Gordon], *Innocence Vindicated*, p. 25.

130 Robert Watson, *The Life of Lord George Gordon* (London, 1795), p. 10.

131 Geoffrey Holmes, *The Trial of Doctor Sacheverell* (London, 1973), pp. 5–6. Sacheverell was much embarrassed by his 'fanatic kindred' (Ibid., p. 5). Furthermore, his maternal grandfather was possibly a regicide! (Ibid., p. 4, n.)

132 Gordon intended to publish a third part, but apparently did not: [Gordon], *Innocence Vindicated*, p. 28.

133 Ibid., pp. 4, 15.

134 Ibid., p. 3.

135 Ibid., p. 24.

136 Ibid., p. 16.

137 Ibid.

138 Ibid.

139 Ibid.

140 Ibid., p. 20.

141 Ibid., p. 25.

142 Ibid., p. 27.

143 Ibid., p. 23.

144 Ibid., pp. 24–5.

145 Ibid., p. 20.

146 Ibid., p. 23.

147 Ibid., p. 16.

148 Ibid., p. 15.

149 Ibid., p. 16.

150 Ibid., p. 23.

151 Ibid., pp. 17, 25.

152 Ibid., pp. 4–5.

153 Ibid., pp. 16, 26.

154 Ibid., pp. 27–8.

155 Ibid., p. 28.

156 Ibid., p. 25.

157 Ibid., p. 20.
158 Ibid., p. 4.
159 Cannon, 'Gordon', p. 514, col. 1.
160 Ibid.
161 Ibid., col. 2.
162 Ibid., col. 1.
163 Ibid.
164 *An Appeal from the Protestant Association to the People of Great Britain* (London, 1779), p. 59.
165 *The Thunderer*, 8 June 1780, p. 1.
166 Ibid., p. 2.
167 *The Reformer. By an Independent Freeholder* (London, 1780), p. 24.
168 British Museum, Department of Prints and Drawings, 5,680. Another print represented Bute as a Papist: Ibid., 5,669.
169 P[ublic] RO, S[tate] P[apers] Dom[estic], 37/20/188.
170 *Memoirs of the Life of Sir Samuel Romilly, Written by Himself ... Edited by his Sons*, I (London, 1840), p. 128.
171 PRO, SP Dom. 37/20/219.
172 L.H. Thraves, 'The Gordon Riots 1780', University of Liverpool MA thesis, 1910, ch. 3, p. 23.
173 PRO, SP Dom. 37/21/77.
174 Historical Manuscripts Commission, *Dartmouth MSS*, III (1896), p. 252.
175 Nicholas Rogers, *Crowds, Culture, and Politics in Georgian Britain* (Oxford, 1998), p. 173.
176 *The Whisperer* lxxxvi (1771), pp. 537–44; Ibid. xc (1771), pp. 565–70; Ibid. xcl (1771), pp. 571–4; Kathleen Wilson, *The Sense of the People: Politics, Culture, and Imperialism in England 1715–1785* (Cambridge, 1995), p. 215.
177 21 Geo. III, c. 49; J. W. Middelton, *An Ecclesiastical Memoir of the First Four Decades of the Reign of George III* (London, 1822), p. 194.
178 *Fanaticism and Treason* (London, 1780), pp. 27–9. Cf. Basil Cozens-Hardy, ed., *The Diary of Sylas Neville 1767–1788* (London, 1950), p. 51.
179 A. Francis Steuart, ed., *The Last Journals of Horace Walpole during the Reign of George III from 1771–1783*, I (London, 1910), p. 362; *Public Advertiser*, 23 June 1774.
180 'S.R.', *Letter*, p. 3.
181 PRO, Privy Council 1/3,097.

Chapter 11

Conspiracy and Political Practice from the *ancien régime* to the French Revolution

Peter Campbell

We think of the revolution as having been obsessed with conspiracy, as so many plots and conspiracies were denounced. Yet when we consult the catalogues of the British Library and the *Bibliothèque nationale*, it is interesting to see that works with *complot, conjuration, conspiration,* or *intrigue*, in the title account for only a tiny proportion of the total numbers. The overwhelming majority of such titles, well over 90 per cent, were published in the nineteenth and twentieth centuries. We discover titles about plots by capitalists, Jews, the duchesse de Berry, Nazis, amorous intrigues, spies, freemasons - it makes one wonder which era has been the most obsessed with this implied mode of historical explanation. Threats to national security seem to have regularly generated speculation and accusations of conspiracy in the modern age. In that context the preoccupation with conspiracy at the time of the French revolution should be less surprising to us. But historians have recently made two significant claims about plots and conspiracies then. The first is that the revolutionaries' obsession helped drive the revolution towards the Terror.[1] The second is that this was new, and grew mainly out of the politics surrounding the Flight to Varennes in 1791.[2] This paper seeks to explore the context of plots and conspiracies at that time by focusing on this type of activity as it was perceived towards the end of the *ancien régime*. No doubt as many questions will be begged as answers suggested, for study of the vision of politics before the revolution is still in its early days - and the very concept of *ancien régime* 'politics' seems open to question.[3]

What then is a conspiratorial explanation? Should it be considered, in the manner of John Roberts and Gordon Wood, as the product of an age, an unhistorical explanation, one that is the consequence of a mind set that cannot cope with the complexities of causation in a large society, one no longer face-to-face but moved by the actions of millions unknown to each other? Full of 1960s scepticism and rationality, Roberts and Wood were interested in exploring what they saw as a collective delusion, a paranoid style of politics.[4] But now that we know so much more about seventeenth- and eighteenth-century politics, should we not ask whether belief in plots had not only its own historically specific rationality, but also a large element of accuracy in its portrayal of *ancien régime* and revolutionary politics? The more we focus on the importance of conspiracy in the revolution as a driving force towards (or simply an aspect of) the Terror, the more important it becomes to understand its context, which means looking at the experience of the revolutionaries before the revolution.

The *mentalité* of the revolutionaries was of course partly constructed in and by the revolutionary experience. But the men and women of the revolution were also formerly men and women of the *ancien régime*. On a conscious level, they may have rejected much of that régime's social and political structures, but unconsciously they must have carried with them older ways of thought. Moreover, the revolution was in some ways responsible for creating the *ancien régime* as an antithesis to its own projected politics and society, and the image of the *ancien régime* played a part in the political culture of the revolution.[5] One way of discrediting the former régime was to show how its politics were corrupt, occult, conspiratorial and plotting. There was a propaganda value to exposing the truth about the old politics, and one historian and geographer, the abbé Soulavie, more or less specialised in producing some apocryphal and several genuine 'memoirs'.[6] Interestingly, as French representative in Geneva, he wrote a number of letters to Robespierre warning him of conspiracies.[7] Moreover, a political purpose was served by stressing that *ci-devants*, aristocrats, continued to behave in typical *ancien régime* ways, plotting against the new régime with their old strategies for old aims: these were the restoration of court society and its politics of corruption. The search for transparency in revolutionary politics thus contrasted sharply with notions of politics before the revolution, and, from this perspective, *ancien régime* politics *was* conspiracy. It was covert, factional, characterised by intrigues for place and wealth, and designed to influence the sovereign behind closed doors; foreign policy was limited by dynastic considerations rather than the national interest.

Let us not forget though, that the actual conspiracies in *ancien régime* France have their own interest, for they can illuminate aspects of its culture and politics. It is of course true to say that fear of conspiracy was an overt or, by the eighteenth century, at least latent part of the political culture of the *ancien régime*. One can cite the religious plots and the dynastic feuds of the sixteenth century; the Day of Dupes and Cinq Mars under Richelieu, the fear of Protestant, Jansenist and Jesuit plots in the seventeenth and even eighteenth centuries; the intrigues and conspiracies of Retz or Condé during the Frondes; in the eighteenth century came the accusations that the Regent Philippe d'Orléans was interfering with the precarious succession (there were claims that members of the royal family had been poisoned and that Louis XV was at risk); there were manoeuvres by Philip V of Spain in the 1720s to secure supporters for his claim to the throne he had renounced; then Damiens was thought to have acted with accomplices, making his blow the product of a conspiracy;[8] Maupeou was accused of having acted against the parlements as a consequence of the influence of the *parti dévôt* who supported d'Aiguillon in the Britanny affair;[9] Turgot felt the grain riots of 1775 were partly inspired by opposition to his reforms, as indeed they may have been. The great plot of the 1780s was that developed by vile courtiers and corrupt ministers to make France into a despotism.[10] That was why France needed the Estates General.

Comparing these practices and rumours from the *ancien régime* with the denunciations during the revolution is an interesting exercise in continuities:

> Another faction existed which schemed and was involved with all the others, which sometimes wanted to usurp [power], sometimes was royalist, sometimes wanted riches, sometimes thought to acquire a great authority, whatever the regime in place, sometimes served foreign states: this faction, like all the others, without courage, led the Revolution like the plot of a play. Fabre d'Eglantine was at the head of this faction; he was not alone there; he was the cardinal de Retz of today.[11]

Reading this accusation by Saint-Just, and his earlier one against the Hébertistes, it is clear that there is considerable carry over between a tacit sense of what *ancien régime* politics was all about (which he assumes his audience shares), and the activities of these alleged conspirators.[12]

So, there are *ancien régime* origins of the revolutionary obsession with plots in terms of the vision of politics and of its implications during the revolution.[13] That is not to say that fears of conspiracy under the revolution were simply a direct continuation of such fears under the *ancien régime*. Far from it, but understanding the context can help us avoid thinking that it was all new in the revolution, and help us to focus on the right questions, such as the fear of certain political practices - faction for example - and the idea that those who employed *ancien régime* methods during the revolution were necessarily counter-revolutionary plotters. It would be a mistake to equate conspiratorial explanations of political activity during the *ancien régime* with a necessarily 'paranoid style' of explanation. Such explanations are only paranoid if they grossly exaggerate the reality. During the revolution there was a basis in fact to some of the accusations, and in pre-revolutionary politics faction, intrigue, plots to discredit ministers and courtiers, are everyday realities. In this paper I am particularly concerned to establish the part played by the image or reality of later *ancien régime* politics in the origins of the revolutionary obsession with conspiracy.

I

Let us first ask whether we are justified in sharing the revolutionaries' views of the way politics worked before the revolution - were they right in condemning the way things were done in the former régime? To do this we need to ask what practices were then thought to be involved in a conspiracy? The area of meaning covers intrigue, covert actions, attempts to achieve political ends secretly by collaborating, caballing, working together. Above all by 1789 a conspiracy involves moral corruption. Here we can perhaps identify a legacy of the heretical elements associated with the earlier idea of doing Satan's work - but let us not make too much of this because much more important in the eighteenth century was the legacy of Greek and Roman history and the influence of the new secular morality of the age. Historical models of conspiracy might be Sallust's account of the Catiline conspiracy, and the assassination of Caesar.[14]

The key words in French are: *cabale, complot, conspiration, conjuration, intrigue, brigue* and their verbs. These words are used in ways which range from the matter of fact to the condemnatory. The *Encyclopédie* does not have an entry for *complot*, but briefly defines a *conjuration* as a 'plot by ill-intentioned persons against the prince or the state' and then has a lengthy dissertation on magic. *Conspiration* is 'a union of several persons with the aim of doing hard to someone or to something. One says a *conjuration* of several individuals, and a *conspiration* in the case of all the orders of a state; the *conjuration* of Cataline... a *conjuration* against the state; a *conspiration* against a courtier'. *Intrigue* is defined as 'the improper conduct of people who are seeking to arrive, or advance themselves, or obtain posts, graces, or honours by a cabal or stratagem. It is the recourse of weak and corrupt souls, just as fencing is the trade of the coward'. There follows eleven and a half columns on plot in drama.

The edition of Richelet's *Dictionnaire portatif de la langue française* revised by de Wailly in 1775 describes a cabal as 'an *intrigue, conjuration, société* [association] in which people act together for common or private interests: it can have an innocuous meaning, as in amusing ourselves in our little cabal'; to cabal means 'to win over a group of people who will support us, and to try to succeed in a plan by means of secret actions, by subtle means'. *Complot* has a negative connotation, being a dark and wicked scheme to do harm to someone, to make him fall [from favour] or ruin him. A *conjuration* is 'a party of people united against the interests of the state, of a sovereign etc'. *Conjurer* retains this sense of acting against the state, but also means to conspire against an individual. For Richelet, *conspirer* has much the same sense as *conjurer*, except that it can be used of either a good or bad intention.[15]

The definitions are largely in agreement, but have in common an area of meaning that goes beyond doing harm to a state or sovereign and incorporates normal practice. Littré (1865) sees a similarity in meaning between *cabale* and *complot*, in that they express the association of several to attain an object, but he discerns a distinction in that a *complot* was directed to a subversive political end and aimed to change by force something in the government, a cabal was not. It is notable that most of these definitions contain the idea of doing harm, and this could be a matter of opinion, in that it supposes the plotters or intriguers were morally corrupt. They are doing more than furthering their own interests: the words for that were *intrigue*, *cabal*. The words *brigue* and *intrigue* are often employed together in the same phrase as near synonyms.

There is thus a wide and somewhat imprecise area of meaning involved, which should put historians on their guard. Clearly writers could exercise a degree of choice in characterising practices as either legitimate factional behaviour, or condemn it as conspiratorial or plotting, even under the *ancien régime*. Indeed, painstaking research by Jean-Claude Waquet has stressed the blurring of definitions by the authors of dictionaries.[16] 'Their use moreover does not suggest any regularity: what is conspiracy with one becomes cabal for another, plot for a third, when it is not intrigue or monopoly. Thus each event does not appear in the texts [of dictionaries] under the name given to it in history books today, but bears in the course of these writings as many as six or seven different appellations' that reflect the political intentions of the author.[17]

II

The idea of conspiracy and plot had a legal use and many people were prosecuted for criminal conspiracy. If we peruse the *arrêts du parlement*, we can see that there were indeed many condemnations for plotting criminal acts, and many of these were linked to some of the famous criminal gangs.

Recognising conspiracy is more problematic when we consider politics: a given historian's assessment can depend upon the meaning of *conspiration, conjuration* and *complot* chosen. Bercé is surely right to argue that there is a decline of conspiratorial activity in the eighteenth century *if by that he means attempts to change the government or system of the state*.[18] This would certainly be true in the sense that the monarchy as an institution seemed well established and more secure by then, and there were no challenges to the legitimacy of the Bourbons. And yet, there certainly were constant manoeuvrings as different Bourbon branches positioned themselves for the possibility of a succession that might be disputed. Indeed, in the other senses of the words (those implying conspiring for positions of power, plotting for places in the system, and intriguing to undermine individuals and policies), in contrast to Bercé and still more recently Timothy Tackett, we should recognise that the type of explanation associated with 'conspiracy' was still a central feature of political life.[19]

Moreover, there were certainly widespread assumptions of plotting and conspiracy. Let us quickly consider some events or cases in which a form of conspiracy was thought to be involved. On the government side was the idea shared by the elite that popular revolts involved the conspiracy of the local authorities against royal authority. The lower orders were thought incapable of leadership and organisation, thus revolt must have involved conspiracy by those entrusted with enforcing order. This idea persisted up to 1789 as evidenced in the Flour War, the Réveillon riots and the Great Fear.[20]

From the other end of the social scale, the famine plot persuasion persisted right up to and into the Revolution.[21] The poor were convinced that the market in grain was being manipulated by capitalists and hoarders in order to make vast profits from the creation or exacerbation of dearth which would drive prices higher. Although the reality of such actions on a grand scale cannot be substantiated, the belief did reflect what happened year in year out on a smaller scale, in that those who could afford it inevitably made profits from their relative wealth by selling their surplus grain towards the summer when prices were higher because the peasants had been obliged to sell just after the harvest to pay their rents and taxes. Prices would usually double over the year and those with sufficient stocks would always profit.

Turning to 'politics' in court society, without dwelling on the several plots of the seventeenth century, we might stress (*pace* Bercé and Tackett) the continuation of conspiratorial practices up to the eve of the Revolution. A far from exhaustive list drawn from the eighteenth century might include the Cellamare conspiracy of 1718 which was a genuine plot. The Regent Philippe d'Orléans was said unfairly to be thinking of poisoning young Louis XV (as he had already been suspected of poisoning Louis XIV's heirs in 1711), in which case he stood to inherit the throne. In 1725 the Pâris brothers and the duc de Bourbon imprisoned the Belle-Isle brothers for some murky financial dealings involving a murder. Montgon's memoirs give an account of the intrigues of the *grands* and Philippe V to secure French throne in the event of the premature death of Louis XV without an heir before 1728 when the Dauphin was born. The *parti janséniste* from the 1720s to the 1760s was behaving in a very organised, some might say conspiratorial, way in publicising, organising and co-ordinating protest at the religious policy of the Crown, which they saw as essentially Jesuit-inspired [and this gave them the opportunity to refer to the old beliefs in Jesuit plots]. The Damiens affair gave rise to a very determined search for the 'other' presumed conspirators, and reminds us that whole aspects of the judicial system were predicated on the assumption of conspiracy. For a long time during the *ancien régime* the Jesuits were believed to have been conspiring to mislead the king, attack their enemies and further the cause of despotism. The plot of Bourgfontaine, invented by Jesuitistical lawyers in 1655, remained a persistent enough theme of conspiracy for a volume to have been published in 1787 entitled *The reality of the Bourg-Fontaine project, demonstrated by its very deeds.*[22]

The expulsion of Jesuits stemming from the trial of 1762 was believed to have been a *philosophe* plot, although many saw it as Jansenist led, which it was in fact, as Dale Van Kley has shown.[23] Also the Brittany affair of the 1760s was based upon the assumption that the *procureur général* of the Rennes parlement, La Chalotais, was conspiring against royal authority. It led of course to another perceived plot, that of the *parti dévôt* and anti Madame du Barry faction, to defend the governor of Brittany the duc d'Aiguillon against the Jansenist-led Paris parlement.[24] Even trying to summarise it shows how murky the waters were! The pamphlet literature following the Maupeou coup sees the idea of conspiracy taking the interesting turn, not unknown before of course (viz Richelieu and Mazarin), of the evil minister conspiring against the citizenry or political system for personal reasons, using underhand court manoeuvres. This was now labelled *unpatriotic*, and Maupeou's opponents were presented as citizens and patriots.

The period from 1774 to 1789 was not without its accusations of plots and conspiracy. Notably there was the idea that Marie Antoinette was a stooge for the House of Habsburg, and here of course there was great continuity with the revolutionary accusations.[25] Then the Diamond Necklace affair of 1785 might be said to explore notions of conspiracy in public rumour and speculation. It links the interests of the state with criminal plotting in interesting ways.[26] Soon after, the notion that the ancient constitution of France was under renewed threat from despotism became one of the great themes of the pre-revolution. The pre-revolution in Brittany from 1788–1789, with its vehement split in the Estates between the nobility and the Third Estate, represented a powerful model for the deputies in the Estates General, fuelling their paranoia in June. In the Estates General, the idea was current in both the chambers of the Nobility and the Third Estate that plots were afoot especially at court and by extension within the D'Epresmesnil faction in the chamber of the Nobility, to subvert the possibility of regeneration or, in July, bring about counter-revolution. This spilled over into the audience in the *Palais Royal* and the cafés of Paris and Versailles.

It is also notable how in both the seventeenth and eighteenth centuries, fears of conspiracy held by the king and his most trusted ministers dictated some of the characteristic political practices of the *ancien régime*. Disgraced courtiers and ministers were habitually exiled to places from which they could not journey to Paris or Versailles. In order to break their network of contacts it was forbidden to visit them without special permission and at the known risk of disfavour. The fear of popular violence and political plotting led in part to the extensive system of spies in Paris and the focus in the police reports is on faction and potential subversion.

Notwithstanding all the evidence of activities that could be broadly defined as conspiratorial, we might still ask were there actual conspiracies in the manner of those of the sixteenth and seventeenth centuries? It is true that words associated with conspiracy are much in evidence, *cabal* and *intrigue* especially. Accusations of corruption are commonly levelled at courtiers and financiers. On some occasions the case might be made. But Bercé is probably right to say that out and out clear and unequivocal acts of conspiracy against powers in the state were rarer in the eighteenth century. And yet, we must still stress that the idea of conspiracy remained strong and that it was in some ways strengthened, since the moral debate had matured. The rise of the concepts of *patrie* and *vertu* provided a standpoint from which to evaluate politics.[27] Conspiracy stemmed from moral corruption, it was believed. Courtiers were of course perfectly suited for this nefarious role. For example, on the subject of *courtisan*, we have in the *Encyclopédie* the following diatribe:

> [Courtier] is the epithet given to those sorts of people that the misfortune of kings and peoples has placed between kings and the truth to prevent it from reaching them, even when they are expressly charged with making it known to them: the foolish tyrant listens to and likes these sorts of people; the clever tyrant uses them and despises them; the king who knows how to behave like

one, dismisses them and punishes them, and the truth then reveals itself, for it is only hidden from those who do not truly seek it.

This characterisation draws upon an important discourse of anti-courtier sentiment, that goes back to the sixteenth century, but which found on the high moral ground of the eighteenth century philosophy even more fertile soil. For more than a century from La Bruyère to Mercier courtiers are condemned in literature, and Beaumarchais had numerous forerunners. This theme carried over into the revolution. We must conclude that even if particular plots did exist, or were believed to, what was perhaps even more important was the general and widespread belief in the later eighteenth century that all court politics was by its very nature corrupt and full of intrigues, plots and conspiracies.

III

So, was *ancien régime* politics essentially conspiracy? There is not a simple answer to this question: such an assessment of 'politics' depends of course on how one sees the state. If it was by this period essentially an administrative monarchy, having been modernised by Louis XIV in particular (as Bercé and many others still appear to believe), then politics was more about administration and policy than other issues - and patronage and clientage would have become relatively unimportant. Now, even one so committed to combating this old orthodoxy as the present writer, would have to admit that the state had evolved in terms of administrative structures and practices. But even if the state is seen as having been partly administrative, its governance still took place within, one must stress, a court society, for the court was the centre of patronage. So any serious analysis of conspiracy has to accept recent research on the nature of politics, and for some this may require a conceptual shift and a reintegration of the court in to the overall perspective.

Recently historians have tended to accept the case for the centrality of the court to the social and political system. In a sense, the social system *was* the political system. The court centred upon the king's household. The focal point of politics was the king, and the king resided at court - more precisely, the court was in attendance on the king. A courtier was therefore a noble honoured with some task in the royal domestic service: gentleman of the bedchamber, master of the hunt, lady-in-waiting or simple page. The administration itself developed from household offices, and the key administrators were also courtiers. The court had a long history but Louis

XIV had expanded it, rendered it sedentary and refined it as a socio-political instrument. Over two centuries the court had developed from a relatively circumscribed household of retainers, friends and clients until it had become a large, unwieldy but sophisticated instrument. On one level, that most noticed by contemporaries, the court now existed to exalt the monarch and concentrate the gaze of observers. An elaborate system of etiquette and hierarchy enmeshed the aristocrats who surrounded the king, making opposition difficult but encouraging quarrels amongst the courtiers. Life at court became a byword for deceit, intrigue and manners refined to the point of absurdity. Everybody watched everybody else for the smallest indication of ambition, intrigue or advancement in royal favour. The courtier thus concealed his true character and motives behind a mask. The memoirs of the duc de Saint-Simon and the duc de Luynes offer well known and privileged insights into these aspects as they operated on a daily basis well into the eighteenth century.

The masking of feelings was one characteristic of the courtier. La Bruyère expressed this very clearly:

> A man who knows the court is master of his every gesture, of his eyes and his face; he is deep, opaque; he dissimulates bad offices, smiles at his enemies, controls his moods, disguises his passions, denies his heart, speaks, acts against his sentiments... to lift the mask for a single moment at court, is to renounce the court.[28]

To be a courtier was thus a full time occupation and one for which it was constantly necessary to wear a mask. The coded language of the court was more than nuanced: every word, every phrase, posture, gesture and expression was significant. To let the mask slip for a moment was to reveal yourself, and this would enable more subtle minds to add to their knowledge and subsequently to triumph over you. Knowledge was indeed power. Complete discretion was essential for success and every mood was adopted in public in the full knowledge of its possible interpretations. This masking of feelings and ambitions means that observers learned to scrutinise faces with skill in order to detect signs of anger or pique that might enable them to deduce the result of an interview or a council meeting. Only long experience and hindsight would show contemporaries if they were right, but they had to act before such confirmation was available.

It is abundantly clear that this world was also of immense political importance. The court was the only central institution for the whole state. Patronage and clientage were fundamental precepts of society and the networks came together at court where the king was the ultimate provider of graces. The village or urban notables had connections with the local bishop, or with seigneurial agents or a seigneur himself.[29] These men in turn had their patrons and networks of friends, and formed a tightly knit if often divided local elite.[30] Every local or provincial elite had links with great provincial landowners, leading magistrates or royal governors, all with close connections or places at court.[31] Grand aristocrats with easy access to the king and his ministers would intervene to secure favours for their clients or would act as brokers to reduce opposition and promote covert compromises over royal policy. It was unbecoming to royal majesty to be seen to negotiate, but the reality of politics was that almost everything was a compromise. (This was of course anathema to many revolutionaries for whom all politics was a matter of principle). As may be seen from its religious, *parlementaire* and financial policies, the royal government therefore relied upon its centralisation of patronage to ensure that the bureaucratic machinery continued to operate. Sometimes it was a question of informal networks parallel to the formal administrative structures, sometimes the patronage system was at the core of the bureaucracy itself.[32] The court provided the inducements and it provided the means for this system to function on the whole fairly successfully.

Demonstrably, every minister was a courtier and had to operate as such, even if his *bureaux* were based in Paris instead of at Versailles.

> Ministers have of necessity become courtiers, and, if they are not, they are quickly disgraced... Thus they have to participate in all the wishes of the courtiers.[33]

Patronage, to be seen by the revolutionaries as corruption, was essential to good and effective government under the *ancien régime*. Within this system, because social rank and privilege were linked, to the extent that social privilege itself conferred a measure of political authority, the high nobility remained essential to the functioning of the socio-political regime. It had never been cut out of government under Louis XIV nor did its importance diminish significantly during the greater part of the eighteenth century. Its role was important because political power can be said to have operated as much through the social system as through the administration, and must not be identified too closely with the bureaucracy. The administrative or courtly offices held by individuals were acquired by them through a process that was as much a reflection of their existing positions of influence as because of the administrative power inherent in the office.

If personal relations were an important part of the social and political system, faction - that anathema to the revolutionaries - was the inevitable by-product. There was bound to be competition to influence the king and his ministers in favour of family, friends and clients. Life was expensive at Versailles and the great families needed royal largesse and profitable financial investments in order to maintain themselves in the proper fashion. In 1790, the famous *Livre rouge*, published to expose this system during the Revolution, mentioned only two million *livres* in pensions, but there is evidence that the true figure was nearer thirty million. So pensions, lucrative sinecures and contracts were hotly competed for by cabals of the most important families.[34]

Courtiers and power brokers also had networks of clients to whose demands they had to accede by acquiring favours. But factional competition was not just for places, it was also over policies - with serious consequences for the monarchy. The priorities of King and courtier were often very different, the king having to concentrate upon the formation and execution of state policy (although this had a strongly familial dimension), while courtiers often were involved in policy as a means to social advancement or the preservation of acquired positions. In politics, faction therefore created a certain inertia as courtiers were more concerned to advance their interests than they were to encourage sound policies. Thus, when a minister began to pursue unpopular measures of economy or centralisation his supporters at court would abandon him. Economy meant fewer opportunities for profit, and centralisation meant pressure from clients in the provinces anxious to retain local power. By contributing to a reformer's dismissal courtiers hoped to remain on the winning side and consequently secure greater influence for themselves - as with the falling away of Bourbon's support in 1726, or Calonne's in 1787. Reforming ministers were sure to run up against powerful vested interests, especially if, like the duc de Bourbon in 1725 and Loménie de Brienne in 1787–1788, they reduced the household expenses. The great reformer Turgot fell foul of this mentality in 1776 and so did Necker in 1781. As Elias so rightly pointed out, all the king could hope to do was balance the factions in order to divide and rule. The court was an arena in which intense competition took place. A king or a first minister had to keep himself fully abreast of the factional interplay, intervening constantly to preserve the necessary equilibrium. One of the main problems during the revolution was how to do politics without getting involved in patronage and clientage. These practices were redolent of faction and the very antithesis of the role of virtuous citizens.

In terms of the emerging doctrine of public and private, the governance of the *ancien régime* state thus saw considerable confusion between the two - a confusion the revolutionaries wished to combat (but could never wholly do). During the *ancien régime* commentators made a distinction between *intrigue*, *complot, cabal, brigue de cour,* and *conspiration* and *conjuration.* But these words refer to practices that the revolutionaries would assimilate to the notion of *conspiration* and *conjuration,* so that from the perspective of the revolution, all the normal political practices of court system of politics became illegitimate and liable to fall into the category of conspiratorial. A search in the *Bibliothèque nationale*'s digital library for the key words *intrigue* and *cabale,* from Retz's *Mémoires* to the Revolution, reveals that Retz uses the words with neutrality, in matter of fact way, but that from the mid-eighteenth century they are increasingly associated with courtier, corruption and inefficiency of government.

We might then conclude this section of the argument with the idea that, from the perspective of the revolution, in many respects politics was conspiracy, especially in terms of political practice. That is to say that much of what took place could later be called conspiratorial, when judged by other standards than those of the courtiers and those in power in society - because practices involved intrigue, corruption and concert to attain ends. To the extent that people in the later regime (or indeed earlier cynics like the early moralists La Bruyère and La Rochefoucauld) had access to the reality of politics they were often justified in their interpretations.

Thus in several senses *ancien régime politics was conspiracy* corruption and conspiracy (to pervert the cause of justice, say, or to get power for member of faction) was under the *ancien régime* either an essential part of the system or a question of degree, but the question of degree is significant too. Under the *ancien régime* there were few political prosecutions for conspiracy, but plenty of actions against corruption, as in the *chambres de justice,* attacks on financiers, dismissal of ministers associated with this, for example Le Peletier Desforts in 1730. It appears to have been accepted that lots of different and, after 1789, incompatible interests could be served at once: king, state, faction, family. During the revolution we have the dominance of the idea that the revolution represented a kind of meta-system of virtue and patriotism within a transparent political system. This takes away the idea of degree of difference and acceptability, replacing it with absolute imperatives for conduct. Thus any form of corruption can be said to undermine the system.

The revolutionaries inherited a rich tradition of conceiving of court politics as essentially corrupt and subject to conspiracy, faction, intrigue, and cabals. The revolutionaries were not altogether inventing the centrality of conspiracy to politics, and were right to be afraid of these *ci-devant* practices. For historians of the revolution, the question is therefore less one of explaining the roots of their 'obsessions', which were in fact not so irrational given their experience and the existence of real plots, than in explaining how and why they made political capital out of what can be seen as a quite natural and even justified fear of past practices that would continue and thereby undermine their revolutionary attempt to create virtuous citizens.

Notes

1   F. Furet, *Interpreting the French Revolution* (Cambridge, 1981), pp. 53–4; Lynn Hunt, *Politics, Culture and Class in the French Revolution* (Berkeley, Calif., 1984), pp. 39–44.

2   See Timothy Tackett, 'Conspiracy obsession in a time of Revolution: French elites and the origins of the Terror, 1789–1792', *American Historical Review*, 105, (2000), 691–711.

3   For some recent attempts at defining politics and the state, see Roger Mettam, *Power and Faction in Louis XIV's France* (Oxford, 1988); Peter. R. Campbell, *Power and Politics in Old Regime France 1720–1745* (London, 1996); and John Hardman *French Politics, 1774–1789. From the Accession of Louis XVI to the fall of the Bastille* (London, 1995).

4   John Roberts, *The Mythology of Secret Societies* (London, 1972); and Gordon S. Wood, 'Conspiracy and the paranoid style: causality and deceit in the eighteenth century', *William and Mary Quarterly*, 3rd ser., XXXIX (1982), pp. 401–41.

5   See Diego Venturino, 'La naissance de l'ancien régime', in C. Lucas, ed., *The French Revolution and the Creation of Modern Political Culture*, II (Oxford, 1988), pp. 11–40.

6   From 1788 to 1801 Soulavie published part of the memoirs of Saint-Simon, the memoirs of maréchal de Richelieu, drawn from his papers; apocryphal memoirs by Massillon and Maurepas, and documents on the reigns of Louis XIV, XV and XVI, as well as a history of the reign of Louis XVI, all of which exposed factional machinations.

7   See also Soulavie's letters to Robespierre, in *Courtois Papiers inédits trouvés chez Robespierre* (2 vols., Paris, 1824), I, pp. 122–32.

8   Dale Van Kley, *The Damiens Affair and the Unraveling of the Ancien Régime 1750–1770* (Princeton, 1984).

9   See Julian Swann, *Politics and the Parlement of Paris under Louis XV, 1754–1774* (Cambridge, 1995), and from the time, one of Pidansat de Mairobert's many works is, *Memoirs of Madame du Barry*, ed. E. Cruickshanks (London, 1956).

10   On the interpretation of this situation developed by one important terrorist, Billaud-Varenne, see John M. Burney, 'The fear of the executive and the threat of conspiracy: Billaud-Varenne's terrorist rhetoric in the French Revolution, 1788–1794', *French History*, V, (1991), pp. 143–63. Tackett's evidence, 'Conspiracy obsession', p. 698, that almost all of the 32 Third Estate Deputies who wrote pre-revolutionary pamphlets did not reflect conspiracy theories is misleading for two reasons. Firstly, because would-be deputies might not have felt in 1788 and 1789 that conspiratorial denunciations of the executive or nobility were the best way to get elected or promote their career. Secondly, because some pamphlets written by deputies later elected to the Legislative Assembly and Convention were more openly radical. Burney demonstrates this in the case of Billaud-Varenne, and refers to the analogous case of Marat. We might add that Breton deputies arrived at Versailles in 1789 already suspicious of the nobility.

11   Saint-Just, 'Rapport sur la conjuration ourdie pour obtenir un changement de dynastie; et contre Fabre d'Eglantine, Danton, Philippeaux, Lacroix et Camille Desmoulins', in C.

Vellay, ed., *Oeuvres complètes de Saint-Just* (2 vols., Paris, 1908), II, pp. 305–32, quotation from p. 312.

12   The official accusations of the *Hébertistes* presented by Saint-Just to the convention was entitled 'Rapport sur la faction de l'étranger'.

13   There is no space here to develop my arguments about the vision of politics in the 1780s, but a further study on this is in preparation and should be published in P.R. Campbell, M. Linton and T. Kaiser, eds., *Conspiracy in the French revolution*, 2004/5.

14   On the use of the classics in the Revolution see Harold T. Parker, *The cult of antiquity and the French revolutionaries* (Chicago, 1937).

15   P. Richelet, *Dictionnaire portatif de la langue francaise. Nouvelle édition entièrement refondue et considérablement augmentée par M. de Wailly*, A Lyon, chez J.-M. Bruyset père et fils, rue St Dominique, 1775.

16   Jean-Claude Waquet, 'La politique des dictionnaires: Langue royale et idiomes monarchiques dans la France moderne', *Società et Storia*, 87, 2000, pp. 19–36. The article focuses on the area of meaning around *cabale, complot, conjuration* and *conspiration*.

17   Any attempt to suggest that belief in conspiracy was in abeyance during the later *ancien régime* based solely on the examination of one word must be doomed to failure. Tackett's attempt to draw meaningful inference from a search for the word *conspiration* in the ARTFL database could surely not give useful results (except to show that *conspiration* very often refers to the past).

18   Y.-M. Bercé, ed., *Complots et Conjurations dans l'Europe Moderne* (Rome, 1996), pp. 1–5.

19   Tackett asserts, 'Conspiracy obsession', 696–9, that conspiracy beliefs in the later *ancien régime* were 'the exception', 'remarkably rare', 'there was a relative absence of conspiracy fears in French political culture', pp. 697–9.

20   We know today that they indeed often did involve planning by the lower orders (conspiracy to their superiors) who might get together at the fair or carnival time, to consider protests. But many were unpremeditated, the product of a culture of revolt.

21   L. Biollay, *Le Pacte de Famine* (Paris, 1901); Steven L. Kaplan, *The Famine Plot Persuasion in Eighteenth-Century France* (Philadelphia, 1982).

22   *La réalité du projet de Bourg-Fontaine, démontré par l'exécution*, two vols in one, Paris, 1787.

23   Dale Van Kley, *The Jansenists and the Expulsion of the Jesuits from France, 1757–1765* (New Haven, 1975).

24   See John Rothney, *The Brittany Affair and the Crisis of the Ancien Régime* (Oxford, 1969), and Julian Swann, *Politics and the parlement of Paris*.

25   Thomas E. Kaiser, 'Who's Afraid of Marie-Antoinette? Diplomacy, Austrophobia, and the Queen', *French History*, XIV, (2000), pp. 241–71; id. 'Ambiguous Identities: Marie-Antoinette and the House of Lorraine from the Affair of the Minuet to Lambesc's Charge', in Dena Goodman, ed., *Marie Antoinette: Writings on the Body of the Queen* (London, 2003).

26   The best recent analysis is by R.A.W. Browne, 'The diamond necklace affair revisited: the Rohan family and court politics', *Renaissance and Modern Studies*, XXXIII, (1989), 21–40.

27   The rise of virtuous discourse is particularly important in this period, providing as it does a moral basis for criticism of political practice. See the important new study by Marisa Linton, *The Politics of Virtue in Enlightenment France* (Basingstoke, 2001).

28   *Caractères*, 'De la cour', Nelson edition (1945), p. 254.

29   At village level this is illustrated by N. Rétif de la Bretonne, in *La Vie de Mon Père*.

30   This elite was often composed of magistrates and judicial officers, with strong ties of vertical solidarity: see for example M. Gresset, *Gens de Justice à Besançon, 1674–1789* (2 vols., Paris, 1978), II, part III, book III; M. Cubells, *La provence des Lumières. Les parlementaires d'Aix au XVIIIe siècle* (Paris, 1984); J. Meyer, *La Noblesse Bretonne* (Paris, 1972).

31   See esp. W. Beik, *Absolutism and Society in Seventeenth-Century France* (Cambridge, 1985) and S. Kettering, 'Patronage in early modern France', *French Historical Studies*, XVII, (1992), 839–62; on Burgundian connections to the governors, the ducs de Bourbon, up to 1740, see P. Lefebvre, 'Aspects de la fidélité en France au XVIIe siècle: le cas des agents du prince de Condé', *Revue Historique*, CCL, (1973), 59–106. During the eighteenth century these links were no doubt conceived of less in terms of clientage and more in terms of sociability, as expressed through provincial academies, freemasonry, and philanthropic societies.

32   For studies of the administration of war and foreign affairs, all of which refer to the continued importance of patronage, see C.-G. Picavet, *La Diplomatie Française au temps de Louis XIV (1661–1715): Institutions, Moeurs et Coutumes* (Paris, 1930); C. Piccioni, *Les Premiers Commis des Affaires Étrangères au XVIIe et au XVIIIe Siècles* (Paris, 1928); J. Rule, 'The *commis* of the department of foreign affairs, 1680–1715', *Western Society for French History, Proceedings*, 8, (1980), pp. 69–80; D.C. Baxter, 'Premier *commis* in the war department in the later part of the reign of Louis XIV', *Western Society for French History, Proceedings*, 8 (1980), pp. 81–9.

33   *Mémoires et Journal Inédit du Marquis d'Argenson*, Janet edition (5 vols, Paris, 1858), V, p. 350.

34   T.J.A. Le Goff, 'Essai sur les pensions royales', in Martine Acerra, *et al.*, eds., *État, Marine et Société* (Paris, 1995), pp. 252–81.

Chapter 12

Burke and the Conspiratorial Origins of the French Revolution: Some Anglo-French Resemblances[*]

Nigel Aston

Explaining the French Revolution was as much of a challenge to contemporaries as it has been to historians subsequently. Just what was going on? What had caused it? How had change on this scale, what Edmund Burke called 'Things... so much beyond the scope of all speculation',[1] been effected and at such a velocity? Burke conveyed his bewilderment to Lord Charlemont on 9 August 1789:

> As to us here, our thoughts of everything at home are suspended, by our astonishment at the wonderful Spectacle which is exhibited in a Neighbouring and rival Country - what Spectators and what actors! England gazing with astonishment at a French struggle for Liberty and not knowing whether to blame or to applaud![2]

Less than one month after the fall of the Bastille, when his main preoccupation was the impeachment of Warren Hastings,[3] Burke found himself ineluctably drawn away to observe unfolding events in France and to register their profound importance in marking a new and deplorable phase of European cultural life, a retrogressive and destructive paradigm shift. Just over a year later, on 1 November 1790, he offered the public his perceptions on the true significance of things in the *Reflections on the Revolution in France*, a comprehensive guide to what had happened so far - and what was likely to happen. This character of the *Reflections* as a guide is often overlaid by emphasis on the emotive rhetoric and the counter-revolutionary character of Burke's great tract for his times. He was trying in the first instance to make sense of what had befallen France and the British public (and, very soon afterwards once the first translations appeared, the European) bought his book to watch him put the key in the lock. That thousands disagreed with his thesis was less significant initially than the fact that he had one,[4] and central to his causational explanation of the Revolution was the notion of a conspiracy pushing an already unstable country further into the abyss.[5]

Burke's discovery of a plot against Christianity and monarchy, actual in France, latent in England, was not original to him, but appropriated (without explicit acknowledgement) many of the politico-theological commonplaces of contemporary Anglican controversialists who were trying to identify and connect patterns of subversion at home as well as abroad, those whose defence of the established Church of England in the 1780s had led them to suspect the existence of a plot - or several plots - to undermine her status and her creeds to the advantage of the unscrupulous and the heterodox. Burke's primary achievement was, of course, to articulate this perception in his own inimitable voice, to apply it to France in the first instance, and to achieve a degree of publicity none of the clergy had enjoyed.[6] Nevertheless, his diagnostic and rhetorical revelation will only be adequately contextualised once Anglican anticipations of the 1790s obsession with the conspiratorial origins of the French Revolution are properly charted. This essay is a modest attempt to begin the process of recovering the religious typology of Burke's theory.[7]

Burke found it impossible to understand the genesis of the French Revolution except in terms of successful conspiracy and plotting by alienated groups.[8] As he noted in the *Reflections*

> I hear on all hands that a cabal, calling itself philosophic, receives the glory of many of the late proceedings; and that their opinions and systems are the true actuating spirit of the whole of them.[9]

This interpretative strategy is partially explicable from Burke's first-hand unfamiliarity with French political life before the 1790s. If his visit to France in 1773 - towards the very end of the previous reign - had not brought him into sustained contact with any of the leading public figures[10] it had left him in no doubt about the spread of unbelief within the French elite. He had spoken of his fears and opinions regarding French infidels in the Commons on 17 March 1773 during a debate on the Dissenters' Relief Bill:[11]

> He pointed out the conspiracy of atheism to the watchful jealousy of governments... those enemies of their kind, who would take from us the noblest prerogative of our nature, that of being a religious animal.... 'Already under the systematic attacks of these men, I see many of the old propos of good government beginning to fail. I see propagated principles which will not leave to religion even a toleration, and make virtue herself less than a name'.

Where others resorted to the contingent or the circumstantial in explaining events in France, Burke insisted on a large degree of conspiratorial purpose. If his evidence for a conspiracy was nebulous, it was at one with much else in the *Reflections*. As one periodical journalist commented:[12]

> The dupe of his imagination or his passions, he despises arrangement or logical precision. He loses himself in a wilderness of words and figures.

Nevertheless, this 'wilderness of words and figures' was immensely persuasive for an audience desperate to understand how Britain's great rival had imploded so quickly. The chaos could not be accidental. Conspiracy as a sufficient explanation of the unexpected turn in public life remained conventional in the late eighteenth century, 'integral to Western thought across the social and political spectrum at the dawn of the modern age',[13] and the French Revolution did much to rejuvenate it as an explanational first resort. The relationship of conspiracy to disclosed politics in the public domain was always going to be problematic, because plotters were plausible in their denial of conspiracy, but the British defenders of Church and state could not permit disclaimers to make them drop their guard. They may seldom in their pamphlets, speeches and sermons have been able to invoke the direct language of conspiracy that was common in France (and that Burke himself invokes in the *Reflections*) with its specific references to plots, hidden agents and dupes, to inner agents and dupes, to inner and outer circles, to former cabals and such like. But the absence of this sophisticated framework was not a sign that conspiracy was not perceived.

From his correspondence and his reading, Burke was quite aware that both noble and non-noble French politicians believed in the existence of plots in 1789 and 1790 to bring about the Revolution in the first place or, subsequently, to destroy it and return to something approximating to the monarchical status quo ante. The theory of *philosophe* conspiracy was already well established in France in 1789 and Burke shared many of the assumptions of the *philosophes'* enemies in that kingdom,[14] they tallied with his perception of the current turn to contemporary British affairs, as well as psychological and moral considerations. From his involvement in English and Irish political life, Burke had seen enough of human nature in 40 years to leave him in little doubt that universal modes of behaviour were more important than the particularities of distinctive political cultures, and recourse to the covert and the concealed had been, was, a mark of selfish, ambitious men in all times and all places.

A conspiratorial explanation or, more properly, part-explanation of the Revolution, was persuasive to Burke on political as well as moral grounds. As a stranger to courts, an outsider in palace politics, it was an article of faith with him that such precincts were the seedbeds of intrigue, and intrigue was but a short step away from plotting. As Burke knew from his experience with Whig grandees, frustrated or discontented courtiers would readily make common cause with those below them in rank, and he discounted the possibility that the latter, on the social as well as the political margins, might have more far reaching reformist objectives. If contemporaries could think readily enough in terms of court conspiracy, then, by the same token, it was persuasive to think of the opponents of a court conspiring. In a French context, restless élite politicians, especially those who gravitated towards that notorious libertine, the duc d'Orléans and his entourage in and around the Palais Royal, had every chance of encountering pamphleteers, polemicists and *philosophe* malcontents in salons, club and masonic lodges, men with no stake in the system but natural-born plotters who, in combination with noble patrons, could do lethal damage to the viability and stability of the polity. Any concern these people professed for the public good was a sham, their sole aim in reality was the satisfaction of personal ambition and desire. These 'literary caballers', these 'intriguing philosophers'[15] were thus only too eager to indulge in activities beyond their proper capacities and, from a combination of incompetence and malice, end up fatally damaging key aspects of the state's fabric.

Political ambition led back to a combination of immoral motives and purposes. What made these unspecifiable networks of destruction so much more objectionable to Burke when he looked at events in France in 1789–1790 was their invariable miring in infidelity as well as immorality: loose livers and unbelievers locked together in an unholy alliance that poisoned the health of the state and relentlessly sought the overthrow of the Church which consecrated monarchy and morality together. Instead of respecting the ordering of things as providentially devised, such men schemed to substitute their own pet schemes in place of the wisdom of the ages. This perversion could only be understood in the light of man's fallen nature, or so it appeared to Burke and the majority of those commentators and onlookers who, even in the 1780s, found it impossible to detach their religious beliefs from their understanding of politics. For these sympathetic first readers of the *Reflections*, it would not be too simplistic to argue that there was something genuinely diabolical about the phenomenon of conspiracy, a natural yoking together of caballers with the cabbalistic.

Burke's sense of the destructive influence of conspiracy stemmed in part from his own perception of being its victim throughout his public career, along with his other erstwhile colleagues among the Rockingham and Portland Whigs. Their - and his - history could be interpreted as one of repeated undermining by secret influences; Burke never doubted that persons as well as polities could be unstitched by the insidious enemies of their country less, in the case of the Rockinghams, by rootless men of letters than by courtiers. Why, in a public career stretching back a quarter of a century, had Burke and his colleagues held office for no more than a few months on three separate occasions? The answer, as Burke saw it, was bound up in conspiracies which originated at court and were sanctioned by George III. Lord Bute may have lasted as first lord of the treasury for less than twelve months but Burke was obsessively convinced that the Scottish former minister had retained privileged, private access to the king well into the North administration.[16] In the early 1770s the bogey figure for opposition politicians was arguably not so much North in the Commons as Mansfield behind the curtain, the country's greatest lawyer (and another Caledonian to gratify the Scotophobes) keeping an irresolute Cabinet committed to waging war in America. Although this culture of 'secret influence' briefly gave ground when Rockingham dictated the terms of forming a ministry in March–April 1782, the system reasserted its force by recruiting Burke's very particular *bête noir*, the Earl of Shelburne, into its clutches after the marquess's death on 1 July. It was Shelburne's protégé, Pitt, who in conjunction with Dundas, the Grenvilles, and Thurlow then engineered the overthrow of the Fox–North Coalition in late 1783 and, with it, Burke's last spell as an office-holder. Pitt's part in ousting the Coalition still stuck in the throats of opposition politicians a decade later, but was he an architect of conspiracy or merely the tool of his royal master? The overthrow of the Fox–North coalition showed that kings could be plotters too. This was the political sin which dared not speak its name publicly until the Regency Crisis of 1788–1789 made it safe for the Whigs to drop heavy hints that they blamed George III personally for their marginalisation and were ready to 'un-Whig' themselves to become secure in power under the protection of his eldest son.

Burke's own prospects of holding office for any length of time had been snuffed out, but personal and financial disappointment was subordinated to his intense sense of moral and political outrage at the violence inflicted on the British constitution by those who posed publicly as its defenders, principally the king, William Pitt, and the East India Company lobby.[17] However, by the close of the 1780s, Burke was more concerned with plots to destabilise and then overthrow the ecclesiastical settlement of the constitution and here the

218　　　　　　*Conspiracies and Conspiracy Theory in Early Modern Europe*

culprits were not courtiers but those restless non-Anglican Protestants whose spokesman, Dr Richard Price, was the occasion for Burke's writing the *Reflections* in the first instance.[18] These rational dissenters were open agitators in and out of parliament for religious reforms from which they could expect to emerge as the principal beneficiaries.[19] Behind the outwardly respectable campaign of the late 1780s for the repeal of the Test and Corporation Acts,[20] Burke, in common with many Anglican clergy, suspected the existence of a barely-concealed layer of frenetic activity with a much more radical agenda: one which sought the outright destruction of the Church establishment and a recasting of the state to permit a confessional free-for-all in which all the barriers to the spread of Socinianism would be down.[21] For the 'rational dissenters' such an achievement would be the most fitting way of commemorating the centenary of the 1688 Revolution; for Burke and most Anglicans, it would be at once the negation and overthrow of that settlement.

Burke read Price's sermon of November 1789 (the *Discourse on the Love of our Country*) less as an encomium on the Glorious Revolution or as another salvo in the campaign for repeal of the Test and Corporation Acts, than as a blind for a much wider scheme of subversion. Given what Burke took to be the absence both of transparency and sincerity among such dissenters, it was not to be expected they would be happy with lawful petitioning and lobbying to gain their ends. It was not as if Priestley, Price and their allies in the 'society of the Old Jewry [the meeting house in the City of London] and the London Tavern'[22] made much effort to disguise the extent of their covert operations, the boldness of their objectives, and their passionate commitment to undermining the state Church. Ceaselessly fomenting schemes for change from what one opponent called his 'theological laboratory',[23] Priestley talked brazenly about lighting a 'train of gunpowder' which would blow away the Church of England, thereby rekindling for Anglicans a whole train of seventeenth-century historic associations centred on plots allegedly fermented by presbyterians, independents and other sectaries which had resulted in the overthrow of the crown in 1649 and the wild republican experimentalism of the 'good old cause' in the 1650s.[24] The original gunpowder plot had been planned as a blow for popery, Priestley's new plot could be seen as a device to demolish any and every form of Christian orthodoxy.[25] The Church of England could be toppled by the rational dissenters as easily as its Gallican equivalent had succumbed. As Burke told a correspondent in March 1790: 'all their words and actions manifest a settled design of subverting it',[26] a point he reiterated publicly in the Commons on the 2nd of that month when he produced an open letter from Priestley with its reference to a 'train of gunpowder'.[27] This was taken from the latter's published *Letters to the Rev.*

Edward Burn (London, 1790), a pamphlet which included the incriminating sentence, 'If I be laying gunpowder, they [his opponents in the established Church] are providing the match'. This ill-advised comment was a gift to those who wanted to retain the Test and Corporation Acts intact.[28]

It was not just Priestley's ecclesiology which Burke loathed, it was his attempt to refashion a historic belief system according to his own misguided, ambitious lights. Central to Priestley's rational dissent was his attempt to resuscitate a purified and 'reasonable' form of Christianity from the 'corruptions' introduced into it by misguided theologians and Newtonian philosophers, in other words a not too dissimilar enterprise to that undertaken by some of the French supporters of the Civil Constitution of the Clergy.[29] Anglican high church apologetic of the 1780s refused to recognise that Socinianism could have any place within a Christian spectrum, viewing it rather as a vehicle of convenience in which extreme unbelievers could travel to achieve their subversive ends. George Horne for one simply would not accept Priestley's good faith in proclaiming himself a Christian:

> Priestley asserts the facts of Xty against the philosophers of France, while he believes no more of its truth than the Sadducees of Jerusalem did, who yet never denied that God had spoken unto Moses.[30]

Burke's views were exactly comparable, his debt to the clergy indubitable.

Thus when Burke spoke in the *Reflections* of a literary cabal that had 'something like a regular plan for the destruction of the Christian religion', manifesting 'A spirit of cabal, intrigue, and proselytism'[31] he thought he could observe at first hand in England just how such men went about their work. For instance, he looked reprehensively at Joseph Johnson's bookshop in St Paul's churchyard. It was here that pro-Unitarian tracts came off the press, as well as being a place in which religious and political reformers gathered, gossiped, and presumably plotted.[32] Burke could not doubt that concealed agitators on either side of the English Channel had traded both talk and tactics to further each other's mutual objectives.[33] For he identified a cosmopolitan dimension to caballing which constantly obtruded itself but was always hard to pin down. In as much as he could locate a focal point, for Burke the finger of suspicion always pointed back to Bowood in Wiltshire, seat of Lord Shelburne, recently created marquess of Lansdowne. 'Tell', as the *Anti-Jacobin* would later put it:

> How Lansdowne, nature's simple child,
> At Bowood trills his wood-notes wild -
> How these and more (a phrenzied choir)

Sweep with bold hand Confusion's lyre,
Till madding crowds around them storm
'FOR ONE GRAND RADICAL REFORM'.[34]

Bowood in the 1780s functioned as a combination of asylum, think-tank and international hotel for those whom Burke both feared and disliked as restless spirits addicted to innovation, moral turpitude and the overthrow of established orders. Over it all presided the most restless and untrustworthy politician of his generation, Shelburne, denied power by Pitt but still desperate to use all the instruments at his disposal to effect change without leaving Wiltshire.[35] Price had been his long time adviser and his son and heir's educator,[36] Priestley his librarian, Paine his regular correspondent, and he had put them all in touch with cheer leaders for the French Revolution like Dumont, Mirabeau and Morellet, all of whom Burke knew personally.[37]

Such circumstantial evidence, dispassionately viewed, did no more than suggest that these individuals were at worst bent on destabilising political life in France and Britain rather than subverting it altogether. Politico-religious reformers like Priestley and Price, Theophilus Lindsey, Samuel Palmer and Robert Robinson (the influential Baptist minister in Cambridge) certainly had an informed interest in events in France, but they also variously possessed a degree of commitment to refashioned Christianity that differentiated them from the majority of the French *philosophes*. That is so long as non-trinitarian Christianity was regarded as a legitimate expression of a faith purged of its historic accretions as Priestley saw it rather than the poisonous heresy Burke and mainstream Anglicans deemed it. On the latter reading, rational dissenters, either as fools or villains, could thus be regarded as the allies of the *philosophes* in England, a stalking horse for transmitting and disseminating atheism across the Channel, and providing the equivalent of the cultural and political degradation which Burke claimed to find in France. The only essential differences he was prepared to concede were that, as far as he knew, there were more members of the cabal in France than in its English counterpart.[38] And that they were better organised.

Burke admitted that there was strictly 'no party in England, literary or political' to compare with the cabal of French atheists and that they acted as individuals rather than 'a faction in the state'.[39] That said, they were the nearest equivalents to the *philosophes* that Britain possessed and it suited the Anglican defenders of the status quo to damn them by association.[40] For Burke and his sympathisers were not inclined to be dispassionate in their diagnosis of Europe's ills in 1790 and they were merely in the vanguard of those who over the next few years came to look upon the Lansdowne circle (especially after the marquess's rapprochement with Fox) as up to no good wherever it exerted its influence. As Burke told Philip Francis, he would not shrink from his duty:[41]

> I mean to set in a full View the danger from their wicked principles and their black hearts, I intend to state the true principles of our Constitution in Church and State, upon grounds opposite to theirs...I mean to do my best to expose them to the hatred, ridicule, and contempt of the whole world, as I shall always expose such calumniators, hypocrites, sowers of sedition, and approvers of murder and all its triumphs. When I have done that, they may have the field to themselves and I care very little how they triumph over me since I hope they will not be able to draw me at their heels and carry my head in triumph on their poles.

Putting aside the hyperbole, the accumulated resentments and the crusading determination, one finds here the same note of unmasking deceit and restating truth that characterises other contemporary voices, particularly those of the clergy. In many sermons and tracts of the late 1780s several influential clerics argued that events in both England and France could only be satisfactorily explained in terms of one or more conspiracies to undermine establishment. It was a conventional perception of unexpected events inimical to the stability of Church and state and reinforced by the Anglican Book of Common Prayer. The Litany, used every Sunday, asked God for deliverance 'From all sedition, privy conspiracy, and rebellion' (the links were presumed). It figured in other acts of worship. The first collect in the Gunpowder Treason service every 5 November talked of conspiracy as 'wicked' and 'unnatural'; a prayer in the 29 May Restoration Day service thanked the Almighty for His 'miraculous and gracious deliverance of thy Church, and ... the protection of righteous and religious Kings and States, professing thy holy and eternal truth, from the malicious Conspiracies and wicked Practices of all their enemies'. Conspiracy, therefore, was no abstract concept but a constant menace as well as an explanation, one constantly before the clergy of the Church of England and connected with every evil which could befall a polity. It was the responsibility of Christian subjects to call attention to signs of spiritual wickedness in high - and low - places and to flush out those glorying in their subversion while there was still time. In France, all the indicators for Burke were that by 1790 it was too late to halt the destruction of the kingdom,[42] in Britain, on the other hand, time was still on the side of the defenders of the established order in Church and state, giving them a respite in which to shore it up against those who were indubitably seeking to imitate the French pattern.

By contrast with rational dissenters, Anglican resort to a conspiratorial reading of the times was not usually (with some significant exceptions), prior to the Revolution, located within the context of impending apocalypse,[43] but rather reflected disquiet at perceived moral collapse (it was no coincidence that the Royal Proclamation on this subject had been issued in 1787) and the creation of a climate open to exploitation on the part of the malign and the malcontented, among whom Price, Priestley and their allies were naturally prominent. Yet churchmen were still bound to offer a theological framework for understanding what was afoot as part of the Church's duty to identify the signs in their own generation making for the fulfillment of scriptural prophecies.[44] The establishment in Church and state lay exposed to its enemies and, in such dangerously unstable times, it made sense to look for signs of conspirators at work. Anglican clerics were doing this in the years immediately before Burke published the *Reflections*. All that the Revolution did was to confirm their worst apprehensions and allow publicists like Barruel and Robison the chance to proclaim the news with a shrillness which obscured the fact that they were by no means the first to find evidence of a plot or plots.

The insistence of Anglican clergy in the 1780s rather than the 1790s, that, whatever the appearances, the enemies of orthodox Christianity had spent many years plotting the overthrow of establishments upholding the historic faith helped shape Burke's insights into the Revolution (initially in the *Reflections*) to an unacknowledged and unappreciated degree. Edward Sayer, writing in 1790, articulated the sentiments of hundreds of parsons:

> That such a Revolution should be thus suddenly introduced, must be attributed to the influence of very powerful and malignant principles, and be feared as the harbinger of worse.[45]

It is, however, unlikely that Burke discussed at first-hand his sense of 'very powerful and malignant principles' with bishops and clergy in the 1780s when he was, anyway, more likely to register them in connection with India. For the most part, they mixed in very different circles and were unlikely to come into familiar contact. Though his own Christian orthodoxy was never in doubt, Burke's latitudinarianism was too marked to endear him to most Oxford educated high churchmen. He had few clergy friends although there was no suggestion of disrespect.[46] He was not their champion until publication of the *Reflections* suddenly revealed what each party owed to the other and how usefully and mutually supportive they could be in what Burke described to one prelate as 'our Common Cause'.[47]

One finds a conspiratorial interpretation repeatedly present in the work of several religious apologists in the years prior to the Revolution, nowhere more so than with George Horne, dean of Canterbury and dean of Magdalen College, Oxford (bishop of Norwich from 1790 to 1792) and his life-long friend and chaplain, the Rev. William Jones of Nayland. Horne honestly feared that the destruction of the establishment in Church and state was impending. Here he is preaching in Canterbury cathedral in October 1788 as celebrations for the centenary of 1688 reached their climax, and the note is despondent:

> We have a church, and we have a king; and we must pray for the prosperity of the last, if we wish to retain the first. The levelling principle of the age extends throughout. A republic, the darling idol of many amongst us, would probably, as the taste now inclines, come attended by a religion without bishop, priest, or deacon; without service or sacraments; without a Saviour to justify or a Spirit to sanctify; in short, a classical religion without adoration.[48]

Jones, too, with the full support of Archbishop John Moore, was using the pulpit of Canterbury cathedral, to unfold his troubled sense of the times. Thus on 20 September 1789 he took 'Popular Commotions considered as signs of the approaching end of the world' as his theme and was scathing in his denunciation of events in France and their domestic cheerleaders, Price and Priestley.[49] He also resumed with a vengeance the chiliastic theme that came easily to him.[50] Horne wanted to compare his friend's sermon with Dr Price's. 'The latter sings his nunc Dimittis, on the subject of paradise returning, the former thinks the devil is just broke loose'.[51] For Jones sermons were but one component of what Brian Young has called 'a coherent counter-revolutionary programme'.[52] Throughout his career he had steadily produced a series of ultra orthodox essays, for instance, *The Catholic Doctrine of a Trinity* (1756) and *An Essay on the Church* (1787),[53] enough to confirm him in the late 1780s as a Burkite diagnostician of the ills afflicting western Europe and, *per contra*, to indicate the extent to which Burke was a Jonesite. He told Thomas Percy of St John's College, Oxford, in 1790 that there was a direct parallel between the 'policy of the French Atheists' and 'our infidels & dissenters; who have been so neglected by the supineness of the honest party, that it is miraculous they have not already overthrown it'. He repeated the point on 5 January 1791:

> Mr Burke's account of our literary cabal in France, applies very closely to the proceedings of our Disaffected Dissenters and Infidels in England. The

> Church and government in France have been ruined by their supineness; may
> better measures be adopted here, ...[54]

The lingering English distaste for French Catholicism had initially dulled
awareness of the secular consequences of overthrowing an ecclesiastical
establishment based on a close working alliance of Church and state: but this
was quickly corrected as the public was reminded by Burke as well as the
clergy that to cast down one was to imperil the other.

While the spread of freemasonry had given conspiracy theorists plenty of
fresh scope,[55] and plotting were wider standard reference points in French
counter-enlightenment polemics as Darrin McMahon has recently reminded
us, and these had their English counterparts. Clerical opinion in the
eighteenth-century Church of England likewise found conspiracy an
indispensable device for comprehending contemporary political and religious
trends, to be considered in the light of historical precedence. Horne and
Jones read their own times in the light of the 1640s, the previous era in which
heretics and republicans had conspired successfully to dismantle an episcopal
Church and a powerful monarchy.[56] They were also very conscious of the
damage done in the decades after the 'Glorious Revolution' of 1688 by
freethinkers, libertines and anticlericalists taking advantage of the lapsing of
the Licensing Act in 1695, and conspiring to further weaken the Anglican
establishment (it had lost its legal monopoly by the Toleration Act 1689) and
its core dogmas in a variety of subversive ways.[57] As Jones had noted, as far
back as 1774, wolves in sheeps' clothing still abounded: '...not a few, who are
very loud in their pretensions, have made the rights of a Christian to consist
in nothing but Heresy, Schism and Rebellion'.[58] In their own generation, they
were encouraged to fight back against the insidious enemy by the example of
predecessors who had done much the same in theirs. The great non-juring
polemicist, Charles Leslie (1650–1722), was a huge influence, especially his
The Socinian Controversy Discuss'd (1708). It inclined them to a view of
conspiracy as likely to express itself in a republican and non-trinitarian idiom,
often covert but utterly destructive of both throne and altar, with brutalising
mob activities going hand-in-glove with the machinations of maverick
members of the elite bent on wrecking the traditional order. What else was to
be expected asked Jones in 1787, for '... it is the business of the apostate spirit
to counter-work the ways of the Divine Spirit by all the efforts of subtilty,
falsehood, pride, malice, and contradiction'.[59]

Although it was not exploited by Burke, there was another rich domestic
vein of conspiratorial culture for British commentators to draw on as they
pondered the fate which had befallen France, that of conspiracy as essentially

popish, even jesuitical: it was no coincidence that Shelburne was known as 'the Jesuit of Berkeley Square'.[60] Not that Horne or Jones or other high churchmen of the 1780s looked on Gallicanism as in any sense a threat to the Church of England. Quite the contrary.[61] But they remained in some sense the inheritors of a post-Reformation anti-Catholic rhetoric which, since the 1750s, possibly earlier, had rather lost its currency among educated men and women. Less so among the populace at large as the 1780 Gordon Riots had demonstrated. Literary attempts were still made to stoke up anti-popish sentiment: *The New and Complete Book of Martyrs* updating John Foxe had been produced by Paul Wright c.1785, but it was not the kind of book likely to appeal to a discriminating purchaser; someone who could not really take seriously the possibility that papists were still planning horrible fates for God-fearing Protestants.[62]

However, the linguistic and cultural treasury of English anti-Catholicism was a resource readily available for application to any new set of enemies. So it was but a short step to load the anxieties, the fears, the craftiness and the moral turpitude associated until recently with the papists on to the *philosophes*, whether in their native French guise or their English equivalents. Socinians, sceptics, infidels of any and every colouring were parcelled together by the orthodox in the 1780s as fears mounted about the viability of establishment and its capacity to withstand indefinitely a combination of overt assault and covert undermining. As high churchmen began to raise again the time-honoured cry of 'The Church in danger!' so they began to reconstruct and update the stage set of Popish plots with which English audiences were ancestrally so familiar into contemporary political theatre: a *philosophe* plot. Any event which could not be readily explained could be given sinister connotations even down to a break in at Lambeth palace at 1788. As an anxious Horne explained it:

> ... our metropolitan, I hear, has lost all his plate: some fanatics, or Socinians, have broken thro' the wall, and carried the spoil on hurdles to a coach, ...[63]

Though their daring was blatant, none should doubt their ultimate intention or their devious organisational skills: if part stood revealed, much was still obscured. Preaching at the consecration of Samuel Horsley, the relentless orthodox opponent of Priestley, as bishop of St Davids, in 1788, the Rev. Dr. Charles Layard noted how '... the enemies of Christianity have changed the mode of their attacks, and have endeavoured insidiously to undermine the fabric, that hath withstood every effort of open force'.[64] These people could never be underestimated. 'Our opponents are shrewd, active, busy, bustling, and indefatigable', preached George Horne in one of his greatest sermons, 'The Duty of contending for the faith', delivered in 1786, urging his congregation to be constantly on their guard.[65] The perception of such Anglican alarmists was that the conspiratorial mode was a primary means to a heterodox end for Socinians, and they were the more dangerous in that while part of their agitation to change public opinion was all too open, the remainder of it was felt to be clandestine, secretive and subversive. Some orthodox apologists were also alarmed that they had what one anonymous sermoniser in 1789 called 'secret friends within the bosom of the church, without shame, fear or interest at present restrain within the bounds of hypocritical profession'.[66] However, should subscription and the Test Act both be set aside then these hypocrites would disclose themselves and the full extent of the conpiratorial chain stand horribly revealed. These forebodings were comparable to those expressed by many of the Gallican higher clergy after the passing of the Edict on non-Catholics of 1787. Such concessions, granted in France, petitioned for in England, were a cover for far more radical gaols.[67]

Confronted with this covert and overt challenge to the integrity of the Church, there were gratifying signs for Horne and his allies that Anglican opinion was at last mobilising both in word and deed. The harrying of Priestley was unremitting. In his episcopal Charge of 1790, Bishop Horsley, in defending the high church identity, branded him and Lindsey as heretics and their religion as sinful.[68] In a more obviously pastoral mode, in the summer of 1789 William Cleaver (1742–1815), bishop of Chester since 1787, was touring his diocese, taking in Lancashire, Westmoreland, and the northern deaneries of Yorkshire and issuing charges to his clergy against Socinianism. Across England and Wales generally by early 1790, clergy and laity were marshalling on a county basis and successfully counter-petitioning Parliament against the repeal of the Test and Corporation Acts.

In France by that date such behaviour would have been regarded as counter-revolutionary since Catholicism had been denied (13 April 1790) status as the sole state religion by the National Assembly. French Protestants may have been the ostensible beneficiaries but high church opinion in England detected the beginnings of an attempt to undermine establishment as was happening at home. France had its own, more numerous pack of restless heretics and unbelievers whose insidious behaviour in that 'monstrous tragicomic scene' as Burke called the Revolution[69] could be interpreted in the light of the British experience because the conspiratorial model had a universal application. It was important to read events within a British as well as French light. The task was always to detect the outward and visible signs of conspiracy, and it was a commonplace of anti-revolutionary preaching and pamphleteering to enjoin the true believer and the patriot (they tended to be opposite sides of the same coin) never to relax his search for them, an echo so often heard in Burke's writings of his last years with all their harping on 'exposing'. At least the coming of the Revolution had served to flush out the enemies of establishment. As Jones preached in a 1791 sermon: 'Sedition, which used formerly to hid its trains of mischief in caverns under ground, now brandishes a torch in broad day-light', while lamenting that 'the policy of the age (too deep for *me* to understand) leaves it to itself, and waits to see what it will do'.[70]

For both Jones and Burke, government could not afford to be dilatory. It must be both vigilant and ready to act promptly against the disaffected, a category which included, as Burke informed the home secretary in the autumn of 1791, that 'nine tenths' of the dissenters who were 'entirely devoted, some with greater some with lesser zeal, to the principles of the French Revolution'.[71] As Burke put it in his speech of May 1792 against the Unitarians' petition for relief

> Above all, he [the magistrate] ought strictly to look to it when men begin to form new combinations, to be distinguished by new names, and especially, when they mingle a political system with their religious opinions, true or false, plausible or implausible.[72]

What had happened in France before November 1790 showed there was no limit to the damage that could be caused by underhand, mischievous intriguers and in England, despite the failure the previous April of the campaign to remove the Test and Corporation Acts from the statute book, nothing indicated that the danger was over from 'societies' agitating for change to the constitutional status quo. The Unitarian petition drove home the lesson that such societies were in effect organised groups of conspirators shaming concern for the commonwealth. All Burke could do in the circumstances, again borrowing from the clergy, was to combine the prophetical and the political and keep on warning whoever would hear him. For Burke, as Priestley himself expressed it, thus to be steering 'the ship of the state through the storm, which we all see to be approaching', was an onerous self-imposed role and, as he sardonically concluded: '... if, in these circumstances, you can save the church, as well as the state, you will deserve no less than canonization, and ST. EDMUND will be the greatest name in the calendar'.[73] Burke certainly did not over-estimate his hopes of success. For him as for other Anglican and Gallican luminaries of the Counter-Enlightenment, given fallen human nature, in the final reckoning only so much could be done to preserve any worldly system from the malignant or to seek preservatives against the workings of Providence, which confounded ready explanation in overthrowing just and unjust alike. That insight, too, was a commonplace of pre-revolutionary high church controversialists and defenders available for appropriation and endorsement.

Notes

* I am grateful to Grayson Ditchfield, Ian Harris, Emma Macleod, Darrin McMahon, Peter Nockles and Richard Sharp for their comments on an earlier version of this essay.

1   To Charles-Jean-François Dupont, November 1789, *The Correspondence of Edmund Burke*, vol. VI, *July 1789–December 1791*, eds. Alfred Cobban and Robert A. Smith, (Chicago/Cambridge, 1967), vi, 41.

2   Ibid., vi, 10.

3   'My particular province has been the East Indies', to Lord Charlemont, 10 July 1789, Burke, *Correspondence*, vi, 2. See, most recently, Frederick G. Whelan, *Burke and India* (Pittsburgh, 1997).

4   As F.P. Lock observes, 'Burke's opponents recognized in the *Reflections* a powerful and credible representation of the Revolution', 'Rhetoric and representation in Burke's *Reflections*', pp. 18–39 at 35, in John Whale, ed., *Edmund Burke's Reflections on the Revolution in France. New interdisciplinary essays* (Manchester, 2000).

5   Cf. Edmund Burke, *Reflections on the Revolution in France. A Critical Edition*, ed. J.C.D. Clark (Stanford, 2001), Introduction, 81. There is a useful discussion of Burke and the causes of Revolution in Michael Freeman, *Edmund Burke and the Critique of Political Radicalism* (Oxford, 1980), pp. 188–203. Freeman argues that Burke never said that the conspiracy of revolutionary leaders 'was the sole or a sufficient cause of revolution' (202).

6   The 1790 edition of the *Annual Register* thus took his charge at face value by having a heading called the 'Political Effects of the Junction between the great monied Interest and the philosophical Cabals of France'. Paul Keen, *The Crisis of Literature in the 1790s. Print Culture and the Public Sphere* (Cambridge, 1999), p. 45.

7   For Burke's indebtedness in the 1790s to Anglican political theology in general, see J.C.D. Clark, *English Society 1688–1832. Ideology, Social Structure and Political Practice during the Ancien Régime* (Cambridge, 1985), p. 249–50.

8   Seamus F. Deane, *The French Revolution and Enlightenment in England 1789–1832* (Harvard, 1988), 10.

9   Burke, *Reflections*, 253. As Seamus F. Deane usefully observes: 'Both "cabal" and "sect" fit into the general context of Biblical allusion and exegesis which was inspired by Price's sermon. Similarly, vilifying the new ideas as "heresy", the parallel with the Reformation, and many other ironically religious references all fit into this background'. 'Burke and the French Philosophes', *Studies in Burke and his Time* 10 (1968–9), 1113–37, at 1121–2n. See also his comments on the cabal 'as essentially the corruption of the family, the basic unit of society', ibid., p. 1124.

10   For his itinerary in 1773, see F.P. Lock, *Edmund Burke. Vol. I, 1730–1784* (Oxford, 1998), pp. 342–3.

11   *The Writings and Speeches of Edmund Burke*, vol. ii, *Party, Parliament, and the American Crisis 1766–1774*, ed. William B. Todd (Oxford, 1981), pp. 388–9; Robert Bisset, *The Life of Edmund Burke* (London, 1798), p. 159; C.B. Tinker, *The Salon and English Letters* (New York, 1915), p. 68.

12   *Analytical Review*, Nov. 1790. Cf. *Monthly Review*, Nov. 1790: 'His reasoning is of that species, which is calculated to affect, rather by the accumulation and combined force of a number of arguments, each of which appears light, and airy, and refined, in itself, than by the strength and solidity of any single and independent proposition'.

13   Darrin M. McMahon, *Enemies of the Enlightenment. The French Counter-Enlightenment and the Making of Modernity* (New York, 2001), 63. Cf. Clarke Garrett, 'Belief in conspiracy, ... was virtually universal among political actors in 1789'. 'The myth of the counterrevolution in 1789', *French Historical Studies* 18 (1994), pp. 784–800, at p. 788.

14   Amos Hofman, 'The origins of the theory of the *philosophe* conspiracy', 'French History' 2 (1988), 152–72; McMahon, *Enemies of the Enlightenment*, pp. 68–9.

15   *Reflections*, 156, 276. For a modern view which has some sympathy for this allegation, see Colin Jones, 'Bourgeois revolution revivified: 1789 and social change', in Colin Lucas ed., *Rewriting the French Revolution* [The Andrew Browning Lectures 1989], (Oxford, 1991), pp. 69–118, at p. 113.

16   Richard Pares, *George III and the Politicians* (Oxford, 1952), 80n., 84n. Burke articulated his suspicions of a court conspiracy against the Rockingham government of 1765–1766 in his *Thoughts on the Cause of the Present Discontents* and in his *A Short Account of a Late Short Administration.* Lock, *Burke*, I, 190, 229, 230.

17   Burke was insistent that 'Indianism' was part of the conspiracy to dislodge the Coalition. Burke later compared Warren Hastings and his allies to the Jacobins. Ibid., I, 526–33. See also Peter Marshall, introduction to *The Writings and Speeches of Edmund Burke.* Vol. 7. *India. The Hastings trial, 1789–1794* (Oxford, 2000), p. 17.

18   For Burke's accumulated resentments towards the rational dissenters see Robert A. Smith, 'Burke's crusade against the French Revolution: principles and prejudices', in Peter J. Stanlis, ed., *Edmund Burke, The Enlightenment and the Modern World* (Detroit, 1967), pp. 27–44 at p. 41, who refers to his attack on them as 'almost pathological'. See also D.O. Thomas, *The Honest Mind. The Thought and Work of Richard Price* (Oxford, 1977), pp. 310–13.

19   Recent scholarship stresses the status and influence of Rational Dissenting ministers in English commercial centres in the 1770s and 1780s. See James E. Bradley, *Religion, Revolution and English Radicalism: Nonconformity in Eighteenth-Century Politics and Society* (Cambridge, 1990); John Seed, '"A set of men powerful enough in many things": rational Dissent and political opposition in England, 1770–1790', in Knud Haakonssen, ed., *Enlightenment and Religion: Rational Dissent in Eighteenth-Century Britain* (Cambridge, 1996), pp. 140–92.

20   See generally G.M. Ditchfield, 'The parliamentary struggle over the repeal of the Test and Corporation Acts, 1787–90', *E.H.R.*, 89 (1974), pp. 551–77.

21   As one prominent Oxford don - and future bishop - put it: 'But though the asperity of his [Priestley's] censures, the ardour of his wishes, and the confidence of his predictions, be levelled chiefly against the Church of England, yet he acknowledges, that he would willingly see the whole established government of his Country subverted for the sake of removing the "Corruptions of Christianity", which it supports'. Thomas Burgess, *The Divinity of Christ proved from his own declarations attested and interpreted by his living witnesses, the*

Jews. A Sermon preached before the University of Oxford at St Peter's, February 28th 1790 (Oxford, 1790), p. 46.

22   *Reflections*, p. 248.

23   [George Horne], *A Letter to the Reverend Doctor Priestley, By an Undergraduate* (2nd ed., Oxford, 1787), p. 11.

24   The 'language of gunpowder' had been drawn on by earlier generations of Anglican controversialists, for instance, [Charles Leslie], *The New Association of those called Moderate Church-men, with the Modern-Whigs and Fanaticks, to undermine and blow-up the present Church and Government, by a True-Church-Man* (London, 1702).

25   George Horne remarked that Priestley 'spoke of this Powder-plot against the Church of England with as much certainty, as if he had *held the lantern*'. William Jones, *Memoirs of the Life, Studies, and Writings of the Right Reverend George Horne, D.D., late Lord Bishop of Norwich* (London, 1795), 144n. For the links between gunpowder and insurrection see Maurice Crosland, 'The Image of Science as a Threat: Burke versus Priestley and the "Philosophic Revolution"', *British Journal for the History of Science* 20 (1987), pp. 287–318, at pp. 285–8.

26   To John Noble, *Correspondence*, vi, 102, 14 Mar. 1790.

27   *Parl. Hist.*, xxviii, pp. 438–9.

28   Quoted in Crosland, 'The Image of Science', p. 286.

29   J.G. McEvoy and J.E. McGuire, 'God and nature: Priestley's way of rational dissent', *Historical Studies in the Physical Sciences*, vi (1975), pp. 325~404; Clarke Garrett, 'Joseph Priestley, the millenium, and the French Revolution', *J.H.I.*, 34 (1973), pp. 51–66.

30   Jones, *Memoirs of Horne*, p. 133.

31   *Reflections*, p. 277.

32   Gerland P. Tyson, *Joseph Johnson: A Liberal Publisher* (Iowa City, 1979).

33   In 1790 Anglo-French reformers were constantly and genially congratulating and encouraging each other. Price was pressed by Treilhard (President of the National Assembly) and his admirer, the duc de La Rochefoucauld d'Enville, to attend the celebration of the *Fête de la Fédération* in Paris on 14 July 1790 but his poor health prevented him attending. Other British revolutionary sympathisers such as Lansdown's son, Earl Wycombe, and the Unitarian, Benjamin Vaughan, were there. See W. Bernard Peach, ed., *The Correspondence of Richard Price, vol. III: February 1786–February 1791* (Durham, N.C.,/Cardiff, 1994), pp. 305–11.

34   Dorus [W. Gifford], 'Imitation, etc. Written at St Ann's Hill', in ed. L. Rice-Oxley, *Poetry of the Anti-Jacobin* (Oxford, 1924), p. 67.

35   Cf. Derek Jarrett, 'If the *Reflections* were the product of an obsession, it was an obsession with the evils of the marquis of Lansdowne as much as with the evils of the French Revolution', *The Begetters of Revolution. England's Involvement with France 1759–1789* (London, 1973), p. 285. Burke's detestation of Shelburne is well discussed in Conor Cruise O'Brien, *The Great Melody: A Thematic Biography of Edmund Burke* (London, 1992), pp. 234–42.

36   For Price's long friendship with Shelburne see Seed, 'Rational Dissent and political opposition', p. 145.

37   Russell Kirk, *Edmund Burke, A Genius Reconsidered* (Peru, Ill., 1987)150–1; Thomas, *The Honest Mind*, pp. 313–14.

38   A royal chaplain in ordinary gave thanks to God that Priestley 'is a missionary without an army to back him'. Browne Grisdale, D.D., *A Sermon preached in Whitehall Chapel, at the consecration of the Right Reverend John Douglas, D.D., Lord Bishop of Carlisle, on Sunday, November 18, 1787* (London, 1788), p. 11n.

39   *Reflections*, p. 253.

40   Burke variously referred to Price as the 'Spiritual Doctor of Politics', 'the Political Divine', 'the Apostle of Liberty', 'the Political Preacher and the Archpontiff of the Rights of Man'. Thomas, *The Honest Mind*, p. 317.

41   Burke to Francis, 12 Feb. 1790, in Beata Francis and Eliza Keary eds., *The Francis Letters: Sir Philip Francis and Other members of the family* (2 vols., London, n.d., ii, 380–6).

42   As early as 12 Nov. 1789 he reckoned that France was 'a country undone', everything pointing to 'the total political extinction of a great civilized Nation situated in the heart of this our Western System'. To Lord Fitzwilliam, *Correspondence*, vi, 36.

43   Jack Fruchtman, Jr., 'The apocalyptic politics of Richard Price and Joseph Priestley: a study in late eighteenth-century English republican millennialism', *Transactions of the American Philosophical Society*, 73 (1983), p. 53; C.D.A. Leighton, Antichrist's revolution: Some Anglican apocalypticists in the age of the French wars, *Journal of Religious History* 24 (2000), pp. 125–42. Dr Leighton argues (136) 'It was, though, the apocalyptic tradition itself, rather than the related propensity to seek out conspiracy, which chiefly allowed the identification of rationalist Dissent as Antichristianism'. Anglicans were slow to resort to millennial explanations until the outbreak of the Revolution because these offered a dynamic of change which they did not seek and would work against them. They had a corresponding attractiveness to rational dissenters. Price, for instance, believed that before the millennium, all Church establishments would be destroyed as part of the downfall of Antichrist: 'Religion must lose that connection with civil power which has debased it, and which now in almost every Christian country turns it into a scheme worldly emolument and policy, and supports error and superstition under the name of it'. Richard Price, D.D., F.R.S., *The Evidence for a future period of improvement in the state of mankind, with the means and duty of promoting it,...* (London, 1787), pp. 19–20.

44   Neil Hitchin, 'The evidence of things seen: Georgian churchmen and biblical prophecy', in B. Taithe and T. Thornton, eds., *Prophecy: The Power of Inspired Language in History, 1300–2000* (Stroud, 1997), pp. 119–39. And, indeed, it would be in such a prophetic mantle that Burke would, in the last seven years of his life, cover himself.

45   [Edward Sayer], *Observations on Doctor Price's Revolution Sermon* (London, 1790), p. 16.

46   Frederick Dreyer, 'Burke's religion', *Studies in Burke and his Time* 17 (1976), 199–212; Nigel Aston, 'A "lay divine": Burke, Christianity, and the Preservation of the British state, 1790–1797', in Aston, ed., *Religious Change in Europe 1650–1914* (Oxford, 1997), pp. 185–212.

47   Burke to Bishop Horne, 9 Dec. 1791. In this same letter, Burke asked to call on Horne when the bishop was next in London, considering that the criticism of the Revolution and the praise for Burke as an [unnamed] 'learned and eloquent layman' in *A Charge intended to have been delivered to the clergy of the diocese of Norwich, at the primary visitation of George, Lord Bishop of that Diocese* (Norwich, 1791), 33, was an 'act of your own goodness to be a title to my ambition to cultivate your friendship personally'. Burke, *Correspondence*, vi, 455–6. Horne died before the meeting could occur.

48   Horne, 25 Oct. 1788, 'The Duty of Praying for Governors'.

49   William Jones, *Sermons on Moral and Religious Subjects* (2 vols., London, 1790), ii, no. 1.

50   It is a recurrent emphasis in his MS Sermons (2 vols.) in Pusey House Library, Oxford. See his Advent 1774 sermon which argues that the contemporary degeneracy of the Christian Church suggests that it is in its last age. vol. I, pp. 22–3.

51   Horne to George Berkeley the younger 15 Dec. 1789, B.L. Add. MS. 39312, fol. 108. Horne had himself preached uncompromisingly on 25 October 1789 on 'Submission to Government'. In his habitual sardonic manner he observed that were the Revolution to spread to England, both he and Jones were likely to be strung up to the same lamp-post. Jones, *Memoirs of Horne*, p. 153.

52   *Religion and Enlightenment in Eighteenth-Century England* (Oxford, 1998), p. 146. See also Robert Hole, 'English sermons and tracts as media of debate on the French Revolution 1789–1799', in ed. Mark Philp, *The French Revolution and British Popular Politics* (Cambridge, 1991), pp. 18–37, especially 19–29 for a contextualised discussion of the post-1789 preaching of Horne and Jones.

53   Many of these were reissued as a 2 volume compendium bulked out with other classic high church apologies under the title *The Scholar Armed against the Errors of the Time; or, a Collection of tracts on the principles and evidences of Christianity* (2 vols., London, 1795).

54   Bod Lib., MS Percy, c.3, fos. 45–6, 47. Jones's remarks also suggest how quickly churchmen were learning from Burke as well as finding in the *Reflections* a confirmation of their own forebodings about the direction of events in France.

55   J.M. Roberts, *The Mythology of the Secret Societies* (London, 1972).

56   The resemblances were not lost on Burke, too, with such comparisons as that of Richard Price to Hugh Peters, *Reflections*, p. 225.

57   See John Redwood, *Reason, Ridicule and Religion: The Age of Enlightenment in England 1660– 1750* (London, 1976); G.V. Bennet, *The Tory Crisis in Church and State 1688–1730: The Career of Francis Atterbury Bishop of Rochester* (Oxford, 1975).

58   MS Sermons, vol. I, p. 21.

59   A Country clergyman [William Jones], *A Preservative against the publications dispersed by Modern Socinians* (4th ed., London, 1787), p. 6.

60   Burke was habitually represented as a jesuitical figure in most contemporary caricatures so it would have been entirely counter-productive for him to have resorted to this explanatory line. See Nicholas K. Robinson, *Edmund Burke. A Life in Caricature* (New Haven, 1996).

61   Nigel Aston, 'The dean of Canterbury and the sage of Ferney: George Horne looks at Voltaire', in. Nigel Yates and W. Jacob, eds., *Crown & Mitre* (Woodbridge, 1993); idem. 'Anglican-Gallican relations, 1740–1790', unpub. paper given at the IHR, 2001.

62   Colin Haydon, *Anti-Catholicism in Eighteenth-Century England* (Manchester, 1993), p. 29.

63   Horne to Berkeley, 13 Oct. 1788, B.L. Add. MS39312, fol. 79.

64   Charles Peter Layard, DD FRS FAS, *A Sermon preached in Lambeth Chapel, at the Consecration of the Right Reverend Father in God Samuel Lord Bishop of St David's, on Whit Sunday, May 11, 1788,* (London, 1788) [Titus, I.9], p. 7–8.

65   Horne 'The Duty of contending for the faith', p. 313, preached Canterbury, 1 July 1786, *Sixteen Sermons on various subjects and occasions* (Oxford, 1793), 313.

66   *Thanksgiving for the King's Recovery* (London?, 1789), p. 16.

67   The 1788 Remonstrance issued by the General Assembly of the Clergy of France spoke in terms of a joint Protestant-*philosophe* conspiracy. McMahon, *Enemies of the Enlightenment*, pp. 45, 71, 78.

68   For a putative link between Horsley and Burke see Clark, Introduction to *Reflections*, p. 59n.

69   *Reflections*, p. 155.

70   William Jones, *The difficulties and resources of the Christian ministry in the present times: A Sermon preached before the chancellor and the clergy of the deanery of Sudbury, at Bury St Edmund's, at the Primary Visitation of the Right Rev. Father in God, George, Lord Bishop of Norwich, on May 31, 1791* (Bury St Edmund's, 1791) [Matthew 28, vv. 18–20], pp. 10–11.

71   To Henry Dundas, 30 Sept. 1791. Burke, *Correspondence*, vi, 419.

72   Debate, 11 May 1792, *Parl. Hist.*, 29:1374.

73   Joseph Priestley, *Letters to the Right Honourable Edmund Burke occasioned by his Reflections on the Revolution in France* (Birmingham, 1791), p. 151.

Chapter 13

'The Tartuffes of Patriotism': Fears of Conspiracy in the Political Language of Revolutionary Government, France 1793–1794

Marisa Linton

I

Belief in political conspiracies was widespread in Europe during the seventeenth and eighteenth centuries. The reasons for this are complex. A somewhat functionalist argument is that in a world that lacked as yet an appreciation of social and economic forces, history was seen very much as a matter of individual agency. Conspiracies were thus one way to explain and interpret events.[1] This was still a society that conceptualised politics in profoundly moral terms: a society within which individual actions were seen as either good or bad. This view of politics owed much to both the Christian tradition and the world of the classical authors.

Before the Revolution there were several political themes that often involved conspiracy theories. One of these was the 'famine plot' which was itself related to the so-called 'aristocratic plot'. This was the belief that wealthy court nobles were literally conspiring to hoard grain and fix prices in order to profit by starving the people, a charge that was played out in popular rumours as well as pamphlet debates.[2] In addition, court factionalism and political intrigue were sometimes seen in terms of conspiracies. For example, Thomas Kaiser has demonstrated that the belief that Marie-Antoinette was the secret leader of a conspiracy to bring down the Revolution had its roots in anti-Austrian sentiment originating in court politics that went back at least as far as the reaction against the treaty of alliance between France and Austria of 1756.[3]

The rhetoric of conspiracy intensified dramatically with the outbreak of revolution in 1789 and played a part in the radicalisation of politics. From as early as July 1789 much of the impulse towards radical politics was inspired by fear of an 'aristocratic conspiracy' directed against the Third Estate. The very fact that a vast political revolution had taken place gave substance to ideas about conspiracy, for it encouraged belief in the efficacy of human agency. Things previously thought to be fixed and unchangeable - absolute monarchy, the authority of the Catholic church, the ascendancy of the nobility - had been brought down, almost overnight, by human will. Subsequent generations of historians have attributed the outbreak of the Revolution to wide-ranging phenomena: to the rise of the bourgeoisie, to class conflict, to modernisation and the formation of the state, or the rise of new forms of political culture. But people who lived through the Revolution did not, by and large, see it in such terms. For them 1789 was the achievement of individuals acting together with a common purpose. These individuals might be cast either as heroes or villains, depending on one's political perspective. Whilst the Revolution's supporters saw 1789 as the achievement of courageous heroes, they were also likely to attribute the subsequent decline in the political situation to the furtive efforts of men of ill-well, conspiring in secret to destroy the Revolution. The rhetoric of conspiracy clashed fatally with some of the fundamental precepts of the Revolution, most significantly, with the ideal of universal fraternity. The revolutionary ideal was founded on virtuous or selfless citizenship, universal standards of human rights, transparency of politics and citizenship as inclusion. But the revolutionary experience simultaneously strengthened ideas about exclusion, nationalism and suspicion of outsiders. In the spring of 1794 the tensions between these two incompatible approaches to the Revolution tore revolutionary government apart and precipitated the end of the radical experiment of the Year II.

In recent years, historians have begun to unravel the links between the rhetoric of conspiracy and the radicalisation of revolutionary politics. This work originated, in part, with Furet who pioneered the idea that revolutionary language did not simply describe events but was itself instrumental in causing them. For Furet, the discourse of conspiracy was the central organising principle of French revolutionary rhetoric.[4] Lynn Hunt has also contributed significantly to this debate. She has stated that 'the narrative of Revolution was dominated by plots', and an obsession with unmasking conspirators. Hunt traced this to an obsession with what she termed 'transparency'. This was an idea of revolutionary politics as an authentic expression of the self, in which there is no room for particular interests or political factions: each deputy should represent only the national good.[5] She sees Rousseau as a fundamental influence here, though such ideas did not emanate from Rousseau alone, indeed, the influence of religious thought from such political forces as the Jansenists may also have played a part. An additional key factor - as Hunt and others have noted - is the relative lack of political experience for revolutionaries who were catapulted in such short space of time from an absolutist system to a self-consciously democratic one. In such circumstances there was scant recognition of the legitimacy of the viewpoints of others, and little sense of the pragmatic need for political negotiation and management. In this context political opponents were likely to have their personal integrity questioned. Their political aims appeared to their suspicious opponents as the opposite of 'transparent' - as 'opaque', cloaked in secrecy, and (fatal word) - conspiratorial.

The part played by conspiracies in the Revolution went beyond a purely rhetorical function. For there were also real conspiracies: that is, groups of people organised clandestinely to undermine the political transformation brought about in 1789. The extent of these conspiracies is hard for historians to ascertain. Much of the relevant evidence either way, if it ever existed in a written form, was probably destroyed at one point or another by the parties concerned who had every incentive to make sure that no incriminating documents remained. This was a problem for the revolutionaries themselves, who naturally lacked access to the records of the hostile foreign powers and had to conjecture on the basis of partial evidence. Whilst revolutionary claims about the existence of networks of conspirators clearly overstated the case, it would be unwise to attribute such suspicions to paranoia or rhetorical construction alone. To seek to explain what took place during the Revolution without consideration of the genuine opposition to it makes little sense. As Sutherland states, 'opposition to the Revolution was real, serious, authentic and legitimate in its own way, and popular' and as such it was central to the way in which the Revolution developed.[6]

From as early as July 1789 a series of plots were launched by active members of the old elite against the political changes that were taking place. This point has been taken up by Timothy Tackett who argues against Furet's contention that by the summer of 1789 real opposition to the Revolution had already collapsed and that revolutionary politics were being conducted in a power vacuum.[7] It could be argued that the pivotal flight to Varennes in June 1791, the king's abortive attempt to flee both Paris and his commitment to the constitutional monarchy, was itself a major conspiracy. Indeed, one of those involved in the attempted escape, baron Klinglin, referred to it enthusiastically as 'our sublime conspiracy'.[8] The flight to Varennes fatally undermined public trust both in the monarchy and in the moderate deputies who became involved in the attempted 'cover-up'. It did more to induce the ultimate downfall of the constitutional monarchy than any other single event between October 1789 and August 1792. It also at a stroke enhanced the credibility of every radical journalist who had been claiming that the new elite put in power by the Revolution were now conspiring with the monarchy to rein in the forces let loose by the events of 1789.

II

Fears of conspiracy haunted the politics of the constitutional phase of the monarchy. They escalated further with the onset of war, the overthrow of the monarchy and founding of the Republic. But they reached their zenith during the period of Jacobin domination of government, from June 1793 to July 1794. Of the many accusations of conspiracy that were made in that year, the most traumatic were those that involved the so-called 'foreign plot'. These accusations simmered throughout the autumn and winter of 1793, and exploded in the spring of 1794 with the arrest and execution of the Hébertists and the Dantonists (or Indulgents). These accusations of conspiracy were directed against men who were, or had been, part of the inner circle of the Jacobins. The indictment of such men went to the heart of the revolutionary government and called into question the validity of the Jacobin vision of the Revolution itself. We shall look more closely at the view of conspiracy as it was portrayed through the language of the 'foreign plot' in a moment. But firstly, the wider Jacobin preoccupation with conspiracy needs to be considered and put into context.

It was a time of extremes: extreme measures and extreme fear. Obsessive fear of conspiracy was a driving force behind the origins of the Terror.[9] In part this was a logistical problem that arose out of the nature of revolution. Revolutionary politics were inherently unstable and the normal methods of enforcing the will of government did not apply. As Robespierre expressed this: 'The aim of constitutional government is to conserve the Republic, that of revolutionary government is to found it. The Revolution is the war of liberty against its enemies; the Constitution is the regime of victorious and peaceable liberty. Constitutional government concerns itself principally with civil liberty, and revolutionary government with public liberty'.[10] One of the most problematic characteristics of revolutionary government was the tendency to assume that any opposition to it constituted a plot. Several of the Jacobin leaders had been engaging in this kind of rhetoric since the early years of the Revolution. Marat and Robespierre both forged their reputations as demagogic leaders partly through their contributions to the conspiratorial vision of revolutionary politics, and their dogged persistence in unmasking plots. For Marat this was something of a sacred duty. In November 1792 he offered an account of the qualities necessary for a 'patriotic denouncer' of plots. Such a man 'must be pure in his morals and irreproachable in his conduct ... he must possess an unassailable impartiality ... he must renounce life's pleasures, sweetness, and repose... he must have an indomitable courage ... and he must carry his self-abnegation to a heroic level'.[11] In order to recognise the true nature of a conspiracy one had to be a 'man of virtue', that is, one must keep oneself pure and sacrifice one's own interests to those of the *patrie*. This was seen as the essential guarantee that the motives of the denouncer were not tainted by self-interested motives such as jealousy or a desire for revenge.

The obsession with conspiracy was inextricably linked to the revolutionaries' propensity to see the Revolution in purely moral terms: the 'patriots' who could be identified by their virtue, and who defended the Revolution, versus the 'conspirators' and 'scoundrels' who sought to overturn it. Denunciation was thus seen as a revolutionary duty. But the difficulties of achieving this in the 'virtuous' manner prescribed by Marat were compounded by the overwhelming complexity of the actual political situation in the Year II, in which very little was clear and nothing was pure. Above all, how could one recognise conspirators when they looked like patriots, talked like patriots and, indeed, claimed to be patriots? This dilemma is one that looms large in all civil wars and counter-revolutionary situations when the enemy is not a convenient 'foreigner' in a distinctive uniform. It was to prove particularly intractable for the French revolutionaries for a number of reasons which we can sketch out provisionally here.

A central problem when interpreting the politics of the Year II is how to make sense of the increasingly ferocious and hysterical language of revolutionary speeches within the context of events of which we may only have a very incomplete knowledge. Conspirators have every incentive to leave few written traces behind them. It seems very likely that some people were actively conspiring against the Jacobin government. Many people had cause to detest it. Even the *sans-culottes* who had put it in power and helped maintain it there throughout the most traumatic year of the Terror were finding that it was disappointing their expectations. For their part, the Jacobins felt beleaguered. The federalist revolts that followed the overthrow of the Girondins, and the murder of Marat in July of that year fed into their sense that no one was to be trusted. One of the most extraordinary consequences of that fear was the readiness of the Jacobins to link together supposed conspirators in 'the foreign plot', a sort of super-conspiracy, in which everyone from British agents, the Dantonists and the Hébertists were all secretly involved. The big political speeches against the factions set out to rewrite the history of their participation in the Revolution, to show that not only were these groups secretly linked but that, from the very beginning of the Revolution, their purpose had been malign. It was not enough to convict people of incompetence, nor yet of having individually disagreed with the political position of the Jacobin leadership. What they did was to try and demonstrate networks of conspiracy in a way that went far beyond the rhetoric of conspiracy as they had envisaged it only a year before.

Any explanation of the obsession with plots in the Year II must take into account a number of factors. Firstly, as we have seen, this obsession can be traced back to long-standing ideas about the nature of political opposition as self-interested and lacking legitimacy. Nor were the Jacobins immune from the *sans-culottes'* preoccupation with the existence of a 'famine plot'. An additional complication is the likelihood that a number of genuine conspiracies were being hatched, and there is evidence that British spies and French royalists were trying to bribe revolutionaries.[12] However, this in itself still leaves much unexplained, for there was much that was irrational about the Jacobins' pursuit of conspirators. Two things stand out in particular: firstly, the revolutionaries showed a lamentable failure to get their hands on the right men; secondly, the practice of lumping people together amidst accusations of super-conspiracies did not correspond to the reality of the situation.

There were also psychological factors, the precise effect of which are hard to measure, but which had a direct impact upon the men directing Jacobin policy. Perhaps the most fundamental of these was the leading revolutionaries' consciousness of the uncertain legitimacy of the Jacobin government which kept its place (and they their heads) ultimately only through a combination of the force of the *sans-culottes* and Robespierre's tenacious faith in the republic of virtue. Both these supports were looking decidedly shaky by the spring of 1794. Combined with this, and linked closely to it, was a pervasive fear and anxiety which surfaced again and again in both public and private pronunciations of the Jacobins. There is no doubt that the men of the Year II were very afraid. They were genuinely afraid of conspiracies (even though not all the conspiracies were real). They were afraid of losing the war. They were afraid of the counter-revolution winning and the monarchy being restored. They were afraid of the *sans-culottes* - of the popular violence that they had sought to master and direct but which, now fully unleashed, might be turned on them. They were afraid of being assassinated, as Charlotte Corday had assassinated Marat. And they were, increasingly, afraid of each other. Some of this fear was misdirected, but its impact was far from negligible and it should not be left out of account. For it is against this background of acute tension, mistrust, fear and hatred that the accusations of conspiracy in the spring of 1794 were played out, with such deadly consequences.

III

Nowhere is this fear more evident than in the language used about the 'foreign plot'. The background to this was complex. There were two principal aspects: the 'foreign plot' itself; and the entangled web of financial corruption and speculation known as the affair of the East India Company. It was Fabre d'Eglantine, former actor and playwright who, in an effort to distract attention from his own financial misdealings in the East India Company, denounced to the ruling Committees the existence of a foreign plot in October 1793. In his frantic attempts to clear himself, he implicated many others, Hébertists, dechristianisers, foreigners in France, and accused them of complicity with foreign governments and royalist émigrés to overthrow the Revolution. One of the men he named, Chabot, an ex-Franciscan monk, in turn denounced the East India Company speculators. He spoke to the Committee of General Security in November (having first approached Robespierre with his story) and implicated Fabre d'Eglantine and Delaunay d'Angers (both friends of Danton and members of the 'Dantonist' faction). The veracity of neither Fabre nor Chabot can be relied upon: they were fighting for their lives. No one, even at the time, could disentangle all the threads.

The history of the 'foreign plot' has been examined in detail, though the lack of conclusive surviving evidence makes interpretation difficult. One of the most asked questions - whether there was a genuine conspiracy - is unlikely to ever have a definitive answer. What is clear is that much of Jacobin politics from the Autumn of 1793 to April 1794 has to be understood in relation to conspiracy - both real and imagined.[13] The probability is that quite a number of revolutionaries were exploiting their political power by making money out of it, and that some were taking bribes. It is not unlikely, too, that some revolutionaries were also 'for sale' to the most interested buyer - the British government. But it is unlikely that there was a concerted political conspiracy. The surviving evidence suggests that the ruling Committees of Public Safety and of General Security were not paranoid in suspecting a plot - but they may not have got the right culprits.[14] The situation was further complicated by the fact that the accusations of corruption coincided with the political opposition of two groups, the Dantonists and the Hébertists, some of whom were also implicated in the financial and corruption scandals. The accusations of corruption thus dovetailed neatly with the charge that these factions were seeking to overthrow the government. But this charge also fitted in with the overall Jacobin conception of politics which in turn drew on the classical republican ideal whereby, in order to be politically virtuous in public life, it was also necessary to be virtuous in private life. A man of virtue ought not to make personal profit from his public position by financial misdealing, or accepting bribes. To do so was to call into question not only his personal but also his political integrity.[15] For some of the Jacobins, such as Robespierre and Billaud-Varenne, financial corruption amongst the national deputies equalled political and moral corruption, which brought the Convention, and hence the Revolution itself, into disrepute.[16] It also proved a way for the Committees to justify to the Convention the elimination of their political opponents. The result was that all these groups were accused of one vast labyrinthine plot against the Revolution.

The Hébertists were self-appointed spokesmen of the *sans-culottes*, their power-base was in the Commune and the Cordelier club. They supported an increase in the Terror, enforced dechristianisation and popular measures in support of the *sans-culottes*. They sealed their fate by an abortive attempt at insurrection. The Dantonists, on the other hand, were working to moderate the Terror and curtail the power of the *sans-culottes*. Both groups were opposed to the policy of the Committees, therefore, and the success of either might well have meant an end of the Committees, certainly a change in their membership. At the same time, both factions were bitter opponents of each other, their policies diametrically opposed. The argument that the Hébertists might make common cause with the Dantonists, and that they in turn were secretly linked to overseas powers and royalists was hardly convincing. The evidence of such links as presented at the trials of the Hébertists and Dantonists was thin in the extreme. It seems clear that both factions were condemned ultimately for political reasons: above all, for having opposed publicly the policies of the Jacobin government.

The war with hostile powers had put a severe strain on the cosmopolitan ideals of the early years of the Revolution. Revolutionary politics were growing ever more nationalist. In this context it is not surprising that some of the people denounced as conspirators were foreigners living in the capital, whose very enthusiasm for the revolutionary cause was now seen as tantamount to a cause for suspicion. These included shadowy figures associated with the (genuine) conspirator the Gascon baron de Batz and the East India Company, men such as the Austrian Jewish Frey brothers whose principal crimes seem to have been financial speculation and corruption. Other foreigners accused included committed political radicals active in the Commune, the Sections and in dechristianisation, such as the wealthy Spanish grandee Guzman, the Portuguese Jew Pereira and the Prussian nobleman Anacharsis Clootz. Linked with them was a rather more plausible conspirator, Proli, who was possibly the illegitimate son of the Austrian chancellor, Kaunitz. He had been at one time at least, an Austrian agent.[17] In spite of, or possibly because of, his radical and Hébertist sympathies he too fell under suspicion.

Still more significant was the inclusion on the list of suspects of a number of Frenchmen who had hitherto been known as patriots and committed revolutionaries, veterans of several years of struggle against the forces of reaction and monarchy. These men included Hébert, Ronsin, Momoro, Danton, Desmoulins (the personal friend of Robespierre), Hérault and Lacroix. The arguments used to attack these men were particularly traumatic and divisive. Their revolutionary credentials were often no less distinguished and long-standing than those of the members of the ruling Committees who now led the formal accusations against them. These were former fellow-revolutionaries, indeed in some cases, erstwhile friends of the men who were now accusing them. How then did the Committees construct the case against them and identify them as 'conspirators'? One of the most striking things about the way the spokesmen for the Committees used the language of accusation was the extent to which they made use of a panoply of signs to identify the characteristics of a conspirator.[18] The ways in which they constructed these arguments, and the kind of signs that they invoked, indicate something of the effect of their own fears and anxieties about conspiracy, and the ways in which conspiracy was conceptualised as the opposing force to what they understood by the Revolution. The rhetoric of conspiracy was the reverse of the ideals of universal fraternity and brotherhood. The signs of conspiracy that they invoked derived from a number of sources: popular fears amongst the lower orders of aristocratic conspiracy and famine plots; *ancien régime* political concepts of factions at court as groups of self-interested conspirators, hiding behind masks; and classical republican rhetorical traditions of conspiracies against the state.

The original account of the 'foreign plot' as it was delivered to the Committees owed much to the inventive narrative powers of Fabre d'Eglantine and his convincing demeanour when he told his story. When the Committees eventually realised that they had been duped by Fabre, rather than assuming that his tale of a plot was false, and that Fabre had implicated other men in order to save himself, they continued to believe that the plot was a reality, for it fitted in with their (especially Robespierre's) ideas about the nature of the opposition ranged against them - a fact of which Fabre had been well aware when he had made his charges. Indeed, for a while at least, Robespierre now believed not only that the story of a plot was true, but that Fabre himself was 'this grand master', who had been one of its chief organisers. Fabre's former career as an actor told against him in Robespierre's eyes for it not only made his skills as a convincing liar more plausible, but the very idea of acting, of dissimulation, was the polar opposite of the ideal of the virtuous patriot, who was honest, straightforward and 'transparent'. According to Robespierre, Fabre had been a kind of spy-master, who had used his trusted position within the ranks of the Jacobins to find out and exploit their weaknesses. 'Fabre is perhaps the man in the Republic who knows best which spring to touch, in order to set in motion the different political machines that intrigue has at its disposal. No mechanic is more skilful at manoeuvring the cogs of the machine he wants to set working, than this artisan of intrigues is at manipulating people's passions and characters, in order to further the execution of his plots'. Fabre had used his theatrical skills to play upon the fears of the revolutionaries: 'It was his principle that fear is one of the great motivating forces in human actions... He continually had the air of a man who is frightened by the very phantom that he himself had created in order to appal the whole Convention...'.[19] The effect of this conspiracy within the ranks of the Jacobins was to eat away at the Revolution from within. 'Thus, like a fruit of superb appearance, that an invisible insect devours in secret, the Republic, undermined silently by the gnawing worm of intrigue, would wither, in spite of its brilliant successes, and die, so to speak, in the midst of its victory'.[20]

Fabre was imprisoned on 12 January (later to be tried and executed along with the Dantonists) but the fears of a 'foreign plot' escalated in the ensuing weeks, to culminate in the arrest of the two political factions deemed to be implicated: the Hébertists and the Dantonists. The official accusations against both these groups invoked signs and indications of conspiracy to incriminate them.

IV

The official speech 'on the foreign factions' that portended the arrest of the Hébertists was made in the Convention by Saint-Just on the 23 ventôse (3 March 1794).[21] He was speaking on behalf of the Committee of Public Safety and his choice of words indicate how those at the heart of the Jacobin government conceptualised conspiracy. The attack included a long peroration on the distinguishing characteristics of the conspirators and asserted the importance of signs. Conspiracy - like everything else in the Revolution - was to be understood in moral terms. 'It is the league of all the vices' against the republic of virtue.[22] All the plotters were secretly united: 'The Indulgent faction that wants to save the criminals, and the foreign faction that howls for blood'.[23] The most significant characteristics of a conspirator were duplicity and hypocrisy. Conspirators sought to disguise their true intentions by feigning loyalty to the Revolution whilst imitating and exaggerating the language and actions of genuine patriots. Again, conspirators were characterised as consummate actors. The kinds of people involved were: 'The nobles, the foreigners, the idle, the orators who had sold themselves. We declare war on these tartufes [*sic*] of patriotism'.[24] Another category singled out as suspect was that of the civil servants who, like old regime officials, used their posts for self-enrichment. Such conspirators could be distinguished from true 'patriots' by external signs: 'The conspirators have signs whereby they recognise one another, at the theatre, in the places where they encounter one another, in the places where they go to eat'. Self-indulgent over-eating, especially when flaunted in public, was a particularly ominous indication of suspect political loyalties. Saint-Just referred tight-lipped to rich conspirators consuming meals in restaurants at '100 écus' a head.[25] It is hard to know what they might have found to spend such a large sum on in Paris in the Year II. He imitated satirically the wife of a civil servant complaining that it was simply impossible to obtain delicacies like pheasants. This was contrasted to the eating habits of the people who lived modestly off simple local fare that they produced themselves, such as chestnuts, bread and vegetables cooked in oil.[26] It was a line of argument calculated to undermine the image of Hébert's alter-ego, *Le Père Duchesn*e and the Cordelier club in the eyes of the *sans-culottes*.

Appearance, too, could be an indication of a conspirator. The Revolution had educated the French in the politics of dress. It too, was a sign or language to be read, but also to be manipulated. To dress like an old regime noble was to flaunt one's rejection of revolutionary principles, to make a statement that was readable by all. But more sinister still to the mind of the Jacobins, were those conspirators who emulated the dress of the *sans-culottes*, the short trousers, the 'bonnets rouges', whilst secretly holding opposing political opinions.[27] Not clothes alone, but even the face could apparently give an indication of one's political allegiance. Physiognomy had been particularly important in the world of the eighteenth-century courtier, a place of masks and deception, where the art of reading someone's true character through their features was considered an essential ingredient of success in negotiating the maze of factional politics.[28] In their anxiety to identify political enemies, the Jacobins, too, now resorted to reading duplicity in people's faces. Other members of the Committee of Public Safety addressed the importance of features and appearances when they in turn spoke on the plot. Couthon stated, '... in Revolutions all the good citizens must be physiognomists; all those people who today have a sinister look, wild eyes, clothes that are evidently a disguise, are bad citizens whom every true republican has the right to arrest on the spot'.[29] Barère added that a number of 'muscadins' (dandies), foreigners and deserters had been seen on the streets of Paris where they 'congregate at the theatre, dressed with ridiculous ostentation and, at the moment of insurrection, show themselves with dirty stockings, large moustaches and long sabres, threatening the good citizens, especially the people's representatives'.[30] The term *muscadin* was of recent provenance, mentioned from May 1793 onwards: it conflated a dandified appearance with counter-revolutionary sympathies. As a sartorial model it was the antithesis of the somewhat dishevelled appearance of the 'true sans-culotte'.[31] An overly ostentatious appearance suggested a lack of appropriate masculine revolutionary virtue, and indicated avoidance of military combat, if not of actual counter-revolutionary sympathies. *Muscadins* were seen as opponents of the *sans-culottes*, so it is significant that according to Barère they were congregating in support of Hébert. This may well have been a tactic for discrediting the Cordelier club in the eyes of the *sans-culottes*.

The two factions who were the objects of the Committees' wrath had themselves been employing similar accusations in the course of the attacks and counter-attacks that they had launched on one another since the autumn of 1793. Such language had been employed in the pages of Hébert's journal, *Le Père Duchesne*, and Desmoulins' journal *Le Vieux Cordelier*. In the course of their mutual recriminations and charges of financial corruption, unidentified sources of income and conspiratorial tendencies, Hébert had accused Desmoulins of having the manners, sentiments and over-refined language of a *muscadin*. Desmoulins saw no reason to apologise for his taste for luxury and pleasure. He countered Hébert's criticisms by a reference to Solon's Athens - for he had always preferred the Athenian to the Spartan republic, though it was the latter, austere, frugal and warlike, that had gained the ascendancy in the Republic of the Year II. 'No one there accused Solon of being a *muscadin*; or thought he was in any way less fit to be a model for legislators, proclaimed by the oracle the first of the seven sages, although he made no bones about admitting to his taste for wine, women and music...'.[32] Hébert was no match for Desmoulins as a skilled manipulator of the written word. But unhappily for Desmoulins, he would have needed more effective weapons than his satirical pen to defend himself against the attack of the Committees. The blow was not long delayed.

V

A few days after the downfall of the Hébertists, the Dantonist faction in its turn was denounced as part of the 'foreign plot'. The question of why the Committees took the fateful decision to eliminate Danton is one that has long preoccupied historians. The break between Robespierre and Danton has been seen as one of the pivotal points of the Revolution. It has divided even professional historians, most famously Aulard (the defender of Danton) and Mathiez (the supporter of Robespierre), both of whom took up strongly partisanal positions. An image which lingers in the popular imagination is that of Robespierre, the icy and ruthless 'Incorruptible', condemning the more attractive and humane, but all too venal Danton. Although this is not without some truth, the politics of the situation were rather more ambiguous than this suggests. The idea that Danton was profiting out of the Revolution was not new. There were long-standing suspicions in revolutionary circles of Danton's personal corruption, and possibly political corruption that dated back as far as his association with Mirabeau. But the real reason why Danton was brought down was his outspoken support for a policy of moderating the Terror which threatened to overthrow the government and, it was feared, bring an end to the Jacobin Revolution. Even then, there is evidence to suggest that Robespierre had some sympathy with the Indulgents' desire to finish with the Terror, and that he continued to defend Danton as long as he dared and tried - without success - to get him to accept a compromise with the Committees. But other members of the Committees such as Billaud-Varenne, Collot d'Herbois and Vadier were determined to move against the Dantonists, and ultimately Robespierre supported them, either because he knew that, even with Danton's support, he was not strong enough to outface the other Committee members, or because he feared the consequences of Danton's success even more than he feared the triumph of the Committees. Whatever the truth of this, once Robespierre had decided to throw in his lot with the Committees against Danton (and even against his childhood friend, Desmoulins) he spared no effort to ensure their deaths.[33]

The official report against the Dantonists was once again delivered by Saint-Just, though this time the Committees (fearing Danton's eloquence) had taken the precaution of arresting the suspects first. Saint-Just had written a preliminary draft of the report, but Robespierre thought this insufficient for the task in hand and himself provided copious notes, in which he made much of his long friendship (or at least association) with Danton, to 'dish the dirt'. Saint-Just incorporated much, though not all, of these notes into the final version of the report. Robespierre's notes against Danton contained very little in the way of substantial allegations. It is notable that almost nothing was made of Danton's financial corruption though there was some circumstantial evidence that could have been invoked. Neither was there any attempt to substantiate the claim that Danton had been in the pay of the British - though for this no solid proof seems to have existed and Robespierre appears to have drawn the line at fabricating evidence.[34] What he did do, however, was to pass under review the history of Danton's actions throughout the Revolution (much of which Robespierre had observed at first hand) and put the worst possible interpretation on Danton's words and actions.[35] The aim seems to have been say enough to cast doubt in the minds of the deputies regarding Danton's revolutionary integrity, in order to make it possible to proceed against him.

In the absence of firm evidence, the allegations that Robespierre provided leaned even more heavily than in the case of the Hébertists on external signs of conspiracy. One such sign was the pursuit of luxury and self-indulgence. Danton's reputation as a 'bon viveur' appears to have been justified. Private dinners were a place where unscrupulous revolutionaries might use wine and food to relax the guard of their more virtuous fellows and influence their political decisions. As proof of this Robespierre offered the following account. 'I recall an anecdote which seemed of little importance at the time. During the first months of the Revolution I was at dinner with Danton, Danton reproached me with hindering our good cause, by not following the line taken by Barnave and Lameth who were at that time starting to deviate from popular principles'.[36] Thus Robespierre remembered something said in friendship over dinner four years earlier, and saw it retrospectively as evidence of conspiracy.

According to Robespierre, Danton mingled conspiracy with the overt hedonism of a man who, on his own admission, knew no virtue better than that 'which he practised every night with his wife'.[37] It is not clear whether the greater crime in Robespierre's eyes was Danton's ignorance of true virtue, or his having made a joke about it. Again, lavish and expensive dinners were seen as the occasion for private plotting. This was reflected in Saint-Just's final version of the report. In the summer of 1793, he said, there was a plot to make the little Capet, son of Louis XVI, king. 'At that time Danton often dined in the rue Grange-Batelière, with some English people; he dined with Guzman, the Spaniard, three times a week, and with the infamous Sainte-

Amaranthe, the son of Sartine, and Lacroix. It's on these occasions that some people partook of dinners that cost a hundred écus a head', he added, using the same extravagant figure as he had previously fixed on for the conspiratorial dinners of the 'foreign faction'. [38] Robespierre's notes refer only in passing to this particular accusation, though later, after Danton's death, he was to go into these 'conspiratorial dinners' at greater length, in some private notes he compiled on deputies he suspected of counter-revolution. Regarding one of these men, Thuriot he mentioned as grounds for suspicion the fact that he, too, had attended the dinners with Danton, Guzman and Lacroix.[39] Robespierre's notes on Danton also recounted how Fabre had continued to take both lunch and dinner with Proli, even though Fabre had secretly denounced him, showing the extent of Fabre's hypocrisy. He also recalled other social gatherings, involving 'known' conspirators. 'One must not forget Robert's tea parties, where d'Orléans himself made the punch, and Fabre, Danton and Wimpffen were in attendance. It was there that attempts were made to attract the largest possible number of deputies of the Mountain, either to seduce or to compromise them'.[40]

Rich food and excessive wine could seduce the unwary deputies of the Mountain. To accept offers of wine and dinner with other suspect characters, could be dangerous, even damning. Like Persephone in the Underworld, by partaking of such food one might be drawn into that other underworld of intrigue and conspiracy. There are several possible reasons for this suspicion of food and wine. Firstly, Saint-Just and, to some extent, Robespierre admired the ideal of the republics of antiquity, where frugality and moderation were seen as virtues. Saint-Just in particular was a devotee of Sparta.[41] Saint-Just's accusation of Danton's personal as well as political shortcomings, his idleness at key moments and self-indulgence, invoked the classical model of denunciation of failures in private as well as public virtues. It recalled Cicero's indictment of the degrading behaviour of Mark Antony, his neglect of politics and abandonment of the soldiers fighting on his behalf in order to engage in dissipation with Cleopatra. Secondly, excessive dining and, especially, the money to pay for it was seen as both aristocratic and frivolous, recalling the values of the *ancien régime*. Indeed, the arch-enemy, Pitt himself, was justly renowned for his remarkable capacity for claret. Thirdly, excessive consumption of rare and expensive delicacies was seen as offensive to the people who were suffering shortages of bread and other essential foodstuffs. Robespierre even used Danton's well-fed look ('embonpoint') against him, saying that Danton and his friends used it to justify his idleness and inaction at key revolutionary moments.[42] This was not quite as trivial an allusion as it sounds. The language of denunciation in the Convention recalled popular anger over the 'famine plot' and echoed the anxiety of the *sans-culottes* over food shortages. As the food queues lengthened in the spring of 1794 the Jacobin deputies in the Convention sought to appease the crowd by using the highly charged language of food consumption to make the argument that neither the Hébertists nor the Dantonists were in sympathy with the sufferings of the Parisians.[43]

Even signs of emotion, such as tears or laughter, might indicate duplicity. In the language of Rousseau (of which so many Jacobins were devotees), tears were the outpouring of authentic emotion, a sign of true sensibility. But in the context of fears of conspiracy, tears might be employed to disguise one's authentic emotions, offering only the appearance of sincere feeling.[44] Robespierre described the occasion when Fabre (that consummate actor again) had seen the issues of *Le Vieux Cordelier* that asked for a policy of clemency, and he had wept tears, deceiving the gullible Desmoulins into thinking that he had 'an excellent heart' and was, in consequence, 'a patriot'. 'Crocodiles weep too' observed Saint-Just laconically in his version of this story. Still more cruelly, Robespierre recalled that Danton had attempted to copy this tactic, in the tribunal of the Jacobins, and at Robespierre's home. According to Robespierre, 'he tried to imitate Fabre's talents' but he was unable even to make a pretence of true feeling: his tears were unconvincing and he succeeded only in making himself ridiculous.[45] This particular charge was omitted in Saint-Just's final version of the report, possibly because it seemed so vindictive an accusation as to undermine the virtuous image of the man making it.

Even laughter might conceal duplicitous thoughts - a point that was used against Hérault de Sechelles. Hérault had turned his back on a privileged upbringing in the ranks of the higher nobility to espouse the revolutionary cause. He had become a radical Jacobin and a member of the Committee of Public Safety. But his wealth and aristocratic background, together with the suave and affected manners of the former courtier, aroused the suspicions of his fellow Committee members who were all of much humbler social origins.[46] He was denounced by Fabre, accused (probably wrongly) of selling the Committee's secrets to the hostile powers, using Proli (who had at one time lived in Hérault's house) as an intermediary. According to Saint-Just: 'Hérault was serious within the Convention, elsewhere he played the buffoon, and would laugh incessantly to cover up the fact that he never said anything'.[47] It is not clear why Hérault's tendency to laugh should so have infuriated Saint-Just, but it is not hard to imagine the unfortunate Hérault laughing out of nervousness, feeling the eyes of his colleagues upon him, scrutinising him for signs of noble mannerisms and suspect allegiances.

VI

In conclusion, the language and imagery of conspiracy are revealing of the attitudes of revolutionary leaders. Suspect friendships, disguised appearances, private dinners, tears, laughter, even facial expressions, all these might be invoked as external signs that called into question inner revolutionary integrity. Possibly one of the most revealing images was that of the conspirator as actor, the 'Tartuffe' who knew the words, the appearance, even the emotions of the genuine 'patriot' but did not share them in his heart. It is an image that suggests an underlying anxiety in the revolutionary mentality, a profound, though unvoiced, uncertainty that anyone could ever entirely prove their revolutionary virtue. We should not exaggerate the significance of this. The decision to eliminate the leaders of both Hébertist and Dantonist groups was taken in both cases on more substantial political grounds: not for being conspirators, but for openly opposing the politics of the Committees. But these more substantive points were played down in the formal accusations of both factions. What remained were the images of conspiratorial actors, who feigned and acted words they did not believe. Ironically, the conspiracy launched against Robespierre in Thermidor was to have many of the characteristics of a theatrical performance - though one with life and death consequences. From Robespierre's perspective, the 9 Thermidor would be the last hopeless stand of the 'men of virtue' against the forces of corruption. But when the victors of Thermidor subsequently rewrote the history of the Revolution in such a way as to exculpate themselves from the guilt of the Terror, it was Robespierre himself, the 'Incorruptible', whom they deemed to have been the arch-conspirator.[48]

Notes

1   On this subject, see the arguments by G.S. Wood, 'Conspiracy and the Paranoid Style: Causality and Deceit in the Eighteenth Century', *William and Mary Quarterly*, 3d ser., 39 (1982), pp. 401–41. Although he is talking principally about American political culture, his points may also be applicable to France.

2   See the article on the 'complot aristocratique' in A. Soboul, ed., *Dictionnaire historique de la Révolution française*, Paris, 1989, p. 274 ; also D. Sutherland, *The French Revolution and Empire : The Quest for a Civic Order* (Oxford, 2003), pp. 54–6.

3   See T.E. Kaiser, 'Who's afraid of Marie-Antoinette? Diplomacy, Austrophobia and the Queen', *French History*, 14, 3 (2000), pp. 241–71, esp. pp. 245–6.

4   F. Furet, *Penser la Révolution* (Paris), 1978, pp. 78–9.

5   L. Hunt, *Politics, Culture and Class in the French Revolution* (Berkeley, California, 1984), esp. pp. 38–45.

6   Sutherland, *The French Revolution*, p. 3.

7   T. Tackett, 'A Conspiracy obsession in a time of Revolution: French elites and the origins of the Terror', *American Historical Review*, 105 (2000), pp. 691–713, esp. p. 701. Similar points have been raised by G. Cubitt, 'Denouncing conspiracy in the French Revolution', *Renaissance and Modern Studies*, 33 (1989), pp. 144–58.

8   Cited by T. Tackett, *When the King Took Flight* (Cambridge, Mass., 2003), p. 78. This book gives a convincing analysis of the political significance of Varennes.

9   See T. Tackett, 'Interpreting the Terror', *French Historical Studies*, 24, 1 (2002), pp. 569–78, esp. p. 575.

10   M. Robespierre, 'Rapport sur les principes du gouvernement révolutionnaire, fait au nom du Comité de Salut Public, par Maximilien Robespierre', 5 nivôse an II, 25th December 1793, in *Œuvres de Maximilien Robespierre*, eds. M. Bouloiseau, A. Soboul *et al.* (10 vols., Paris, 1910–67), X, p. 274.

11   J.P. Marat, *Le Journal de la République Française*, No. 46, 16 Nov. 1792, in *Œuvres de J.P. Marat*, ed. A Vermorel (Paris, 1869), pp. 255–7.

12   On the development of the British secret service in the course of espionage to undermine first the monarchy, and later the Jacobins, see A. Cobban, 'British secret service in France, 1784–92', and 'The Beginning of the Channel Islands correspondence' in Cobban, *Aspects of the French Revolution* (St Albans, 1971), pp. 192–238.

13   The classic study of conspiracy in the Year II was by A. Mathiez, *La Conspiration de l'Étranger* (Paris, 1918). His research was meticulous, but his interpretation was one that leaned towards a vindication of Robespierre, and a condemnation of Danton. A more dispassionate analysis of the evidence for the existence of a plot is detailed in N. Hampson, *The Life and Opinions of Maximilien Robespierre* (London, 1974), pp. 201–23.

14   See Hampson's conclusions, *Robespierre*, p. 215.

15   On the long-standing classical republican idea that public and private virtue were linked, see M. Linton, *The Politics of Virtue in Enlightenment France* (Basingstoke, 2001).

16   See Billaud-Varenne and Robespierre's criticisms of Amar for failing to make this connection between the financial corruption of deputies and the political integrity of the Convention (and hence the nation) in his report on the East India Company affair, *Archives parlementaires*, LXXXVI, 26 ventôse an II, 16th March 1794, pp. 553–7.

17   Hampson, *Robespierre*, p. 202.

18   On the problems of interpreting the languages of signs, see S. Rosenfeld, *A Revolution in Language: The Problem of Signs in Late Eighteenth-Century France* (Stanford, 2001).

19   M. Robespierre, 'Discours non prononcé sur la faction Fabre d'Eglantine', in *Œuvres de Maximilien Robespierre*, X, pp. 339–40. This manuscript was also published in E.B. Courtois, *Papiers inédits trouvés chez Robespierre, Saint-Just, Payan, etc., supprimés ou omis par Courtois* (3 vols, Paris, 1828); republished Geneva, 1978, II, pp. 21–49. Robespierre did not, in the end, deliver this speech, either because of illness at the critical time, or because it explicitly attacked both factions at once, and it was decided that such a tactic would be excessively dangerous.

20   Ibid., p. 341.

21   On the Hébertists, see M. Slavin, *The Hébertistes to the Guillotine: Anatomy of a "Conspiracy" in Revolutionary France* (Baton Rouge, 1994). The case for Hébert's involvement with the baron de Batz was made by A. de Lestapis, *La 'Conspiration de Batz' (1793–1794)* (Paris, 1969), but even he admits that the evidence is inconclusive. He thought that the fault lay partly with Robespierre, for wanting 'to save the honour of the Mountain' by suppressing

the consideration in court of the full evidence against Hébert and Chabot, thus allowing a lingering doubt to remain, pp. 236–47; 256–7.

22 Saint-Just, 'Discours sur les factions de l'étranger', delivered before the Convention, 23 ventôse an II, 13 March 1794. Republished in L.A. Saint-Just, *Oeuvres complètes de Saint-Just*, ed. C. Vellay (2 vols, Paris, 1980), II, p. 259.

23 Ibid., p. 266.

24 Ibid., p. 261.

25 Ibid., p. 260.

26 Ibid., pp. 269–70.

27 On the politics of dress, see R. Wrigley, *The Politics of Appearances: Representations of Dress in Revolutionary France* (Oxford, 2002). On Jacobin suspicions that the 'bonnet rouge' was being worn by men with aristocratic sympathies to mask treacherous intentions, see pp. 199–202.

28 This was an old-established idea: physiognomy as a science had a venerable history that dated back to the Aristotelian school. In the eighteenth century it had gained new popularity through writers such as Lavater. But it came into pre-eminence in the world of *ancien régime* politics. On the court as a place where everyone wore a metaphorical mask to disguise their true features, see P.R. Campbell, *Power and Politics in Old Regime France, 1720–1745* (London, 1996), chapter 8, esp. pp. 187–8.

29 *Archives parlementaires*, LXXXVI, 25 ventôse an II, 15th March 1794, p. 502. See also the text of Couthon's report, Ibid., 'Pièces annexes', pp. 512–13.

30 Ibid., p. 503.

31 See N. Pellegrin, *Les Vêtements de la Liberté: Abécédaire des pratiques Vestimentaires Françaises de 1780 à 1800* (Aix-en-Provence, 1989), pp. 131–2.

32 C. Desmoulins, *Le Vieux Cordelier*, ed. A. Mathiez and H. Calvet, Paris, 1936, No. 7, p. 232; also No. 5, p. 156, note 4.

33 For a point by point consideration of the allegations made in Robespierre's notes for the accusation of Danton, see, J.M. Thompson, *Robespierre*, this edition, Oxford, 1988, pp. 463–70. On Robespierre's ideas regarding conspiracy and corruption, see G. Cubitt, 'Robespierre and conspiracy theories', in C. Haydon and W. Doyle, eds., *Robespierre*, Cambridge, 1999, pp. 75–91.

34 Such evidence as there was against Danton was marshalled by Mathiez in his *La Conspiration de l'étranger*. There is nothing here that would have convicted Danton in a more scrupulous law court than the Revolutionary Tribunal. It is true that much evidence disappeared or was suppressed, but what remains can amount to no more than conjecture.

35 One can compare Robespierre's notes with what he had said publicly about Danton at the Jacobin club the previous December. 'I have observed Danton with regard to his politics, I have observed him with severity, and the differences in our opinions have meant that I even observed him with a kind of anger; but I have never discerned in him any inclination towards treason'. 13 frimaire an II, 3rd December 1793, in Robespierre, *Oeuvres Complètes*, X, p. 223.

36 M. Robespierre, 'Les Notes contre les Dantonistes', published in A. Mathiez, *Etudes sur Robespierre (1758–1794)* (Paris, 1958), p. 134. See also Saint-Just, *Oeuvres*, II, p. 316.

37 Robespierre, 'Les Notes contre les Dantonistes', p. 138.

38 Saint-Just, 'Rapport sur la conjuration ourdie pour obtenir un changement de dynastie, et contre Danton…', delivered before the Convention, 11 Germinal an II, 31 March 1794.

Republished in Saint-Just, *Oeuvres*, II, p. 329. To situate this accusation within the wider context of the development of the restaurant as a 'public/private' space where secrets might be discussed, see R. Spang, *The Invention of the Restaurant: Paris and Modern Gastronomic Culture* (Harvard, 2000).

39   Robespierre, 'Les Notes contre les Dantonistes', p. 131. On Thuriot, see Courtois, *Papiers inédits*, II, pp. 18–19.

40   Robespierre, 'Les Notes contre les Dantonistes', pp. 138 and 151. Saint-Just referred to these 'confabulations' briefly in the final report: see Saint-Just, *Oeuvres*, II, p. 320.

41   On the adoption of the classical (and particularly Spartan) model of republicanism in the Year II, see M. Linton, 'Ideas of the future in the French Revolution', in M. Crook, ed., *Enlightenment and Revolution* (Aldershot, 2004).

42   Robespierre, 'Les Notes contre les Dantonistes', p. 143. The 'embonpoint' did not feature in the final version of the report, possibly because Saint-Just thought it too petty to be a serious accusation.

43   On the politics of food shortages in the spring of 1794 see Slavin, *The Hébertistes to the Guillotine*, chapter 2, esp. pp. 40–1.

44   On the growing suspicion of tears during the Revolution, see A. Vincent-Buffault, *The History of Tears: Sensibility and Sentimentality in France*, originally published as *Histoire des Larmes XVIIIe–XIXe siècles*, Paris, 1986; translated, Basingstoke, 1991, pp. 92–6.

45   Robespierre, 'Les Notes contre les Dantonistes', p. 135. Saint-Just, 'Rapport sur la conjuration … et contre Danton…', *Oeuvres*, II, p. 326.

46   According to Palmer, Hérault, despite his antecedents, was a Hébertist in his politics. See R.R. Palmer, *Twelve Who Ruled: The Year of the Terror in the French Revolution* (Princeton, 1941), pp. 116, 192–7.

47   Saint-Just, *Œuvres*, II, p. 325.

48   See B. Baczko, *Ending the Terror: the French Revolution After Robespierre* (Cambridge, 1994), pp. 1–32.

Chapter 14

The 'Foreign Plot' and the French Revolution: A Reappraisal

Munro Price

Early in the morning of 14 November 1793, Maximilien Robespierre was woken from his sleep by his colleague in the national convention, the former Capuchin monk François Chabot, with an extraordinary tale about a vast financial and political conspiracy to destroy the revolutionary government. The brains behind the plot, Chabot alleged, was the royalist financier and spy the baron de Batz. He claimed that Batz, backed by English gold, had conceived a plan to undermine the Revolution from within by setting its leaders against each other by means of corruption. The first stage, Chabot went on, had already taken place with the inveigling of several deputies into a shady scheme to hold the French East India Company to ransom over the terms of its liquidation. Having joined the plot in order to learn its secrets, he was now performing his patriotic duty in denouncing it.[1]

Chabot's motives, of course, were neither so pure nor so simple. His early-morning confession to Robespierre was at least partly an attempt to escape his own pursuers. On 12 October, he himself had been denounced before the committees of general security and public safety by another deputy, Fabre d'Eglantine, as being implicated in a similar counter-revolutionary conspiracy. The cast of Fabre's plot was even more exotic than Chabot's. It included the Belgian financier Proli, who was rumoured to be the illegitimate son of the Austrian chancellor prince Kaunitz, and two wealthy Moravian Jews, the Frey brothers (whose sister Chabot had married the previous week).[2] According to Fabre, this group and its associates were in reality *agents provocateurs* in the pay of Austria, whose aim was to discredit the Revolution by pushing it ever further to extremes.

This 'foreign plot' conjured up by Chabot and Fabre, English or Austrian or both, may seem absurdly fanciful today. Yet its importance for the French Revolution was huge. Over the next six months, on the basis of Fabre's and Chabot's accusations, Robespierre and his allies eliminated their rivals for power first on the left, then on the right. Hébert and his leading associates were arrested, tried as foreign agents, and executed on 24 March 1794. Just a week later, it was the turn of Robespierre's more moderate rivals, led by the great orator Danton. On the evening of 2 April, and looking, in the words of one observer, 'as if he were emerging from the tomb rather than about to enter it', Danton went to the guillotine.[3] Neither Fabre nor Chabot managed to save themselves; both accompanied Danton to the scaffold.

The 'foreign plot' did not merely add to the Revolution's already high body-count of illustrious corpses. The execution of both Dantonists and Hébertists dangerously isolated the revolutionary government both from the Convention and its base of popular support. It thus marked a turning-point in the Revolution itself. By plunging its leaders into internecine strife, it prepared the way for the coup of Thermidor, the fall of Robespierre, and the ending of the Reign of Terror.

Even today, much about the 'foreign plot' remains mysterious. As with most conspiracies, the remaining evidence is inconclusive and fragmentary. The most incriminating documents, if they did exist, have been destroyed. As a result, historians have always been divided on whether the plot had any basis in reality, or whether it was simply a convenient fabrication to enable Robespierre and his faction to discredit their enemies. For Albert Mathiez, Fabre and Danton were guilty as charged, while Michel Eude was much more sceptical. Norman Hampson concludes that there probably was something to the 'foreign plot', but that it is impossible now to determine its precise outlines given the lack of surviving evidence.[4] It does seem clear that there was a corruption scandal surrounding the liquidation of the East India Company, but how far, if at all, this had political and counter-revolutionary overtones is a very murky question indeed.

In revisiting the 'foreign plot' here, I have two aims. The first is to probe once more the vexed issue of how much, if any, of the 'plot' was reality, and how much politically-inspired fantasy. After all the efforts of contemporaries and historians to discover the truth of the matter, I have no illusions about being able to provide an answer. However, very little scholarly work on the 'foreign plot' has been produced since the 1960s, and much of this has been of mind-boggling complexity.[5] As an antidote to this, it seems worthwhile to review the most important evidence for and against the existence of the 'plot', and separate it from the mass of detail that has since accumulated around it.

The second aim is to reassess the role played by the baron de Batz himself. It may well be that Batz was merely a shady financier, rather than, as Robespierre himself alleged, the mastermind of the whole conspiracy. Yet before this conclusion is reached, some new, and some neglected evidence linking Batz to an important counter-revolutionary network outside France in the 1790s should be examined.

The first, and still the most important, testimony about the 'foreign plot' is Chabot's original confession to Robespierre of 14 November 1793. Chabot claimed that his involvement had begun some time the previous August, when his fellow-deputies Delaunay d'Angers and Julien de Toulouse invited him to an elegant dinner at a country house at Charonne just outside Paris, where he was surprised to find that his host was Batz. The conversation soon turned to various possible ways of extorting money from the bankers of Paris, and it was from these beginnings that the plan to hold to ransom the directors of the East India Company was born. First, the Convention would be persuaded to suppress the Company (it was, in fact, Delaunay d'Angers and Julien de Toulouse who led this campaign), then the directors of the Company would be allowed to liquidate their assets on favourable terms in exchange for a large bribe.[6]

It is certain that this scheme really did exist. The decree of the Convention liquidating the East India Company was indeed illegally altered to favour the Company, and the difference between the two versions can be clearly seen in the copies of the projected and the falsified decrees in the Archives Nationales. Chabot's chief role in the fraud was to bribe the one hostile member of the commission charged with drawing up the decree, Fabre d'Eglantine, not to oppose the plot, and in this he succeeded; Fabre's signature appears along with all the others at the foot of the page.[7]

The real difficulty comes with Chabot's further allegations. Soon after the dinner at Charonne, he claimed, he had realised that the financial plot was only one part of a much wider and more dangerous political one, 'to corrupt the strongest patriots, and to discredit them if they could not be bought'. He amplified this at the end of his confession: the conspirators' aim, he concluded, 'was to dissolve the Convention, and all those who are working to undermine and corrupt it, or to discredit those of its members who have done the state some service, appear to me to form part of this plot'.[8]

How far, if at all, can this dramatic but frustratingly vague accusation be substantiated? It would obviously be strengthened if some of those who dined with Chabot at Charonne also had counter-revolutionary connections. This was certainly the case with Batz. Born in 1754 and by 1789 a successful Parisian speculator, the baron had been elected to the Estates General and in 1790 become president of the National Assembly's important committee for the liquidation of the national debt. He had used this position to siphon off a percentage of the sums that passed through his hands to create an emergency secret fund for Louis XVI. By July 1792 he had raised 512,000 *livres* in this way, as the king himself noted in his diary.[9] Batz even claimed later to have made an attempt to rescue Louis from the scaffold on the morning of his execution. He may have been exaggerating, but the Committee of General Security believed the incident had taken place, as it made clear in a letter of 22 April 1794 to Fouquier-Tinville, the president of the revolutionary tribunal.[10] The Committee also believed that Batz had helped organise a plot to enable Marie Antoinette to escape from the Temple. This was echoed by Chabot, who claimed he had at first been reluctant to meet the baron, knowing him to 'have been involved in the plan to spirit away the former queen'.[11]

In view of this, it is surprising that in the separate trials of Hébert and Danton and their associates, for both of which Chabot's confession provided evidence, Batz was very rarely mentioned. At the Hébert trial, although several potential witnesses offered evidence linking Batz to Hébert, Fouquier-Tinville called none of them, while the only one of Danton's co-defendants to be directly accused of working for Batz, Lullier, was also the only one to be acquitted. As Norman Hampson comments: 'It is difficult to resist the conclusion that some members of the revolutionary government were protecting Batz, whatever their reasons'.[12]

The baron only moved centre-stage two months later, after the failed assassination attempts of Ladmiral and Cécile Renaud against Collot d'Herbois and Robespierre. On 14 June 1794, in a speech to the Convention, the deputy Elie Lacoste cast Batz for the first time as the moving spirit behind all the recent plots against the republic. In Lacoste's purple prose, the baron emerged as an 'atrocious brigand ... resting one hand on the guineas of Pitt and holding in the other the electric current with which he galvanized the Vendée, Lyon, Bordeaux, Toulon and Marseille' whose ultimate aim was the overthrow of the Convention and the triumph of the counter-revolution.[13]

It remains unclear why, after being so carefully kept out of the trials of the Hébertists and the Dantonists, all the political allegations against Batz first made by Chabot should suddenly have been unveiled two months later by the revolutionary government. It may be, as Batz's descendant René de Batz argued in his 1911 biography of his ancestor, that Robespierre and his allies had discovered that the baron really was at the head of a major counter-revolutionary conspiracy.[14] Equally, it could simply be that the Committee of Public Safety wanted to dissuade any more would-be assassins of its leading members by fabricating a suitably all-embracing conspiracy and staging a spectacular show trial of those allegedly involved.

Whatever the precise motivation, the result is clear. On 17 June 1794, fifty-four suspected accomplices of Batz, convicted of plotting to overthrow the state, went to the guillotine dressed in the red robes reserved for parricides.

Amazingly, Batz was not among them; thanks to a remarkable network of secret helpers and safe houses, he remained at liberty in and around Paris until after 9 Thermidor. He survived into the restoration, dying peacefully at his château of Chadieu in the Auvergne in 1822.

To complicate matters still further, if that is possible, Batz left behind two contradictory accounts of his involvement in the upheavals of 1793–1794. The first was a pamphlet, *La conjuration de Batz ou la journée des soixante*, which appeared in 1795 but was probably written at the time of the events it described, in the summer of 1794. It was a vehement defence against the charges made against him by Elie Lacoste in his speech of 14 June; while acknowledging his links with many of those executed as a result, Batz formally denied that he had had 'in France any form of correspondence or relations, direct or indirect, with the kings, princes, generals and ministers of whom it has pleased the two Committees [of Public Safety and General Security] to cast me as the principal agent, nor even with any foreigner or émigré whatsoever, and if anybody proves me wrong they may drag my honour in the dust!'[15]

Twenty-two years later, however, Batz told a different story. Writing from Chadieu to the publicist Eckard on 10 March 1817, he confirmed that he had indeed tried to rescue Louis XVI and Marie Antoinette, and claimed that in the second case he had come close to success. He added some tantalising hints: 'I had a lot of important material on the great crimes and secret policies of the two Committees, but I lost most of it on two occasions when I would unquestionably have perished if these papers had been discovered, and I could only avoid this danger by destroying the majority of them'.[16]

Given the current state of the evidence, it is impossible to tell on which of these occasions Batz was telling the truth. He may of course have been lying on both: in 1795 to avoid further pursuit by the revolutionaries, and after the restoration to present himself as an unsung royalist hero. There is, however, one further source that implies he did at least consider a plan to undermine the Convention through corruption of the type Robespierre and Lacoste attributed to him. In a manuscript foreword to his 1795 pamphlet, also written in 1794 but not published at the time, he outlined just such a scheme and how it might work:

How can such a formidable power [the revolutionary government], before which all heads are bowed in silence, be brought down? I would reply that such a regime is by its very nature a form of delirium, a convulsive state; and that any such violent action is by definition, according to the immutable laws of nature, of short duration, and that the jealousies, suspicions, hatreds and divisions it produces will set the participants against each other and drag them towards the abyss they themselves have opened; that preparing these divisions and accelerating them by sowing mistrust and exacerbating rivalries is, in the absence of armed force, the only effective way of conspiring against such a government and hastening its prompt collapse.[17]

The one thing Batz never revealed was whether any of this visionary project was carried into effect. It may be a mistake to take his indignant denials of counter-revolutionary plotting in the published version of the pamphlet at face value. Beneath the polemic, it is noticeable that he did not deny having tried to rescue the king and queen, or having used corruption to discredit members of the Convention. Yet this is speculation. The only way at present of judging whether Batz was directing a political, as opposed to a purely financial, conspiracy is to examine the actions of those Chabot originally accused, and see how far, if at all, they matched the motivation he ascribed to them.

Chabot's central allegation was that the plot had two branches: one set of conspirators would corrupt prominent deputies, and when this was done another set of conspirators would in turn denounce them, sowing dissension within the Convention and dragging its reputation through the mud. The principal *corrupteurs* were Chabot's fellow-guests at Charonne, Delaunay d'Angers and Julien de Toulouse, who may not have been told the full political details of the plot and assumed that it was simply a financial speculation. The *diffamateurs*, on the other hand, would have had to have at least some knowledge of the subtext in order to perform their task effectively; Chabot accused them directly of being royalist *agents provocateurs*, and both Fabre d'Eglantine and Robespierre suspected the same thing.[18] The key figures here were Dufourny and Lullier, president and *procureur syndic* respectively of the Department of Paris, Desfieux, a leading member of the Jacobin club and his friend the cosmopolitan banker Proly, and Hébert himself, *procureur général* of the Commune of Paris and editor of the radical newspaper *Le Père Duchesne*.[19]

It is certainly true that within days of Chabot's dinner at Charonne, Dufourny and Lullier at the Jacobins, and Hébert in the *Père Duchesne*, denounced him as the accomplice of a gang of corrupt speculators.[20] It may be that these accusations were sincere (Chabot's lifestyle certainly lent itself to such suspicions) and should be taken at face value. On the other hand, the actions of these men, and some of the circles they moved in, did not always match their reputations as pillars of the revolutionary Left. Dufourny, Lullier and Desfieux certainly had dealings with Batz, and these aroused suspicion at the time.[21] Evidence recently discovered indicates that Desfieux's friend and lodger Proly really was, as his enemies suspected, an Austrian spy.[22] It is thus conceivable that, as Chabot himself alleged, this group was attacking him to further not the Revolution, but the counter-revolution.

At first sight, it seems extraordinary that Hébert, one of the key leaders of the radical sans-culottes, could have been mixed up in these intrigues. Yet aspects of his behaviour, too, remain curious. On 27 September 1793, just a fortnight before Marie Antoinette's trial, he proposed to the Jacobins that she be transferred from the Conciergerie prison back to the Temple, which was certainly far more comfortable, and from where Batz had already made attempts to rescue her.[23] Coming from the man who was simultaneously leading the campaign for the queen's swift trial and execution in the *Père Duchesne,* this suggestion was extraordinary. Yet at Hébert's trial, several witnesses were prepared to come forward and testify that he had links with Batz, although they were never called.[24] None of these scraps constitute conclusive evidence, but taken together they give off a very fishy odour.

After a century of assiduous combing, the archives of the revolutionary government have probably yielded up all the secrets of the 'foreign plot' that they ever will. Yet the overwhelming concentration by historians on the 'official' side of the story has led to a neglect of the other side, that of the alleged conspirators themselves. In particular, their links with the royalist emigration, and with the important European network of spies and informers it is known to have set up, have only rarely been examined. The sources for this are more scattered than those for the first republic, but if examined and put together with them shed revealing new light on the 'foreign plot' and its principal figures.

The most important material here concerns Batz himself. Despite his assertions to the contrary in 1795, there is strong evidence that Batz was in fact closely linked to a powerful group of émigré royalist politicians based in Brussels. This was headed by one of the leading figures of the counter-revolution, the baron de Breteuil.

Louis-Auguste le Tonnelier, baron de Breteuil, played a crucial role in shaping Louis XVI's and Marie Antoinette's response to the French Revolution. A distinguished diplomat who became minister of the royal household in 1783, Breteuil was made leading minister on 11 July 1789 when Louis XVI decided to reassert his authority in the face of an increasingly revolutionary situation. The storming of the Bastille three days later transformed the political landscape, and forced Breteuil to flee abroad. Yet from exile in Switzerland and then Brussels, he continued to act as the royal couple's secret spokesman, negotiating with the European powers for the restoration of the king's authority. In this capacity, he was the principal organiser of the flight to Varennes. When the revolutionary war broke out and

the Austrians and Prussians invaded France in August 1792, Breteuil
accompanied their general staff. Had the invasion been successful and the
king and queen rescued from their captivity in Paris, the baron would have
resumed his post as chief minister.[25]

For such a pivotal figure in counter-revolutionary intrigue, Breteuil has
been strangely neglected by historians. Even more neglected is his long
association with Batz. This dated from before the Revolution, when both men
had joined the same syndicate speculating on the Paris stock-market. The
partnership may have been sealed by a more intimate bargain - an English spy
later claimed that for a time Batz shared the favours of the baron's mistress
the duchesse de Brancas.[26] When Breteuil briefly became prime minister in
July 1789, it was Batz who was charged with raising the emergency loan made
necessary by the situation.[27]

Throughout the Revolution, Breteuil maintained a network of highly-
placed contacts in Paris, of whom Batz was the most important. Breteuil's link
with Batz assumed particular significance when the Austrians and Prussians
invaded France. Just before the invasion began, Batz slipped across the
border. Two months later, in early September, he surfaced in Brussels, where
he had a long discussion with count Fersen, Marie Antoinette's probable
lover, about ways of ensuring the royal family's safety as the allies advanced
on Paris. He then crossed back onto French soil, to find Breteuil at Verdun
with the duke of Brunswick's Austro-Prussian army. From Breteuil's
correspondence with Fersen at this time, it is clear that he was thinking of
using Batz to negotiate secretly with his revolutionary contacts for the royal
family's safety as the army neared Paris. 'If the duke of Brunswick gives
battle', he wrote to Fersen on 16 September, 'we shall see what opportunities
a victory might open up for ... a conciliation. Perhaps the baron de Batz will
make the sacrifice of going to Paris, yesterday at least he seemed willing to do
so, and I shall try to keep him to that decision. I can think of no-one with
better contacts on the spot'.[28]

Brunswick's defeat at Valmy, four days after this letter was written, made
Batz's proposed mission irrelevant. Yet it is significant that, several months
before his more famous attempts to rescue Louis XVI and then Marie
Antoinette from the scaffold, Batz was making clandestine efforts to save the
royal family, and specifically on the instructions of Breteuil.

Even more important, as far as the 'foreign plot' is concerned, there is
evidence that by this time, Batz had already begun his campaign to undermine
the revolutionary government by corruption and espionage. Again, his
schemes had close connections to Breteuil. From early 1792, it seems that
Batz, in conjunction with other royalist bankers in Paris, maintained a highly-

placed informer in the Jacobin club, and passed on the information gleaned from this source to Breteuil, who was then in Brussels, along with the queen's friend Fersen. Proof of this comes in an entry for April 1792 in Fersen's diary, concerning French war preparations:

> The baron de Batz writes from Paris that nothing is ready nor will be before 20th May, that resignations are flooding in from all directions ... that the revolutionaries are in great difficulties and will be lost if Prussia joins with Austria and if their troops arrive by 20th May, that there is only 17 million left in the royal treasury. This baron de Batz is an intriguer, but he, Laborde de Méréville, Boyd and Company and Walckiers (all prominent bankers) have a member of the Jacobins' secret council on their payroll who tells them everything.[29]

This is only one source, but it is an extremely important one. It indicates that individual Jacobins were not averse to taking bribes from counter-revolutionaries, and that more than one may have been playing a double game. It also shows that in April 1792 Batz maintained at least one paid informer who moved in the highest revolutionary circles. Bizarrely, although a full edition of Fersen's diaries was published in Sweden between 1924 and 1936, this particular passage was omitted, and has never been published. The diaries' editor, the eminent Revolutionary scholar Alma Söderhjelm, did not even insert the customary dots to indicate that it had been left out.[30] One wonders why she would not admit that perhaps all was not as it seemed at the Jacobin club.

By the end of 1792, the connection between Breteuil and Batz had moved beyond simple espionage, and broadened out into large-scale economic warfare against revolutionary France. That December, Breteuil sent the Austrian government an elaborate plan to destroy the credit of the *assignats* by flooding France with forged notes. According to Breteuil, a secret fund had been set up to aid Louis XVI, which was still in the coffers of various Parisian bankers. It consisted of the equivalent of 150 million *assignats* in gold, silver and letters of exchange. However, since the *assignat* had gone up in value since the fund had been created, selling it off now would involve a loss for the bankers concerned. The latter were, claimed the baron, prepared to deliver their holdings to the Austrians and Prussians in exchange for 150 million forged *assignats*. At a stroke, Vienna and Berlin would gain a massive sum in real effects, and France's new paper currency would be wrecked by a wave of counterfeit notes.[31]

There are obvious links between this plan and Batz's earlier scheme to set up a fighting fund for Louis XVI. Between the autumn of 1791 and the summer of 1792, Batz had continued his efforts to raise money for the king, making several trips abroad on behalf of the French government to negotiate the sale of *assignats* on the international money market against solid cash. Some of these solid effects had gone to make up the reserve earmarked for Louis. It was surely to these that Breteuil was referring in his memorandum when he spoke of the 'fund of 150 millions in gold, silver and bills of exchange ... constituted by the efforts and through the credit of the greatest banking houses of Paris, to be paid for in *assignats* by Louis XVI'.[32]

Most remarkable of all, Breteuil also claimed in his memorandum that he would be able to get hold of the actual plates and type-moulds currently being used to manufacture the *assignats*. 'Certain devoted servants of the king of France inside the country', he wrote, 'are in a position to procure the type-moulds produced by the very plates from which the *assignats* are printed'.[33] Although this statement cannot be corroborated, it does point to close links between counter-revolutionaries outside France and well-placed financial interests within.

Breteuil's plan was submitted to the emperor Francis II for his approval. However, the underhand means outlined horrified Francis, and he killed off the proposal with one sentence: 'Such an infamous project is not to be considered'.[34] Without the backing of the Powers, the scheme for flooding France with forged *assignats* had to be abandoned. Yet the episode shows well before the beginning of the Reign of Terror, royalist and *émigré* circles inside and outside France were considering undermining the Revolution by financial means.

From this point on, evidence linking Breteuil to Batz becomes much sparser. Forced to flee Brussels in the face of the French invasion of Belgium, Breteuil became extremely peripatetic, and this alone must have made it more difficult for him to keep in touch with Batz. It is possible, however, that the authorisation Batz carried during his attempted rescue of Louis XVI in January 1793 came from Breteuil - certainly it is difficult to see who else would have felt himself authorised to issue such wide-ranging powers, or have addressed them in the first instance to Batz. It is also likely that Breteuil met Batz a month later in London, where the latter had fled immediately after the attempt's failure.[35] This implies, although it cannot constitute proof, that the first phase of Batz's activities in 1793 and 1794, his plotting to free the king and queen, had Breteuil's blessing.

It is much harder to judge what role, if any, Breteuil played in Batz's next set of intrigues over the East India Company. If he did have a part in them, this would be significant, since it would suggest that there was indeed a counter-revolutionary subtext to Batz's financial manoeuvres. There is certainly no direct evidence of this. Yet Breteuil did have plenty of experience of the East India Company. Just before the Revolution, he and Batz had been partners in a financial syndicate speculating heavily on a downturn in the company's share price.[36] Given this knowledge and experience, if they had indeed conceived a plan to involve leading revolutionary figures in a corruption scandal, then the East India Company was an obvious place to begin.

There are only two other pieces of evidence linking Breteuil to Batz and the 'foreign plot', but they are important. They both appear in the series of secret bulletins from Paris sent to the British government between September 1793 and June 1794?, and published in 1894 as part of the Dropmore papers. These reports were the fruit of the remarkable intelligence network set up by the émigré spymaster the comte d'Antraigues, who claimed they were the work of one of his agents who was actually a member of the Committee of Public Safety. Just how authentic or accurate these reports were is still controversial among historians, but they do have to be taken seriously.

Several of the Dropmore bulletins discuss the 'foreign plot'. Significantly, whenever Batz is mentioned it is as the agent of Breteuil. The first reference to him comes in a bulletin dated 15–21 March. This is almost entirely devoted to the Committee of Public Safety's attack on the Hébertists, who are presented unambiguously as royalist plotters. The report goes on to state that 'on 16th (March) the Committee of Public Safety arrested Batz (misspelled as Bath), the baron de Breteuil's agent in Paris, the Spaniard Gusman and baron Frey, three bankers who had supplied Hébert's faction with 1,800,000 francs for the initial stage of the rebellion'.[37] In fact, although a warrant was made out for his arrest, Batz escaped. This error, coupled with the misspelling of Batz's name, might cast doubt on the bulletin's reliability. On the other hand, it is revealing that in one sentence it connects Batz with both Breteuil and Hébert. By no stretch of the imagination is it proof that Hébert really did have links with Batz, but it does underline the fact that many well-informed contemporaries thought that he did.

The next reference to Batz, in the bulletin of June 14–22, is much more detailed. It is a report of some highly unflattering comments allegedly made by Carnot in the Committee of Public Safety about his career up to that point. It emphasises Batz's close collaboration with Breteuil before the Revolution, and states explicitly that this was still continuing in 1794. Since the dissolution of the Constituent Assembly, it claims, Batz had 'remained in Paris as the baron de Breteuil's agent, and there is no doubt that his multiple intrigues hastened the king's death.[38]

These allegations need some qualification. Firstly, the bulletin's main thrust was that Batz's plotting was totally ineffective, and was simply being used by the Committee as a pretext 'to implicate everyone it wished to destroy'.[39] This is the line that many subsequent historians have taken; yet it is noticeable that the report only deals with the final version of the 'foreign plot' denounced in June 1794, which Batz himself denied, and not with the fall of the Hébertists and the East India Company Scandal.

Secondly, d'Antraigues, who collated all the bulletins and sent them on to the British government, loathed Breteuil as the head of a competing spy network, and one of the major aims of his voluminous secret correspondence was to discredit his rival.[40] To portray Batz's actions both as completely counter-productive and as inspired by Breteuil was to kill two birds with one stone. On the other hand, though d'Antraigues hated Breteuil it does not follow that he simply invented his link with Batz. There is too much other evidence to the contrary, and d'Antraigues had every interest in knowing what his principal royalist adversary was up to.

None of this fragmentary evidence justifies the claim, first made by Robespierre and his allies themselves, and subsequently echoed by some royalist historians, that the baron de Batz did indeed mastermind a vast conspiracy that struck at the heart of the revolutionary government. It is, however, quite possible that he did try to implement some sort of plan to discredit the Revolution through the use of corruption, though on a much more limited scale than his opponents believed. Ironically, in the short term Batz's intrigues may even have benefited the revolutionary government, since they lent just enough substance to the charges it levelled against its enemies to make them believable. In this sense, as d'Antraigues was at such pains to point out, the baron may have achieved the exact opposite of what he intended.

The divisions that split the revolutionary camp from June 1793 to July 1794 owed little if anything to Batz's various intrigues. Danton challenged Robespierre not because Batz was manipulating him, but because he himself came to the conclusion that the Terror must be ended. While Hébert and some of his associates may on occasion for whatever reason had dealings with royalists, it was as representatives of the radical sans-culottes that they launched their ill-fated insurrection. Yet one aspect of Batz's plan did succeed. The knowledge that there were royalist conspirators, however ineffective their actions may have been, operating on the margins of the revolutionary government contributed powerfully to the galloping paranoia that eventually crippled the Committee of Public Safety and provoked the Convention to overthrow it. Here at least, the baron may have had the last laugh.

Notes

1   The principal works on the 'foreign plot' are N. Hampson, 'François Chabot and his plot', *Transactions of the Royal Historical Society*, fifth series, vol. 26 (London 1976); A. de Lestapis, *La 'Conspiration de Batz'* (Paris, 1969); Baron de Batz, *La Vie et les Conspirations de Jean, baron de Batz* (Paris, 1908) and *Les Conspirations et la fin de Jean, baron de Batz* (Paris, 1911), G. Lenotre, *Le baron de Batz* (Paris, 1896) and A. Mathiez, *Un Procès de Corruption sous la Terreur: L'Affaire de la Compagnie des Indes* (Paris, 1920). I am grateful to Professor Hampson for his comments on an earlier draft of this chapter.

2   On the Frey brothers, see G. Scholem, *Du Frankisme au Jacobinisme: la vie de Moses Dobruska, alias Franz Thomas von Schönfeld alias Junius Frey* (Paris, 1981).

3   Cited in C. Hibbert, *The French Revolution* (London, 1982 edition), p. 244.

4   A. Mathiez, *La Révolution Française* (Paris, 1924), iii, 104; M. Eude, 'Une interpretation "non-Mathezienne" de l'affaire de la compagnie des Indes', *Annales Historiques de la Révolution Française*, liii (1981), N. Hampson, 'François Chabot and his plot', *Transactions of the Royal Historical Society*, fifth series, vol. 26 (London, 1976).

5   See, for example, Lestapis, *La 'Conspiration de Batz'*.

6   Robespierre's account of Chabot's visit to him is printed in Mathiez, *Une Affaire de Corruption*, pp. 77–8, and Chabot's formal denunciation of the 'plot' to the Committee of general Security in ibid., pp. 79–93.

7   Reproduced in ibid., p. 121.

8   Ibid., pp. 80, 93.

9   Batz, *La Vie*, p. 393.

10   Batz, *Les Conspirations*, pp. 546, 316.

11   Mathiez, *Une Affaire de Corruption*, p. 91.

12   Hampson, 'François Chabot', pp. 11–12, 13.

13   Batz, *Les Conspirations*, p. 335.

14   Ibid., pp. 288, 342–45.

15   Cited in ibid., pp. 361–2.

16   Ibid., p. 546.

17   Ibid., pp. 30–1.

18   Mathiez, *Une Affaire de Corruption*, pp. 79, 246; Hampson, 'François Chabot', p. 9.

19   Batz, *Les Conspirations*, pp 35–46. For Hébert and the *Père Duchesne*, see M. Slavin, *The Hébertistes to the Guillotine* (Baton Rouge and London, 1994), pp. 9–32.

20   Mathiez, *Une Affaire de Corruption*, p. 79.

21   Batz, *Les conspirations*, pp. 35–46, 263–70, 305–10.

22   'Le correspondant de Paris dont vous lisez quelques faibles bulletins est un nommé comte de Proli fils d'une Madame Deproly qui a été maîtresse de prince de Kaunitz, auquel [les?] bulletins sont adressés de suite...'. Fragment addressed to Calonne: 'Extrait d'une lettre de Bruxelles, le 30 octobre 1791', Calonne Papers, Public Record Office, London, PC 1/124 piece 263. This evidence is discussed in S. Burrows, *French Exile Journalism and European Politics, 1792–1814* (Woodbridge, 2000), p. 44. I am grateful to Simon Burrows for drawing my attention to this document.

23   Hampson, 'François Chabot', p. 8, Batz, *Les Conspirations*, pp. 125–44.

24   Hampson, 'François Chabot', pp. 11–12.

25   For a study of Breteuil and his activities during the Revolution, see M. Price, *The Fall of the French Monarchy: Louis XVI, Marie Antoinette and the baron de Breteuil* (London, 2002).

26 *The manuscripts of J.B. Fortescue, Esq., preserved at Dropmore* (2 vols, London, 1892–1894), vol. 2, p. 589 (bulletin no. 28, June 14th–22nd 1794).

27 *Journal du marquis de Bombelles* ed. J. Grassion and F. Durif (4 vols, Geneva 1978–1798), vol. 2, pp. 343–4.

28 Baron von Klinckowström, *Le comte de Fersen et la cour de France* (2 vols, Paris 1877–1878), vol. 2, p. 372.

29 Fersen diary, entry for 25th April 1792, Stockholm, Riksarkivet, Stafsundsarkivet vol. 5.

30 A. Söderhjelm, *Axel von Fersens Dagbok* (4 vols, Stockholm 1924–1936), i, pp. 192–3.

31 Breteuil's memorandum is published in A. Ritter von Vivenot, *Quellen zur Geschichte der Deutschen Kaiserpolitik Österreichs während der Französischen Revolutionskriege, 1790–1801* (5 vols, Vienna 1873–1890), ii, pp. 440–4.

32 Ibid., p. 442.

33 Ibid.

34 Ibid., p. 437.

35 Batz, *Les Conspirations*, p. 546.

36 A. de Lestapis, 'Agiotage et corruption sous le baron de Batz', *Miroir de l'Histoire* (1956), pp. 110–11.

37 The manuscripts of J.B.Fortescue, vol. 2, p. 551.

38 Ibid., p. 589.

39 'C'est sur cet échafaudage que Robespierre et l'abbé Siéyès ont absolument voulu qu'on échafaudât une conjuration qui put atteindre tous ceux qu'on voudrait faire périr.' Ibid.

40 On this and many other aspects of d'Antraigues' activities, see the important work by J. Chaumié, *Le Réseau d'Antraigues et la Contre-Révolution, 1791–1793* (Paris 1965) pp. 35–42, 191–4.

Index